**"Stop talki[ng]
someone i[...]"**

In a rush of adrenaline Lydia a[...]
him. "James, I made the terms of our
relationship clear at the beginning. I
will not make love to you. I will not
marry you. Now will you please leave
me alone!"

After a long silence James said heavily,
"A relationship on those terms won't
work for me. I found that out tonight.
So I will leave you alone, Lydia. And I
won't be seeing you again."

Within her something small and
shining and precious shattered into a
thousand pieces.

At the door he said, "I'm sorry it's
ended this way. You're a fine person,
Lydia, but you'll never be a whole
person unless you can break out of
this cage you've built around
yourself."

When the door closed, Lydia leaned
her forehead on the cold wood panels
and began to cry....

SANDRA FIELD, once a biology technician, now writes full-time under the pen names of Jocelyn Haley and Jan MacLean. She lives with her son in Canada's Maritimes, which she often uses as a setting for her books. She loves the independent life-style she has as a writer. She's her own boss, sets her own hours, and increasingly there are travel opportunities.

Books by Sandra Field

HARLEQUIN PRESENTS

HARLEQUIN ROMANCE

writing as Jan MacLean

writing as Jocelyn Haley

HARLEQUIN SUPERROMANCE

Don't miss any of our special offers. Write to us at the following address for information on our newest releases.

Harlequin Reader Service
901 Fuhrmann Blvd., P.O. Box 1397, Buffalo, NY 14240
Canadian address: P.O. Box 603,
Fort Erie, Ont. L2A 5X3

SANDRA FIELD

single combat

Harlequin Books

TORONTO • NEW YORK • LONDON
AMSTERDAM • PARIS • SYDNEY • HAMBURG
STOCKHOLM • ATHENS • TOKYO • MILAN

Harlequin Presents first edition December 1987
ISBN 0-373-11034-0

Original hardcover edition published in 1987
by Mills & Boon Limited

CHAPTER ONE

It was Lydia's twenty-ninth birthday.

She was applying her make-up in front of the bathroom mirror. The bathroom had navy blue wallpaper flecked with tiny white flowers, a white-painted trim, and tomato-red accessories, which included a pot of flamboyant silk poppies on the floor and heaps of fluffy red towels on the wicker shelves. Lydia herself looked as flamboyant as the poppies, for she had jet-black hair, cropped short, shining under the lights, and eyes an unusual shade between blue and green; at the moment she was artfully enlarging them with mascara and eyeliner, her movements deft and quick. She was wearing a red velour robe; the dress she was planning to wear for her dinner date with George Cumberland still hanging in her closet.

She was not particularly looking forward to the evening. George, she was almost sure, was going to produce as her birthday gift a ring. An engagement ring. It would undoubtedly come from the most exclusive jewellers in town and would consist of diamonds and platinum, neither of which she cared for. The diamonds would represent an exquisite compromise between ostentation and good taste, large enough to denote the considerable family fortune of the Cumberlands, but not so large as to be vulgar. Lydia sighed. She would, of course, turn down both the ring and the offer of marriage.

She frowned at herself in the mirror. Twenty-nine. One year from today she would be thirty. She brought her face closer to the mirror, so that her breath made tiny clouds on its surface, and scrutinised her features one by one. Her skin

5

was as clear and smooth as it had ever been, her throat as firm, her eyes unlined. Twenty-nine was young, she told herself. Nothing to worry about. And even if she were thirty-nine, she would not accept George's proposal.

Resolutely pushing thoughts of her advancing years to the back of her mind, Lydia picked up her lip brush and outlined her lips in fuchsia, then inserted gold drop earrings into her lobes. Her watch announced that she had exactly five minutes before George would arrive at the door of her town house. George was depressingly punctual.

She hurried into her bedroom, flung the robe over the pine rocker and took her dress from the closet. The dress was a favourite, made of silk in blended shades of pale pink and dazzling fuchsia, its full skirt whispering as she walked. She was fastening the straps of very high-heeled, delicately fashioned sandals, also fuchsia, when the intercom rang.

George Cumberland, junior partner in MacPherson, Copwell, Cumberland and Jones, one of Toronto's most prestigious accountancy firms, was good-looking, well-mannered, and correctly turned out. His overcoat was cashmere, his shoes handmade Italian leather; his teeth had been straightened by an orthodontist and his hair cut by a very expensive, if conservative, man's stylist. Lydia always felt she should be flattered that George considered her suitable to grace his dinner table.

She was aware of something else. Just as she fitted George's criteria for a female companion, so did he fit hers for a male. George was safe. He didn't crowd her or attempt to take over her life, nor could he be considered in her wildest imaginings as a passionate man. She found herself hoping, as she greeted him and was helped into her coat, that he would not propose to her and thereby alter the tenor of their relationship. It suited her very well as it was.

The restaurant he had chosen was one of the fashionable places in Toronto that autumn, where one went to see and be seen. While the food was delectable, Lydia privately thought the tables were too close together; however, she and George were led to a corner table by the maître d', with whom she had done business and whom George knew well, and the table next to theirs was empty. She sat in the corner, was handed a tasselled, leather-covered menu and began perusing its parchment pages, which were covered with a calligraphy that was astonishingly difficult to read.

She was not one to agonise over decisions. Smoked salmon, Salade Niçoise and medallions of veal would do her nicely, and if she had dessert, she would play an extra game of tennis tomorrow. She put down the menu as George turned to the list of entrées, which he proceeded to study as seriously as if they were a complicated tax file.

She felt a rush of affection for him. They had had some good times together over the past year, skiing in the Laurentians at his mother's chalet, sailing in the Muskoka, dining and dancing in the city. Endearingly, for it did not fit his image as the businesslike, emotionless accountant, he was an ardent fan of chamber music, and had taught her a genuine appreciation for an art form she had known nothing about. If there was any passion in his nature it was directed towards music; Lydia had never slept with him, and his occasional, half-hearted attempts to seduce her had been easily turned aside. That was another thing she would miss about him: so many men seemed to feel they had to prove their virility on the very first date.

George put down the dinner menu and picked up the wine list. Another lengthy silence. Then the waiter brought their cocktails, they gave him their orders, and George finally looked across the table at his companion. Raising his whiskey sour, he said, 'Happy birthday, darling.'

'Thank you, George.'

He gave her his slow smile. 'The next one will be the big three-oh.'

'I was thinking about that while I was getting ready.'

'You'll only get more beautiful as you get older, Lydia. Good breeding always shows.'

She winced. Her parents, Judith and Maxwell Winsby, were two people she thought about as rarely as possible. 'I'm not in any hurry to prove you right,' she said lightly.

'And you would have beautiful children.'

Lydia took a gulp of her Martini. 'That would depend at least partly on the father, I would think.'

'So it would.' As if she had given him his cue, he reached into the pocket of his charcoal-grey suit and pulled out a small, square jeweller's box. 'I haven't yet given you your birthday present.'

With a flourish of his black-jacketed arm the maître d' seated a customer at the small table next to Lydia's and George's. The customer was a man, Lydia saw in a quick, comprehensive glance. An extremely attractive man, who was seated facing her and who would be able to hear every word she and George were saying. With an effort she brought her attention back to George. 'Why don't you save it until——?' she began.

But George, once launched, was not easily deflected, a trait that stood him in better stead in the boardroom than at the dinner table. 'I chose your gift over a month ago,' he said. 'But I thought it would be appropriate to wait until your birthday.' He flipped the box open, holding it out to her across the table. 'I'm asking you to marry me, darling.'

The ring was a solitaire diamond set in platinum. Suppressing a ridiculous urge to giggle, and keeping her hands firmly in her lap, Lydia gulped, 'It's beautiful, George. But——'

'Hold out your hand and I'll see if it fits.'

'But I can't——'

The waiter put a plate of thinly sliced Atlantic salmon in front of her, and presented George with a ramekin of *escargots.* He then positioned himself at the table of their neighbour to take his order. Lydia seized her chance. Leaning forward, unconsciously putting her hands on the cloth, she said as softly as she could, 'It was sweet of you to buy me a ring, and I can see it's a very fine one, but I can't accept it. I don't want to get married.' She stopped abruptly, wishing she knew the correct etiquette for turning down a proposal.

George smiled at her indulgently, seized her left hand, straightened her fingers, and slid the ring on her third finger. 'It's perhaps a little large—do you agree?'

Out of the corner of her eye she saw the waiter move away. She hissed, 'You're not listening to me.'

'All women want to get married, darling.' He made one of his rare attempts at humour. 'Especially when they reach the ripe old age of twenty-nine.'

As she clenched her fists on the linen tablecloth, the diamond flashed its cold, white fire. The man at the next table discreetly cleared his throat. Lydia shot him a furious glance, and met eyes of so deep a blue that briefly her mind went blank. Then one of the eyes winked at her. As she gasped in outrage George said, 'Try your salmon, Lydia. It looks excellent. For some reason the Atlantic salmon seems of a better quality than the Pacific this year.'

Lydia took a long, steadying breath. 'How are the *escargots?*' she asked.

'Magnificent.'

She squeezed lemon on the salmon and took a mouthful. The salmon, also, was magnificent. She chewed thoughtfully, watching George devote his entire attention to the garlic-laden snails. George considered the matter of the ring closed: he and she were engaged to be married, and no more need be said. Her protestations he presumably attributed to maidenly modesty. Temporarily forgetting the listener at the nearby table, she said, 'George, do you love me?'

The snail he had been about to impale on his fork rolled back into its pool of melted butter. 'I asked you to marry me, didn't I?'

'I'm not sure that's necessarily the same thing.'

'Well, of course I do.'

'You've never told me so before.'

'I assumed that you knew. After all, we've been dating for nearly a year.'

'So did you equally assume that I loved you back?'

'Really, Lydia, I don't understand what you're getting at.'

She put down her fork. 'George, I'm sorry, but I don't love you. And therefore I can't marry you. That's what I'm getting at.'

He met her gaze squarely. His eyes were an indeterminate shade of grey and rather too close together, one of his less attractive features. 'Romantic love is a highly over-rated commodity—I've spent enough time sorting out the financial disasters of the divorced to know that. We like each other, Lydia, we enjoy doing a lot of the same things, we come from similar backgrounds and we're financially independent. We could do a lot worse.'

She felt another of those unsettling surges of affection for him, for essentially she agreed with him. She said slowly, 'I suppose you're right. But you see, George, I don't want to marry anyone—it's not just you. I like being single, and I see no reason to change my status for the sake of——' she moved her hand and smiled at him apologetically '——a diamond ring.'

'There are all kinds of reasons to get married, Lydia——' George broke off, scowling, as the waiter removed their plates. Lydia took the opportunity to glance over at the man with the deep blue eyes, who was eating pâté and drinking red wine with an air of concentration that she was almost sure was bogus. His hair was straw-coloured, thick and a little untidy; there was strength as well as character in the long, straight nose and cleft chin. She couldn't imagine why he was eating alone. He would surely only have to crook his little finger and any number of women would flock to his side.

He looked up and gave her a bland smile. She flushed, aware that she had been caught staring, and hurriedly said to George, 'What did you order next?'

'A spinach salad. And you?'

'Salade Niçoise, then the veal. I'm hoping I'll still have room for dessert.'

George looked uncomfortable. 'Actually my mother invited us back to the house for dessert. As it's your birthday,' he finished lamely.

'George, you didn't tell her you were going to ask me to marry you?'

'Well, I did, as a matter of fact. Couldn't see any harm in it. And you know how Mother likes to be involved.'

Likes to know everything that's going on, you mean, Lydia thought irritably. 'But George, we can't go. Because I turned down your proposal.'

'No, you haven't. You're wearing the ring.'

She pulled it off her finger and thrust it back in the box. 'No, I'm not.'

'Lydia, please—oh, thank you.' The waiter had brought their salads.

Lydia looked at hers without appetite. 'I don't want to marry anyone, ever,' she announced.

'So I'm not to take this personally?' George asked with pardonable sarcasm.

'I don't like what marriage does to people, George. Besides, I like being single.'

George stabbed a sliver of mushroom. 'So are you never

going to have children?'

'*I* don't know. Twenty-nine isn't forty; I don't have to decide yet!'

'Surely you don't feel this way just because your parents happen to be divorced?'

She said coldly, 'That has nothing to do with it. We're a new generation of women, George. We don't have to marry for financial security or for societal approval in the way our mothers did. We're independent of all that.'

'Been to any nice consciousness-raising groups lately?' George said nastily.

Through a mouthful of lettuce she mumbled, 'Don't be petty.'

'And what am I supposed to tell Mother?'

'Tell her the truth—that I don't want to get married.'

'She approves of our relationship, Lydia. She'll be very upset.'

Lydia said coaxingly, 'I can't marry you just to avoid upsetting your mother, George, now can I?'

'She'll miss your visits.'

She hesitated. 'You mean we won't be dating any more?'

'How can we? After this?' And he took the jeweller's box and shoved it back in his pocket.

'So we're no longer friends?' she said with dangerous calm.

'You've turned me down, Lydia.'

He was very much on his dignity. She gave an exasperated sigh. 'That doesn't say much for our friendship.'

'I thought we shared more than friendship,' he responded coldly.

They were sitting in a stony silence when the waiter came to remove their salad plates and bring the main course. Lydia began to eat as fast as she could, anxious only to leave the restaurant and be home, alone, in her house.

She had not handled the situation very well, she decided, but how could she have handled it differently with a waiter popping up every five minutes and the man next door listening to every word? Surely even Emily Post's diplomatic skills would have been stretched by such a situation?

George finished his *filet* before she had dealt with all the veal. He pushed back his chair. 'Excuse me, please,' he said. 'If the waiter comes back, order me some coffee.' He stalked away in the direction of the rest rooms.

A voice to her right said, 'You're doing absolutely the right thing.'

She met the Delft-blue eyes. 'I beg your pardon?'

'In turning him down, I mean. He's not the right type for you at all. Too much of a stuffed shirt. My name is James Connelly, by the way.' And he half rose in his seat, sketching a bow.

Lydia gave him a long, thoughtful look. 'Did your mother never teach you that it's very bad manners to eavesdrop?'

'Impossible not to,' James Connelly remarked apologetically. 'Anyway, it was interesting. What's his mother like?'

'Much as one would expect the mother of a stuffed shirt to be. George is her only son, and duly to be prized.'

Not until his mouth quirked did Lydia realise how feelingly she had spoken. 'I see,' he said. 'One should choose one's mother-in-law almost as carefully as one's husband, you know. The name Lydia suits you, incidentally—a Lydia should have black hair. Does your last name suit you as well?'

She discovered that she was enjoying herself. Keeping an eye out for George's return, she said sweetly, 'I'm afraid you will have to remain in ignorance of that.'

'But as of this evening you will be date-less.'

She widened her eyes with the utmost innocence. 'Are

you suggesting yourself as the saviour of my demolished social life?'

The smile faded from his lips. 'Yes. As a matter of fact, I am.'

Determined not to show that he had disconcerted her she said calmly, 'This seems to be my evening for saying no, doesn't it? Ah, here comes George.'

James Connelly raised his wine glass. 'You look like a very beautiful rose in that dress, Miss Lydia whatever-your-name-is ... a rose equipped with thorns, though. Don't let his mother change your mind, will you?' He drained his glass and signalled to the waiter.

Hoping she was not blushing, Lydia gave George a bright smile. 'Here comes the waiter now, you can order your coffee. Perhaps I'll have some as well, I'm not even going to look at the dessert menu. How's that for strength of mind?'

George sat down. 'I shan't return the ring for at least a month, Lydia. I feel we should think this over. Possibly I was too abrupt this evening.' He looked up as the waiter began clearing their table. 'Two coffees, please. Colombian, if you have it. And I'll have Courvoisier. Lydia?'

'Just coffee, thanks.' Recklessly disregarding the waiter and James Connelly, she added, 'George, you were not too abrupt. I had anticipated you might ask me to marry you— and I won't be changing my mind. I'd like to think that we can still get together as friends, though.'

'You can say that because your feelings aren't involved,' he replied with the astuteness that occasionally overcame his pomposity. 'We'll see, Lydia. Did you get the MacArthur contract?'

Lydia was one of the Toronto representatives of a firm that supplied indoor plants to businesses and stores; she had an office in her town house, and was good enough at her job to be given a great deal of freedom by the head office, a situation that suited her well.

'They're to call me tomorrow,' she said. 'I hope I do get it.'

Shop talk kept her and George safely occupied until the waiter brought their bill, tactfully enclosed in a leather folder. Without looking at the total, George put one of his credit cards in the folder and the waiter whisked the whole thing away. George described, at some length, the ill-health of his mother's African violets. The waiter brought the bill back, George added a tip and signed it. The waiter removed himself.

'Shall we go?' asked George. 'I'll take you home and then I'll have to drop in to see Mother, as she's expecting us.'

Feeling guilty, as perhaps he had intended she should, Lydia stood up. George had turned and was nodding at an acquaintance on the other side of the dining-room. She had intended to ignore James Connelly completely, but sneaked a sideways glance at him and was rewarded with a second wink and a smile of complicity. He inclined his head and said, 'Good evening, Miss Bennet.'

Just as graciously, she said, 'Mr Darcy,' and swept past him in a rustle of pink silk.

George, fortunately, had not noticed this interchange. At the doorway he helped her on with her coat, then hailed a taxi, giving the driver her address. When they pulled up outside her town house, he asked the driver to wait as he accompanied her to the door.

When she had unlocked the deadbolt, Lydia turned to face him. 'George, I'm sorry,' she blurted. 'I know I've hurt you. But I had to be honest. I do hope you'll call me some time—maybe we could go to a concert, or to a movie.'

He bent his head and kissed her, an atypically fierce kiss from which he emerged looking ruffled. 'I'll give your regards to Mother,' he said stiffly.

'You'd better wipe the lipstick from your chin before you

do. George, I'm flattered and complimented that you asked me to marry you, even though I did say no. Take care of yourself, won't you ... goodnight.'

She gave him a little wave of her hand, stepped indoors and locked the door on the inside, standing there until she heard the taxi drive away. Then, with a sigh of relief, she hung up her coat and climbed the two flights of stairs to her bedroom. By the time she got there she was no longer thinking of George. She was thinking of a blond-haired man with laughing blue eyes and a cleft chin. A man who read Jane Austen and ate alone in a fashionable Toronto restaurant. A man who had wanted to ask her for a date.

It was a pity she would not see him again. Although, she thought, as she reached for the zipper in the back of the silk dress, it was probably just as well. She was quite sure James Connelly would not be nearly as easy to handle as George.

CHAPTER TWO

THE next morning Lydia was hard at work at her desk in the office when the telephone rang. She glanced at the digital clock on the filing cabinet. Nine forty-two. MacArthur Computer Sales opened at nine-thirty. 'Torrington's Exotic Plants,' she said pleasantly. 'Can I help you?'

'I'd like to speak to Lydia Winsby, please.'

Her lashes flickered; she would have known that voice anywhere. 'This is she,' she replied, somewhat less pleasantly.

'James Connelly speaking, Lydia.'

'How did you get my name?' she demanded.

'From the maître d'. I pretended you'd dropped a glove.'

'How very enterprising of you. If a touch dishonest.'

'You know the old saying. All's fair in love and war.'

She should have hung up. Instead she heard herself say, 'So which is this?'

'War, by the sound of your voice. Did you visit Mother last night?'

'I did not.'

'I knew you were a woman of character. You'll like my mother a lot better. What are you doing this evening?'

'Playing indoor tennis.'

'Tomorrow?'

'Going to the theatre with a friend.' A woman friend but she didn't have to tell him that.

'Friday?'

'A house party.'

17

'Dear me ... how did you find time for the estimable George?'

She wanted to laugh. She said severely, 'Mr Connelly, I'm a very busy woman and I'm not, contrary to your belief, on the look-out for a new——'

'Do you always go out with men like George?' There was genuine interest in his voice, as if he were a journalist interviewing a particularly fascinating personage.

'Besides teaching you not to eavesdrop, your mother should have told you not to interrupt,' Lydia said.

'I obviously need the softening influence of a woman, Lydia Winsby. How about Saturday?'

'No, thank you. I'm going to stay home on Saturday night and water my plants,' she said demurely.

'Let me help. I'm a mean hand with aspidistras.'

He would, she was convinced, be a mean hand with more than aspidistras. For a wild moment she was tempted to allow him to visit her. But she always did date men like George, safe and predictable men who made no demands on her; and on the basis of a very limited acquaintance with James Connelly she knew he was not to be compared with George. Her voice expressed her exasperation with herself as much as with him. 'You don't take a hint, do you? I don't want to date you, Mr Connelly. Is that clear?'

'Clear, if misguided. Goodbye, Miss Lydia Winsby.'

The receiver clicked in her ear. She put down the phone. He had sounded cheerful rather than disappointed, matter-of-fact rather than upset. Nor had she expected him to give in quite so easily. Trying to rid herself of a sense of deflation, she frowned at the latest bill from the greenhouse. She had purchased only one *Spathiphyllum* last week, not three. Terence Strong, who ran the greenhouse, might be a wonder with plants, but he was no good at book-keeping. With a sigh, she began to dial his number.

Over the next few days, Lydia's life proceeded along its normal lines. She played tennis, went to the theatre and the house party, watered her plants and gave the town house its regular weekly cleaning. She did not hear from George, nor did James Connelly phone again. She was not, to her disappointment, awarded the MacArthur contract; it went to her main competitors in the city, Beazley's Indoor Plants, a company that spent far more on advertising than did Torrington's. However, on Monday she received a call from a Mrs Payzant, the purchasing agent for a company called Finlay and Madson. 'We would like to place an order for half a dozen aspidistras. You do deliver?'

'Certainly, Mrs Payzant. And if you wish, I can arrange weekly visits to look after the plants. Thursday afternoon, say around four, would be the earliest I could supply them.'

'Thursday would be excellent.' Mrs Payzant gave Lydia concise directions, said a pleasant good afternoon, and rang off.

Lydia checked the phone book, discovered that Finlay and Madson was a shipbuilding company, and presumably a prosperous one since it was located in a prime area of the city. She made a note on her pad of the order, which she could deliver at the same time she visited one of her regular customers, a chartered bank only a block from the shipbuilders. She frowned to herself, trying to visualise the building, which she must have driven past dozens of times. She would probably recognise it when she saw it.

And so she did. The frontage of Finlay and Madson was predominantly Greek, being adorned by two friezes of classical origin and four fluted columns, as well as a number of pigeons huddled together against the November cold. It was an imposing building; she hoped the aspidistras would lead to more business. Lydia parked the company van in a loading zone and grinned at her young assistant, Pete, who had freckles and cheerful disposition and a tendency to whistle out of tune. 'We'll have to make two trips,' she said. 'I'll go ahead and see if I can locate the purchasing agent.'

The foyer had a preponderance of marble and cried out for the softening effect of some umbrella trees or weeping figs. The receptionist was expecting Lydia, directing her towards the brass-plated elevators and Room 401 in the chief engineer's department. With the aspidistras loaded on to wheeled trolleys, Lydia and Pete went up in the elevator, which had plush carpeting and more brass. But when they stepped off at the fourth floor and started down a long corridor towards Room 401, they entered another world. The carpeting stopped at the elevator. The corridor was lined with large, well lit offices; an air of urgency, of important things under way, permeated the men and women bent over the draughting tables and computers.

Room 401 was empty. It was a corner office, with tall windows and a massive oak desk cluttered with rolled-up blueprints. Nautical charts were pinned on the walls.

'This must be the right place,' Lydia said. 'Although six plants are going to be at least three too many. I guess we might as well unload them, Pete.'

As Pete walked past one corner of the desk with a pot in his arms, his leg brushed against the blueprints, shifting the pile so that Lydia saw a gold nameplate on the desk. It read JAMES D. CONNELLY.

Footsteps were approaching down the corridor. She composed her face to a professional calm, turned, and as a tall, blond-haired man walked in the door, she held out her hand and said, 'Good afternoon, Mr Connelly. This is quite a surprise.'

He was in his shirt sleeves, his hair considerably more untidy than it had been in the restaurant, his eyes just as blue. His handshake was firm and brief. 'Oh? I thought you'd guess I was the one involved when the order was for aspidistras.'

'Any number of my customers order aspidistras, Mr Connelly.'

He grinned. 'Where shall we put them?'

She said briskly, 'They shouldn't be exposed to direct sunlight. They'll require only moderate amounts of water all winter; the compost can almost dry out in between waterings; but in the spring and summer they'll need more water, as well as plant food. And you must keep dust from the leaves. I'll give you a little sponge; dip it in water to which you've added a few drops of milk. That will keep the leaves shiny.'

He looked dazed. 'I had no idea aspidistras were so complicated.'

'But I thought you were a mean hand with them,' she said gently.

Pete put a plant on a small table in the corner and said cheerfully, 'She'll look after them for you, sir. For a price.'

Lydia shot him a dirty look. 'I'm sure——'

James's face brightened. 'You mean you'd visit occasionally, complete with sponge?'

'I rarely do the maintenance work myself,' she said repressively. 'And for so small a number of plants the monthly charge would be quite high. I'm sure you won't find it necessary; aspidistras can stand a lot of mistreatment.'

'God forbid that I should mistreat a poor dumb plant,' James Connelly said. 'I'll make the arrangements for the extra charge with the purchasing agent.' He glanced at his watch. 'What are your plans for the evening, Miss Winsby?'

Ostentatiously Pete began to whistle as he flanked the teak table with two more aspidistras. Very much aware that as the representative of Torrington's Exotic Plants she must behave herself, Lydia said with immense cordiality, 'I have a date with a sumo wrestler.'

'Cancel it. I have to make a quick check of a hydraulic system; you could come along, then I'll take you out for dinner.'

He was smiling at her guilelessly; he looked extremely handsome, very sure of himself, and not at all like George. 'And what if I don't want to go?' said Lydia.

'I think you do.'

She did. Rationalising, she decided November was a dreary month and she needed a change. And she was twenty-nine, not nineteen: she could handle Mr James Connelly. 'I know as much about hydraulic systems as you know about aspidistras, Mr Connelly—absolutely nothing. So I'd be delighted to accept.'

He flipped his tie off the chair. 'Great. We'll go right now. I'll call the company limousine.'

'But it's not even four-thirty!'

'Oh, it'll take us a while to get there,' he said vaguely. Shrugging into his jacket, he picked up the phone and told someone called Rose he was ready for the limousine. 'All set?' he said to Lydia.

She thrust her hands into the pockets of her scarlet coat. This disorderly office, now bedecked with aspidistras, was a strange place in which to be suddenly struck with fear. She had the impulse to grab one of the empty carts, run down to the van and drive back to the town house, her sanctuary and haven, where there was order and solitude and she was in control.

Pete, who had met George once and disliked him, said, 'I'll take the van home, Lydia. We got a couple of morning deliveries, don't we?'

The moment of choice. She tried to relax her hands. 'Yes. You could pick me up around ten-thirty.'

'Sure thing.' He stacked the carts one on top of the other. 'See you. Afternoon, sir.' He wheeled the carts through the door, whistling his own unique version of *Yesterday*.

'He's tone deaf,' said Lydia unnecesssarily.

'He likes you.'

She blinked. 'I suppose he does.'

James was stuffing papers in a briefcase. 'Says a lot about you. Good bosses are rarer than a ship without rats.' He pulled on his duffle coat. 'Let's go.'

In silence Lydia accompanied him along the corridor and down to the foyer. They got into the Cadillac limousine parked outside. The driver, who was separated from them by a sheet of glass, touched his cap and pulled away from the kerb. James said easily, 'Did you play tennis this week? I play at the club on University.'

They moved from winning strategies and the vagaries of tennis stars to the world of the theatre. Besides being a most amusing and well informed conversationalist, James was that rarity, a good listener; Lydia heard herself being far wittier than usual and much more insightful. More alive, she decided recklessly, ignoring the small twinge of alarm this paricular insight produced. It was dark outside and she had been paying no attention to where they were going; when the limousine came to a stop, she said artlessly, 'Oh! Have we arrived already? That didn't seem to take long.'

James opened his door and helped her out. She looked around her in consternation. 'But we're at the airport! I thought you had to check a ship's hydraulic system.'

He indicated a sleek, ten-passenger jet parked on the tarmac on the far side of the limousine, and said in a voice that was slightly too casual, 'That's the company jet. The hydraulic system is on a freighter in Montreal. We'll have dinner there afterwards.'

Lydia took a backward step as the fragile bubble of intimacy that had enclosed them in the limousine burst, and she was exposed to the cold, seeking fingers of the wind. 'I'm not going to Montreal!'

'It's only a little over an hour, Lydia.'

'You deliberately deceived me, didn't you?' she said, and heard pain in her voice. 'No wonder you were so interested in everything I said in the car—you didn't want me to notice where we were going!'

Anger tightened his mouth. 'I was genuinely interested in everything you said. But I didn't tell you our destination because I figured you wouldn't go.'

'You were right,' she retorted, holding on to her temper with an effort. 'I know absolutely nothing about you. Do you honestly think I'd get on a plane with you and take off to God knows where?'

'God and the pilot, Lydia.'

The half-smile in his eyes was too much for her. She abandoned restraint. 'For all I know you could be a white slaver!' she cried.

'Don't be ridiculous!'

'Better to make myself ridiculous now than to end up at midnight in some sleazy hotel in Montreal.'

James gripped her by the arms, a light from the terminal shining full on his face. 'We're flying to Dorval, getting a limo to the docks, making a thirty-minute stop at the freighter, having dinner in the old city, then coming straight home. We'll be back by midnight. One at the latest.'

'That's a marvellous itinerary—I do hope you enjoy yourself. Because *I'm* not going with you!'

'We're making a spectacle of ourselves in front of the crew, I hope you realise that.'

'A man with your imaginative ability should have no problem thinking up an explanation,' she retorted. 'Now will you kindly let go of me?'

His hands dropped to his sides. 'I do wish you'd come, Lydia.'

Her temper died. A jet screamed overhead and the beam of the searchlight swept the sky. 'I'm sorry, James, but I can't. I really don't know anything about you. I don't know what your job is, whether you're married or single——'

Behind them a voice said apologetically, 'He's the company's head engineer, miss. East coast and west.'

Slowly Lydia turned her head. The uniformed chauffeur, a middle-aged man who looked the ultimate in reliability, was standing by the limousine; she coloured as she realised he must have heard her ravings about white slavers. She said very reasonably, 'Genghis Khan was the head of an army. But no woman in her right mind would jump on a pony and follow him.'

'I'm a much nicer man than Genghis Khan,' James interposed.

'And he's never been married, miss. Last winter he sent the wife and me to the Bahamas when she'd been sick.' That, for the chauffeur, obviously clinched the matter.

Lydia looked from one to the other. Then, wondering if she was being an absolute fool, she announced, 'I shall need a very strong drink when I get on that plane. If I'm going into white slavery, I shall do it in style.'

'Champagne?' James suggested with a lift of one brow.

Did he have any idea how devilishly attractive that made him look? 'Champagne will do,' she said graciously, marched ahead of him to the metal steps, and climbed up into the plane.

It was elegantly appointed in dove grey and burgundy. Two men in business suits and another in orange coveralls were seated near the back. James waved to them and ushered Lydia into a seat as far from them as posible. 'Once we get airborne you'll get the champagne,' he said, and fastened his seat belt. 'Will you excuse me for a few minutes, Lydia? I want to glance through these papers. There are some magazines in the rack.'

Within twenty minutes the lights of the city had been left behind and Lydia was indeed being served champagne by the extra crew member. She took a couple of swallows, feeling the bubbles tickle her nose, and turned in her seat to look directly at her companion. 'James,' she said quietly.

He put down the report he had been reading. 'Yes?'

She hesitated for a moment, playing with the stem of the champagne glass. 'This has been all very amusing—you asking the maître d' for my name and then getting me to your office along with six aspidistras and on to your jet for dinner in Montreal . . . but why are you doing it? I don't understand.'

As he took a sip of champagne, she felt certain he had not anticipated her query. 'It's a fair question,' he admitted.

'To which I'd like a truthful reply. I don't like being deceived.'

'I'm not normally deceptive. But I was quite sure if I invited you to Montreal you'd turn me down flat. And I very much wanted you to go.'

'Why?' she persisted. 'You saw me that one time having dinner in a restaurant with another man. We've never even been properly introduced.'

'Is that important to you?'

'I was brought up to believe it was.'

He drank some more champagne, taking his time. 'I was intrigued with you from the beginning,' he said slowly. 'I sat down at a table in a restaurant and facing me was a woman in a pink dress with hair black as night and eyes like the sea. You're very beautiful, Lydia—yet even as I say that, I'm aware of the inadequacies of the word beautiful. It's such an over-used word. Those vapid Hollywood starlets are called beautiful. You're not like them.' He let his eyes wander over her features. 'There's a purity to your face, an untouched look, yet at the same time character and passion—as I said, you intrigue me.'

She swallowed, complimented, embarrassed, and again aware of the brush of fear. George had never quite

approved of her looks, of her startling colouring and
dramatic dress sense; George, and his mother, would have
liked her considerably more subdued. 'My looks aren't
fashionable,' she mumbled. 'Nowadays you're supposed to
be tanned all year round with a mane of streaky blonde
hair. I don't tan. I go red and blotchy.'

James laughed. 'Much more interesting to be unique
than fashionable . . . But your looks aren't the only reason I
worked so hard to get you here beside me. I said you
intrigued me—you also puzzled me. You and George were
so blatantly mismatched. I'm sure he's a very fine man
who's full of probity and votes Conservative. But he's not
the man for you. I couldn't understand why you'd been
dating him. And presumably for some time, since he'd
worked himself up to ask you to marry him. I would not
characterise George as a man of impulse.'

She had to smile. 'Far from it.'

'I'd be willing to bet you never slept with him.'

He had given her the opening she had been looking for. 'I
don't indulge in affairs, James Connelly,' she said, looking
straight into his eyes. 'So if that's one of your motives in
pursuing me, you're out of luck.'

His expression gave nothing away. 'Nor do you want
marriage. Or so you said to George.'

'Nor do I want marriage. Or any other kind of
commitment.'

'Do you,' he said delicately, 'prefer women?'

'No! I simply dislike intimacy, and all the emotional
entanglements that go along with it.'

'Because your parents are divorced?'

'You really didn't miss a word, did you?' she said crossly.

'Answer the question, Lydia.'

It was the one question she would not answer with any
degree of truth, and oddly enough, she found herself
reluctant to lie to him. 'I'm a single woman, James, who

likes being single,' she equivocated. 'For so many generations it's been perfectly acceptable—even romantic—for a man to be a bachelor, and yet socially disastrous for a woman to be a spinster. Spinster. Horrible word! But that's changing, thank goodness. I'm a woman of the eighties who likes being single. I enjoy my freedom, and I have no intention of giving it up for a set of good china and a man underfoot.' She broke off, aware that she was sounding too vehement.

'What about children?' he said equably.

'Motherhood is a highly over-rated pastime.'

For a moment her veneer of words, words she had used with more than one man, cracked, and she had a split-second image of her mother in the nursing home. She thrust the image away, burying it deep in her psyche where it belonged, and saw James watching her. Little as she knew him, she had no doubt of his perceptiveness. She lifted her chin, gave him a cool stare and said, 'Is there more champagne?'

He signalled to the steward, who refilled their glasses. Deciding she should keep the initiative, Lydia raised her glass and said, 'To the single life.'

'I'm not sure I'll drink to that, Lydia.'

'You're older than I am and you're single—at least, according to your chauffeur, you are.'

'He was telling the truth. I've never been married. Never really came close to it. I apprenticed on a freighter when I was eighteen, knocked around the world for a couple of years, took my engineering degree, specialising in marine engineering, and joined up with Finlay and Madson. For ten years, I was based on the east coast and in each of those years, I was lucky if I spent a month in my apartment. Not a life-style that encourages—or even enables—one to foster a serious love affair. Then six months ago I was appointed to head office, in a position that's geared more to administration and training. My whole life-style's changed. The first thing I did was buy a house. And now I'm ready to put down some roots and cultivate a long-term relationship.'

The positions had been stated. Lydia said, 'It would seem that you and I are as mismatched as George and I.'

'In a very different way. You want to be single, I want to settle down. But other than that we're alike, Lydia, I sensed that the moment I laid eyes on you.'

'We're not at all alike! You build ships, I sell plants.'

'You're honest and direct and you have a temper and a sense of humour. This is only the third time we've talked, and look at the depth of the conversation we're having.' He added as an afterthought, 'And we both play tennis.'

'I play to win,' she said obliquely.

'So do I.'

Excitement stirred within her. For many years she had avoided emotional challenges, venting her energies on her business and on the tennis courts. James Connelly challenged her in a new way. Naturally she would never marry him, or get involved with him on a serious level. But it might be interesting to get to know him better. She took another sip of champagne and said, 'Did you make reservations for dinner?'

'I wasn't quite that sure of my powers of persuasion. I'll phone from the airport.'

'I'm not dressed for dinner.'

He glanced at her tailored black suit and frilly white blouse, with which she was wearing high black leather boots. 'I would be proud to escort you to any restaurant in Montreal,' he said.

She flushed. 'You flatter me.'

'No, Lydia. I'm telling the truth. No more deceptions.' A glint of laughter appeared in his eye. 'And now that we've settled the problem of marriage, may I go back to my blueprints?'

Lydia was far from sure that anything had been settled: rather, the battle lines had been drawn. 'Certainly,' she said. She leaned back in her seat, crossing her legs, delighted that she was wearing patterned black stockings. They were unquestionably sexy. She was not averse to using that most basic of weapons.

She closed her eyes, decided that she had had more than enough champagne on an empty stomach, and drifted into a doze.

CHAPTER THREE

THE freighter was Greek, and to Lydia's eyes very large. The limousine that had met the jet at Dorval waited on the concrete dock as Lydia and James walked up the gangplank. James and a uniformed officer, who was short and exceedingly handsome, exchanged stiff bows and a few phrases in Greek. Lydia's presence was ignored.

She smiled inwardly, and at a duly respectful distance followed James and the officer along a maze of narrow passageways to where the captain awaited them in an elegant panelled boardroom. The captain bowed. James bowed. Then James introduced her to the captain, who kissed her hand with garlic-scented fervour. From a bottle on the table he poured a clear liquid into tiny glasses. He and James tossed theirs back. Lydia, determined to uphold the honour of womankind, did likewise, managed not to choke, and stood very still, her eyes watering and her throat on fire.

James and the captain, now speaking a broken mixture of Greek and English laced with technical terms, bent over the papers. They talked for quite a while before James gathered up the blueprints and followed the captain from the room, throwing an apologetic grin at Lydia over his shoulder.

Lydia sat down. The label on the bottle depicted some jolly-looking peasants picking olives. They would indeed be jolly, if they drank much of that stuff. Jolly, or flat on their faces.

The captain and James returned, looking as pleased with themselves as the peasants. The glasses were refilled and

31

drained, Lydia's hand was kissed again, and the same officer appeared in the doorway to escort them back to the deck. Under her breath Lydia muttered to James, 'You'd better take my arm. I'm drunk.'

Through the thicknesses of her coat and suit she felt the firm grip of his fingers. He was walking very close to her, an altogether pleasurable sensation. You *are* drunk, she scolded herself.

So what? said a second voice. Enjoy yourself!

And for the rest of the evening it was this second voice that she obeyed. She sparkled with witticisms and epigrams; she drank more than was wise; and in between courses she danced with abandon. Not surprisingly, she fell asleep in the jet on the way home. When the limousine arrived at her town house at quarter to one, and James walked to the door with her, she was able to say with perfect truth, 'I had a wonderful time, James! Thank you.'

'My pleasure.' He smiled down at her. 'Are you free on Saturday by any chance? Would you like to go to Roy Thomson Hall with me? The Toronto Symphony's regular series.'

He had brought her home at the time he had promised, and he had made no attempt to take advantage of her somewhat befuddled state after the visit to the freighter. 'I'd like that,' she said.

'Good! I'll pick you up at seven . . . I hope you won't be too tired tomorrow.'

Without attempting to kiss her, he waited until she was indoors, gave her a salute of his gloved hand and strode back to the limousine.

Lydia was not at all tired the next day. Rather, she felt buoyed up and exhilarated, feelings that carried over into the weekend. She accomplished wonders at work, typing bills and contracts, and hiring two new maintenance workers, one for the head office of an insurance firm that had ordered nine hundred trees, the other for several smaller businesses. She spent Friday afternoon in an intensive, on-location training session with them, as well as submitting tenders to do the interior landscaping for a newly constructed trust company.

Saturday evening at seven found her dressed in a pale pink evening suit with a dramatic black blouse, waiting for James with a smile on her lips.

In some respects the evening was a replica of many Lydia had spent with George: a concert, and a light meal afterwards. But there the resemblance ended. Tonight the music had a peculiar poignancy, as if speaking to her directly. As she and James wandered through the crowds in the intermission, she felt as if she were the most beautiful woman in the hall, vibrantly alive, aware through every nerve in her body of the man at her side, whose arm protected her from being jostled and whose voice was murmuring in her ear. Food had never tasted so delicious nor wine so crisp; again she felt as if she were intoxicated, although this time it was nothing to do with alcohol.

They left the restaurant and James drove her home. As he pulled up outside the town house, Lydia said, without premeditation, 'Why don't you come in for coffee?'

'I'd like to.'

She unlocked the door, hung his coat in the closet, and led him upstairs to the first level, which comprised kitchen, dining-room, office and bathroom; her bedroom and the living-room were on the top floor. She plugged in the kettle, turned to get the coffee beans from the jar on the counter and saw James leaning against the refrigerator, watching her. His intention was quite clear, for she could read it in his face: he wanted to kiss her. Like a woman in a dream she watched him cross the parquet floor, take her by the elbows, and bend his head to hers. The pressure of his lips was warm and sure.

The air of unreality, or of super-charged reality, which had surrounded her all evening, dropped from her like a discarded garment. She was standing in her own kitchen kissing a man she scarcely knew, a man who had a most disturbing effect on her. A man who made up his mind what he wanted and went after it. In a terrifying flash of insight she thought, I'm what he wants, and felt the colour drain from her face.

'Lydia, what's wrong?'

She backed away from him. 'Why are you here?' she said stupidly.

His eyes were very watchful; had she looked, she might have seen calculation in their depths. 'You invited me in for coffee, remember? Come on, Lydia, you're twenty-nine years old, you've been kissed before.'

The small of her back was pressed against the edge of the counter. 'I told you I don't have affairs!'

'I haven't asked you to have an affair.'

She closed her eyes and took a deep breath, knowing she was making a fool of herself, and heard him say, more gently, 'Where do you keep the coffee?'

She indicated the glass jar with the red lid, a red that accentuated the red of the strawberries in the wallpaper. 'The grinder's beside it.'

With a minimum of fuss he ground the beans, poured them into the filter and added boiling water. Lydia got out cups and cream and sugar, putting everything on a small teak tray. 'Let's go up to the living-room,' she said politely.

The living-room was her favourite room in the house. It had a cathedral ceiling with skylights and long windows that faced south, in which she grew begonias, azaleas, and cyclamen. Around the fireplace she had grouped a velvet-covered chesterfield set and some graceful palms. The clean lines of the teak bookshelves and stereo console, and the softly hued abstracts on two of the walls added to the sense of space; it was the room of a woman sure enough of her own tastes to live without clutter.

James stopped in the doorway, and after a small silence said, 'This room says a great deal about you.'

She was kneeling by the hearth, touching a match to the wood, her back to him. 'Oh?' she said, not sounding very encouraging.

'You have an appreciation of texture, colour and form. A love of living things, and of quietness. Lydia, look at me.'

She stood up, brushing off her hands as the flames took hold, and said pleasantly, 'This room is the main reason I bought the house.'

'Are you a virgin? Is that what you're trying to tell me?'

Her fists clenched at her sides. 'No, I'm not.'

'What have you got against sex?'

Her eyes were cold, those of an enemy. 'Like motherhood, it's an over-rated pastime.'

'Then you've never done it with the right person.'

'You must allow me to be the judge of that!'

'You acted tonight as if a man had never even touched you before. Didn't George ever kiss you?'

'Of course he did,' she said sharply. 'Why don't you sit down? The coffee's getting cold.'

Moving closer to the fire, James helped himself to cream. 'Did you react to him the way you reacted to me?'

'James, I feel like a prisoner of war hauled in front of the enemy commanding officer—I don't have to answer all these questions. And you don't have the right to ask them!'

He passed her the other cup of coffee and sat down on the rug in front of the fire, staring into the flames. 'I've already said you intrigue and puzzle me, haven't I, Lydia? I'm going to add a third word—you worry me. You're a beautiful woman, intelligent and talented, yet you seem to have walled yourself off from the very normal needs of love and intimacy. I don't understand why.'

She had perched herself on the arm of one of the chairs, as if poised for flight. 'I told you, I like being single.'

'This is the twentieth century, not the nineteenth. You can be single and still have a lover.'

'If you choose to do so. I choose not to, that's all.'

'You didn't make love with George, did you?'

'No, I didn't.'

'Would you with me, Lydia?'

'No.'

His face tightened, so that he looked suddenly older. 'You've left me with one obvious question. If you aren't a virgin, then you've had at least one lover. Was it so bad an experience that you've never cared to repeat it?'

She attempted an indifferent shrug. 'Neither particularly bad nor particularly good,' she said.

She sometimes had difficulty remembering the name of the young man she had slept with at the age of nineteen, only a few months after her escape from the big house by the lake. His face was hazy, his body a blur. She did remember meeting him at a university frat party; she also remembered deciding it was time she lost her virginity. The experience itself remained as hazy as her memories of him. Something had been done to her, something had happened to her, and although she had been willing to participate, in one sense she had never been touched. She had been left with a faint feeling of bewilderment . . . was there no more to making love than this awkward, uncomfortable grappling in the dark? The young man—Roy had been his name—had seemed happy enough. The fault—or the lack—must have been hers. Certainly she had been left with no desire to repeat the experience.

'Then you did it with the wrong person,' James said.

'Look, there's no point in this conversation,' Lydia said impatiently. 'And no point in us seeing each other again. Because I'm not going to change.'

She was choosing the safe and sensible course of action, as she had done for many years, yet even as she spoke she was torn by an acute pang of loss. Somewhere deep within her, rebellion stirred. She was tired of safety and of undemanding men like George who allowed her to do exactly as she pleased.

'I'd like to see you tomorrow,' James said steadily. 'We could drive out to the country, it's supposed to be a sunny day.'

Something changed in Lydia's face: a sense of strain superimposed on the delicate features. 'I can't.'

He hesitated. 'This really is none of my business. But are you seeing another man?'

She shook her head. She was to visit her mother in the nursing home tomorrow, which would ironically, involve driving out to the country. She had been making these visits faithfully for five years, yet they never seemed to become any easier. For a moment she was tempted to tell James the whole sorry story, so that he would understand why she shied away from intimacy and the demands of love as a horse shies from fire. If he understood, then he would leave her alone ... wouldn't he?

As if he had heard her inner question, he said quietly, 'I'd like to continue to see you, Lydia. If I accept your terms, will you allow that?'

She could say no. She should say no. For the antonym for safety was danger. She heard herself whisper, 'Yes,' and saw the tension ease from his shoulders. He had been afraid of her reply.

His voice was almost normal as he said, 'I'll call you early in the week. I think I can get tickets to Tarragon's new play through the firm.'

They talked very sedately of plays and movies they had seen, and of the difficulty of transmitting a book from the printed page to the screen, just as if the other conversation had not taken place. Lydia had finished her coffee. She reached up to place the cup on the mantel, a move that inadvertently pulled the black chiffon of her blouse tightly against her breasts, and glanced over at her companion.

He got to his feet and said abruptly, 'I'd better go.'

She suddenly realised what he must have seen and flushed scarlet. 'A relationship between us will never work, James,' she said helplessly. 'Not on my terms.'

'Yes, it will.' He gave her a wry smile. 'You could consider wearing bulky sweaters, though.'

After that, there seemed nothing more to say. Lydia trailed down the stairs behind him, watched him put on his coat, and was not surprised when he didn't try to kiss her. 'Take care,' he said briefly. 'See you soon.' Then he was gone.

She was exhausted, as tired as if she had run five miles then played three sets of tennis—and had a fight with her mother afterwards, she added ruefully. She'd better go to bed. Because she had to face her mother tomorrow.

The nursing home, which was east of the city, was not a place for ordinary citizens, for its rates were astronomical. Lydia's father paid these rates regularly, if not cheerfully, and had never once visited his former wife in the five years she had been in residence there. Judith Winsby was, and had been as long as Lydia could remember, an alcoholic, who had done such damage to herself that she had been reduced to a shadow of a woman who spent most of her time in bed and on occasion did not even recognise her only child. Today, Lydia was glad to see, was not one of those days.

'Hello, Mother,' she said, as she advanced into the room.

'Hello, Lydia. Is it Sunday already? I thought it was Friday.'

Lydia merely smiled. 'I brought you some flowers.'

'Thank you, darling. There's a vase in the cupboard. If that bitch of a nurse hasn't stolen it,' Judith added viciously. 'You've got to keep an eye out all the time. Things disappear.'

The cupboard to which her mother was referring was a scrolled Victorian armoire; the dresser and the high four-poster bed were of the same ornately carved mahogany. The heavy flowered curtains shut out most of the sun; to Lydia the room was like an expensively appointed cage, airless, lifeless, joyless. She sometimes dreamed about it, and would awaken crying for the pretty, blonde-haired woman of a quarter of a century ago whose photograph was in a silver frame on her dresser in the town house. Judith Winsby was not pretty now. Her make-up was as garish as a clown's on a face like a crumpled mask.

Lydia arranged the freesias and irises in the crystal vase and placed it near her mother's bed. 'Would you like me to take you for a walk?' she asked gently.

'No. I'm very tired today. I didn't sleep well. There was such a racket in the middle of the night, nurses laughing and talking, no consideration at all for us poor guests, particularly when you consider what we pay for this place . . .'

Lydia listened with half an ear, for more than once she had heard this litany of real and imaginary complaints from a woman who had too much time on her hands and lacked, as she always had, resources to fill it. In the middle of her tirade, Judith fell asleep. She whimpered in her sleep like a child; as always, Lydia felt the tug of a helpless, guilt-ridden love. She sat quietly, her hands folded in her lap. She always stayed for tea.

In half an hour one of the attendants brought in a silver tray with fragile porcelain cups and a plate of tiny cakes. As if a bell had rung in her ear, Judith Winsby woke up. 'Good,' she said, eyes darting over the plate, 'mocha cakes.

They don't have them nearly often enough.'

Lydia passed her mother a cup of tea and began describing, as amusingly as she could, her visit to the freighter with James. She had reached the second round of drinking in the boardroom when her mother said, 'What about George?' and took the last mocha cake.

'George and I aren't seeing each other any more, Mother.'

'You'd better settle on a man sooner or later, Lydia. You're not getting any younger.'

They had had this conversation before as well. 'I lead a very full and happy life.'

'Nonsense—we all need a man. You don't want to end up like me, do you? All my troubles started when your father got that job that took him away so much.'

Lydia did not want to talk about her father. 'I'm dating James now. He's very handsome, you'd like him.'

'Ring for some more cakes, Lydia.'

Lydia sighed and did as she was told. The visit wore on. At five o'clock, when the nurse came to pull the curtains shut, she got up to leave. 'I'll see you next week,' she promised. 'Is there anything you need?'

'Have you heard from your father?'

'No, Mother.'

Judith's eyes flooded with easy tears. 'I've never understood why he won't come to visit me.'

'He's very busy, you know that.'

'I still love him,' Judith quavered. 'I always will.'

'You'd be happier if you could forget him,' Lydia said as kindly as she could, patting her mother's hand. The gnarled fingers, ornate with rings, were cold to the touch.

Judith's eyes closed. Lydia stayed until her mother fell asleep again, then drove home through the dark streets, as always aware of the dead weight of the visit crouched like a vulture on her shoulders. She almost wished James would be at the town house, waiting for her. Almost.

He was not. But he phoned her first thing Monday morning. 'The aspidistras are flourishing,' he announced.

Lydia laughed. 'Aspidistras do not flourish, James.'

'Well, they haven't died yet.'

'I'm delighted to hear it.'

'I have two theatre tickets for Thursday. Are you interested?'

'Very. Thank you.'

'What about Monday, Tuesday and/or Wednesday?'

She said promptly, 'I'm giving a talk to a garden club tonight, I have meeting with my maintenance workers tomorrow night and I play tennis Wednesday.'

'Friday, Saturday and Sunday?'

'Not Sunday,' she said. 'And on Friday, I'm visiting my friends Malcolm and Annabel.'

'Consider yourself booked for Saturday then.'

'James——'

'I'll pick you up on Thursday at seven. Take care, Lydia.'

The receiver clicked in her ear. A man who knows what he wants, she thought drily, and goes after it. She frowned at her order sheet, trying to bring her attention back to *Schleffleras* and rubber plants.

As the week developed Lydia was glad she had got an early start on Monday. Two of her maintenance crew caught the 'flu, and as she could only get a replacement for one of them she spent the better part of Tuesday and Wednesday in the head office of a chartered bank which had twenty-five floors, each with plants that required watering, dusting, spraying, and clipping. Her answering service was consequently plugged with calls, all of which had to be dealt with. In the meantime, Peter, whistling tunelessly, coped with the minor deliveries. Another worker called in on Thursday with a problem at the model suite of a building contractor that was located at the very boundary of Lydia's territory. She fought her way out there through the traffic, which with Christmas a little more than a month away was already getting congested, found the plants infested with scale insects, and had to sponge all the leaves with a mixture of water and an insecticide. On the way home an accident on the Parkway held her up for half an hour, and three more calls required an immediate response. At ten to seven she got out of the shower and threw on some clothes, not wanting in the least to meet James at the door artistically draped in her housecoat. The bell rang at three minutes to seven. She ran down the stairs in her stockinged feet, her hair damp and tousled, her face bare of make-up, and swung open the door. James was standing on the step in a navy blue overcoat clutching a cellophane-wrapped bouquet of red roses. Her heart gave an unexpected leap. With a shy smile she said, 'Come in. As you can see, I'm not ready.'

Standing close to her in the hallway, he held out the bouquet. 'I suppose it's a bit redundant to bring you flowers. But I've always loved red roses. Trite of me, I know.'

The roses were long-stemmed, with dusky petals just opening from the bud. 'They're beautiful,' she said sincerely. 'Thank you.'

He leaned forward and kissed the tip of her nose, which was shiny. Her skin smelled of soap and her hair of shampoo; without make-up she looked younger than her twenty-nine years, with an unguarded and innocent quality. He said, 'I've never understood why women feel they have to plaster their faces with powder and lipstick.'

'War paint,' she replied.

'It's a weapon you don't need . . . particularly when you blush like that.'

She pulled a face. 'But if I don't soon put some on, we'll be late for the theatre.'

He took her by the shoulders. 'So if it's war paint, Lydia, am I the enemy, or the prize to be captured?'

Both, she thought silently. Both.

Her ambivalence must have shown. He leaned forward, kissed her hard, then immediately turned away to hang up his coat, taking rather a long time about it. 'Busy day?' he asked, his voice sounding carefully detached.

'Hectic,' she gulped. 'I'll pour you a drink while I dry my hair.'

The play was a one-man show about an elderly musician and his double bass, and was both comic and profound. They discussed it at great length over a meal afterwards, then James took Lydia home. He did not kiss even the tip of her nose.

CHAPTER FOUR

Two weeks passed. James went to Newfoundland for two days to supervise repairs on one of the CN ferries, but other than that dated Lydia every evening she was free. They went to movies and concerts, dined in ethnic restaurants, skated in front of the city hall, and talked about almost everything under the sun: the exceptions being that Lydia did not talk about her parents or what she did on Sundays. She thoroughly enjoyed James's company and should have been happy. But she wasn't.

The problem was sex. She knew it and he knew it.

Although James was a mature man with very adequate self-control, Lydia was under no delusions. He wanted her; more and more as time went on. Increasingly he was avoiding even casual touch, the brush of a sleeve against her arm, the grabbing of her hand on an icy sidewalk; and increasingly, when he left her at night, there was tension in the line of his mouth, a guarded frustration in his eyes. He was conducting the relationship scrupulously on her terms. But the terms were not without cost.

She was very much afraid of becoming involved with him sexually, for she knew she couldn't have a casual affair with James; he was not a casual man. The alternative was, sooner or later, to lose him, a prospect that genuinely appalled her. On a Friday early in December the conflict came into the open.

James had suggested they see the Japanese movie *Ran*. Although not wholly convinced that nihilism went with Friday nights, Lydia had agreed. But at quarter to six her phone rang. It was Annabel Doherty, a friend from college days, who lived a few blocks from Lydia with her husband Malcolm, an executive in a computer company. 'I'm so glad you're home!' Annabel cried. 'Lydia, I'm stuck. You're not free tonight by any chance, are you?'

'Well, we were going to the movies. But——'

'Oh, no! *What* am I going to do?' Annabel had always been what one could politely call volatile.

'Why don't you start by calming down and telling me what's the matter?'

'The annual Christmas dinner and dance for Malcolm's company is tonight. Have you been out today? It's a *terrible* day, pouring rain and windy, not at all the right weather for a Christmas party. But it's absolutely *essential* to attend, the only acceptable excuses are death or terminal illness, Lydia, you have no idea. The president greets everyone at the door, he has a computer for a brain, that man, and if you're not there, he *notices*. Actually, once you get there, it's rather fun, the food is out of this world and the music's always good, even Malcolm usually manages to get on the dance floor, and *that's* an accomplishment, believe me. And I've got a new dress, it's very sexy, Lydia——'

'Annabel,' Lydia interrupted, 'get to the point. You don't sound dead or terminally ill, and when I bumped into Malcolm at the mall one day last week he looked in very good health. Give.'

'It's the sitter!' Annabel wailed. 'We arranged for her to come tonight two weeks ago, and she left it until an hour ago to phone and tell me she had the 'flu. I could absolutely *kill* her, Lydia, really!'

'So you'd like me to babysit.'

'I've tried *everywhere*. My parents are out of town this week and Malcolm's sister declined to give up a party she's been invited to, she didn't seem to understand this is life and *death*.'

'I'll come,' Lydia said.

'Malcolm's not home yet, he'll be furious when—*what* did you say?'

'I said I'll come.'

'But what about your date?'

'He'll understand.'

'Are you still going out with George?'

'No. This one's name is James.'

'Bring him along,' Annabel suggested. 'I always like to meet your new man to see if he's as deadly respectable as the last one. I never think it's possible, but somehow you always manage it. Lydia, do you really mean it? You'll stay the whole evening? It'll be late.'

'Certainly I will.'

'You're an *angel*, a positive angel. Cocktails are at seven, so we should leave about quarter to seven. Can you make it by then?'

'We'll be there by six-thirty sharp.'

'Darling Lydia, I love you! Now I must tear and make myself beautiful. As one gets older, it takes longer, doesn't it? Nicolas will be pleased you're coming, he likes you better than any of the sitters. I really must go. See you soon.'

'Goodbye,' Lydia said into the empty receiver, chuckled to herself and put down the phone. It was only as she was showering, the water sluicing her breasts, that she began to have second thoughts about the change of plans. Nicolas, who was three, would be in bed by seven or seven-thirty, after which she and James would be alone in the apartment until at least two in the morning.

Wrapping a towel around herself, she hurried to the phone in her bedroom and dialled his number. 'I thought you might already have left,' she said breathlessly. 'James, something's come up.' She explained the situation of Annabel and Malcolm. 'Maybe we could go to the movies on Sunday instead, would you mind?'

'We can do that, sure. Why don't I bring a book or some

paperwork along this evening; your friends are likely to be late home, aren't they?'

'Are you sure you want to come? It'll be a bit boring for you, won't it?'

'I've never yet been bored with you, Lydia. Unless you don't want me there?'

'Oh no, that's fine,' she said weakly. 'I said we'd get there at six-thirty; it's only five minutes from my place.'

James arrived promptly at quarter past six. Under his raincoat, which was already wet, he was wearing cords and a V-necked blue pullover over an open-necked shirt; he did not look deadly respectable. Lydia had chosen jeans and two sweaters, a loose pink mohair over a crew-necked navy knit, a combination that she hoped would qualify as bulky in James's view.

She picked up her knitting bag, which contained pieces of a sweater she had been working on for six months, locked the door behind her, and ran through the rain to the car.

Malcolm, carrying Nicolas, met them at the door. Malcolm was dark and thin and clever, with a quiet sense of humour that seemed to take his wife's volatility in stride. Nicolas, who immediately flung himself forward into Lydia's arms, had Annabel's caramel-coloured curls and dark brown eyes. Lydia hugged him, feeling his hair tickle her cheek. Into her collar he crowed, 'Peek-a-boo!' then suddenly looked up, eyes bright in anticipation. She burrowed her nose into his chest, and growled, 'Peek-a-boo.'

He screamed with laughter. 'Do it again, Lyddy!'

'In a minute,' she promised, looked up, and found James watching her with an enigmatic expression. 'James, this is Malcolm Doherty,' she babbled. 'And his son, Nicolas. Malcolm, James Connelly. James is a marine engineer.'

As the men shook hands, Lydia and Nicolas went through their ritual again. Then they all moved into the living-room, which was cluttered with toys, magazines, and various cast-off garments belonging to both Nicolas and Annabel. In a rustle of taffeta Annabel entered.

Her dress was black moiré, straight, full-length, slit to the knee. From its high collar her heart-shaped face with its cluster of curls looked deceptively innocent. She kissed Lydia on the cheek, enveloping her in perfume. 'Hello, darling.'

Lydia said demurely, 'Annabel, I'd like you to meet my friend, James Connelly.'

Annabel's big brown eyes took in James's height, his rugged good looks and the air of confidence that he wore as casually as his clothes. She took his hand and breathed, 'I'm *delighted* to meet you, James. You're so kind to do this for us, I was in such a panic, Malcolm's career would go down the *drain* if we didn't go, and if one of us went without the other, they'd have us instantly *divorced*. Do you live in the city, James?'

'Not far from Lydia,' said James, smiling at Annabel in a way that Lydia, personally, always found devastating.

'You must both come for dinner soon,' Annabel replied. 'Malcolm and I would like that, wouldn't we? It would be a way of saying thank you for this evening. Darling, do I look all right?'

This last was to Malcolm, who looked her up and down, brushed a hair from her shoulder and said with his grave smile, 'You look very beautiful.'

Annabel dimpled up at him and said without affectation, 'I do adore you. Shall we go?'

In deference to her carmined lips, Malcolm kissed his wife's cheek. 'Let us go and make obeisance to the president.'

Annabel frowned. 'Do you make obeisance or pay obeisance?'

'Whichever it is, we shall do it. Goodnight, Nicolas. In

bed by seven-thirty at the latest.'

With no respect for her black dress, Annabel gave her son an extravagant hug. "Night, darling. Sweet dreams. Be a love and don't wake up *too* early in the morning.'

With his parents gone, Nicolas settled down on the carpet to play blocks with Lydia and James; he was already wearing his blue sleeper suit. Lydia was very fond of him, and his parents were her closest friends in the city. Contentedly she erected towers and bridges, listening to the rain beat against the window behind the curtains, and to Nicolas's cheerful prattle; he had his mother's ingenuous good nature. At quarter past seven she read him a story, then carried him into his room and put him to bed. She turned on the night light before shutting off the overhead light, for Nicolas did not like being in the dark. 'Sleep well, love,' she murmured.

He mumbled something, clutched his teddy bear to his chest, put his thumb in his mouth, and closed his eyes.

James was standing in the hall; she hadn't realised he had followed her. He said quietly, 'You'd make a good mother, Lydia.'

A warning bell rang in her brain. She said as casually as she could, 'Malcolm was away when Nicolas was born—he arrived two weeks early. So I was with Annabel in the hospital, and I've felt close to Nicolas ever since. I'm his godmother, too.' Brushing past James, she went into the kitchen.

'Doesn't he make you want one of your own?'

'Maybe. Some day,' she said vaguely, looking for the kettle. 'Goodness, listen to the wind!'

James gripped her by the elbow, pulling her round to face him. In a low, angry voice he said, 'I think we've avoided this issue long enough, Lydia.'

She tried to shake free. 'I don't know what you're talking about!'

'Oh yes, you do. What the hell have you got against the very ordinary institutions of marriage and child-rearing? It's connected with your parents, isn't it? And don't bother denying it, because I know I'm right. You never mention them. Ever.' She opened her mouth to say something, but he ignored her. 'Do you remember last weekend? I told you all about my parents, and my brothers and my sister, and described their house to you and invited you to go there with me. You'd rather not do that, you said, although you couldn't produce a reason that made any sense. I'd given you a perfect opening to talk about your parents—but did you take it? Oh, no! You changed the subject as quickly as if I'd been talking about something obscene. You've got one hell of a hang-up about your family, Lydia Winsby, and I want to know what it is!'

She stared at him, open-mouthed. He was not a man to swear. She said, for want of anything else to say, 'You'll wake Nicolas.'

He let go of her arm and ran his fingers through his hair. 'For God's sake, Lydia!'

She said defiantly, 'If you choose to tell me about your parents, that's your decision. Equally, if I choose not to tell you about mine, that's my decision.'

'So you do admit that you avoid the subject?'

'Yes, I admit it,' she said wildly. 'But I have a perfect right not to talk about them. I don't like talking about them. I don't want to talk about them!'

He hesitated. 'Are they both alive?'

She thought of her mother's cold, slack fingers. 'You could say so . . . James, please don't push me.'

James stared at her, frowning. 'I could find out. Toronto's not so large that a few questions in the right quarters wouldn't give me all the information I need.'

'Go ahead,' she said coldly. 'But don't bother phoning me again if you do.'

'I may not. There are plenty of women out there who are willing without choosing one who's frigid.'

'I'm *not*!'

'No?' He seized her waist with one arm, took her chin in his other hand, and kissed her hard on the mouth.

His body was tight with anger, his lips a weapon. She held herself rigidly, refusing to struggle, giving him nothing back but her own anger, and was not surprised when he thrust her away. She could see the pounding of the pulse at the base of his throat; his eyes impaled her like bayonets. 'No?' he repeated furiously.

'I'm a single woman—I'm free!' She flung the words at him, not caring whether they made sense or not. 'I don't have to go to bed with anyone if I don't want to. If you can't handle rejection, that's your problem.'

'Not when the rejection is grounded in some kind of Freudian neurosis.'

'How typically male to drag in Freud—if ever there was a male chauvinist, Freud was one. And how typically male to label me frigid just because I've turned you down!'

Said James, flatly, 'I need a drink.'

She heard the echo of her angry words, saw the effort he was making to regain control, and felt desolation curl around her heart, cold as the sea. She had not had a fight like this for years, because she had always been careful to choose the kind of man who would not fight her. Men like George. She had know from the beginning that James was different. She should also have known that, given the kind of man he was, this clash was inevitable. But the pattern of her life was set; she could not change it. Not even for James.

She said, attempting to move back from the abyss that had opened between them, 'I need a drink, too. Preferably a double. The alcohol's in the dining-room; I'll get it.'

She almost ran into the little dining area, where tarnished silver candelabra kept watch over the dusty table; Annabel was no housekeeper. She grabbed a bottle of rum from the hutch, and found herself staring at the printed label as if she had never seen a bottle of rum before.

When she went back in the kitchen, James had put two glasses on the counter and was taking ice cubes from the freezer. 'I'll be finished in a minute,' he said, his back to her.

She went back into the living-room, sat down on the far corner of the chesterfield and picked up her knitting. The wool was teal blue and very soft; she had just finished the ribbing in the front and started the pattern. Lips moving, she counted her way along the row.

James put her drink on the coffee table and sat down at the opposite end of the chesterfield, taking some papers from the briefcase he had brought with him.

'Thank you,' she said.

He nodded.

Her needles clicked, his papers rustled, the rain rattled against the window and the wind moaned. To an outsider looking in, the scene in the living-room would have looked very peaceful, a young couple spending a stormy evening at home. James, quite possibly, was at peace. Certainly each time Lydia sneaked a sideways peep at him he was absorbed in his work, scribbling in the margins of the pages, occasionally using a small calculator or consulting a book of tables. She envied him his ability to concentrate; she had dropped three stitches, and had had to unravel four rows when she made a mistake in the pattern.

Outdoors a new sound added itself. Lydia said incredulously, 'Is that thunder? In November?'

James did not look up. 'I heard on the news that we could expect some freak storms.'

Lydia did not like thunder. Scowling, she began to knit again.

By the time she had reached the arms she had decided

teal blue was far from her favourite colour and that the pattern was not very exciting. James had put away his calculator and the book of tables and was now reading a report. A thick report. She said with a touch of desperation, 'Are you hungry? Or would you like another drink?'

He glanced over at her. 'I am hungry, as a matter of fact. I didn't have time for supper.'

'Oh James, why didn't you say so?'

He smiled. 'We started fighting instead.'

Ridiculously his smile made her want to cry. 'We did, didn't we? James, what are we going to do?'

He purposely misunderstood her. 'We're going into the kitchen to forage.'

She managed to smile back. 'That's a very appropriate word to use in Annabel's kitchen.'

He put the report face down on the coffee table and stood up, stretching to his full height and yawning unselfconsciously, his sweater pulled taut across his chest. With a sudden sharp longing Lydia knew she wanted to be held by him, to feel his arms go around her and draw her close, into security and warmth and comfort.

That's what you always wanted from your father and never got, she derided herself, bundling her knitting into the bag. James is definitely not your father. Don't confuse the two of them, Lydia. 'A cup of tea would taste good,' she murmured.

The refrigerator contained a great many little plastic containers, the contents of several no longer edible. 'Here's some cheese,' Lydia said, 'and this bacon looks OK. We could broil them on toast.'

James headed for the bread box and peered inside. 'The choice is white bread with mould or wholewheat without.'

She laughed. If only she didn't like him so much. 'Wholewheat is better for you,' she said, and began slicing the bacon. The knife was very sharp; obviously Malcolm's department.

Directly overhead there came a peal of thunder, like giant hands clapping in the sky. With dramatic suddenness the lights went out. Lydia's hand slipped and the steel blade bit into her nail. She gave an exclamation of mingled fright and pain. 'James?' she quavered.

'Stay put—did you hurt yourself?'

'Nothing serious.' The darkness was absolute, as if she had been muffled in a thick blanket. 'Where are you?'

She reached out her hand, felt the softness of his sweater and latched on to it. He put his arms around her, just as a few minutes ago she had wanted him to. She leaned against him, hearing the steady thud of his heartbeat and feeling the warmth of his body seep through his sweater, and in the concealing darkness closed her eyes, allowing herself to luxuriate in sensations from which she had deprived herself for years.

'Lydia,' he said huskily.

She lifted her head. His lips brushed her cheek, seeking her mouth. She gave it to him willingly, totally bemused. His arms tightened their hold.

It was a long kiss that started gently and then deepened into intimacy. Lydia forgot the darkness and her sore finger. She forgot George and her father and the rules she had laid down for herself years ago. She forgot everything but the sweetness of James's kiss and the slow, sure roaming of his hands over her back, and her own surging pleasure. When his mouth left hers to explore her face in tiny, feather-light caresses she brought her hands up to rub the hard bone-and-muscle contours of his shoulders, as, she now realised, she had subconsciously wanted to do for days.

He kissed her again, tongue to tongue. His heart was racing now beneath her palm; she felt power and desire mingle in her blood, drowning the careful, protective rules.

Her fingers sought the silky thickness of his hair. Her lips were as hungry as his. Then his hands, at her waist, pulled back the thicknesses of her sweaters and sought the smoothness of her flesh.

Her whole body went still, concentrating on the splayed fingers searching the curve of her spine, rounding her ribs, then arriving at the soft, swelling breasts.

'Lydia,' he whispered against her mouth. 'My beautiful Lydia.'

He was stroking her breasts, teasing the tips to hardness until she could scarcely bear the agonising wonder of his touch. She strained upwards to reach his mouth, telling him of her hunger, and felt him seize one hand and thrust it beneath his shirt. His skin was hair-roughened and very warm, his belly taut beneath the arching ribcage; she thought she could die from such pleasure. The darkened kitchen vanished from her consciousness; she was in a sun-dazzled meadow adrift with flowers, where she would lie down and he would take her, her yellow-haired lover, gentle as the whispering grass, fierce as the sun ...

From the bedroom down the hall Nicolas gave a piercing scream. Lydia jumped. The sunny meadow was swallowed up in darkness; the flowers vanished. 'He's frightened of the dark,' she said, stumbling over the words as if she were speaking a foreign language. 'I'll have to go.'

She had been in the apartment often enough to be able to find her way in the dark, even if she had not been guided by Nicolas's shrieks. She hurried into his room, stepped on something soft, realised with a jolt of relief that it was his teddy bear, and picked it up. 'Hush, Nicolas, it's OK, I'm here. You dropped your teddy, didn't you? Here it is. Up you come.'

'Don't like the dark,' Nicolas sobbed.

'The power went off, sweetie, so all the lights went out.'

Nicolas burrowed his face into her sweater. 'I want my mummy.'

'Your mummy will be home a little later. James is in the kitchen, let's go and find him.'

Over Nicolas's diminishing sobs James reported that the street lamps were still on but all the buildings appeared to be in darkness. 'Any idea where the matches would be?'

'Matches are bad,' Nicolas snuffled. 'Dang'rous.'

'Where does your mummy keep them?'

'Up high,' said Nicolas helpfully.

'One of the rare times I'm sorry I don't smoke,' James muttered, as he began searching through the cupboards that were at eye level.

The matches were eventually located in the cupboard to the right of the sink, in a screw-cap jar. James brought in a candelabrum from the dining-room and lit each of the three candles in it. The flames threw shadows across his face, so that he looked like a stranger. Lydia stared at his hands in fascination, remembering how intimately they had touched her, and said in a voice that sounded false even to her own ears, 'There are two or three more sets of candles in the dining-room. Ever since Annabel turned thirty, she insists on eating by candlelight.'

James looked over at her. The pointed flames were reflected in her eyes and shone on her hair, which was as black as the night. Her cheeks were still flushed, her lips kiss-softened; the blond-haired child was cuddled at her breast. 'You're so beautiful, Lydia,' he said. 'More beautiful than any woman I've ever known.'

She hugged the child closer, her eyes as brilliant and unrevealing as glass. 'I'd better put him back to bed. If we can find a single candlestick, I'll put it in his room.'

James's jaw tightened. He led the way into the dining-room, lit a candle and put it on Nicolas's dresser. Nicolas allowed himself to be tucked into bed. He was gazing wide-eyed at the candle when Lydia left the room.

She waited while James lit more candles and carried them into the living-room. She felt cold and very frightened, for she had learned a great deal about herself in the last hour. Somehow she had always assumed that she was a woman without much taste for passion, for her monastic life had rarely discontented her. But James, in a few short minutes, had taught her differently. Under his hands her body had sprung to life. She had wanted him as badly as he had wanted her.

It had happened once; it could therefore happen again. The inevitable corollary was that James had power over her. Just as her father had had—and still did have—power over her mother.

She said, 'Why don't I get you some crackers and cheese? We'll have to forget about the bacon.'

'Good idea.'

She escaped to the kitchen, where she took her time arranging crackers and cheese on a plate and pouring each of them a second drink. But she could not hide in the kitchen for ever. After gathering everything on a tray, she went back into the living-room. 'It's not very much,' she said dubiously. 'You must be hungry.'

'Not for food, my love,' he said lightly.

Her lashes flickered, and she moved fractionally away from him on the chesterfield, reaching for a piece of cheese and a cracker. '*I'm* hungry,' she said, just as lightly.

'I owe you an apology, Lydia. I should never have called you frigid. You're not. You're a woman who's passionately alive.' As calmly as if he had been discussing the weather, he helped himself to a wedge of Brie.

'We all have our moments of weakness,' Lydia replied with a laugh that could only be called nervous.

He looked her straight in the eye. 'We shared a moment

of truth out there in the kitchen, Lydia. You know it and I know it.'

Deliberately she held his gaze, trying very hard to pretend that he was just another man like George. 'No, James. The true Lydia is the woman you've known all along.'

'I don't believe you.'

'You must. The terms haven't changed.'

He put down the piece of cheese, untasted. 'You can't ignore what happened a few minutes ago. If Nicolas hadn't woken up, we'd probably have made love on the floor.' He gave her a singularly sweet smile. 'Unless I'd have managed to hold you off long enough to bring you in here to the chesterfield.'

She fought against the charm of his smile. 'Look, what happened in the kitchen was a temporary aberration, a slip-up. My—my animal nature coming out. The libido that Freud is always ranting on about.'

'You're playing with words.'

'I'm telling the truth!' she cried, and knew somewhere deep within her that she was not.

He carefully preserved the distance between them on the chesterfield. 'I want to make love to you, Lydia,' he said steadily. 'As part of our relationship. An important part, but by no means the only part. Because eventually, you see, I expect I'll ask you to marry me.'

'No,' she whispered. 'No, James.'

His face was inflexible. 'Yes, Lydia.'

'I can't marry you any more than I could marry George. That won't change—not even for you.'

'Then tell me the problem.'

'Telling you won't make it go away.'

'How do you know, you've never tried. Have you?'

'James, I warned you from the beginning that I wouldn't have an affair with you. That I didn't want commitment. I can only assume you didn't listen.'

'I was sure enough of myself—and of you—that I thought I could change your mind.'

'Well, you can't.' More to avoid looking at him than from any motive of thirst, she took a gulp of her drink.

'So what am I to do now?'

Her nerves were rubbed raw from the unrelenting pressure he was applying. 'Eat your crackers and cheese,' she said.

'Don't be facetious. Lydia. I can't force you to make love to me.'

'I'm glad to hear it.'

'Goddammit, will you stop talking like a character in a soap opera!'

In a rush of adrenalin she said, 'James, I made the terms of our relationship clear from the beginning. If you didn't like them, you didn't have to get involved. I will not make love to you. I will not marry you. Now will you *please* leave me alone!'

There was a long, charged silence. Then James said heavily, 'A relationship on those terms won't work for me. I found that out this evening. So I will leave you alone, Lydia. Once I take you home tonight, I won't be seeing you again.'

Within her something small and shining and precious shattered into a thousand pieces. And she was responsible for the destruction, not him. She felt like a little girl who wilfully breaks a toy and only afterwards realises how much the toy meant to her. Broken pieces, splintered fragments. Beyond repair.

Unable to think of anything to say, she picked up her knitting, began to decrease the raglan sleeves, and prayed that Annabel and Malcolm would come home soon.

They arrived home at two-fifteen, an hour after the power was restored. Annabel was flushed and laughing,

Malcolm had a twinkle in his eye. 'Once we got past the president we had a marvellous time,' Annabel exclaimed, kicking off her high heels and wriggling her toes. 'Malcolm, you stepped on me. More than once.'

'At least I danced with you, my darling.'

'So you did.' She reached up and kissed him on the cheek, giving him a brilliant smile. 'So what if I'm crippled? It was worth it.'

It was obvious to Lydia that once she and James were gone, Annabel and Malcolm would make love. Desperate to remove herself, she said brightly and inaccurately, 'Everything went fine here. The power was off for a while so Nicolas helped us find the matches. He was frightened for a few minutes, but he went right back to sleep.'

'You were angels, both of you,' Annabel said. 'Next year I swear I'll line up a dozen sitters.' She smiled prettily at James. 'It was lovely to meet you, I'm sure we'll see you again. Lydia, I'll talk to you in a day or two. Thanks for everything.'

Lydia had been pulling on her raincoat and boots. She picked up her knitting bag, waved goodbye, and hurried out of the door, James on her heels. The wind had died, although it was still raining, the puddles dimpled, the streets slick and wet.

She got in the car. James drove her home. As always, he accompanied her to the front door. It took her three attempts to insert the key in the lock, by which time her nerves were at the screaming point. 'Thank you for the drive,' she said stiffly.

He took her by the sleeve, ignoring the drips from the gutter that were pattering on his hair and shoulders. 'I'm sorry it's ended this way. You're a fine person, Lydia—but you'll never be a whole person unless you can break out of this cage you've erected around yourself.' He leaned forward and kissed her briefly on the lips. 'Goodbye.' Then he turned and strode down the path to his car.

She went inside and locked the door with a vicious snap of the key. Then she leaned her forehead on the cold wood panels and began to cry.

CHAPTER FIVE

A WEEK passed. Lydia worked morning, noon and night, coping with all her regular work as well as going through files she had not touched for years, following up calls she had neglected, tracing new contracts, and, on Wednesday, playing some extremely competitive tennis. Every night she slept like a dead woman.

James did not call. But she hadn't expected him to.

Annabel phoned on Wednesday evening after Lydia had played tennis. 'Tried to get you earlier,' she said innocently. 'You must have been out with that perfectly gorgeous man. *Where* did you find him, Lydia? Is he there now?'

'We're not going out together any more,' Lydia said baldly.

'Lydia—you're joking!'

'I wish I were,' Lydia heard herself say.

'What *happened*? Malcolm, who notices a lot more than I give him credit for, thought James was in love with you. Don't tell me he's married or something dreadful like that—although it would be a wonder if he weren't,' Annabel added thoughtfully.

'We just had a fight, that's all.'

'You don't want to talk about it.'

'No, I guess I don't.'

'And I'd called you up to invite you both for dinner!' Annabel wailed. 'Oh, Lydia dear, couldn't you make up?'

'I don't think so.'

'You must come for dinner anyway. On Sunday. And I promise I won't say a word on the subject of James Connelly.'

Nor would she, Lydia knew, for under her scatterbrained exterior Annabel was both tactful and kind. 'You're a sweetheart,' Lydia said with more warmth than had been in her voice all week. 'Thanks, I'd love to come. I'll see you then.'

Consequently Lydia visited the nursing home on Saturday rather than Sunday. It was a dull December day, the sky leaden grey with impending snow, pressing down on the grey-brown landscape. Lydia wished it would snow. Maybe a good storm would lift the heaviness from her spirit, the heaviness that had been there all week. For she missed James. Missed him acutely.

Her frenetic activity all week had not succeeded in keeping his image at bay. She missed his sense of humour, his decisiveness, his swift, penetrating judgments. She missed his deep blue eyes, so often full of laughter. She missed his phone calls and their outings. And at a deeper level she missed the sense of security he had given her even as, paradoxically, he had challenged her. But because he had wanted what she could not give, he had gone away.

As she parked outside the Victorian mansion and clumped up the steps between the ornate metal railings she tried to shake off her mood. Although sprays of pine and holly held by red velvet ribbon decorated the oak-panelled halls of the nursing home and a tastefully trimmed Christmas tree glimmered in the sitting-room, she didn't feel much better. Christmas had not been her favourite season for many years. Nor, of course, had it been her mother's.

She had brought her mother a pretty arrangement of anemones this week, as well as a box of bonbons. Fixing a smile on her face, she climbed the second flight of stairs.

A nurse was coming out of Judith Winsby's room. She saw Lydia and beckoned her aside. 'She's having one of her little upsets,' she confided, patting Lydia's sleeve, then, lowering her voice still further, 'Yesterday she got hold of a bottle—don't ask me how, dear, we watch them like hawks, you know. So today she's not quite up to par.' Three more pats. 'The doctor will be along in an hour or so; I expect he'll give her a needle to quiet her down. My, what pretty flowers!'

Lydia managed to withdraw her arm. 'Perhaps they'll cheer her up,' she said diplomatically. 'You've already phoned the doctor, have you?'

'Oh, yes. At noon. But it is the weekend, you know.'

The doctor was paid handsomely for his attendance at the nursing home. 'Thank you,' Lydia said, and walked into her mother's room.

Judith Winsby was lying in bed crying. She had been crying for some time, Lydia decided, because her eyes were red-rimmed and puffy. 'Mother,' she said gently, 'what's the matter?'

Judith flung an arm dramatically across her forehead, opened her eyes and said flatly, 'Oh. It's you.'

'Who were you expecting?'

'The nurse said Dr Warner would be in to see me.'

'He will be, later on. Tell me what the trouble is.' While Judith might be prepared to dramatise her tears for the benefit of the doctor, a good-looking man, Lydia knew the tears were genuine enough, as was the quiver in her mother's voice as she began to talk.

'I'm not feeling very well today, Lydia. This place gets me down. Oh, everybody's very nice, I suppose, but I get so bored, there's absolutely nothing to do, day after day goes by and they're all the same.'

Lydia had heard this complaint many times before. 'You could go on the outings they have every week.'

'And be seen in public with some of the old scarecrows that are in here? No, thank you!'

'There's always a bridge game going on. And there's

television and the library.'

'I hate to read.' Judith gave her a sly look. 'Lydia, why couldn't I go home with you? I could look after your meals, do a little cleaning. I'd be happier in a real home.'

Which is within walking distance of the liquor store. 'You know Dr Warner doesn't think that's advisable, Mother,' Lydia said, racked as always by guilt that Judith had to be confined in this expensive, elaborate prison. Once, three years ago, she had brought her mother home with her, paying for a housekeeper to be with her during the day. Judith had fired the housekeeper, drunk herself almost to insensibility, and set off the fire alarms in the building by turning on a pot of stew and forgetting to turn it off. She had been in the nursing home ever since.

Judith began to cry again. 'Dr Warner doesn't understand.'

'I brought you some flowers, Mother. And some of those candies you like so much.'

But Judith was too miserable to be wooed by her sweet tooth. She pressed a lace-edged handkerchief to her eyes. 'Nobody ever comes to see me,' she wailed, ignoring the presence of her only child. 'Lydia, have you heard anything from Maxwell?'

Maxwell was Lydia's father, divorced from Judith for eleven years. 'No, Mother, I haven't. Not since the summer.'

'Why couldn't he come and see me? Just once. It wouldn't hurt him to do that, and it would mean the world to me.'

Judith was crying in earnest now. Lydia sighed. They had come to the crux of the matter, for she had long ago realised that Judith's unrequited, limpet-like adoration for Maxwell, and his equally determined avoidance of her, were at the root of her mother's drinking problem. Judith loved Maxwell. And for Judith love had meant dependency, a clinging, stifling dependency that had existed for as long as Lydia could remember. Although Maxwell had betrayed her at every turn—by his prolonged absences from home, by his other women, by his cruel tongue and occasional flashes of rage—Judith had never been able to break free of him. As an adult Lydia had been able to assess more objectively the cost to her father of such dependency; but she had never been able to forgive him his cruelty.

'I haven't seen him for over two years, Mother, and then only because I happened to be in Paris at the same time as he.'

'I'd give everything I owned for him to walk in that door. Why can't *he* bring me flowers and candies? It's y-years since he's sent me as much as a card. I wish I were *d-dead* . . .'

Lydia took her mother's hands. 'You mustn't say that. *I* love you, Mother. The people here care about you. Let me get you a clean handkerchief——'

Judith's nails dug into Lydia's hands with diabolical strength. 'If you loved me, you'd bring your father here, I know you're in touch with him all the time. The two of you keep me in here, I know you do. If you asked him, he'd come to see me. But you don't ask him, do you? You'd rather I suffered.' Her voice rose to a shriek. 'You hate me, Lydia! And you've taught him to hate me!' Her teeth bared, she suddenly ripped her fingernails across the back of Lydia's left hand.

Lydia cried out in shock, looked down, and saw thin trails of blood left by the long red nails. She backed away from the bed, sick to her soul. She had never learned how to cope with her mother's rages, her twisted accusations, her lack of love for her only daughter. For deep in her heart Lydia had never felt loved by her mother; there had been no room in Judith's life for anyone but Maxwell.

Judith's face was contorted by hate and by what Lydia recognised, horribly, as jealousy. 'Go away!' Judith screamed. 'Go away and leave me alone to die.'

With an authoritative rap on the door, Dr Warner entered. Quickly Lydia hid her left hand against her coat. Although she normally found the doctor's sleek good looks and unctuous manner unappealing, today she was heartily glad to see him; and to his credit he took in the situation in a glance. 'Perhaps you could wait outside, Miss Winsby,' he said, putting his black alligator medical bag on the dresser. 'Now then, Mrs Winsby, no more of that.'

Lydia fled. Even half-way down the hall she could still hear her mother screaming; she wanted to thrust her hands against her ears and run down the stairs and never come back.

Yet she could not do that. A sense of duty brought her here week after week. Duty, and perhaps a faint, deeply buried hope that some day Judith Winsby might acknowedge that she loved her daughter.

The strident voice subsided to a harsh weeping and then even that died away. Her shoulders rigid with tension, Lydia waited, staring at the Audubon prints on the wall without really seeing them, aware of pain in her hand. She had worn a new outfit today, for if Judith had ever had a genuine interest in anything other than herself, it had been in clothes; Lydia's coat was black with red trim, close-fitting over a red knit dress, a colour she had presumably hoped would cheer her mother up. She grimaced to herself. How wrong she had been. She would be willing to bet Judith hadn't even noticed what her daughter was wearing.

'Miss Winsby?'

Lydia started. 'Oh, Dr Warner ... how is she?'

'I gave her a sedative, she'll sleep now until morning.' He directed a professional smile at her. 'Sleep is the best thing for her right now. As you're no doubt aware, she got hold of some alcohol yesterday.' He drew himself up to his full height; he was not a tall man. 'I am having security measures stepped up, I cannot allow that sort of thing. In your mother's condition alcohol could be fatal. Her heart is not strong.'

Lydia said with sudden, bitter truth, 'Maybe that would be the best thing for her.'

'Now, Miss Winsby, we mustn't talk that way.' He paused delicately. 'If you could persuade your father to visit her, the effects would be salutary, I'm sure.'

'Contrary to what my mother believes, I am almost never in contact with my father.'

'I see.' He gave a pompous nod. 'I see. Such delusions are very common in patients like your mother. Most unfortunate. Well, I must be going. Good afternoon, Miss Winsby. Compliments of the season to you.'

'Thank you, Dr Warner. Goodbye.'

She watched him march down the hall towards the nurses' office. Then she walked downstairs and out of the front door. The early dusk of December was creeping over the trees; the air was still. She drew a deep breath, feeling the cold bite into her lungs, and began to shiver.

She was still shivering as she drove home with the car heater on high and the windows closed. When she got home she would have a hot bath, start a fire in the fireplace and turn on some soothing, undemanding music. She'd wear her old red housecoat and curl up by the fire with a book . . . she wouldn't think about her mother or her father. Or about James. Fighting back tears, Lydia turned on to the expressway.

The town house had never looked so good. She parked on the edge of the road, unlocked the garage and drove the car inside. Then she went indoors, pulling off her leather boots but keeping her coat on for warmth. She was half-way up the stairs when the doorbell rang.

Frozen to the step she thought, it's Dr Warner. My mother's dead.

The doorbell rang again. She forced herself to move, her body as stiff as a doll's. Through the peephole in the door she saw that her visitor was not Dr Warner, but James. *James ...*

He was speaking to her. With another part of her brain she heard the words through the door. 'Lydia, please let me in.'

Obediently she unlocked the door, standing very still in the shadowed hallway. 'Lydia, I was——' He stopped. 'What's wrong?'

'What are you doing here?' she asked politely.

'I had to see you. What's happened? You look terrible.' Without waiting to be asked, he entered the hall and closed the door behind him

She retreated a couple of steps. 'James, I can't see you now,' she said in the same polite, dead voice.

'Are you expecting someone else?'

She frowned. 'Of course not.'

'You're shivering.'

'I'm cold. I was just going to start a fire.'

'Then I'll help you.'

'No. I don't want you to.'

'Sweetheart, you don't have a choice.'

She said raggedly, 'I'm *not* your sweetheart!'

'OK, OK—but you are my friend, Lydia. So I'm not leaving until you're settled in front of the fire.'

He looked large and immovable; she lacked the energy to fight him. Without waiting to see if he was following her, she began once more to climb the stairs.

She had reached the first floor when the telephone rang; it was fixed to the wall between the kitchen and the dining-room. 'Excuse me, please,' she said vaguely, and picked up the receiver.

An operator's voice said, 'Hold on a minute, please, madam. Long distance.'

Mother's had a heart attack.

Don't be silly. The nursing home would dial direct.

A self-assured, cultured male voice said crisply, 'Thank you, operator,' and in exactly the same tone added, 'Is that you, Lydia?'

'Hello, Father.'

'Speak up, I can scarcely hear you.'

She gripped the receiver a little more tightly with her right hand, putting her left hand against the wall to steady herself. 'Where are you?' she said.

'New York. At the head office.' Her father controlled the Western Pacific operations of a worldwide drug company based in New York. 'Lydia, I've had a letter from the nursing home, there's been some kind of mix up in the payments. They say I owe them for the last three months. But those payments have already been deducted from my account. Will you look into it for me? I don't have the time to bother with it.'

Maxwell had not spoken to her for over six months. He had not asked how she was, or how her mother was; and the implication was that her time was far less valuable than his. 'I was there today,' she said, 'visiting Mother.'

He gave an impatient exclamation. 'I tried to call you last night, but your line was busy. You'll look into it, will you, Lydia?'

Trying very hard to keep the anger from her voice, she said, 'Why don't you get on a plane and come up here? You could sort out the money and we could see each other as well.'

'I really don't have the time, you know how busy I am. Can't you do a simple thing like phone the accounts department at the nursing home and find out what's going on?'

'Yes, I can do that. But there's something else. Mother was really upset today. She'd so much appreciate a visit from you; it would make such a difference to her. You must know she still cares about you.' Care *was* an inadequate term for Judith's obsessive love for her husband, but Lydia did not want to use any of the stronger, more accurate words.

'Visiting your mother is the last thing in the world I'd be likely to do. We've been divorced for eleven years—are you forgetting that?'

Lydia abandoned restraint. 'No, I'm not,' she said curtly. 'I'm asking you for once in your life to show a little decency towards a woman who was your wife and is my mother. It wouldn't hurt you to take two days to come up here; I'm quite sure the Acton Drug Company wouldn't collapse if you were to do so. *Please*, Father . . . after all, it will soon be Christmas.'

'That reminds me, your gift should be delivered early next week.'

Silence hummed along the line. Lydia said finally, 'So will you come?'

'Of course not. You should know by now that I refuse to dance to your mother's tune.'

'You've never danced to anyone's but your own!'

'That is a ridiculous thing to say.'

'No, it's not! You haven't seen me for two years. You haven't talked to me for six months, but do you ask how I am? Do you even care? For all you know I might have broken my leg or had triplets or gotten married——'

'The latter before the former, I trust,' said Maxwell with wintry humour.

'With the example you and Mother set, I'm not likely to consider matrimony as a pathway to happiness. Father, please come up here and visit Mother, Dr Warner says her heart is bad and——'

'That's the most obvious form of blackmail, Lydia.'

She sagged against the wall. 'It wasn't intended to be,' she said in a low voice. 'How will I get in touch with you about the money?'

'A letter to head office will reach me.'

'I hope you understand I am doing it only for Mother's sake.'

'I shall ignore that statement, Lydia.'

Another silence. 'Where will you spend Christmas?' she asked.

'In Fiji with a number of friends. One of them a most attractive woman whom I am thinking of making my wife.'

'I see,' Lydia said. Why should Maxwell come to Toronto in December to visit his alcoholic former wife when he could be in Fiji with a most attractive woman? Why, indeed? 'Congratulations,' she said drily. 'Goodbye, Father.'

'Lydia——'

She replaced the receiver on the hook and felt the sobs crowd her throat. Thrusting her fist into her mouth, she tried to force them back, for she had vowed years ago never to shed another tear because of her father.

Someone touched her on the shoulder. She whirled, terrified, saw that it was James, and said foolishly, 'Oh, it's you. I'd forgotten you were here.'

'Who did that to your hand?' he said.

She looked at the three parallel scratches, now crusted with blood. 'My mother did it,' she said. Blindly she looked around the kitchen with its pretty wallpaper and its polished oak cabinets. 'I—you'd better go, James. I can't——'

When he took her by the shoulders, he must have felt her trembling. Under her make-up her face was drained of colour and her eyes were empty of expression, as though the real Lydia had retreated deep into herself. 'I'm not leaving,' he said. 'Why did she do that to you, Lydia?'

In her mind's eye Lydia could recall every detail of her

mother's face, distorted with rage. Tears flooded her eyes and spilled down her cheeks. She turned her face away, not wanting James to see her cry. 'She hates me,' she whispered. 'She always has.'

She began to weep, the ugly, raw sounds of grief tearing at her throat. James took her in his arms and pressed her face into his chest, his big hands very gentle.

Lydia cried for a long time, her body shuddering with the intensity of her grief. He stroked her hair, and held her close, and waited. He had already noticed the box of tissues on the counter by the sink, so that when she showed signs of quietening he said calmly, 'Hold on a minute. I'm going to get you something to blow your nose.'

Lydia stood still, her head bowed, knowing that she had wept tears that had been held back for months. She took a handful of Kleenex from James, keeping her head down, and mumbled, 'I'm going upstairs to wash my face. Won't be long.'

He waited until he heard the bathroom door shut before making a phone call. Then he went up to the living-room to wait for her.

When she came out of the bathroom she had removed her old make-up and put on new in a brave attempt to hide the marks of her weeping. Her nose was pink. He said, very seriously, 'That looks better.'

She managed a smile. 'Flattery, James—I look dreadful. Why don't you light a fire? Have you eaten?'

'I have a better idea. Throw a nightdress and your toothbrush into a suitcase, change into your jeans, and we'll take off.'

'Why?' she demanded. 'Where are we going?'

'To the country,' he said blandly. 'Don't look so suspicious, Lydia. You will sleep in one room and I will sleep in another.'

'The country?' she repeated.

'To stay with my mother and father.'

'Oh, no! I've had enough of mothers and fathers for one day.'

'I've already phoned—Mum will have a late dinner ready for us in about an hour and a half. So hurry up and get changed.'

Her face was troubled. 'But, James——'

'I want to get you out of here, Lydia. Away from your house and away from the city. We'll come back tomorrow evening. And you'll enjoy yourself. Trust me.'

Although he was smiling she sensed he meant those last two words literally. Trust me. She said with total honesty, 'I'm tired out, James. I don't know that I can face a whole lot of new people.'

'I told Mum you needed twenty-four hours of cosseting. Now that her children are all grown up, there's nothing she likes better than to spoil someone. You can go to bed as soon as you've eaten if that's what you want to do, and I'm sure breakfast in bed could be arranged.'

She did want to get away from the phone, and it was years since she had had breakfast in bed. 'It's supposed to snow,' she murmured.

'We'll go snow-shoeing tomorrow.'

'You're a very determined man,' she said slowly.

'My mother uses ruder words. Like pig-headed.'

This time Lydia's smile was more convincing. 'Maybe I should meet your mother; we could see eye to eye on a number of things.'

He laughed. 'Jeans and a toothbrush. Hurry up.'

Ten minutes later they were in James's car, heading east. Despite James's casual talk of the 'farm' where his parents lived, Lydia had put on a very smart shirt under a designer-knit sweater, and was wearing her best leather boots with her newest jeans; her hiking boots were in the trunk. The scratches on her hand were too widely spaced to hide with band-aids, so she had washed them and was trying to behave as if they were not there.

In the city streets the first snowflakes were drifting from the sky. James said non-committally, 'What does your father do, Lydia?'

In a voice that was just as non-committal she described Maxwell's job. 'He has a very responsible position with a great deal of travel. He's only fifty-seven . . . I'm sure he has ambitions to go higher yet.'

'How did he meet your mother?'

She was well aware that, obliquely, James was leading her back to her mutilated hand. She had soaked the front of his down jacket with her tears; she supposed he had the right to know. 'My father was born with ambition but no money or social position. My mother had old family money that carried with it access to the country clubs and the world of society. He must have been very handsome when he was younger, and she was a pretty woman. They had a huge wedding, my father settled in to work his way up in the business world, and within a couple of years I was born.'

They had pulled up at a traffic light. She watched a snowflake meander past her window as aimlessly as if gravity did not exist. 'You understand that what I'm telling you now I've pieced together myself over the years . . . my father decided that the country property was the place to bring up a child, so my mother, who loved parties and crowds and shopping, was more or less confined to the house by the lake. I grew up there. It's very beautiful, but for my mother, deprived of society and, more importantly, deprived of my father's company most of the time, it must have been excruciatingly lonely. She was never a woman with interior resources. So she started drinking. To pass the time. To give a little lustre to a succession of empty days. And the more she drank, the less my father came to visit her. Naturally. I don't think he ever loved her. He uses people as if they were things.'

'You haven't seen him for a while.'

'Two years.' She looked down at her lap. 'I'm sorry if I sound self-pitying; I don't mean to. I'm trying to be factual. You see, I don't think he ever loved me, either. When I was a little girl I could be produced at strategic intervals to complete the picture of the perfect family man. But when I turned into a gangly adolescent, I was no longer an asset. Besides, by then he'd made his own way. He didn't need me or my mother.'

'So you grew up in the house by the lake with your mother.'

'Yes. She had convinced herself that her pregnancy and my birth were what drove my father away . . . so from the beginning she resented me. I think she was wrong. I think my father would have found another excuse had I not been born—because, of course, he had other women in the city and he wanted the freedom to do as he pleased. A clinging wife was not part of the picture. But to my mother I was the wedge between her and her adored Maxwell. I suppose that's why she hates me to this day.'

They were on the 401 now, driving very fast through the darkness. 'She's the reason you were never free on Sundays.'

'I visit her on Sunday afternoons. She's in a nursing home near Lawley Park.'

'You're very faithful . . . a daughterly sense of duty?'

'I suppose so.' Lydia added so quietly that he could scarcely hear her, 'I keep hoping that one day she'll tell me she loves me.' She had never admitted this to another living soul.

James's eyes were bleak as he pulled out to pass another car. 'That doesn't seem very likely, Lydia . . . why did you visit her on Saturday this week?'

Her eyes widened. 'I'd forgotten—I'm invited for dinner at Annabel's and Malcolm's tomorrow night!'

'I'll phone Annabel when we get to the farm and explain that I've kidnapped you,' James said, glad to see a more normal emotion on Lydia's face. 'Annabel will appreciate that.'

Annabel would. Lydia countered, 'Why did you turn up at my house this evening? You said you weren't going to see me any more, remember?'

'Yes, I remember. A very short-sighted declaration on my part.' He peered through the windscreen, flipping on the signal light. 'This is our exit . . . I could tell you I just happened to be driving past when I saw you arrive home, but it wouldn't be the truth. Not the whole truth, anyway. I'd been phoning all afternoon and getting that damned answering machine of yours . . . leave a message at the sound of the beep—no, thanks. So I'd been driving around hoping to see you, and there you were. Alone, which is more than I deserved.' He gave a humourless laugh. 'By Tuesday morning I knew I'd made a mistake in walking out of your life. It just took me until Saturday to swallow my pride.'

Lydia said nothing; she couldn't cope with this on top of everything else. She leaned her head back on the seat and closed her eyes. Within five minutes she was asleep.

James drove on. The snowflakes veered from the windscreen with hypnotic speed. The city had been left behind; the road was narrower, more hilly, with trees and widely spaced houses on either side. He knew every corner and bump in the road, every landmark along the way. He was going home. . .and he was taking Lydia with him.

CHAPTER SIX

LYDIA woke when James slowed to turn off the highway. Rubbing her eyes, she saw stone gateposts, and a picket fence as white as the snow that covered the ground and bowed the branches of the patient fir trees. The driveway curved up a hill and down into a hollow. A house built of stone and wood with a slate roof and three stone chimneys nestled in the hollow. Light spilled from the square-paned windows.

She said in wonderment, 'It's like a Christmas card. It must be very old.'

'Early 1800s. Dad had it restored about thirty years ago.' His smile was uncomplicated. 'I'm glad you're here, Lydia.'

Lydia was not sure if she was glad to be here or not. She pulled her sheepskin jacket around her and took her overnight bag from the back seat of the car, then followed James down the steps to the back door. The snow was falling steadily now, silent and purposeful; tiny flakes melted on her skin and powdered James's hair. When they reached the door and a dog started barking inside she said in sudden mischief, 'You'll look very handsome as a white-haired old man.'

'You're going grey yourself, Granny.' Then he opened the door, shouting, 'We're here!'

A Labrador retriever and a very large mongrel came gambolling up to him, leaping up with every evidence of joy. James buffeted them around in what must be a time-honoured game, then commanded, 'Down!' The dogs obeyed, sinking back on their haunches, tongues lolling. 'Ben on the left, Heinz on the right,' James said. 'Now come and meet Mum and Dad.'

He ushered her across a large porch cluttered with coats, boots, snowshoes and skis, and opened the door to the kitchen. A delicious smell of roast beef and apple pie wafted to Lydia's nostrils. She blinked in the light, watching James stride across the room in his boots, pick up the grey-haired woman by the stove and whirl her around before kissing her on both cheeks. 'Hi, Mum,' he said, his grin like a small boy's.

'Haven't I ever taught you to take your boots off?'

'Clean snow, Mum.' He dipped a finger in the gravy. 'Mmm—not bad.'

The kitchen was large and friendly and even more cluttered than the porch. In one quick survey Lydia tallied three cats, innumerable plants and bunches of herbs, piles of books, battered copper pots hanging by the stained glass windows, a pair of lovebirds in a cage, and an artist's easel. But beneath the muddle all the furnishings of the kitchen were extremely expensive.

Ben and Heinz sidled past her, sneaking under the circular oak table. Feeling like a spectator to a scene where she did not belong, Lydia bent and pulled off her boots.

James said, 'Mum, I'd like you to meet Lydia Winsby. My mother, Betty Connelly, Lydia.'

Betty Connelly walked towards Lydia, holding out her hand, and Lydia was drawn into the scene. 'Hello, Lydia. I'm happy to meet you.'

Betty Connelly was unmistakably a happy woman, tall, handsome, as untidy as her kitchen. Impossible not to contrast the warm blue eyes and elegant cheekbones with Judith's wrinkled, tragic mask. Lydia swallowed. 'It's very kind of you to have me at such short notice.'

'James—once he's taken off his boots—will show you to your room. Then come down and have a drink by the fire before dinner,' Betty suggested. 'I've put Lydia in Julie's room, James.'

Julie's room was under the eaves at the far end of a long hall. It had a tiled fireplace and two white-painted beds with hand-made, brightly patterned quilts. Like the kitchen, the room was instantly friendly, and like the kitchen it was cluttered: dolls, teddy bears, books, dried flowers, posters and family photographs, all the paraphernalia of a young girl growing to adulthood. Lydia already knew that Julie was the only girl in a family of four, and had been widowed a year ago. This pretty, unassuming room made Julie into a person; the armour of this house and a loving family had not protected her from tragedy.

'I'll light the fire for you after dinner,' James said. 'The bathroom's two doors down.' He drew the curtains, shutting out the whirling snowflakes, then turned to face her. 'It's strange seeing you in my sister's room.'

She heard herself say, 'You'd rather see me in yours.' And could have bitten off her tongue.

He ran his fingers down her cheek. 'Of course I would. But we'd have to get married first; Dad's very old-fashioned.'

'Then I'd better stick to Julie's room.'

'At least you're here. In the house where I grew up. The last few days I'd given up hope of that ever happening.' As if he could not help himself, he put his arms around her and rested his cheek on her hair.

Lydia could feel the tension in his body and knew he was holding back, that what he really wanted to do was kiss her, caress her, make love to her. She held herself just as still, and after what seemed like a very long time he released her, stepping back, his face unreadable. 'Come down whenever you're ready,' he said.

After he had gone, she sank down on one of the beds, wishing she could lie down and sleep until morning. Why had James brought her here? To show her that not everyone had had a childhood as lonely and loveless as her own? She knew that already, knew that her upbringing was an aberration, but knew too how deeply it had marked her. Was James, not very subtly, trying to cure that hurt? You're too late, she thought. Years too late. I'm terrified of trusting myself to love. My mother loved my father. I loved them both. And the end result was nothing but unhappiness and betrayal. Better by far to be self-sufficient. To need no one but yourself.

In the bathroom she re-applied her make-up. Then she went downstairs. James was in the kitchen, carving the roast. 'Mum's gone to oust Dad from the study,' he said. 'He's writing a book on aboriginal land rights, and he often seems to forget which century he's in.'

Charles Connelly was shorter than his wife. His face was weathered, his voice vigorous and his opinions strong. The bond between father and son was also strong, and again Lydia was aware of a complicated mixture of anger and bittersweet longing, neither of which she revealed. She had very good manners. She talked amusingly about her job, intelligently about the last election and superficially about her background. No one mentioned the scratches on her hand. But by the time the four of them had moved back to the fireplace in the living-room—the tidiest room she had seen so far—she was feeling light-headed with tiredness; the visit with her mother seemed to have happened days ago.

James disappeared briefly. When he came back he said, 'I lit the fire in your room, Lydia. You've had a long day, feel free to go up any time you want.'

She smiled at him gratefully. 'I think I'll go now if you'll excuse me. Thank you, Mrs Connelly, that was a wonderful meal. Goodnight, Mr Connelly. Goodnight, James.'

James kissed her chastely on the cheek. "Night, Lydia. Sweet dreams.'

She went upstairs, got into bed, and turned out the light. The flames danced and swayed on the ceiling. The dolls smiled at her benignly from the shelf. She would like Julie, she thought drowsily. How lucky James was . . .

Downstairs, Charles had escaped to the study and Betty was saying to her son, 'She's lovely, James. I'd like to paint her—that incredible colouring.' She hesitated. 'But what happened to her hand? It looked like scratches.'

Restlessly James threw another log on the fire. Then he picked up his brandy snifter. 'Her mother did it. This afternoon.'

'Her *mother*!'

'She's in a nursing home.' Succinctly he described Lydia's upbringing, ending with the angry exchange of words with her father. 'He hasn't seen her for two years. But he's sending her a Christmas gift,' he finished savagely.

'The poor child . . . may I invite her for Christmas, James?'

'You're a doll, Mum. She might accept if you invite her. She almost certainly wouldn't if I did.'

Betty said placidly, 'You're in love with her.'

'You know me too well.'

Betty's wide mouth broke into a smile. 'You're being rather obvious about it. But I'm delighted—I've waited long enough. You *are* thirty-five, you know.'

'Don't start planning the wedding,' James said gloomily. 'She's not into commitment.'

'Understandably so. You'll have to be very patient, dear.'

He did not look overjoyed at the prospect. 'I want her now. On any terms.' He had always been able to be honest with his mother. 'She's not into affairs, either.'

'If she comes here for Christmas, she'll see how happy your father and I are when you're all home. A different view of family life. She's certainly sensitive to atmosphere.'

He patted Betty's knee. 'Ask her. Tomorrow. And now I must go and make a phone call.'

When he rang the Dohertys' number, Annabel picked up the receiver. 'It's James Connelly, Annabel. Lydia's friend.'

'Hello, James,' said Annabel, her voice an interesting blend of politeness, pleasure and outright curiosity.

'I'm calling from Scranton. I brought Lydia up here to stay at my parents; she had a very upsetting visit with her mother today.'

'You mean she *told* you about it?' Annabel said blankly. 'I know the basic situation with her parents but she hardly ever discusses either of them with me. Shuts up like a *clam* if you ask even the most *innocent* questions.'

'The point is, I'd like her to stay here tomorrow, I think it would do her good. Would you mind very much if she doesn't turn up for dinner?'

'Goodness, no! I'm just so *delighted* she's with you.' Annabel's voice suddenly dropped its rather exaggerated mannerisms. 'She needs you, James. But she'd be the last person to admit it. Lydia is scared to death of allowing herself to need anyone.'

'You're right, of course,' he said slowly.

'Children need their parents. But Lydia's mother was always getting soused and her father was always pulling fast deals or sleeping with other men's wives. So Lydia retreated from ever needing anyone. You've got your work cut out for you—it goes deep with her.'

When James hung up a few minutes later he had a deepened sense of respect for harum-scarum Annabel; and, under the plans he was making and the strategies he was considering, an uneasy edge of fear that in the end Judith and Maxwell Winsby might be the winners, and Lydia would never allow him any closer than she already had.

'Lydia, I've brought you breakfast.'

She had been dreaming about James ... smiling to herself, Lydia opened her eyes and saw James standing at the foot of her bed. He looked very solid and real, limned in the clear white light that comes from sun on snow. 'It's morning!' she said in surprise.

'Did you sleep well?'

'Wonderfully! I meant to stay awake to enjoy the fire, but I think I fell asleep right away.'

Her hair was like black satin against the pillow, her mouth sleep-softened. He tried not to stare at her white, finely boned shoulders as she reached for her housecoat.

Lydia pulled the folds of velour around her, glanced up, and saw in the blue eyes all James's desire for her. What would it be like to waken in the morning and find him beside her, his tousled blond head on the pillow, his big hands clasping her body? Colour crept up her cheeks. 'I—I hope your parents didn't think I was rude going to bed so early last night,' she said.

'No, they didn't think you were rude, Lydia. In fact, Dad took the chance to hightail it back to the study.' As if he was long accustomed to being in her bedroom, he sat down at the foot of her bed. 'I hope you're feeling energetic. Mum wants to get the Christmas tree today. We could hike to the woodlot on snowshoes.'

She drank her orange juice. 'Sounds like fun.'

'We'll take the dogs.' He began describing some of the exploits of Ben and Heinz, his big body relaxed, his ready smile very much in evidence.

Lydia did not feel nearly as relaxed. She had not pulled her housecoat closely enough about her body; it gaped at the front, exposing her cream satin nightgown, which in turn exposed her cleavage. Yet if she put down her knife and fork to adjust the housecoat she was admitting her own self-consciousness.

But there was more. Because it was a single bed, James was sitting very close to her. He was wearing a faded denim shirt and jeans, more casual clothes than she was used to, clothes that gave him a rakish air; the sleeves were rolled up, the neck of the shirt undone, and every now and then she could catch, tantalisingly, the sharp tang of his aftershave. Eating the fluffy mushroom omelette more quickly than it deserved, she wished she could obliterate from her memory those frantic few minutes of discovery in Annabel's kitchen. If only she could forget the probe of his tongue, the slide of his fingers at her breast . . . she gulped down her coffee.

'There's no rush,' James said lazily. 'The tree will wait for us.'

Lydia neatly refolded the linen napkin and put it back on the tray. 'A shame to waste the sunshine,' she said lightly.

He reached forward, took the tray from her lap, and placed it on the other bed. Resting his hands on her shoulders, a move that made the velour gape a little more widely, he kissed her.

She tried to push him away. But the denim shirt was thin from many washings, so that the heat of his skin touched her fingers almost as if there was no barrier between them. His hands were moulding her shoulders through the red velour. In a burst of longing as primitive as it was fierce, she wanted him to strip her of her robe, to fondle her naked flesh and to cover her with his body.

And then the pendulum swung to the other side. What am I thinking of? I must be mad.

Terrified, she shoved at his chest with all her strength and wrenched her head free—and found herself held by the depthless blue of his eyes.

'When are you going to stop fooling yourself, Lydia?' he demanded. 'You want me as badly as I want you.'

She pulled the robe tightly across her chest. 'No, I don't!'

'You can't lie about that kind of thing.'

She had yielded to him; only for a few minutes, but that had been long enough. For James was attuned to her every mood, her every move. She should know that by now.

Refusing to be stared down, she said, 'Maybe I did want you. But I pushed you away—that was my decision.'

'At least you're admitting there's a choice.'

'You give no quarter, do you?'

'I'm fighting for my life. And for yours.'

'I do my own fighting, James.'

'You always have, yes. But that's a lonely road, Lydia.'

'It's a safe road.'

'Oh, safety!' he said impatiently. 'There's more to life than safety. If you were totally committed to safety, you wouldn't be here now.'

'You've got all the answers,' she said irritably.

'Not all of them,' was the dry response. 'And now I'm going to get out of here before I start kissing you all over again.'

'That was a lovely breakfast,' she said meekly. 'Thank you.'

Fifteen minutes later, showered and dressed, Lydia made her way downstairs, following her nose to the kitchen. Wrapped in a huge red apron, Betty was vigorously stirring the contents of a bowl with one hand and pouring in brandy with the other. 'Come and hold the bowl, Lydia,' she said cheerfully.

'Smells heavenly. What is it?'

'Mincemeat.' Betty poured in another generous dollop of brandy. 'The plum puddings are cooking, too. I'm late with them this year. Lydia, Charles and I would very much like you to join us for Christmas.'

Lydia's hands slipped on the bowl. 'That's very kind of you,' she temporised, and thought to herself with a flicker of admiration, James put her up to this. Clever James.

'All the children will be home. I'm sure you'd enjoy yourself.'

'I usually go to my friend Annabel's for Christmas.'

Betty tasted the mincemeat, frowning thoughtfully. 'Tastes good,' she said. 'One could get drunk on that. Perhaps you'd better check with your friend first?'

'I'll do that, and let you know at the first of the week.' Which would make James suffer a little, Lydia thought meanly.

As if on cue, James came in the back door, the dogs at his heels. He was holding a pair of mukluks. 'These are Julie's. I hope they'll fit you, Lydia.'

With two pairs of socks, the mukluks were a snug enough fit. Lydia pulled on a windbreaker over her sweater, added a white fur hat and mittens, and went outside. Blue sky, brilliant sun, sparkling snow; she drew a deep breath of the cold air and was glad she was miles from the city, where the snow would already be grimy and the streets coated with salt. She bent to adjust the soft leather bindings on the snowshoes.

James straightened, whistling to the dogs. He had a coil of nylon rope over one shoulder and was carrying a saw. 'All set?' he asked.

She nodded, taking a few experimental steps; it was years since she had worn snowshoes.

The snow was dry and fluffy, well over a foot deep, blindingly bright in the sunlight and blue-shadowed in the hollows. They left the house, crossed the gently rolling meadows, then entered a grove of maple and birch. The incline was steep. The dogs chased each other through the trees, Heinz barking hysterically. Although she would never have admitted it, Lydia was glad James was going ahead of her, breaking the trail, and glad, too, that she was in reasonably good physical condition. She called, 'You do realise that the further we walk, the further we have to carry the tree?

He stopped, looking back at her and laughing. 'Only three more miles.'

His jacket was scarlet against the snow, his long-limbed body relaxed; the sky was no more blue than his eyes. 'I don't even see any fir trees,' Lydia said, trying to keep her mind on their errand.

'Just over the next hill. Cross my heart.'

'Oh, sure.'

'Can't keep up the pace, eh, Lydia?'

She sensed a double meaning to his words, and said calmly, 'I can snowshoe just as fast as you.'

His smile acknowledged her acuity. 'So you can,' he said amiably. 'When you were a little girl did you get your Christmas trees from the woods?'

'The chauffeur would buy a very expensive pine tree and the maids would decorate it,' she replied with a grimace.

'So what was Christmas like for you, Lydia?'

She kicked at the snow. 'Father being away and no one ever sure whether he'd arrive home or not. Some years he did, more often he didn't. Mother getting drunk if he didn't and fighting with him if he did. Food ... elaborate, rich food enough for ten families. I usually ate Christmas dinner with the cook and the maids; they felt sorry for me, I suppose. I hated Christmas. I was always glad when it was over.' Her smile was self-deprecating. 'Classic picture of the poor little rich girl—Charles Dickens would have had a heyday with a Winsby Christmas.'

'Classic picture of a very lonely child,' James said soberly. He gave his shoulder a sudden shake. 'Come on, Lydia, let's find this tree.'

He set a faster pace, as though pursued by thoughts he

did not care for, and within five minutes they had reached a stand of fir trees, whose feathered branches were weighed down with snow. They circled the trees, eyeing them critically, deciding that this one was too straggly and that one lopsided. 'Has to be a fir,' James said. 'Spruce drops its needles too quickly. How about this one?'

She walked around it, knocking some of the snow from the branches, the mongrel Heinz following in her steps. The boughs were bushy and well spaced, and the tree was even on all sides. 'Isn't it too big?' she said doubtfully.

'We could always take a foot or two off the bottom. Mum likes some extra boughs for decorating.'

He began to saw through the trunk in smooth, even strokes. The tree leaned, then swished to the ground. The trunk started to bleed a clear, sticky sap.

James looked at the tree with satisfaction. 'Once we get out in the open we'll put the rope on it. But for now we'll just have to pull it.' He grabbed one of the bottom branches, waiting for Lydia to do the same on her side. 'Let's go.'

She discovered very rapidly how awkward snowshoes could be when pulling a very large tree between other trees over uneven ground. Within a few minutes she was gasping for breath. 'We'll never make it back to the house!'

'Sure we will—watch out!'

She had brushed against an overhead branch which proceeded to dump its burden of snow down her neck. She yelped, stepped sideways, tripped on a snag, and sat down, abruptly. James began to laugh.

Peeling off one mitten, Lydia scooped the melting snow from the neck of her jacket. 'It's not funny, James Connelly! I'm beginning to think our chauffeur had the right idea—picking out a nice tree at the market.'

He knelt beside her, brushing more snow away. 'You're having fun,' he said firmly.

She had never been able to resist the charm of his smile.

'And we're going to have so much more fun before we get this darn tree back to the house. Go away, Heinz!'

James bent and kissed her cold, wet lips. 'We can always add to the fun, you know.'

The edge of one of the snowshoes was digging into her calf, water was trickling down her neck and the seat of her jeans was soaked. Yet she felt very happy, the man's blue eyes one with the sky, the coldness of his lips part of the bright, glistening snow. She said spontaneously, 'I like you!'

'That's a good start.'

Her face clouded, but before she could say anything, he added quickly, 'I shouldn't have said that. Let's stop worrying about tomorrow, Lydia. Right now I'm kissing you in the snow and I'm happy, and so are you, I'd be willing to bet—— and that's enough. More than enough. To hell with tomorrow.'

She had a feeling there was a fallacy in his reasoning, but she too was content with the present moment. 'I'm getting very wet,' she said.

He heaved her to her feet, not without difficulty, for their snowshoes were entangled. They grabbed the tree again, hauling it through the undergrowth; when they reached the hardwood grove, James tied the rope to the trunk, which made their job much easier. As they walked in stride across the first meadow, the tree gouging parallel tracks in the snow, James remarked, 'We pull well together.'

'We are pulling this particular Christmas tree across the snow very well together,' Lydia replied agreeably.

'So you don't like my metaphor?'

'Only as it relates to the present.'

'You're too clever, Lydia, my love.'

'I am not your love!'

'You're cute when you're cross—and you must allow me my occasional flights of hyperbole.'

'As long as each of us recognises them as hyperbole.'

Their dialogue was light enough. But Lydia was well aware of the undercurrents, and was not surprised when James stopped in his tracks to reach across and kiss her, clumsily because of the snowshoes. She was discovering, and was shocked with herself, that she liked fighting with him. That it made her feel fully alive in a way she didn't often feel.

Not saying a word, she began pulling on the rope again. Twenty minutes later they reached the house. James stored the tree in the garage, the dogs flopped down in the porch, and Betty produced cocoa and a plate of cookies once Lydia had changed into dry clothes.

Lydia unashamedly fell asleep on the chesterfield for half an hour. Then she and James were put to work decorating some plain pine wreaths Betty had bought at a local bazaar, after which dinner was served in the dark-panelled dining room. Then Lydia and James got ready to go home. James hugged his father and kissed his mother; Lydia shook their hands and thanked them sincerely for her stay. 'We'll hope to see you at Christmas if not before,' Betty said with a smile that reminded Lydia of James's. 'You're welcome any time, Lydia.'

For the first half of the journey home Lydia was very quiet. James put on the radio and left her to her thoughts. Finally she said, 'James . . .'

He lowered the volume. She began again. 'James, I understand why you took me home to meet your parents . . . apart from the fact that I was upset on Saturday, that is. You wanted to show me that all families aren't like my family, that Christmas need not be an occasion to be dreaded, that one's father and mother can love each other years after they're married and still welcome their children home . . .'

She seemed to have run out of words. 'Not very subtle of me, I agree,' he said. 'But it seemed an obvious thing to do.'

'I saw all those things. I envy you your parents and your brothers and sister and . . . and the *warmth* in that house. Your parents made me feel very welcome, don't get me wrong. But I don't belong there, James. I can't see myself as part of such a family.'

'That was only one short visit.'

'I'm not so naïve that I think all families are like mine. At least my head tells me they're not. But the rest of me doesn't pay any attention to my head. The rest of me feels like an outsider who can't imagine herself giving and receiving love, or trusting and needing others . . . I'm not explaining myself well, James.'

'Stop trying to undo the damage of years overnight, my dear.'

His endearment caught at her heart. Panic-stricken, she said, 'You should stop seeing me, James. I'll only bring you pain.'

'I can look after myself, Lydia.'

'Don't fall in love with me—*please*,' she said with sudden desperate honesty.

He was silent for a few seconds. 'You're the one we should be concerned about,' he said finally. 'Not me. Look how far you've come since you met me. You're still going out with me, no doubt against your better judgment, you've visited my parents and you've told me about your parents. Those are all big steps. Things take time. Be patient, it will all work out in the end.'

'I don't feel as sure of that as you do,' Lydia said in a low voice.

'As I said to you once before, trust me.'

She said sharply, 'The terms haven't changed, James.'

'They will. When the time is right.'

She had the sensation of battering her head against a brick wall. 'There's no talking to you,' she said, and couldn't have guessed that he was not feeling nearly as confident as he sounded.

'Oh, the battle's still on, Lydia.'

In a lightning flash of prescience she said, 'Maybe neither of us will win,'

'I prefer my version. That both of us will win.' James shifted restlessly in his seat. 'Did Mother ask you for Christmas?'

'Yes. I'll have to check with Annabel, I usually spend Christmas with them.'

'Phone her tonight, will you?'

'What's the hurry?'

He banged his palm against the steering wheel. 'I'd like to know you'll be there. So I can look forward to it.'

'You *have* fallen in love with me.' She said it like an accusation.

'Of course I have,' he said shortly.

'That's crazy, James! You scarcely know me. You've admitted yourself you've had no social life for years because of your job—all you've done is fall in love with the first available woman.'

'I would hardly say you're available.'

'Then date other women. Some of them will be available.'

He was getting angry. 'Are you trying to say that all I want from you is sex?'

'*I* don't know what you want from me!'

'I want you to put your childhood in proper perspective, and then get on with ordinary living. Hell, Lydia, I've said all this before!'

'You're putting too much pressure on me.'

'Any pressure would be too much. Go on, admit it!'

She glared through the windscreen. They were on the 401 again, being swept along in the parallel lines of cars. Just as James is trying to sweep me along, she thought, and turned her head to look out of the side window.

When they arrived at the town house she said evenly, as if they had never argued in the speeding car, 'Thank you, James. I enjoyed meeting your parents.'

His face gave nothing away. 'I'll call you tomorrow.'

He did not kiss her, nor did he accompany her to the door. Carrying her overnight bag, she let herself in the house and waved at him. He drove off. She locked the door, said out loud several pithy words that would have shocked George's mother, and went to bed.

CHAPTER SEVEN

LYDIA's telephone started ringing at eight forty-five the next morning. 'Torrington's Exotic Plants,' she said.

'Lydia? It's George.'

'Oh ... hello, George. How are you?' she said lamely.

'I'm well, thank you. And yourself?'

They discussed his mother's health and the weather, neither of which Lydia felt was the reason for the call. Then he said, 'Lydia, I have two tickets for Ofra Harnoy on Friday. Would you like to go?'

George's placid, undemanding nature suddenly seemed very attractive. 'I'd love to,' she said, more warmly than perhaps was wise.

'Excellent. I'll pick you up at seven-fifteen.'

After another exchange of pleasantries, he rang off. I'm not going steady with James, Lydia told herself defiantly. I have a perfect right to date anyone I please.

Her next phone call involved delivery of forty trees to a newly opened mall in Leaside. The mall manager wanted the trees planted on Saturday night after closing, and on Sunday, so as not to inconvenience the Christmas shoppers. She made all the necessary arrangements and put down the telephone, which immediately rang again.

'James here, Lydia. I'm out at the airport, on my way to Vancouver. I'll be there most of the week. Can I see you Friday?'

'I can't see you until Monday,' she said, and because she was trying not to sound guilty, sounded cold instead.

'Why not?' he rapped.

'I'm going to a concert on Friday——'

'Who with?'

95

'George.'

'For heaven's sake, Lydia! Why are you doing that?'

'Because he asked me.'

'You know what his motive is. The month is up—he's going to produce the diamond ring again.'

'In which case I shall refuse it again.'

'Then what about Saturday?'

'I have to work Saturday night and Sunday. At the Eglinton Mall. I could call you when I get home on Sunday, if you like.'

'Yes, I like,' he said caustically.

'You're jealous,' she said in surprise.

'Damn right I am. It would serve me right, wouldn't it, if I've broken down your opposition to marriage just enough for you to marry someone safe and dull like George.'

'James, I am not going to marry George! Get that through your head once and for all.'

Silence. Finally he said in a mollified tone, 'My mother *is* much nicer than his . . . isn't she?'

'Much. No comparison.'

'What about me?'

'Oh, you're much nicer than his mother, too,' she said wickedly.

Reluctantly he laughed. 'You'll call me Sunday?'

'Promise. Enjoy Vancouver.'

Lydia put down the receiver and told herself that a week away from James would be good for her. Give her the sense of perspective he was always talking about.

Restlessly she left the office and went upstairs to water her plants. Her living-room, which had always satisfied her with its orderly, carefully chosen furniture and sense of space, now seemed bleak and sterile. Did she want the clutter and confusion of the stone house in the hollow, along with all its attendant emotional demands? Or did she want the control, the self-sufficiency, of the life she had built for herself?

I don't know what I want, she thought miserably, plucking two dead blooms from the cyclamen.

She discovered on Friday—or rediscovered—that she didn't want George. James had chosen exactly the right description: safe and dull. She could not imagine how she had ever contented herself with his company for over a year, and realised, inevitably, how much James had expanded her horizons. She wasn't the same woman she had been a month and a half ago. She had changed.

This thought stayed at the back of her mind during her Saturday afternoon visit with her mother, a visit that was as tranquil as last week's had been harrowing, and during the tree-planting at the mall. Pete was there to help her, as well as the delivery man from the greenhouse in his heated truck. One of her maintenance workers should have turned up and did not; on Saturday night the greenhouse sent only five trees, not ten, and on Sunday morning the truck was two hours late arriving at the mall. These were more or less normal contretemps of Lydia's job; but it meant that at seven o'clock on Sunday evening there were still six trees left to plant.

She straightened her aching back. 'What'll we do, Pete? Go for dinner and come back, or work straight through?'

He grinned at her. 'No restaurant'd take you in, Lydia.'

She looked down at herself in rueful agreement. The cement planters had first to be tamped with a layer of charcoal to prevent soil odour; a fair bit of the charcoal, which was black and clinging, had transferred itself to her person, along with some of the soil, also black, in which the twelve-foot trees were planted. Her boots, jeans and long-sleeved shirt were all very dirty; her face, which she could not see, was no doubt the same. 'Let's finish, then,' she said wearily. 'I'll dump the charcoal if you'll help Mario unload the last six trees.'

Whistling 'Tannenbaum' out of tune, Pete strode off down the deserted mall, his steps echoing eerily on the tile floor. The store fronts, barred and unlit, massed with shiny tinsel, reflected his skinny outline. Lydia shivered, for the scene evoked all the loneliness of Christmas to her as a child: the isolated figure surrounded by tinsel. Stop it, she told herself. You're over-tired. And you're twenty-nine, not nine. Grow up, Lydia. As James keeps telling you.

She cut open six bags of charcoal, tipping the black chunks over the edge of the planter, then climbing in to level them off with her boots.

From far down the long corridor she heard 'O Come, All Ye Faithful'. At least she thought it was 'O Come, All Ye Faithful'. With Pete it was often difficult to tell. She climbed out of the planter and hauled some bags of charcoal over to the next one. Five more to go. Pete would have to help her with the soil; it was much heavier than the charcoal.

She was climbing out of the second planter when Pete called cheerily, 'Brought a visitor along, Lydia.'

Without any presentiment she turned around, pushing back a strand of hair with a finger that was equally black.

Her boot slipped. She fell back, grazing the side of her leg on the rough concrete. Clutching her leg, wondering if she had broken the skin, annoyed with herself for being so clumsy, she said weakly, 'James! What are you doing here?'

'Did you hurt yourself?'

'No.'

He could have laughed at her appearance; he could have made any number of wisecracks. But he must have seen the pallor under the dirt on her face, and the way she unconsciously eased the ache from her shoulders as she looked at him. 'I was worried about you,' he said. 'So I drove out here. Can I help?'

She had never heard three more lovely words 'Yes,' she said. 'Provided you don't mind getting dirty.'

He shrugged off the jacket he was wearing over jeans and an old shirt. 'Tell me what to do.'

With four of them, the work seemed to go much faster. They spread charcoal, emptied bags of soil, stood the trees upright and stamped down the earth around them, then covered the ground with chips of bark. Mario departed. Pete, James and Lydia gathered up their tools and the empty bags, carrying them the length of the mall to where the van was parked outside. The security guard locked up behind them. James said firmly, 'Pete can drive the van and you can come with me, Lydia.'

'Sure,' said Pete.

'I'm too dirty,' said Lydia.

'That's settled, then,' James said. 'See you, Pete.'

Every bone in Lydia's body seemed to be aching; certainly she didn't have the energy to argue. 'Thanks, Pete. No need to bring the van round until one-thirty tomorrow. See you then.'

James spread his jacket on the passenger seat and she collapsed on to it. 'I feel ninety-nine, not twenty-nine,' she mumbled. 'How was Vancouver?'

'Wet and foggy. How was George?'

'Safe and dull.'

'Are you coming to us for Christmas?'

'Yes.' Annabel's comment had been, 'Darling, of *course* you'll go with him. If you're in any doubt whatso*ever*, then I withdraw our invitation—so you'll have to go to his house, won't you? Darling, he's gorgeous, not a bit like your usual. It's about time. You'll have a *wonderful* Christmas, I know you will.'

Lydia did not share any of this with James. 'I wrote a note to your mother and accepted her invitation.'

'Good,' was all he said. But she was not deceived; she had seen his smile.

He didn't speak again until they reached the town house. As he helped her out of the car he said, 'You're getting in the shower, I'll make something to eat, and then you're going to bed.' He grinned crookedly, keeping a hand under her elbow. 'Alone. I want a little more life in you when I take you to bed.'

Her head seemed to be floating above her body. She said curiously, 'Does it ever occur to you that I may not go to bed with you?'

'Yes, it does,' he said flatly. 'Scares the hell out of me, if you want the truth.'

Somehow comforted that James too had his doubts, she allowed herself to be led indoors. She took off her boots and headed for the bathroom. In the white-framed mirror she gazed at her face in horror, not sure whether to laugh or cry. She looked like a clown, black daubed on white around blank turquoise eyes. Had she been purposely trying to discourage James, she could not have looked worse.

Soap, shampoo and hot water accomplished wonders. She dried her hair and dressed in an unsexy nightshirt under her red velour robe. Cheeks glowing from the steam, she went downstairs to the kitchen, where James was tossing pancakes with considerable expertise; when he served them with hot maple syrup in front of the fire in the living-room she said, licking her fingers, 'You can always get a job as a short-order cook if shipbuilding palls.'

Sipping her tea, she put her feet up on the coffee table. The red robe fell back, revealing the bruise on the inside of her leg. Oblivious, she gazed contentedly into the flames.

'Did you do that when you slipped on the planter?' James demanded. She followed the direction of his eyes, and quickly flipped the robe over her leg. 'It's nothing.'

He knelt beside her, drawing back the hem of her gown. 'It's quite a bruise. Does it hurt?'

'It'll be fine.'

There was tension in her voice. He looked up, one hand resting on her bare knee. The robe fell open still further, revealing the brevity of her nightshirt; her eyes were trained on him as if she had never seen him before. He said hoarsely, 'Lydia.'

In a single lithe movement he got up from the floor. As he took her in his arms on the chesterfield, they began kissing with a fierce, desperate hunger, a hunger that was altogether mutual. Lydia clasped him by the shoulders, feeling his lips on her mouth, her closed eyes, her throat, hearing his voice repeating her name with the same hunger.

Somehow they were lying side by side on the soft, yielding velvet. James took her face in his hands, kissing her even more deeply until she felt nothing but the intense, all-encompassing ache of desire. Drowning in it, she rejoiced in the slide of his hands down her body to her breasts, in the probe of his fingers through the soft cotton of her shirt.

She could not bear that he not touch her flesh. She fumbled for the buttons on the shirt, opening them, and heard him say her name again, a sighing breath against her cheek.

Between her thighs she felt the press of his manhood. He raised his head, looking straight into her eyes as his fingers teased her nipples to hardness. 'You're so beautiful and I want you so much.'

And she, who had locked away passion for years, said softly, her eyes shining like jewels, 'I want you, too.'

He put his arms around her pliant, yielding body and hugged her to him, burying his face in the sweet-scented line of her throat. 'I never thought I'd hear you say those words ... I feel as though I've waited for them forever.'

'Not even two months,' Lydia said in wonderment, running her nails down the long curve of his spine, glorying in the weight and warmth of his body. 'Such a short time ... how you've changed me.'

Again he raised his head; she had never seen such tenderness in a man's face before. 'How could I not change you?' he said huskily. 'I love you more than life itself, Lydia. I love you with all my heart.'

The brilliance faded from her eyes, leaving only the flat

opacity of fear; her body tensed in his arms. 'Don't say that, James—please.'

He didn't understand. He kissed her lips, his mouth lingering. 'Why ever not? Every word is true, and needs to be said.'

'No!' The embrace that had convulsed her with desire now convulsed her, claustrophobically, with fear. She pushed him away with frantic strength. 'We can go to bed, that's one thing, but I don't want you to fall in love with me.'

There could be no mistaking her sincerity. His body went very still. 'Lydia, I can't separate them. I want you because I love you. And part of the reason I love you, I suppose, is because I find you so desirable. How can I separate them?'

She sat up, huddling into her robe, crossing her arms over her breast. 'They're different,' she said fiercely. 'Yes, I want to go to bed with you—the terms have changed. But I don't want to love you. Not now or ever. Love destroys people!'

He pulled himself upright. 'What you mean is, love destroyed your mother.'

'Yes, that's what I mean! I'll never do that to myself. Never.'

'A month ago you said you wouldn't go to bed with me.'

'That's different,' she flashed back. 'That's lust or passion or whatever you want to call it. Straightforward. Simple. Not like love.'

'That's where you're wrong, Lydia. Sure, there's a healthy amount of lust in my feeling for you. But I'd never take you as one animal takes another. Because I love you. So there's emotion involved, feelings, caring.' His voice was clipped with extreme anger. 'If all you want is to get laid, you've got the wrong man.'

She flinched. 'Don't be crude!'

'You started it.' He got to his feet, tucking in his shirt.

'Where are you going?' she faltered.

'Home.'

'But——'

'But what?' He ran his fingers through his hair. 'You think over everything I've said, Lydia. Because the terms have changed. *I* won't make love to you until you can accept my love for you. As part of me. The whole man.'

She felt numb all over, and could think of nothing to say. She followed him across the carpet and down the two flights of stairs, watching in silence as he pulled on his boots and jacket. He took his car keys from his pocket and looked over at her. The hall light shone on the bruised shadows under her eyes and on the soft, vulnerable mouth.

Briefly he closed his eyes. 'Lydia, I shouldn't have lost my temper—you're tired. But it had to be said. Go to bed, dear, and get some sleep.'

She could have maintained her composure had he remained angry. But his unexpected gentleness disarmed her. 'I'm sorry,' she whispered. 'I didn't mean to hurt you. But *I* had to say what I said, too, James.'

He took her in his arms as a father might take a wayward, much-loved child. 'I understand,' he said. 'Sleep well, and I'll talk to you tomorrow.'

When she locked the door behind him the action seemed horribly symbolic, as if her inability to love was locking him out of her life. Clutching for comfort his promise to phone her, Lydia trailed upstairs to bed.

CHAPTER EIGHT

James kept his promise to phone Lydia the next morning. All too literally. The telephone rang at six-thirty.

At first she thought it was the alarm clock. She grabbed for its fluorescent face in the darkness, saw the time, and shook herself awake. The telephone. It was the telephone ringing.

'Hello?' she croaked.

'Lydia? James. Sorry to wake you. I'm at the airport, I've got to go north—to the Beaufort Sea. Trouble on one of the oil rigs ... are you there, Lydia?'

'Yes, I'm here,' she said dazedly. 'I thought you said this new job didn't involve much travel.'

'This is nothing compared with what I used to do. And it's only until I get a couple of new guys trained. I should be back tomorrow afternoon at the latest; I'll get in touch as soon as I'm home. Are you free tomorrow evening?'

'Yes ... you still want to go out with me?'

'I've got to go, they're waiting for me. Yes, of course I do. Take care, Lydia.'

The busy signal buzzed in her ear. She had wanted to say, be careful. She had wanted to say, you're my best friend, I care about you. But he had gone.

She burrowed her head into the pillow and tried to go back to sleep. But her leg was sore and her mind was crowded with images of James. Taking her arm on the Greek freighter. Laughing at her as she sat in the snow with ice-cold water trickling down her neck. Gazing into her eyes as he stroked her breasts ... I want you, she thought. I want you. I'm willing to risk physical intimacy with you, and all that it implies. As for the rest, I don't know. I'm so frightened of becoming dependent on you, of needing you, of being vulnerable to you.

Trust me, he had said.

She pulled the blankets over her head, trying to close out the voices, and instead remembered the slide of his fingers on her flesh. Neither memory was conducive to sleep. Wincing from various aches and pains, she got out of bed and stumbled to the shower.

Lydia arranged her work so that she was in the office all Tuesday afternoon. However, James did not phone. Nor did he that evening. As the hours passed she moved from anticipation to annoyance to anxiety, an anxiety that multiplied drastically when she watched the ten o'clock news and heard that a crew member had been killed that afternoon in an accident aboard an oil rig in the Beaufort Sea. The name was being withheld pending notification of next of kin.

James was not a crew member. Therefore James was not the dead man. Holding firmly to these two facts, Lydia watched the rest of the news, the weather, and the sports, and couldn't have repeated a single item. If anything had happened to James, would anyone let her know? No one at Finlay and Madson knew she was a friend of James's. His parents knew. But her phone number was listed under Torrington's Exotic plants, not under Lydia Winsby, a set-up which had always suited her in the past. So Betty Connelly would not be able to reach her either.

It was eleven o'clock by now. She could not justify calling the Connellys to ask if James was all right. They'd think she was crazy. Worse, they'd think she was in love.

She turned off the television set and went to bed, where she dreamed of an oil rig adorned with Christmas wreaths, whose captain could not tell her where James was because he only spoke Greek.

At five past nine her office telephone rang, and a businesslike female voice asked for Lydia Winsby.

'Speaking,' said Lydia.

'This is Lynn MacLeod of Finlay and Madson, Miss Winsby. I have an official request here from Mr Connelly. He'll be arriving at Toronto International Airport at eight-twenty p.m. on an Air Canada flight from Montreal.' She gave Lydia the flight number. 'He asked if you could meet him.'

'Is he all right?'

'I believe there was some trouble on the rig,' Lynn MacLeod said evasively. 'I'm not sure of the details.'

Nor would you tell me if you knew, thought Lydia. 'Certainly I can meet him,' she said. 'Would you give me the flight number again?' She jotted it down on her pad. 'Thank you.'

She quickly called her tennis partner and cancelled her game that evening, and then tried to concentrate on work. Why was James not returning on the company jet? Why was he coming from Montreal? And why was he a day late? All were questions to which she had no answers. What she did have, apart from her concern, was a small, warm glow that he had arranged for Lynn MacLeod to telephone her, and that he wanted to be met.

The temperature was dropping steadily as she drove to the airport under a star-studded sky. She had tucked a red silk scarf in the neckline of her new coat, and her cheeks were flushed with an uncomfortable mixture of anxiety, excitement, and uncertainty. Very clear in her mind was the anger with which they had parted; equally clear was the tenderness in James's blue eyes.

She parked the car and hurried to the Air Canada arrivals area. The monitor announced that the Montreal flight was on time. She waited at the barrier. A baby was crying monotonously. Two shrieking children chased each other up and down, darting in and out of the crowds, ignored equally by a voluble Italian family and a majestic black man in a long cotton robe and a maroon turban. The minutes ticked by. A group of passengers straggled through the doorway and stationed themselves around the luggage carousel posted for the Vancouver flight. Ten minutes later there was another surge of people.

Lydia saw James immediately, for he was taller than average. He was carrying a briefcase and headed straight for the sliding doors, his eyes scanning the crowd. She squirmed her way forward, seeing an intense, crushing disappointment settle on his face. 'James!' she called, waving a black-clad arm. 'James, over here.'

She smiled apologetically as she squeezed past an Italian matron stationed, arms akimbo, at the very front of the crowd, and nearly tripped over one of the yelling children. James caught at her sleeve. 'Take it easy,' he said with his crooked smile. 'You don't have to fall at my feet.'

He was wearing a navy duffel coat with dark green work pants and steel-toed boots, and was carrying a yellow hard-hat along with his briefcase. But it was his face that held her attention. She said, 'James, you look awful!'

The harsh fluorescent lighting fell impartially on his untidy blond hair and on the ugly graze on his cheek. His eyes were sunk deep in their sockets; the shadows under them were as dark as bruises.

She said, 'You were on the oil rig where the man got killed, weren't you?'

'Yeah.' He looked around at the jostling crowd. 'Will you take me home?'

She heard the thread of desperation under the prosaic words. 'Of course. Do you want to wait here while I bring the car up?'

'I'm not an invalid, Lydia.'

She bit her lip, for his irritability was totally out of

character. Something was wrong. Badly wrong. Keeping her thoughts to herself, she led him outdoors into the cold December night, and efficiently threaded her way through the parked cars to her own. Unlocking the passenger door, she took his briefcase and hat and put them in the back seat. He lowered himself into the seat rather too carefully. 'Do you need a doctor?' she asked in a neutral voice.

'No. Saw one on the oil rig.' He leaned back and closed his eyes. 'God, I'm tired.'

He was asleep before she left the car park, the dead sleep of total exhaustion. She paid the parking attendant and accelerated smoothly along the exit ramp. Although she had never seen his house, she knew the general area where he lived; she would have to wake him when she got there for exact directions.

He was not easy to waken. In the end she had to pull over to the side of the road and shake his arm. 'James, wake up!'

He jerked upright with a muffled exclamation. She said more gently, 'I don't know where your house is.'

He squinted at the traffic lights. 'Turn right, then second to the left and first to the right. Number thirty-seven.'

Number thirty-seven was one of a row of remodelled Victorian brick homes. Lydia turned off the ignition. 'I'll get your case,' she said, suddenly terrified that he wasn't going to invite her in.

She locked the car and followed him up the stone steps to the front door, which was painted a dark bottle green, an attractive contrast to the brass accessories. James fumbled with the key, then stood aside and gestured for Lydia to precede him.

Hoping her relief did not show, she entered the high-ceilinged hallway. James closed the door, enveloping them both in darkness. He said, 'Lydia, come here.'

She went to him without hesitation. He put his arms around her, muttering, 'Don't squeeze too hard, my ribs are sore,' then letting his cheek rest on her hair. He let out his breath in a long sigh.

Lydia stayed very still. Although he was leaning rather more of his weight on her than was comfortable, she would not have complained for the world, and was rewarded when he said, several minutes later, 'You don't know how I needed this, Lydia. Just to hold you. Thank you for meeting me—I know it was your regular tennis night, but I wanted so badly to see your face at the airport.'

'I was glad when Lynn MacLeod phoned,' she said. 'I was worried about you.'

He straightened, resting his hands on her shoulders as much for support as from affection. 'We ran into some trouble . . . would you make me a sandwich, Lydia, while I shower? I feel as though I've been in these clothes for days.'

'Of course I will.'

He kissed her hair. 'My refrigerator's probably in much the same state as Annabel's.'

She worked contentedly in the kitchen, hearing James moving around upstairs, refusing to analyse why she should be so happy. She had produced a creditable club sandwich when the telephone rang. The water was still running in the bathroom overhead. She bounded up the stairs and knocked on the door. 'Telephone!'

The taps were turned off. James opened the door, his hips swathed in a towel, and padded across the hall to his bedroom. Lydia stood frozen to the spot as steam billowed out of the bathroom, one part of her brain registering his curt, monosyllabic replies on the telephone, the other part recalling, with shocking clarity, the red welts across his chest and arm.

She heard him say, 'I'll file the report tomorrow morning, it'll be on your desk by ten . . . OK. Goodnight.' He slammed down the receiver.

She was still standing motionless when he came back into

the hall. 'James,' she whispered, 'what happened?'

Water was trickling down his chest and legs; his hair clung wetly to his scalp. 'It looks a lot worse than it is,' he said. 'No bones broken, I'll just have Technicolor ribs for a while. Don't look so worried, Lydia.'

'You'll tell me about it?'

'Downstairs,'

She was all too aware of the nearness of his bedroom, and of his naked, beautifully proportioned body; had she reached out her hand, she could have touched him. 'The sandwiches are ready,' she said, striving for normality.

'I'll be down in a couple of minutes.'

She set the table in the kitchen, which was spartanly decorated in black and white with no relieving touches of colour, not the kitchen she would have expected of a son of Betty's. She located some serviettes in the drawer, some pickles in the cupboard, and poured the tea. James walked in, buttoning his shirt. 'That looks good, Lydia. Thanks.'

His voice had lost its leaden exhaustion. Lydia sat down across from him, and although she wasn't hungry, ate half a club sandwich. James finished eating and cupped his hands across the mug of tea. 'The problem with the hydraulics, which is the reason I went, was easily solved,' he said, gazing at his hands. 'I was watching a roustabout lay pipe when a connecting link from a chain and hoist line ruptured. Caught this young fellow across the throat. I grabbed for him—I was the closest one—but it was too late, he must have been killed instantly. The chain caught me across the ribs and I guess I scraped my face when I hit the deck ... it all happened so fast, you only piece things together after it's all over.' Absently he swirled the tea in the mug. 'He was twenty-three years old, the man who was killed. Got married two months ago. I was more or less nominated to accompany the body back to Montreal. His wife was a pretty little creature, totally distraught. Luckily her parents were with her. Eight days before Christmas,' he finished heavily.

Any words of sympathy sounded facile and insincere. 'Did you spend the day in Montreal?' Lydia ventured.

'I stayed around for a while, looked after a few practical things for them. Figured it was the least I could do.' He added flatly, 'If I'd been a split second faster or a few feet closer, maybe I could have saved him.'

'James, you can't blame yourself,' she said. If James had been closer, he might have been the one to be killed.

'Maybe that's why I needed you here—to hear you say that.' He drained his mug and pushed back his chair. 'Let's clear up the dishes.'

Sensing that he needed the activity, she put away the food while he loaded the dishwasher. He gave a rather exaggerated yawn. 'I've got to catch up on some sleep, I was up most of the night. And the boss wants a full report on his desk by ten.'

He had given her a not very subtle hint that it was time for her to leave. She should put on her coat and go home. She gripped the back of the chair. 'James, let me stay.'

Very slowly he hung the dishcloth over the chrome tap. 'I'm tired, Lydia,' he said deliberately. 'I want to go to bed.'

'So do I.'

'You're feeling sorry for me. That's no motive for lovemaking.'

'I'm sorry for all you've gone through the last day and a half. But that's not the reason I want to stay.'

His smile was ironical. 'Don't tell me you've fallen in love with me.'

She flushed. 'No, I haven't,' she said steadily. 'But I care about you. You're my friend. And I very much want to make love to you.'

She had taken him aback. 'You're certainly honest.'

'I want to renegotiate the terms, James. If you're willing.'

There was a half-smile on his lips. 'Oh, I'm willing. It's debatable right now whether I'll be able.'

She laughed outright. 'We could sleep together in the literal sense of the words.'

'I don't often think of sleeping when I'm with you, Lydia.'

She remembered the tapered waist and the long, muscled legs, and felt a shiver of anticipation. 'We could negotiate that as well.'

He hesitated. 'I'm very much in love with you, Lydia; that hasn't changed. Can you accept that?'

'I can try.'

He nodded, as though her answer had pleased him. 'Then let's go upstairs,' he said.

The stairs were carpeted in wool the colour of oatmeal, and the same carpeting extended into his bedroom, which had a spartan air like the kitchen. 'You could do with a couple of aspidistras in here,' Lydia said lightly, hoping her nervousness didn't show.

James switched on the brass bedside lamp. The bed was queen-sized, not very tidily made; the light seemed excessively bright. Lydia stood at the foot of the bed, fiddling with the belt of her red dress. When she had been sitting in the snow in the woods James had kissed her and said let's not worry about tomorrow, the present is more than enough. The present is certainly more than enough for me now, she decided. How did I get myself into this?

James was very casually unbuttoning his shirt; Lydia envied him his nonchalance and knew she could not possibly imitate it. Matters were not helped when he said over his shoulder, 'The bathroom's through that door, Lydia. Lots of clean towels on the shelf.'

She scurried into the bathroom, closed the door, stared at her face in the mirror with wide, frightened eyes, ran the tap for a few minutes, and, reluctantly, decided she couldn't stay there all night. She went back in the bedroom.

James was now stripped to his briefs. She could see the bruises on his chest and realised once again how horrifyingly close he had been to not coming home at all. She could have been weeping for his death rather than standing in his bedroom waiting to make love to him. And suddenly everything was all right. She said in a voice that was almost normal, 'James, would you give me a hand with my zipper? It sticks near the top.'

He walked over to her, close enough that she saw the thrumming of the pulse at the base of his throat and the intensity in his blue eyes; she exclaimed as if making a discovery, 'You're nervous, too!'

'Of course I am. Did you think I wasn't?'

She could feel his fingers warm on her nape. 'You seemed so casual. As though you do this kind of thing every evening of the week.'

He drew the zipper down her back, then turned her around, easing the dress from her shoulders. 'I don't, Lydia.'

She gave him a smile of great sweetness. 'I know you don't. I know I'm special to you, James.'

It was her way of apologising for last time, and he accepted it as such. 'Very special,' he said.

After she had stepped out of her dress and slipped off her stockings, James took her hands, saying gravely, 'Come to bed with me, Lydia,' so that it seemed very natural to sit down on the edge of the bed and slide under the sheets with him. He reached over for her, winced at the pull on his ribs and said wryly, 'Don't give me any bear hugs, will you, love?'

'Bear or bare?' she said innocently.

He was laughing as he undid her bra. Laughter, she thought, as he gathered her into his arms, was not a bad way to begin a love affair. And then she stopped thinking altogether.

She had said to him once, weeks ago, that sex was an over-rated pastime. Perhaps he had remembered. Certainly he seemed intent upon proving her wrong. His hands lingered upon the curves of her body until she moaned with pleasure; his lips explored and tasted and teased, so that when he finally entered her she opened to him as naturally as a bud unfolds to the sun. He watched her face change, saw all her passionate hunger and her joy; felt her gather him in and hold him until the rhythms overcame her and broken cries pierced her throat. Only then did he allow himself to lose control.

From an immense distance that was yet immensely close, Lydia saw his eyes darken and his face convulse. She wrapped her legs around him until her whole body was filled with him, and felt his throbbing, agonised release deep within her. He collapsed across her, his heart pounding, his back slick with sweat. With a tenderness she had not known she was capable of, she held him to her.

'James,' she whispered. 'Oh, James . . .'

He raised his head and with desperate honesty said, 'Darling Lydia . . . I love you.'

The tenderness in the turquoise eyes did not falter. 'You were so good to me.'

Fleetingly she spared a thought for that long-ago experience with Roy, when her needs had been ignored and her inhibitions had been allowed to shackle her. She had a very different feeling now. Inexperienced as she was, she sensed James had treated her with exquisite control, intent upon giving her the most profound pleasure. Yet the roles had not been so simple that he was the giver and she the receiver. Her first shy advances had delighted him. He had guided her hands across his body, letting her share every nuance of passion. He had freed her to boldness and encouraged her to risk.

She said, a lift in her voice, 'I feel wonderful!'

He switched off the light, then eased himself on to his back, drawing her against his good side. 'I don't feel so bad myself,' he murmured. 'Are you comfortable?'

Her cheek was resting in the hollow of his shoulder, her arm lay across his belly. 'Blissfully so.'

He fell asleep as suddenly as a child does. In the light from the street that filtered through the vertical blinds Lydia could see the cleanly moulded lips and long, straight nose; under her cheek his chest rose and fell. She felt warm and secure. She felt loved.

Her lashes drifted shut and she slept.

CHAPTER NINE

LYDIA was doing some book-keeping the following afternoon when the doorbell rang. Maybe it's James, she thought, getting up from the desk, a smile already curving her lips.

But through the peephole in her door she saw a delivery man standing outside. Disappointed to an extent that startled her, she opened the door.

The delivery man was smartly uniformed in dark grey and was carrying a large maroon box emblazoned with gold. His van was labelled Armview Furs. 'Miss Lydia Winsby?' he asked.

'I'm Lydia Winsby.'

'Could you sign here, madam? And would you have some identification?'

'But I haven't ordered a fur coat.'

He frowned at his form. 'Ordered by Mr Maxwell Winsby, madam. For delivery before Christmas.'

In instinctive protest she said, 'But I don't want it!'

The man gaped at her; presumably the women to whom he delivered fur coats did not turn them down. 'It's mink, madam,' he said in shocked tones.

'I don't care if it's polar bear—I don't want it. You'll have to take it back.'

'I can't do that, madam. It's been paid for. You'd have to speak direct to Mr Maxwell Winsby if you don't care for the coat.'

'He's in Fiji,' she said with a helpless kind of irony.

He sensed her weakening. 'It's a beautiful coat, madam. You'll love it. I'd advise you to arrange for insurance, though. I can leave you this card; the gentleman will be very happy to serve you.'

Her lips compressed; she knew when she had been beaten. She went back in the house, found her wallet and presented her driver's licence. The big maroon box changed hands. It was heavy.

She carried it upstairs to her bedroom and lifted the lid. There was no card or message inside the box. Were you expecting one, Lydia? she jeered at herself. You should know better by now.

She tore the heavy gold seal on the tissue paper. The coat was mutation mink, pale as cream: a shade that did not go with her colouring at all. She had never liked fur coats, and having once visited a mink farm, had a particular aversion to mink.

It's a very generous gift, Lydia.

It's a gift typical of my father. Expensive, yes, but also thoughtless. Given with no consideration for the receiver.

She lifted the coat out of the box and shook its soft, gleaming folds. No card fell out. She would in all honesty have preferred from her father a Christmas card with a personal note to this elegant, extravagant garment.

She telephoned the Armview Fur Company, discovered that she would need Maxwell Winsby's consent to return the coat, and was again advised, rather snippily this time, for the sales clerk appeared to take her dislike of the coat personally, to insure her gift.

She hung the coat in the closet, shut the door, and went back to work. But the serenity that had been with her ever since she had left James's house that morning with his kiss warm on her lips was gone. Maxwell, even by so indirect an intrusion in her life, had destroyed it.

During the years of his marriage to Judith, Maxwell had often bought his wife expensive gifts. Guilt-offerings? Symbols of the correct thing for a wealthy businessman to do? Attempts at appeasement? Lydia had never known. Judith, of course, had interpreted them, quite wrongly, as signs of undying love.

Lydia went back to her ledgers and her calculator. At four o'clock she was interrupted by the doorbell again. Another delivery man, this time with a white florist's box. She accepted it without argument and took it upstairs to the kitchen. It contained a card signed 'Love, James', and two dozen long-stemmed red roses.

She looked at the glossy green leaves and curling petals and felt the stirrings of panic. Had the mink coat not arrived she would probably have been delighted with James's gift. But Maxwell had intruded himself and now the roses filled her with fear. Last night she had blithely broken a rule that had stood her in good stead for ten years. She had made love with James. She had slept in his bed. And now he was sending her gifts.

With scant ceremony she shoved the roses in a vase and left them on the kitchen counter. She would go out to the Eglinton Mall and check that the trees were being watered on schedule. Any excuse to get out of the house.

It was after six when she got home. The telephone began ringing almost as soon as she was in the door.

'James here, Lydia. How are you?'

She clutched the receiver and heard herself say, 'I wasn't sure you'd call.'

'I said I would.'

'I—I thought you might just have disappeared.'

'Disappeared—why?'

She rubbed at her forehead, aware that she had a headache. 'I don't know,' she said lamely.

'I'm coming over. Be there in ten minutes.'

Eight minutes later he was standing in her hallway, kissing her with a nicely tuned mixture of passion, reassurance and love. Then he said, rubbing his hand against her cheek, 'I'm here. In the flesh. Tell me what's wrong.'

'It'll sound so silly.'

'Spit it out, Lydia.'

'My father always disappeared. He'd come for a visit, and they'd share a room at night and then he'd go. He used to give her a present. Although orchids were more his line.'

'I am not going to disappear. Nor am I going to stop sending you roses.'

She stared at the stripes in his tie. 'He sent me a fur coat today. Mink. For Christmas. But he didn't even put a message in with it.'

James swore under his breath. 'I'm sorry he did that. Although from what you've told me, I'm not surprised. Lydia, all your life you've been starved for love from your parents. Maybe it's time you realised you'll probably never get from them what you want. They are not loving people.' He tilted her chin up. 'Because of them you've walled yourself off from love. Most particularly from the opposite sex. Don't ever confuse me with your father, Lydia— because that's what you're in danger of doing. I am not your father. I'm very different from your father. Because I love you deeply and I'm not afraid to say so.'

Her turquoise eyes were opaque and her expression unreadable. He gave her a little shake. 'Do you hear me?'

'Yes,' she said in a dead voice. 'Yes, I hear you. But I'll have to think about it, James.'

He took a deep breath and let it out slowly; she could not have realised that he was remembering his mother's counselling to patience. 'May I take you out for dinner? There's a new Chinese restaurant that's supposed to be very good.'

Her smile was almost natural. 'I'd like that.' She felt as if she had walked to the very edge of a cliff and almost fallen over; only at the last minute had she been pulled back.

That night they made love in her bed, with more confidence and ease than the night before.

Behind the closed closet door the fur coat hung mutely in the darkness.

Four days before Christmas Lydia and James went to the Dohertys for dinner. The Christmas tree twinkled in the living-room, Nicolas was in a state of high excitement and Annabel had cleaned the refrigerator. 'I had to,' she said, taking out a bowl of eggnog. 'Only way I could make room for all the Christmas goodies. Malcolm, can I tell them?'

'You could wait until I've poured their drinks,' Malcolm said mildly.

'We're pregnant!' Annabel announced, patting the waistline of her brown velvet jumpsuit. 'Next summer. I was suspicious the night you babysat, but I didn't say a *word*.' She dimpled at her husband. 'Malcolm was impressed.'

'Amazed would be a better word,' her husband rejoined.

Lydia kissed Annabel and then raised her glass. 'To the new little Doherty.'

'Let's go into the other room,' Annabel suggested. 'Lydia, could you take these crackers for me? Malcolm made this delectable pâté; I do love it when he cooks.'

'I'll take them,' said James, reaching across for them. His other arm was casually resting around Lydia's shoulders. As he gave her a quick smile, she smiled back; they had made love an hour ago, and she felt as relaxed and contented as a cat.

She thought nothing of the incident, and unsuspectingly agreed to help Annabel serve the soup in the kitchen while the men stayed in the living-room; Nicolas had been put to bed.

Annabel let the adjoining door swing shut. 'You're sleeping together, aren't you?' she said, eyes bright.

'How do you know? Not that it's any of your business.'

'Darling, it's obvious, you can see he adores you. I think it's wonderful. Will you marry him?'

'No.'

Annabel put down her spoon with a clatter. 'You must marry him, Lydia. You don't know how *scared* I've been that you'd marry someone like George. I always wanted to say something, but Malcolm said I mustn't interfere, nature must take its course and all that.' She lifted the lid from the soup. 'Nature took its time, I must say. I was beginning to give up. You are twenty-nine, after all.'

'Twenty-nine is not over the hill, Annabel.'

'It's time to be thinking of marriage,' Annabel said firmly. 'I put the soup bowls over there, Lydia, pass them to me, would you? Especially if you want children.'

'I haven't said I'll marry James. So a discussion about children is a bit premature.'

'At least you're finally indulging in the activity that produces them,' Annabel said darkly. 'That's a start. Mmm, the soup does smell good—new recipe.' Her guileless brown eyes fastened themselves on her friend. 'Children are *important*, Lydia.'

'Your pregnancy's put you in a militant mood,' said Lydia, annoyed.

'It's because I'm happy. I love Malcolm and we've made another baby and I'm *happy*. I want you to know that happiness, Lydia.'

'Think of the genetics involved,' Lydia protested, trying to make a joke of the conversation. 'My black hair and his blond. The poor child would probably have mud-coloured hair.'

Annabel tossed her curls. 'It would have gorgeous blue eyes,' she retorted.

'Annabel, serve the soup.'

Annabel hugged her impulsively. 'You look so much

more *human*, Lydia. You've lost that untouchable look. And he is a hunk, you have to admit that.'

Lydia gave a confused laugh; James's body entranced her. 'Yes, I do admit that,' she said, and with pink cheeks carried in the first two bowls of soup.

James gave her a shrewd glance. But all he said was, 'Malcolm was asking when we were going to my parents. Is Christmas Eve all right with you?'

Lydia was glad of any subject unrelated to sex and babies. 'I'd like to visit my mother on Christmas Eve. We could go right after that.'

'I'll come with you,' James said casually. 'Time your mother met me.'

Lydia had been assiduously planning to keep them apart. She glowered at him, then hastily smoothed her features as Annabel entered with the rest of the soup.

Malcolm said in a resigned voice, 'Annabel's parents and my mother arrive on Christmas Eve. My mother is convinced the woman isn't born who's good enough for her son, and Annabel's mother can't imagine what Annabel sees in me.' He made an endearing grimace. 'The usual peaceful family Christmas at the Dohertys'. Lydia knows all about it, don't you, Lydia?'

Lydia laughed. 'I told Annabel's mother one year that you had a beautiful soul, Malcolm—she's regarded me with suspicion ever since.'

'Malcolm's mother is the other reason I cleaned the refrigerator,' Annabel remarked. 'We love them all *dearly*, James, but three days of togetherness when we're all supposed to be overflowing with the milk of human kindness are about two days too many . . . Christmas can be a little difficult, can't it?'

'This is going to be a special Christmas for me because I'm taking Lydia home with me,' James said.

Annabel looked totally smitten with him, Malcolm

quirked a quizzical eyebrow at Lydia, and Lydia drank her soup. Not until they were on their way home did she say, 'You're sneaky, James Connelly. You save your most outrageous remarks until we're not alone. That way I can't argue.'

'I can't imagine you allowing Annabel to inhibit you,' he said lazily. 'This is going to be a special Christmas. And I do want to meet your mother.'

So on Christmas Eve James and Lydia drove up to the Victorian mansion in James's car, the back seat loaded with gifts.

Lydia was tired and edgy. It had been a rush to finish off the loose ends at work so that she could take three days off, and she was nervous at the prospect of meeting all of James's family: two brothers and a sister plus the wife and children of one brother and the girl-friend of the other.

She selected the three prettily wrapped packages for her mother and said inadequately, 'Well, we're here.'

'And you wish I weren't,' James said drily. 'It's important that I meet your mother, Lydia. If your father ever visits you, I'll want to meet him, too.'

'Don't pressure me too much, James.'

He looked at her downbent head. 'Let me tell you something. Since we've become lovers I alternate between happiness because of the closeness between us, and moments of sheer panic when I'm afraid I'll wake up one morning and you'll be gone. I suppose the pressure stems from the panic.'

She had moments of panic, too, although for very different reasons from his ... so how could she reassure him? She said coolly, 'I have no idea how my mother will behave towards you.'

'Let's go and find out.'

Judith was dozing when they arrived, her mouth open, her diamonds flashing with the restless movements of her hands on the lace-edged sheets. Lydia watered the poinsettia she had brought the week before, and straightened the toilet articles on the bureau. Behind her back her mother said querulously, 'Who's this man? Did you bring him, Lydia?'

'Hello, Mother.' She kissed Judith's cheek. 'This is James Connelly; you've heard me speak of him.'

James had been at the office that morning, so was still wearing a dark business suit and a striped tie. He took one of Judith's hands in his much bigger one. 'I'm pleased to meet you, Mrs Winsby.'

Judith hoisted herself up in the bed, twitching at her housecoat. 'Lydia, you should have told me you were bringing someone.'

'I didn't know I was, until a couple of days ago.'

'Pass me my brush and my lipstick.'

Lydia held the small mirror she had given her mother the Christmas before while Judith patted at her curls with the brush and jaggedly outlined her mouth in red. She seemed more alert than usual. 'Perfume,' she said peremptorily to her daughter.

Lydia passed the antique crystal flask. Judith sprayed herself copiously with Scheherazade. 'So, Mr Connors,' she said.

'Connelly, Mother.'

'James,' said James.

Judith's red-veined eyes looked him over from head to foot, a scrutiny he bore with equanimity. 'So you're Lydia's new man. You're the first one she's ever brought here.'

'I insisted.'

'Why, Mr Connelly? It won't do you any good to meet me, you know. Lydia never marries her men.'

'I'm glad she never has.'

Something close to a smile lifted the garish red mouth.

With a pang of compunction Lydia realised that Judith would possilbly have enjoyed meeting her various men friends. Perhaps over the years she had deprived her mother of a source of entertainment, of male company, however sporadic; although it was difficult to imagine George coping with this inquisition as urbanely as James.

'She changes men every few months,' Judith remarked, as if Lydia were not even in the room, let alone standing beside the bed. 'Says her father and I have put her off marriage.'

'That's probably true enough,' James said equably.

Judith's eyes narrowed. 'How long have you known her, Mr Connelly?'

'Two months.'

'Oh, she'll keep you around a while longer, I'd say. She says it's a nuisance changing men.'

'I plan to stay around a good while longer. Like for ever,' said James.

'You want to *marry* my daughter?'

'That's the general idea, Mrs Winsby. I like Lydia, I'm in love with Lydia, I want to raise children with Lydia and grow old at her side.'

His voice was impassioned. Lydia felt curiously humble; it was she who had aroused that passion, she whom he loved.

'Well!' said Judith.

More quietly James said, 'Yes, I want to marry Lydia. I hope I'll have your blessing.'

This had gone far enough. 'You're forgetting something, James,' Lydia intervened. 'Or I should say someone. Me. You've never directly asked me to marry you. If you had, I would have refused. So my mother's blessing, or lack of it, is irrelevant.'

James had the audacity to wink at Judith. 'How do you suggest I get around that?' Abruptly he sobered. 'Nor do I believe that your blessing is at all irrelevant, Mrs Winsby.'

Judith leaned forward and said harshly, 'Love that is not reciprocated is a dreadful burden, Mr Connelly.'

There was compassion in James's blue eyes. 'I understand that . . . but you see, I'm convinced that deep down Lydia is capable of loving me—once she comes to terms with the past. Her childhood experiences of love were not happy ones.'

Judith glared at him. 'I loved my husband!'

'I know you did,' he said gently.

Judith looked up at her daughter. 'Have you heard from Maxwell?'

Lydia's smile was twisted. 'He sent me a very expensive fur coat, Mother, with no note, no card, no message of any kind.'

Judith seemed to shrink in the bed. 'I didn't get a card, either.'

Judith had not received a Christmas card from Maxwell for a dozen years; yet each year she hoped for something. A crumb from the rich man's table, thought Lydia bitterly. She sat down on the bed and put her arms around her mother, shocked, as always, by how frail she was. 'I love you, Mother . . . doesn't that help?'

Judith gripped Lydia's wrist. 'You're a good child, Lydia,' she said. 'You should marry Mr Connelly, he'll be good to you. Better than Maxwell ever was to me.'

Tears crowded Lydia's eyes. You're a good child, Lydia . . .

'I don't think Father has ever loved anyone but himself,' she said levelly, and knew in her heart that she and her mother had never shared so much truth before. And James had been the catalyst. No question of it. She added quickly, 'We brought you some presents. Would you like to open them now?'

Judith's head sank back on the pillow. 'Tired,' she

muttered. 'After tea.'

She wheezed as she slept. Lydia got up from the bed, wandering over to the window. 'She keeps losing weight,' she said helplessly. 'But you were good for her, James, I haven't seen her so bright for a long time ... She never wants me to visit her on Christmas Day. Says she prefers to be alone.'

He joined her at the window of the over-heated room, putting an arm around her shoulders. Outside, the garden was dark and still, the trees black against the week-old snow. 'Then you must allow her that choice,' he said. 'She doesn't have many left.'

Lydia suddenly turned to face him, wrapping her arms around his waist and rubbing her cheek against his lapel. 'Hold on,' she said, her voice not quite steady.

He raised her chin and kissed her with a fierce and passionate intensity that she more than matched. Slowly they separated and again Lydia buried her face in his chest, holding him tightly. She had youth and talent and beauty, and a man who deeply loved her; and against her was arrayed the pathetic shrinking of her mother's world and all the blackness of the night. Marry him, her mother had said. Marry him ...

'Sorry.' she said shakily, easing herself free. 'I don't know what came over me.'

She should have known James would not let her get away with that. 'The need for comfort. The need for love,' he said roughly. 'One of these days you'll look me in the eye and say, I need you, James. And then I'll know I've won.'

'So it's still a battle?'

'Of course. You're fighting for your life, Lydia ... or do you want to end up like your mother?'

'I wouldn't!'

He moved away from her, aimlessly picking up knick-knacks from the bureau and putting them down again. 'We all need to be loved.'

From the hallway came the discreet rattle of the tea trolley. Lydia said brightly, 'Tea time, Mother.'

Judith woke up. 'They always have special cakes at Christmas,' she said. 'Help me sit up, Lydia.'

The uniformed maid brought in a silver tray with extra cups and a plate of cakes. Lydia set the tray on the dresser, poured the tea and passed her mother the cakes. She began telling Judith about James's family. Judith listened with half an ear, more interested in the mince tarts and shortbreads.

Eventually James passed over the presents. Lydia had bought her mother an assortment of books and magazines, some exorbitantly expensive and very beautiful Swiss chocolates, and a blue satin négligé. James had given her a pear-shaped crystal pendant to hang in the window, where it would catch the rays of the sun. Judith was pleased to have a gift from a man, Lydia could tell, and insisted that he hang the pendant in the window immediately. Again Lydia felt that pang of compunction.

They stayed a little longer, until they could see that Judith was visibly tiring. James leaned over the bed and kissed Judith's withered cheek. 'I'm glad to have met you,' he said with undoubted sincerity.

Judith summoned the strength to stare him in the eye. 'You look after her,' she ordered. When Lydia bent to kiss her she added, 'Marry him, Lydia—don't make a fool of yourself and waste your life. Like I did.'

'Oh, Mother . . .'

Lydia straightened, removing the gifts from the bed and putting them on the dresser. The pendant was hanging motionless in the window; she hoped it would flash all the colours of the rainbow in the morning.

She turned and left the room, James following her.

CHAPTER TEN

IT WAS cold outside the nursing home, little flurries of snow whirling in the wind like wraiths. Lydia shivered from more than the cold, and with sudden longing knew she wanted to be part of the noise and confusion of James's family. 'Let's go,' she said. 'Let's go.'

She spoke very little on the drive to the old stone farmhouse, and was grateful to James for leaving her to her own thoughts. Although the traffic was heavy and the snow at times made visibility difficult, she had total confidence in his driving. When he turned between the stone gateposts, she said quietly, 'I'm glad you met my mother.'

'Thanks, Lydia,' he said, allowing his smile to say the rest.

Every window seemed to be lit in the farmhouse. Coloured bulbs glowed against the snow on the spruce trees by the front door, and the lights of the Christmas tree shone through the living-room windows. One of the wreaths that she and James had decorated was hanging on the back door. Ben and Heinz were barking inside.

Before he opened the door James kissed Lydia on both cheeks. 'Better not arrive with lipstick on my face,' he grinned. 'Happy Christmas, Lydia.'

He looked as excited as a small boy. She might have kissed him back regardless of the lipstick had the door not burst open and a blonde young woman catapulted herself into his arms. 'James! It's wonderful to see you!'

As he threw his arms around her the porch was suddenly crowded with people. Dazedly Lydia picked out two large young men, both fair-haired, who must be James's brothers,

129

a startingly made-up redhead, a sweet-faced brunette, a bespectacled young man, two small boys, and, lastly, Betty, Charles, Heinz and Ben. The brothers were pounding James on the back. 'Take it easy!' he protested, laughing. 'I've got sore ribs. Hello, Mum. Dinner ready? I'm starving. Hi, Dad . . . Merry Christmas.' He looked around. 'Lydia, come and meet everyone.'

Alan, Julie, Ralph, Brenda, Davey, Russell, Michael, Michelle . . . Lydia gave a breathless laugh, knowing she would never remember all the names. But she would remember the welcome in Charles's smile, Betty's motherly hug, and all the confusion in the kitchen, where dinner was being served. Someone—Ralph or Alan—thrust a mug of mulled wine in her hand. Someone else passed her a platter of hot, flaky sausage rolls. 'Glad you arrived safely,' Betty smiled. 'The roads must be getting slippery. Charles, carve the roast, darling. Brenda, you look after the potatoes and the squash and I'll make the gravy.' The redhead, who had sparkling green eyes hedged with mascara and layers of eyeshadow, offered to drain the beans. 'Everyone else out of the kitchen,' Betty ordered.

In the living-room a fire was blazing in the hearth. In deference to the two little boys, who turned out to be Davey and Michael, James's nephews, there were no presents under the tree and the row of stockings along the mantel were empty, awaiting the arrival of Santa Claus. There was a stocking there with her name on it, Lydia saw with a lump in her throat. James said heartily, 'Fine-looking tree, eh, Lydia?'

'Little skimpy,' said James's younger brother, Alan, whose girl-friend was the decorative, redheaded Michelle.

'Lydia chose it,' James said innocently.

'It didn't feel skimpy when we were pulling it to the house,' she rejoined.

Ralph, the older brother, remarked, 'Remember the

year we cut down the big pine tree and Mr Wandlyn from next door arrived breathing fire because it had been on his property?'

'The trunk was half on his property and half on ours,' Alan said.

'Not according to him.'

Lydia sat contentedly in the armchair by the fire, drinking the hot wine, listening to the brothers reminisce about other Christmases, feeling her anxieties evaporate. James's family had accepted her without fuss, and Charles and Betty, whom she already liked very much, had been genuinely pleased to have her back.

A hand grabbed her knee. She smiled and said, 'You're either Davey or Michael.'

'Davey. Do you have any little boys?'

'No, I don't. But I babysit for a friend's son. He's three.'

'I'm four-and-a-half,' said Davey.

She lifted him on her knee. 'Tell me what you want Santa Claus to bring you.'

Ben had flopped at her feet; James was perched on the arm of her chair describing his new house to Ralph and Alan; the child felt solid and comfortable in her arms. What if he were her child? Hers and James's?

As Michael scrambled up on the other arm of the chair, she allowed the question—which was unanswerable—to drop to the back of her mind. She felt very happy, as though she had no need to keep her guard up. When James casually took her arm on the way to the dining-room, he looked down at her and said so quietly that no one else could hear him, 'You look very beautiful, Lydia.'

'I'm happy,' she said simply.

He steered her beneath the mistletoe and kissed her soundly. Alan emitted an ear-splitting wolf-whistle, Ralph yelled, 'Enough of that, little brother!' and when Lydia looked up, pink-cheeked, she found the rest of the family regarding her with interest and speculation. Were she a character in a play, she would produce a sparkling witticism that would set them all laughing; however, no witticisms, sparkling or otherwise, came to mind.

Betty rescued her. 'James, you're sitting across from Julie. Lydia, come here next to Charles.'

Brenda, the brunette, was sitting on her other side. Brenda was the wife of Ralph and the mother of Davey and Michael. Russell, Julie's friend, was across the table from her; he had beautiful grey eyes behind his spectacles, a dry sense of humour, and worked in the same government department in Ottawa as Julie. Julie looked exactly as Lydia had always wanted to look: lithe, blonde, tanned, brimming with confidence. Yet when Charles raised his wine glass in a toast to family, friends, and absent loved ones, Lydia saw Julie blink back tears and knew she must be remembering her dead husband. Lydia was glad that Russell had accompanied Julie from Ottawa; she would not have wanted her to be alone.

After dinner Charles and Betty were sent to sit by the fire while everyone else cleaned up the kitchen. Then Ralph read 'T'was the Night Before Christmas' to the two little boys, and Brenda took them up to bed. When the boys were safely asleep, all the presents were brought downstairs and heaped under the tree. James and Lydia pulled on jackets and went outside to unload the gifts from the car. It was still snowing and very quiet.

Said James, 'We usually go to church at eleven. We could walk, if you like. It's only half a mile.'

'I'd love to.'

'Had enough of family?'

'No,' she said honestly. 'I'm enjoying them all. But I'd like to be alone with you for a while.'

'Come here,' he said. 'I can't hug you because my arms are full of presents. But I can kiss you.' Which he did.

From the door Alan called, 'You guys don't need mistletoe!'

'Or privacy,' James yelled back.

'Remember the time you caught me kissing my first girl-friend on the back step?'

'Nothing gets forgotten around here,' James complained. 'Have we got everything, Lydia?'

While the rest of the gifts were being piled under the tree, Betty rambled through some Christmas carols at the old upright piano; her playing reminded Lydia of Pete's whistling. Then everyone except Alan and Michelle, who had volunteered to stay home and babysit, got dressed for church. James and Lydia left before the rest. They slid down the driveway, fired some snowballs at each other, then began to walk along the road more sedately. 'I feel a long way from home,' Lydia said experimentally. 'A long way from my normal self.'

'It's hard to be detached in the midst of my family.'

With the same tentative note in her voice she said, 'Everyone seems to love everyone else.'

'They do. Don't be misled, Lydia—everything hasn't always been idyllic in the family. Dad wanted me to go to medical school in Toronto, not take off on a freighter. Ralph and Brenda nearly split up a year after they got married. And then Julie's husband died . . . she was on the verge of a breakdown eight or nine months ago. But you're right—the love is there. We know we can depend on one another.'

'You're very lucky,' Lydia said, then busied herself brushing some snow from her sleeve. 'It's cold, isn't it? I'm glad I wore my hat.'

Against her white fur hat her hair was raven-black; her cold cheeks picked up the red of her coat. James said, 'It doesn't seem possible that I've only known you for two months.'

How was she to answer that? She herself had days when George's proposal seemed years ago. 'How simple your life must have been before you met me,' she teased.

'Simple but dull. You do realise we can't sleep together for the next two nights?'

She had already been shown her bed in Julie's room; Russell was sharing James's room. 'I do,' she said.

'Too much snow to make love in the woods.'

'We'd melt it,' she said demurely. 'James, this doesn't seem a very suitable topic to discuss on the way to church.'

'The sacred and the profane?' He stopped dead in his tracks. A car drove past in a swirl of snow. 'Lydia, I can't see my love for you as in any way profane.'

'James, please——'

'Oh, I know, you hate it when I talk about love.'

'Don't let's argue, James. Not tonight.'

Reluctantly his face softened. 'A Christmas truce?' He took her arm and they walked on, the snow crunching under their boots; they talked about Christmas carols in a very determined way.

The service was beautiful. The church was lit entirely by candles, dozens of candles, which flickered on the scarlet and white poinsettias, on the red-robed choir and the lifted faces of the congregation. As the two-thousand-year-old drama was unfolded in word and song, Lydia felt its message of hope and love speak directly to her: Judith's health would improve; Maxwell would visit his wife; James would remain her dear and trusted friend. She sang her heart out in the carols and allowed the benediction to enfold her in peace.

Back at the house the whole family sat around the fire in the living-room, eating fruit cake and drinking the cocoa that Michelle had made. Charles and Betty were the first to leave for bed. 'I'll lock up, Dad,' James said casually, and within ten minutes he and Lydia were the only ones left in front of the fire. He flipped off the lamps and drew her into the circle of his arm. 'The best part of Christmas,' he said lazily. 'Everyone under one roof, yet everything quiet.' Very gently he kissed her.

She could see the coloured lights on the tree reflected in his eyes. It seemed a long time since he had kissed her. With a little sigh she gave herself up to the pleasure of his embrace, her lips soft and welcoming.

His kisses grew more demanding. He fondled her breasts and stroked her hair as the flames died in the hearth and the golden sparks blinked out in the chimney. When he pulled free, his breathing was ragged. And Lydia, who as a child had often dreaded Christmas Eve, said truthfully, 'James, I wish we could sleep together tonight. I'd like to wake up on Christmas Day and find your arms around me.'

He said huskily, 'That's the nicest Christmas present you could possibly have given me.'

Because she was happy, and very far from home, she pulled his head down and kissed him with an abandoned sensuality that surprised them both. James said shakily, 'We'd better go to our separate beds, or we'll be making love on the chesterfield.'

Her desire for him was a fierce, burning ache. She said, no more steadily than he, 'We can't risk frightening Santa Claus.'

'Davey and Michael would never forgive us.' He kissed her more moderately and pulled her to her feet. 'I'm going to lock up. I'll see you in the morning.'

They kissed again, lingeringly. Then Lydia went to bed, the narrow single bed in Julie's room. Julie was already asleep. Lydia undressed in the dark and slid between the sheets. The bed was cold. She closed her eyes with great determination and eventually fell asleep.

Looking back a week later, when her hopes in the church

had been revealed to be as fragile as the ornaments on the tree and as easily shattered, Lydia could nevertheless recognise Christmas Day as the happiest day in her life. Crystal-clear in her mind she carried a series of images: Davey's ecstatic face when he saw the tree in the morning; James's eyes watching her as she unwrapped his gift to her, a tiny jade carving on a fragile gold chain; the laughter around the laden table as Betty inadvertently set fire to the holly on the plum pudding; the frolic in the snow afterwards and the impromptu sing-song around the piano in the evening. She had been one of the family. A cliché and a profound truth.

Boxing Day was bitterly cold, the temperature well below zero with a wind chill factor that made venturing outdoors a most unattractive option. Late afternoon found Julie, Russell, Alan, Michele, James and Lydia at the dining-room table playing a highly complicated board game. Betty was in the kitchen rolling out pastry and listening to *Messiah* on the radio; Charles was in the study. 'Sleeping,' Alan had reported with a grin.

When the telephone rang in the kitchen, Lydia paid it no attention; it was her turn to throw the dice. Betty called, 'Lydia, it's for you.'

Because she was happy, she said spontaneously to James, 'Maybe it's my father calling from Fiji—wouldn't that be nice? I left your mother's phone number on my answering machine.'

He gave her that special smile that never failed to touch her. 'I hope it is your father. I'll keep an eye on Alan while you're gone, just to make sure he doesn't cheat.'

She took the receiver from Betty's floured fingers and said blithely, 'Hello.'

'Dr Warner here, Miss Winsby.'

Her smile faded. 'Is something wrong?'

'I'm afraid so. Your mother has suffered a heart attack.

She went by ambulance to the Merton General Hospital half an hour ago.'

'A serious heart attack?' Lydia faltered.

'Because of your mother's poor health, any attack is serious. She'll be in intensive care for at least twenty-four hours while they monitor the situation. I would suggest you visit her as soon as possible.'

'You mean she could *die*?'

Dr Warner seemed shocked that Lydia should mention such a possibility. 'Not at all, not at all, Miss Winsby. Although, of course, there's always the chance of a second attack. But we must look on the bright side.'

Thoroughly confused, and very frightened, Lydia muttered, 'You had said her heart was weak.'

'That's correct. A heart attack has been a very real possibility for months.'

'I—I'll have to come. I know where the hospital is, I was there once before when my mother had pneumonia.'

'Fine,' Dr Warner said heartily. 'She's under the care of Dr Langley; he's an excellent cardiologist.'

Lydia tried to gather her wits. 'I'll leave right away.'

'I shall alert the hospital that you're coming. I'm indeed sorry to have been the purveyor of such bad news at this season of the year, Miss Winsby.'

Pompous man. Yet Lydia found herself trying to reassure him. 'I appreciate your care of my mother, Dr Warner; she always speaks well of you.' This was stretching the truth a little, but Dr Warner's fine-sounding phrases seemed to be contagious.

'I shall be visiting her in hospital, so may see you there. Goodbye, Miss Winsby.'

'Goodbye, Dr Warner.'

Lydia put down the phone and walked blindly into Betty's arms. Betty was large and soft and smelled of lavender and flour: the way a mother should smell, Lydia

thought confusedly, remembering all the times when her
mother's expensive perfume had been unable to mask the
sharpness of gin. 'My mother's had a heart attack,' she said,
and felt Betty's arms enfold her.

'Lydia, dear, I'm so sorry.'

From the doorway James asked sharply, 'What's wrong?'

As Betty told him, Lydia was dimly aware that James
was trying to take her into his arms. Reluctant to surrender
Betty's warmth for a more complicated embrace, she raised
her head. 'I'll have to go to the hospital.'

'Of course. I'll take you there. Come here, love.'

His chest was hard, his arms very strong. She held herself
rigidly. 'I must pack.'

'Julie will pack for you.'

'I'd rather have something to do,' she said stubbornly.

'Why don't I come up with you?' Betty suggested. 'James,
maybe you should warm up the car.'

Fifteen minutes later they were ready to leave. After the
various members of the family had bidden Lydia subdued
and sympathetic goodbyes, Betty and Charles hugged her.
'Come back soon,' Betty said. Lydia smiled and thanked
them and made no promises. As James drove on to the
highway, she closed her eyes and feigned sleep.

The intensive care unit was on the fifth floor of the Merton
General. The head nurse, having explained that Judith was
holding her own exceptionally well, led them to her bedside
and left them there.

Judith's face was a white as the sheets. She was wired to
various machines; her eyes were shut.

Lydia sat down by the bed, taking her mother's flaccid
hand in hers. Judith's rings had been removed; somehow
this brought the reality of the whole situation home to
Lydia in a way the telephone call had not. 'You mustn't die,
Mother,' she whispered childishly, as if Judith could hear

her. 'You mustn't. Because you've never told me that you
love me.'

James said softly, 'She loves you, Lydia.'

'How can you say that?'

'She cares what happens to you, she doesn't want you to
end up like her, she wants you to have a normal, happy life.'

But instead of responding, Lydia said, 'I suppose I should
tell my father she's ill.'

'Can you reach him?'

'I imagine he's still in Fiji. I can probably locate him
through the company.'

'He didn't leave you his number?'

She said wryly, 'He wouldn't do that—he'd be afraid I
might give it to Mother.'

'He probably should be notified, Lydia.'

'He never comes to see her, so I don't suppose he will now
that she's ill . . . but maybe I should give him the benefit of
the doubt.'

James looked down at her unhappy little face. 'There's
not much point in staying here,' he said gently. 'We can
leave your phone number at the nursing station.'

'I'd like to stay for a while,' she said, her chin set, and for
nearly an hour sat by the bed, holding her mother's hand,
trying through that insubstantial contact to transmit the
will to live.

Judith did not waken. The little green blips on the screen
at the head of the bed traced the same, monotonous pattern.
Finally James said, 'Lydia, it'll take us over an hour to get
home, and you've got to call your father. I think we should
go.'

'Oh. All right,' she said obediently. Releasing her hold,
she kissed her mother's cheek and stood up.

Outside the cold was brutal, snatching the breath from
her lungs, numbing her gloved fingers. The windows of the
car were fronded with frost. James scraped them off, then

got in the car beside Lydia. Her face looked pinched and frozen. He said, 'Lydia, it's all right to cry.'

She looked at him as if he were a creature from another planet. 'Let's go,' she said. 'I have the number for a couple of the company directors in my files. I should be able to get hold of my father through them.'

'I can do that for you.'

She huddled deeper into her coat and said politely, 'I can manage.'

Her house was cold inside, empty and cheerless after all the laughter and confusion of the old stone farmhouse. Lydia went directly to the telephone, where after a number of false starts she reached Roger Bryson, one of the other senior partners of the drug company. She explained her predicament, and ten minutes later Roger Bryson called her back with the number she needed. 'Maxwell's supposed to be there for ten days, I don't think you'll have any trouble reaching him, Miss Winsby. I do hope your mother's health will improve.'

She placed the call to Fiji; the operator would ring her back. She paced up and down in the living-room, her coat still on, her arms hugged across her breast. James had lit a fire, and brought her a cup of tea, which she accepted with an absent smile. The telephone rang. She put the tea down on the stereo and went into her bedroom.

Her father's voice, distorted by distance, said, 'Lydia? This is unexpected. Why are you calling?'

Even allowing for the distortion, he sounded accusatory. 'Mother had a heart attack today, Father. A serious one.'

Silence—an extremely expensive silence—hummed along the wires. 'I see,' Maxwell said. 'What is the prognosis?'

'They won't really commit themselves. They say she's doing as well as can be expected.' Lydia waited, but he added nothing more. 'I thought I should let you know. In case you wanted to see her.'

He said testily, 'I cannot possibly leave here, Lydia.'

'I know it's a long way. But there must be flights available.'

'I'm on my honeymoon.'

It was her turn to be silent; she felt sick. Finally she said, 'You didn't tell me you were getting married.'

'I told you I was with the woman I hoped to make my wife. We were married yesterday.'

Lydia could not bring herself to congratulate him. 'Why could she not come with you?'

'I have been divorced from your mother for eleven years, Lydia, there is no possible reason why I should want to visit her in hospital. Besides, I would be putting Marion in a most awkward position.'

So her name was Marion. 'Judith was the mother of your only child,' Lydia said coldly, 'and she was a great help to you in the early years of your career. Don't you think you owe her at least one visit when she's ill?'

'No, I do not. I shall be in New York by the first of January. That will give you the opportunity to meet Marion under more normal circumstances.'

I don't care if I ever meet Marion, Lydia thought viciously. 'I can see that your second wife takes priority over your first,' she retorted. 'How silly of me to think otherwise.'

Her father ignored her. 'I shall have to visit the nursing home as well to straighten out their account. Over the years that has been a great drain financially.'

In a flash of white-hot fury Lydia snapped, 'So you can visit the nursing home but not my mother!'

'I've never known you to be so difficult!'

With commendable restraint she said, 'I'm upset.'

'Then there is little sense in prolonging this conversation. I shall get in touch with you once I get to New York . . .

Marion and I will see you then. I shall trust you to behave towards her with the courtesy she deserves. Goodbye, Lydia.'

'Goodbye.'

She replaced the receiver, wondering with real bitterness how you could say goodbye to someone to whom you have never really said hello.

James had come to the doorway of her room. 'I couldn't help overhearing. He's not coming.'

She was rhythmically thrumming her fingertips on the bedside table. 'No, he's not coming. But he wants me to meet his new wife.'

'If I were you,' James said carefully, 'I'd throw something at the wall.'

Lydia turned to face him, her eyes brilliant with emotion. 'Oh, it's not that easily dealt with. I wish it were.'

'Throw something anyway. It might help.'

She suddenly bent her head. 'No. It wouldn't help.'

He strode over to her, taking her chin in one hand, seeing the sheen of tears. She stared at him in defiance, head held high, and the tears did not spill over.

She was the first to speak. 'James, I think you should go.'

He bit his lip. Thrusting his fists in his pockets, he walked over to the tall south-facing windows, where purple and white hyacinths were blooming in earthenware pots, their scent heavy on the air. 'Go where?' he said.

Lydia stared at his hunched shoulders. She knew he was angry; but not yet angry enough to leave. 'Home. Back to Scranton. Wherever you want. I'm not in the mood for company.'

'What you mean is, you need to be alone.'

'All right. I need to be alone.'

He was facing her now, across the width of the room. 'Good for you,' he said evenly. 'You've actually used the word need.'

'James, I don't want to fight with you. Not right now.'

'Don't you? I get the distinct impression you're trying to make me angry enough so that I'll storm out of here.' He moved his shoulders under the supple leather of his jacket, as if trying to ease the tension from them. 'You should know me better than that. Do you think I'm so childish that I'd lose my temper and leave you alone when your mother's ill?'

Her chin still had its defiant tilt. 'All right—so I behaved foolishly. I'd still like you to leave.'

'Why, Lydia?' Slowly he walked towards her. 'Spell it out for me. Because I'm a little stupid, you see. In my family, when there's trouble, we gather round. We don't shut each other off. So tell me why you need to be alone.'

She gripped the edges of the bedside table, feeling very much at bay. 'I come from a very different family than yours. I'm a product of that family, and my need—yes, need—for solitude springs from that family. You've never been insensitive, James. You must allow me to know my own feelings.'

He was standing only a foot away from her. With his crooked smile he said, 'You're a worthy opponent, Lydia.'

She suddenly found she was able to smile, too. 'James, I can't explain why I have to be alone. I only know it's necessary. Don't fight me on that one.'

'I could tell you why.'

Her smile vanished. 'I wish you'd stop analysing me!'

'It's because you're deathly afraid of admitting you might need another person. So you push me away, get rid of me, rather than face the fear.'

'How very clever of you!'

'Not really.' He rested his hands on her shoulders. 'You know me well enough to know I won't force myself on you. So I'll go. I'll be at home, Lydia. Call me if you need me—I mean that. Promise?'

She could read the strain in his face. James didn't want to leave her alone; it went against his whole nature. It was for him a defeat. But he would do it. She said shakily, 'You're not living up to your dictum.'

He frowned. 'I don't understand.'

'You told me once that all's fair in love and war. If you really believed that, you'd be staying. You're much bigger than I am, I couldn't possibly get you out of here if you didn't want to go.'

Another crooked grin. 'I've ruined my own case, haven't I?' He leaned forward and kissed her on the mouth, without hurry. 'I'm so glad that I had the chance to meet your mother on Christmas Eve and I'm truly sorry that she's ill. I'll let myself out. Lock the door behind me, won't you?'

He left the room; Lydia could hear his footsteps on the stairs, then a few moments later the sound of the front door opening and closing. She sagged against the bedside table. She had wanted to be alone ... and now she was alone. Why then did she have this crazy urge to run down the steps and call him back?

CHAPTER ELEVEN

THE city stayed in the grip of the same bitter cold as the year drew to an end. Lydia spent as much time as she could at the hospital, where Judith had been transferred from intensive care to a regular ward. 'I asked for a private room,' she sniffed. 'They said they had none available. A very poorly run hospital, I'd say.'

But inwardly Lydia thought the ward with its five other patients was good for Judith because there was lots of activity. Nurses and visitors and cleaning staff were in and out all day, and in all of them Judith took a sly, surreptitious interest.

On her third day in hospital she asked Lydia to go to the nursing home to get an envelope of papers from her dresser. 'I know it's a long way for you to go,' she said fretfully. 'But I would like to have them. They're Maxwell's letters, you see.'

Lydia sighed inwardly, wishing for the thousandth time that her mother could relinquish her obsessive hold on Maxwell, but knowing equally that she could not refuse Judith's request. 'I'll go this afternoon, Mother. Then I could bring them in this evening.'

She got back from the nursing home about six, after battling traffic the whole way, and went to Annabel's for dinner. Annabel hugged her tightly and said, 'Darling, you look *dreadful*. The best thing you could do is sit down on the floor and *bawl* your eyes out. That's what I do when things get too much for me, don't I, Malcolm?'

'Noisy but effective,' her husband agreed. 'A whole school of therapy's grown up around it. Primal Scream,

145

they call it. Should have called it Annabel's Scream.'

Annabel ignored him. 'Anyway, Lydia, I'm so glad you've got James,' she said. 'He's a hunk, of course, and those *incredible* eyes, but he's solid, too. Like an oak tree. There when you lean on it. Malcolm's like that, too.' She nodded sagely. 'If anyone asked my advice about getting married, I always ask them if he's like an oak tree or an alder bush. Lean on an alder bush and you fall flat on your face.'

Lydia had been seeing as little of James as possible, although he was to accompany her to the hospital that evening. She made a non-committal noise and began playing with Nicolas.

Judith was wearing a new bedjacket that evening, and visibly perked up when she saw James, who had brought her a huge bouquet of red and white carnations. 'How kind of you,' she murmured, blinking at him. 'Lydia, pass me my perfume. The nurse was in and out of here so fast at dinner-time that I didn't have time to even think about perfume.'

Lydia passed over Scheherazade and the envelope from the nursing home. Judith put the crystal flask on the white spread and opened the envelope, taking out a package of letters tied with a frayed velvet ribbon: a painfully small package for an eighteen-year marriage. 'I like them near me,' she said. 'Oh, I'd forgotten this was in here too—you should have it, I suppose, Lydia.' And she passed over another envelope, tattered and rubbed.

'What is it, Mother?'

Judith said petulantly, 'Just some papers I've kept for years. Don't bother with them now,'

So Lydia did not open the envelope until she was back in her own living-room with James. She tipped out its contents: two smaller envelopes, several photographs, school report cards, a couple of yellowing newspaper articles. The photographs followed her progress from babyhood to her eighteenth birthday, the articles described the two school plays she had participated in. The smaller envelope was labelled *Lydia, one month*. It contained a silky curl of black hair, fine as a baby's hair is fine. The other envelope contained a long black strand; she had had her hair cut when she was ten.

In silence she spread everything on the coffee table. Then she said, very quietly, 'She must love me, after all.'

James picked up the envelope with the long strand of hair. 'How old were you when your hair was this length?'

'Ten. Mother was drinking heavily by then. Yet she kept all these things. Oh James, why could she never show me that she loved me? Why did she never tell me?'

He shook his head, smoothing the black ribbon of hair with one finger. 'You may never know the answer to that.'

'James, how lonely she must have been! The only person she could reach out to was my father. And he didn't want her.'

'But she does love you, Lydia.'

'Yes . . . she loves me.'

Tears flooded her eyes, the unshed tears of a lifetime. She said in a choked voice, 'I've wondered sometimes why I visit her every week; lots of times she doesn't seem to care whether I'm there or not. But I'm glad now that I've kept up those visits. I'm so glad that I have . . .'

The tears were streaming down her face. She made a helpless gesture with her hands. James put his arms around her, drawing her against his chest. She cried for her mother, that lonely woman in the big empty house by the lake, and she cried for herself, a little girl left too much on her own, an introverted teenager whose parents had alternately humiliated and abandoned her. She cried until there were no tears left. Then she said in a muffled voice, 'That's twice I've done this.'

'I choose to be flattered,' James said lightly.

Lydia was not deceived, well aware of the strength of his embrace, of his cheek resting on her hair, of the concern under his flip comment. 'Annabel's right,' she murmured.

She felt the laughter deep in his chest. 'And what has Annabel been saying?'

'Annabel says you're like an oak tree. You can lean on oak trees and they stand firm. Unlike alders.'

'Which grow in swamps. I'm glad she doesn't think I'm like an alder.'

Lydia's arms tightened around his waist. With her face still buried in his shirt-front, she mumbled, 'James, please stay tonight.'

His body went still. 'What do you mean, Lydia?'

She raised a tear-ravaged face in which her eyes shone a clear turquoise. 'Stay with me all night. I don't want you to leave. I know I've been avoiding you the past few days and that I'm not behaving very logically ... but please stay.'

He said deliberately, 'We could go to bed right now.'

She wanted to be held and comforted and loved, to banish from her mind, even temporarily, Judith's appalling loneliness. 'Yes,' she whispered. 'Yes.'

He picked her up and carried her into her bedroom where the only light was reflected light and the hyacinths stood like purple candles against the sheer white curtains. When he put her down by the bed, Lydia began to undress, her movements slow and graceful, for there was no hurry: they had all night.

When they were both naked, he clasped her to him, blond head bent to black, the two bodies merging in the shadows. Then they lay down on the bed. In an elemental need that shocked her in its intensity, Lydia opened to him, kissing him with a wantonness that three months ago she would have thought foreign to her nature. Her hands roamed over his body, exploring the taut planes of his back, the curve of his ribcage and the hollowed belly; she arched her hips against his, feeling his desire with a primitive pride that she could so affect him.

She had thought there was no need to hurry; but their bodies, frantic for each other, dictated the rhythm of their lovemaking. Although they had made love before, so they knew how to tantalise and excite each other, they had not made love for several days, so that the peak of excitement was mounted swiftly and release became a pulsing, agonising necessity. James cried out her name, once. She threw back her head and gave herself up to the plunge of his body into hers. The waves crashed over her, drowning her in him, two as one, the very heart of love . . .

From a long way away she heard him say her name. 'Lydia . . .'

He was above her, his weight held on his palms; they were still joined. She said in a voice he had never heard before, 'It's like death, isn't it? Death and re-birth. I lose myself to become part of you, yet I am most surely myself when I am most lost—oh, I can't explain. Hold me, James, don't let go.'

He lowered his body, resting more of his weight on her, so that her fragile white curves were covered by him and protected by him. 'You are my life,' he said huskily. 'I love you so much, Lydia.'

She brought his head down and kissed him, the passion of a few minutes ago replaced by a tenderness she was suddenly not afraid to share, even if she couldn't articulate it. She was aware of a deep happiness that was yet hedged with sadness . . . for had Judith ever been loved with the same generosity and care that James had shown to her? She said quietly, 'Thank you, James.' and knew she was thanking him for far more than their lovemaking.

He rolled over on to his back, drawing her into the curve of his shoulder. 'Why don't you try and sleep?'

'But it's early,' she protested, and five minutes later was sound asleep.

She woke around midnight, grabbed at James, muttered, 'Don't go—please don't leave me,' and fell asleep again. In the small hours of the morning, in total darkness, they made love again, a loving of touch without sight that was suffused with a passionate, gentle sensuality. At five they went downstairs and made themselves something to eat, then went back to bed.

At ten minutes past nine James reared up on one elbow and looked at the clock. 'My God! I was supposed to be at the office at nine, I'm expecting a call from the head office in Sweden.' He ran for the shower. Nine minutes later— Lydia counted them—he was gone.

She locked the front door and tracked back upstairs. The bedding was in a crumpled, untidy heap. Her clothes were in a similar heap on the floor, where she had dropped them the night before. The morning sun touched the petals of the hyacinths, and she knew she would always associate their fragrance with a man's hands igniting her body and a man's voice saying *I love you*. James's hands. James's voice.

She sank down on the edge of the bed. The house had the quietness that comes from solitude, the stillness of one person alone. She looked over her shoulder at the two pillows, angled because she and James had slept so closely together. I don't want to be alone, she thought. I want James. I need James. He completes me. He makes me whole.

She got up and prowled around the room. She lay down on the bed, her head on his pillow so that she caught, elusively, the scent of his body. She remembered how the darkness had freed her to express through her body what she was afraid to express in words. I love him, she thought. I love James. And to her nostrils drifted the scent of the hyacinths.

For a few minutes she lay still, tangled in the sheets that

had covered him, savouring the wonder of her discovery. She had never thought she would fall in love. Other women did, but not she. She ran the words experimentally over her tongue. I love James. Then, pretending he was standing in front of her, she said them out loud. 'James, I love you.'

Panic struck her as swiftly as a plummeting hawk strikes a dove. Love was not the ennobling emotion that the romantics would have it be; love brought in its train degradation and despair, each as deadly as the talons of the hawk. As clearly as if it were yesterday rather than twenty years ago, she could remember her mother screaming *Maxwell, I love you, I love you* . . .

It had been the Christmas when she was nine. Maxwell had arrived at the country house on Christmas morning, when both Judith and Lydia had given up hope that he was coming. He had stayed the whole day. As an adult looking back, Lydia could see he had tried his best to be pleasant, to construct with his wife and child the fiction of a normal family spending Christmas in the country. She had gone to bed happy, hugging the Parisian doll he had given her. But she had woken in the night, gone to the bathroom, and then, attracted by the noise, wandered down the hallway in her white nightgown towards her parents' suite. Standing in the shadow cast by the door, she had gazed into their bedroom.

Judith was also in her nightgown, another gift from Paris, a seductive gown of grey-blue chiffon; she had been beautiful then. But her face was livid with rage and her voice a rasp of pain and fury. 'You can't go, Maxwell, you can't—you've only just arrived. At least stay overnight, you can't possibly have business to do tomorrow, it's a holiday——'

Maxwell shook her clinging fingers from his arm. 'Don't make a scene, Judith, for heaven's sake,' he said impatiently.

'Then stay. Stay with me tonight. You can leave in the morning.'

'I am leaving now.'

Judith's eyes had darkened with jealousy and spite. 'What's her name this time, Maxwell? Are you so enamoured of her that you can't spend a night away from her?'

He straightened his tie in the mirror. 'You're making a fool of yourself. Of course there's no other woman.'

'Then why can't you stay?'

'I have business to attend to. It's my efforts that keep you in this place.'

'*My* money looks after this place,' Judith said venomously.

'You have to throw that up at me, don't you?' he snarled.

'How else can I hold you? I'm not enough. Neither is our child. If I have to use the money to hold you, I will!'

'No, Judith,' Maxwell said with deadly calm. 'You can no longer use your precious money to keep me in line. Because I have money of my own now. Money I've made on the stock market that's more than enough for my needs.'

'You do have a woman—don't you?'

Fastidiously he brushed a hair from his sleeve. 'Yes. As a matter of fact, I do.'

Judith wilted. 'How can you do that to me?' she moaned.

He said contemptuously, 'Unless you stop drinking, I'll be here even less often than I am now.'

'I drink because I'm lonely. Because you're not here.' Her voice rose. 'Maxwell, I love you!'

He took his overcoat from the closet and adjusted it on his shoulders. 'You're behaving very badly, Judith.'

As she dug her hand into his sleeve, the diamonds on her finger winked coldly. 'I love you,' she cried. 'You can't go. I beg you not to go.' She began to sob. 'Oh God, Maxwell, don't leave me . . . don't leave me, I beg you.'

He struck her across the cheek with the flat of his hand. Judith collapsed on the bed, weeping hysterically. And the child watching at the door fled to her own room, and silently vowed that she would never marry, that she would never love a man . . .

I kept that vow for twenty years, Lydia thought wretchedly. And now I've broken it. I've allowed myself to fall in love. I need James, I'm vulnerable to him. I'm no longer self-sufficient. He has power over me, as Maxwell had power over Judith.

She was shivering as if she had a fever, and she felt as frightened as if she were nine, and not twenty-nine.

An hour later when the telephone rang, she was still lying in bed. 'Lydia? James. I've got to go to St John's again. Damn nuisance, we're short-staffed because of the holidays. Why don't you come with me? I'm booked into a hotel and I'll be free by early evening.'

'Oh, no, I can't do that.'

'Because of your mother?'

Gratefully she seized upon the excuse he had given her. 'Yes. I want to visit her today. You'll be back tomorrow, won't you?'

'I should be. Why don't you call Annabel and stay there overnight? I hate leaving you alone.'

'I may do that.'

'I wish you could have come . . . I'll call you as soon as I get back. I love you.'

Three small words that struck a chill in her heart. She could no more have said them back to him than she could have piloted the jet to St John's. 'Take care,' she said.

As she replaced the receiver she was conscious of a deep sense of relief. She had thirty-six hours' breathing space before she had to face James and dissimulate her new-found knowledge.

CHAPTER TWELVE

LYDIA worked all the next day, glad to be busy; she had dinner with Annabel and Malcolm, parrying Annabel's questions about James with a duplicity that rather horrified her, and in the evening she visited her mother.

James's carnations were prominently displayed on the dressing-table.

Lydia and Judith discussed Judith's day and the weather, which was still very cold, then Lydia took her courage in her hands and said, 'Mother, that envelope you gave me—I never thought you were that interested in me. All those clippings about the school plays and concerts, and my report cards . . .'

Judith avoided her daughter's eyes. 'I couldn't very well throw them out. You might have needed them when you went to university. Would you make me a cup of tea, Lydia?' She gave an artificial little cough. 'The air is so dry in here.'

'You didn't have to keep my baby hair for university. Or the photographs.'

'I don't know what you're getting at,' Judith said fractiously. 'And I'm really very thirsty. The carnations are lasting well, aren't they?'

But Lydia refused to be side-tracked. 'The reason I can't marry James is because of you and Father and the total lack of love in that house by the lake. I never thought you loved me, Mother. But you did, didn't you? The envelope you gave me last night proved that you did.'

Judith let her head flop back on the pillow. 'I'm too tired for all this,' she fretted. 'Don't you realise I'm ill? It's not fair of you to badger me.'

Then say you love me and I'll leave you alone.

For a moment Lydia thought she had spoken the words aloud. Hopelessness bowed her shoulders like the snow bowing the branches of the fir trees. So the childhood mementoes had meant nothing; scraps shoved into an envelope to lie forgotten in a drawer. She stood up. 'I'll make your tea,' she said.

She slept alone in her bed that night, closing her mind to the scent of the hyacinths, dully grateful that James was not there. And late the next day she had two unexpected visitors: her father and his new bride.

Maxwell phoned from the airport to say they would be arriving in an hour. Lydia raced around the house, tidying and dusting; then she dressed with considerable care in a paisley skirt and silk blouse with her newest Italian shoes, and still had time to arrange a tray of drinks and canapés and to light the fire.

None of this furious activity showed in her face when she opened the door to her guests. She offered a cool cheek to Maxwell. 'Hello, Father,' she said, then held out her hand to the woman at his side. 'You must be Marion,' she said. 'I'm Lydia. Do come in.'

She took their coats and ushered them upstairs. Indicating the bottles on the tray she said, 'Father, why don't you do the honours?' adding guilelessly, 'I hadn't expected to see you quite so soon.'

'There was a cancellation on a flight from Fiji,' her father explained. 'Under the circumstances we thought we should take it.'

Marion crossed her exquisite ankles and asked the question that Maxwell should have asked. 'How is your mother, Lydia? The last few days can't have been easy for you.'

Turquoise eyes met lambent brown ones and neither

dropped. With a touch of genuine amusement Lydia
recognised that Maxwell's second wife was no replica of his
first. Marion Winsby would not beg for anything. She was
a glossily packaged woman of forty-five or so who looked as
though she would give to any situation exactly what she
deemed fit and no more.

'She's progressing well,' Lydia said. 'She's still very weak,
but that's to be expected.' She passed serviettes and canapés.
'You must both be tired. You've had a long journey.'

'We arrived in Vancouver last night and stayed in a
hotel,' her father replied, pouring himself a Scotch and
water.

He looked well, Lydia thought. Without ever having
been in the military, Maxwell cultivated the image of a
retired brigadier: clipped moustache and highly polished
shoes, upright bearing and brisk, authoritative pronouncements. He disapproved of youth, any form of sexual
deviation, and all music composed since 1900.

Lydia raised her glass, deciding she had better get it over
with. 'My congratulations to both of you. Where did you
meet?'

'In Hong Kong,' Marion said. 'In one of the country
clubs. My former husband was a diplomat.'

Lydia would not have been surprised had Marion had
more than one former husband. 'Of course, you spend quite
a bit of time in Hong Kong, don't you, Father?'

'Yes, our Western operations are based there.' He made a
stiff little bow in Marion's direction. 'And a very happy
time it was.'

Marion acknowledged this gallantry with a faint
ironical smile. She was beautifully dressed in suede and silk
and the kind of gold jewellery whose price tag is always
discreetly hidden. Lydia wondered why she had married
Maxwell, for it did not seem likely that Marion was in love.
Maxwell was rich. There was that.

In a light, amusing way Marion described several incidents in their travels from Hong Kong to Fiji. Maxwell hung on to every word, occasionally giving the short bark which passed for laughter with him, and gradually Lydia came to the conclusion that while Marion was not in love with Maxwell, Maxwell most certainly was with Marion. She felt a twinge of unholy amusement, for it would seem a kind of poetic justice was unfolding; Marion could lead Maxwell a merry dance, no question of that.

Maxwell poured more drinks, and into a lull in the conversation said, 'Did you like your Christmas gift, Lydia?'

The mink coat had been pushed into the corner of Lydia's closet and forgotten. She said, 'Do you want the honest answer to that question, Father?' and saw antagonism flare in Maxwell's eyes and as rapidly be smothered; Maxwell didn't want any father-daughter conflicts in front of his new bride. 'Of course,' he said manfully.

Lydia included Marion in her smile of apology, for Marion had arrived swathed in a silver fox. 'I'm really not a fan of fur coats,' she said. 'I'm wondering if you'd mind very much if I returned it?'

'It was not cheap,' Maxwell huffed.

'It's a beautiful coat—I just don't happen to like fur coats.'

'Certainly I could arrange for you to return it. What would you get instead?'

She thought of all her ambivalence towards James and said, 'If I could find someone to take over the business, I'd go away for a month. Go south. Lie on a beach in the sun.'

'Wonderful idea,' Marion said. 'I could suggest some lovely places that are a little out of the way.'

They discussed the Virgin Islands and the Bahamas, the dreadful weather in Toronto and skiing in Vermont, a safe, superficial conversation, which was interrupted by the telephone. It was James.

'Just got in. Can I take you out for a late dinner?'

The sound of his voice had made her heart thump with an unsettling mixture of pleasure and panic. 'I don't think so. You see, my father and Marion are here. How about tomorrow?'

'Can I come over?'

'I'd rather you didn't.'

'Are they staying overnight?'

'I don't know.' She was almost certain they were not; they would be booked into the Four Seasons or the Sheraton.

There was a moment's silence. 'Are you all right?'

'Oh, yes. And you? How was your trip?'

'Routine stuff,' he said impatiently. 'How are you getting along—any fights?'

'No,' she said pleasantly.

He gave a frustrated sigh. 'I hate the goddamn telephone! We spend too much time on it, you and I. You'll call me if you need anything?'

That word *need* again. 'Yes.'

'Then I'll see you tomorrow. Shall we go to Scranton? It's New Year's Eve.'

She had totally forgotten the date. 'Not tomorrow.'

'Take care of yourself, Lydia, I know all this is difficult for you. I'm thinking about you—and I'm on your side, don't forget that. Love you.'

Slowly Lydia put down the phone, aching to feel his arms around her yet deeply relieved that she did not have to see him until tomorrow. And how's that for inconsistency, she scolded herself as she went back into the living-room to her two guests.

Maxwell tugged at his moustache. 'I am contemplating visiting your mother tomorrow,' he announced.

Marion preserved a diplomatically bland face; Lydia's

face in swift succession went from shock through dismay to anger. Fighting to match Marion's control, she said tightly, 'Do you think that's a good idea after all these years?'

'My marriage to Marion has made me realise it's time Judith and I buried the hatchet,' he said pompously.

The end of the old year, the beginning of the new ... Lydia said, 'It could be a tremendous shock for her.'

'I shall phone ahead and check with the nursing staff.'

'Will you tell her you've remarried?'

'Certainly. Although I don't think Marion should accompany me to the hospital—it would be most awkward for her.'

Lydia was sure Marion could handle far more awkward situations than a meeting with a former wife. But she could see that Maxwell was determined upon this visit. Because he stood to lose a lot of money if Judith altered her will? Because he wanted to impress Marion with his magnanimity? Both reasons seemed possible; a change of heart to true, disinterested kindness much less so. 'Do be careful,' she said, and knew she had said both too little and too much. 'When will you go?'

'Tomorrow evening. I have some business to look after during the day.'

Lydia's head was beginning to ache, for Judith, pathetic, obsessed Judith, seemed very much a presence in the room; certainly Judith was no match for Marion. And tomorrow evening she, Lydia, would be faced with James.

The conversation laboured on with excruciating politeness on all sides. Eventually Maxwell invited Lydia to join them for dinner; when she gracefully declined, he couldn't quite disguise his relief. 'Well,' he said heartily, 'once we're settled you must come and visit us. You'd enjoy Hong Kong.'

She smiled her thanks and knew she would not visit them, in Hong Kong or anywhere else. The usual hackneyed New Year's greetings were exchanged, cheeks were kissed, and finally, after waving goodbye at the front door, Lydia went inside. She went straight upstairs, stripped off the paisley and the silk, wrapped her old red velour robe around her, and lay down on the bed.

She felt desolate. Judith and Maxwell seemed to hang over the end of the bed. Judith, as much as she was capable, loved her daughter, yet was unable to express that love in word or deed, whereas Maxwell had never been anything but a stranger to Lydia. Physically he had conceived her, and emotionally aborted her; a father in name only. Neither one had ever said to Lydia, I love you.

She pulled the duvet around her, huddling into its softness, and eventually fell asleep. She woke at three in the morning, that blackest of hours, thinking not of Judith and Maxwell but of James, knowing in her heart she had to get away from him, that she had nothing to give him. Or rather, she corrected herself wearily, that she was afraid to give him anything. Afraid that she would end up like Judith, raw and vulnerable and unloved.

The decision was a relief. She fell asleep again, went through the motions at work that day, and agreed to meet James for dinner. 'I'm going to surprise you,' he said cheerfully. 'I'll pick you up at seven.'

Surprises all around, she thought with a dreadful kind of humour, and was waiting for him at the door when he arrived. She was wearing the same paisley skirt and silk blouse, for their sombre colours suited her mood.

Before she fastened her seat belt James reached over and kissed her, the kiss of a man hungry to touch the woman he loved. She bore it as best she could, fighting back her body's instinctive response, and was not surprised when he drew back and said, 'Are you all right? That's a damn fool question—you're not, are you?'

'No. I'm not. Can't we talk about it later?'

'Did you have a fight with your father?'

'Oh, no. He had his new wife with him, so he was on his best behaviour.'

'But his visit has upset you. I'd hoped to meet him, Lydia.'

'There's no necessity for that,' she said more sharply than she had intended.

He gave her a long, considering look. 'He didn't stay long.'

She said ruefully, 'Long enough to visit my mother this evening.' Trying to lighten the conversation—and her mood—she gave him her impressions of Marion, who reminded him of a cousin of his father's who had gone through four husbands and died a very rich woman.

They had arrived at the restaurant. 'But this is where we met!' Lydia said, trying to mask her dismay.

'I'm indulging my sentimental streak. Unfortunately I couldn't reserve either of the two tables where we sat.'

Tonight their table was near the fireplace and gave the most privacy of any in the restaurant. Lydia buried her nose in the menu until the waiter arrived. They ordered and were served cocktails. James raised his glass. 'Better days ahead, Lydia.'

She stared at him, thrown off balance. She had carefully rehearsed her speech this evening and already it was going awry. She blurted, 'I can't drink to that, James.'

'Why not?'

'I—I'm going away.'

He put down his glass, untasted, his blue eyes wary. 'Why?'

Anyone else would have asked where, or for how long. But not James. He had chosen the most relevant question, the one most difficult to answer. Lydia took a mouthful of sherry and tried to get her rehearsed speech back on track. 'It's a little complicated,' she said. 'My father gave me the fur coat for Christmas, which I really don't want, so I'm going to return it and use the money to go south for a month. Providing I can find someone to take over the business—I have a couple of candidates in mind. I want to lie on a beach in the sun.'

James took a long swallow of his own drink. 'And what if I were to take a couple of weeks off and join you down there?'

In her rehearsals he had not asked such awkward questions; instead, he had been very understanding about her need to get away. 'I want to be alone,' she said.

'Let's get real, Lydia,' he said harshly. 'The issue isn't a beach in the sun, is it?'

'What's wrong with wanting to get out of the snow and the ice?'

'The issue's me,' he said ungrammatically and correctly.

Good rehearsal, bad opening night: all very true, she thought wryly. 'I need a holiday. I've worked very hard all autumn and my mother's illness has been a shock.'

'Of course it has,' he said more gently. 'Seeing your father has probably upset you, too. And when it's ten below outside, any beach not knee-deep in snow looks good. Which does not address the question of why I can't join you.'

She said slowly, 'It's uncanny that you brought me to this restaurant tonight. Replay of the whole scene, substituting you for George.' She gave the waiter a false smile and looked down at the cream of broccoli soup he had brought her; it was a very bright green.

'If you're trying to insult me, you're succeeding beyond your wildest expectations,' James said. 'I refuse to consider myself as a substitute for George! Nor am I offering you a damned great diamond. I'm not discussing marriage. I'm discussing two weeks in the Bahamas.'

'The answer's still no.'

He dipped a piece of pickled herring into sour cream and

ate it thoughtfully, a pause Lydia used to brace herself for whatever was coming next. 'When are you leaving?' he asked pleasantly.

'I don't know yet. I haven't made any bookings.'

'So it won't be tomorrow.'

'Of course not.'

'Then we'll go to Scranton tomorrow.'

'James, I can't,' she said with desperate honesty.

He put down his fork. 'We're getting a little closer to the truth, aren't we?' he said grimly. 'What's wrong, Lydia?'

'I can't keep on seeing you.'

Now that the words were out, she had the feeling he had been expecting them. 'Have you met someone else?'

'No, James, I haven't met anyone else.'

'Then what's the problem?'

'You're in love with me—you said so. You want to marry me. I don't love you and I don't want to marry anyone. So I don't want to go out with you any more.'

He said with dangerous quietness, 'Or sleep with me any more?'

That subject had somehow never been mentioned in her rehearsals. She stirred her soup, watching it swirl in the bowl, wondering why she had ordered it. 'I guess not,' she mumbled.

'You *guess*?' he said furiously.

She looked up. 'No!' she said over-loudly, and saw their nearest neighbours glance over at her curiously. 'James, can't we talk about this later?'

'I think that might be advisable,' he snapped. 'What I would like to do to you right now would not be suitable behaviour in a restaurant.'

She didn't ask whether he wanted to make love to her or strangle her. She drank half of her soup, and then ate less than half of the tenderloin of pork. She heard James say to the waiter, 'No dessert or coffee, thanks. If we could just have the bill,' and decided, not for the first time, that she would never eat in this restaurant again.

She insisted on paying half the bill, knowing that she didn't want to feel in any way indebted to James tonight, and said, as they left the restaurant, 'I'd like to go to my place, please.'

He raised a brow. 'Conducting a war on one's own territory gives one a psychological advantage.'

'Good,' she said spiritedly, 'I need all the advantages I can get,' and was comforted when he actually laughed.

Once home, she put on the coffee pot and busied herself with mugs and cream and sugar while James, without asking her permission, lit a fire. When she carried the tray of coffee upstairs, he said, glancing at his watch, 'Two and a half hours to clear this up, Lydia. And then it'll be the New Year, and a clean slate.'

'It's not that simple, James.'

He sat down beside her on the chesterfield. 'I have a feeling I know what the problem is tonight—we talked about it before. Because of your upbringing, you're afraid of loving someone, or of needing someone. Specifically, you're afraid to fall in love with me. But, Lydia, just look at the progress you've made in the last two months and be patient—because I'm not asking you to marry me tomorrow, or even next month. I'll give you all the time you need. You're capable of love, I know you are.'

'I'm terrified of love,' she said flatly. 'I don't want the kind of pressure you're putting on me, James. That's why I won't go out with you again.'

'You're stubborn, I'll say that for you. You're scared to death of admitting you need me.'

'I *don't* need you.'

'You're wrong. You need me very badly. And if you can't admit that need, do you know what'll happen? You won't end up like your mother, because at least she loves someone, however wrong-headedly. You'll end up like your father, incapable of loving anyone.'

She flinched. 'That's a cruel thing to say!'

'It's the truth. Come on, Lydia—say you need me. The world won't come to an end.'

'No!' she cried. 'Because when you need people, they're never there. Let me tell you something. When I was growing up there were lots of times I needed my parents. There'd be a play at school or a parents' day, and I'd tell my father way ahead of time so he could plan for it, but something would always come up at work and he'd have to stay in the city or he'd be off to New York. Sometimes Mother would show up instead; occasionally she'd be sober but more often she'd have been drinking, so that you couldn't depend on how she'd behave, and I'd be humiliated by her in front of all my school friends. I wised up after a while and stopped inviting them. Because I'd learned my lesson—don't let yourself need people. That way you won't get hurt.'

'You might as well be dead,' James said.

'So I have to have a man in order to be alive?' she flashed back.

'You have to love other people and allow yourself to be loved.'

He sounded very angry. She said coldly, 'I have my job and my house and my friends. I have a full life.'

'So we're back to the glorification of the single life, are we? It's a red herring, Lydia. The real issue is that you're confusing me with your father. You think if you allow yourself to fall in love with me, to need me, that I'll disappear. That I'll never be available, just as he never was. I'm *not* your father. I'm a very different man.' His voice roughened. 'I would do my level best always to be there when you needed me—because I love you.'

'So what do I do, marry you and hope you're telling me

the truth?' she cried.

'Keep on seeing me. Allow trust to build between us. But for God's sake, don't run away!'

'The longer we keep on seeing each other, the harder it will be to break up.'

'You're not even listening to me!'

She was gripping the arm of the chesterfield so tightly that her knuckles were white. 'I know I'm doing the right thing,' she said.

'Do you?' he snarled. 'Then allow me to do what I wanted to do in the restaurant, and see if I can change your mind.' He seized her by the elbows, pulling her towards him, and fastened his mouth on hers.

Lydia braced herself against his chest with her palms and tried to pull her head away, but his hand was tangled in her hair; his other hand was fondling her breasts through the thin silk blouse. Anger, desire, and fear attacked her in equal measure.

But his hand on her flesh was gentle, with no wish to hurt her, and insensibly his lips gentled as well. Anger was eaten up by desire and fear was flooded by it.

Dimly her brain chided her for surrendering so easily. But surrender was a pleasure so exquisite as to border on pain. She took his head in her hands and drifted her tongue across his lips and arched her breasts to the touch of his fingers, and forgot her rehearsals and all the reasons why she should not be doing this.

With brutal suddenness James pulled back from her, stood up and went to stand by the fireplace. Lydia slowly lowered her arms and tried to wipe the stunned expression from her face. When she had her voice under control she said carefully, 'Why did you do that?'

'I wanted to prove something to myself. That you're not the cold-blooded bitch you pretend to be.'

'*James!*'

'Didn't take me long, did it?'

She straightened her blouse with fingers that shook. 'That was a horrible thing to do. You manipulated me as if I was a—a doll!'

'Is it any worse than what you've done? You slept with me when it suited you, but when emotion entered into the picture, you backed right off. How do you think *I* feel?'

She stared at him in dismay. 'You feel manipulated, too?'

'Used is more like it.'

'James, I'm sorry. I've hurt you, and I didn't mean to. But you've just proved my point—it's better to break this off now rather than later.' Her nerves were over-stretched; she knew she couldn't take much more. 'Please, will you go now?'

The firelight flickered on the deep lines in his face as the force of his will battered against the dead weight of her childhood years and fell back, defeated. 'Is that how I'm to begin the New Year? By losing you?'

'Better now than later,' she repeated, her chin set, her hands clasped in her lap to still their trembling.

He had been leaning on the mantel. He straightened, his movements those of a much older man. 'You really mean it, don't you?' he said quietly. 'I'll go, Lydia, yes—I can't fight you any more.' He gave a shadow of his crooked smile. 'In the old days I'd have dragged you out of here by the hair and thrown you across my horse, wouldn't I? Unfortunately I'm a twentieth-century man ... I can't do that, much as I might want to.'

Lydia stood up, not sure how much more she could bear. She was the one responsible for that deadness in his voice, for the blank look in his eyes. 'I did warn you,' she said helplessly. 'From the beginning I warned you.'

'So you did.' He was still standing by the fireplace, as if not quite sure where he was. 'If you change your mind, you promise you'll let me know? Don't let pride stand in your way, Lydia.'

'I won't change my mind.'

He looked at her for a long moment, as though he was imprinting her image in his memory. Then he said, 'I'll let myself out,' and left the room.

Lydia sat down abruptly on the nearest chair. It was only ten-thirty. She felt as if it should be two in the morning. I've done the right thing, she thought. I know I have. So why do I feel so unhappy?

CHAPTER THIRTEEN

ANNABEL didn't think Lydia had done the right thing.

Lydia phoned her on New Year's Day at a suitably late hour in the morning. She herself had been too restless to sleep after James left. She had turned on the television, found its blend of old-year nostalgia and new-year revelry insupportable, and turned it off again. She had tidied the kitchen and watched the fire die in the hearth. At eleven-thirty she had gone to bed, trying to pretend unsuccessfully that this particular midnight was just like any other midnight. She had not slept well.

Malcolm answered the phone. 'Lydia—Happy New Year!' he said warmly. 'How nice of you to call.'

'May I drop over for a while?' she asked in a small voice.

'Why don't you come now? I think we have to go out a little later. But don't expect brilliant conversation, will you; we didn't get much sleep because we were out late and Nicolas elected to waken earlier than usual. Will James be with you?'

She felt a sharp pang of loss. 'No, he won't. I'll be over in ten minutes,' she said, and quickly put down the phone.

Annabel had circles under her eyes but produced her usual bright smile. 'Hello, darling, Happy New Year! Isn't it *cold*? Can I get you a drink? I won't have one, I got a little carried away last night and don't you say a word, Malcolm, I'm suffering for it this morning and it's all my own fault. But hangovers are so *lowering*, aren't they? Where did you go last night, Lydia? How's that hunk of a James? I thought he'd be with you?' And she raised her eyebrows in innocent enquiry.

169

'Yes, it's cold, and yes, I will have a drink,' said Lydia. 'A strong one. James and I broke up last night, that's why he's not with me.'

Annabel's jaw dropped. 'Broke *up*?' she squeaked. 'Malcolm, I've changed my mind. I'll have a drink, too. What do you mean, broke up?'

Malcolm had led them into the kitchen, where Lydia sat down on a stool, schooling her expression to a casualness she was far from feeling.

'We're not going to see each other any more,' she said.

'I don't believe you!' Annabel announced. 'If this is your idea of a joke, I don't think it's very funny.'

'She's not joking,' Malcolm interposed, giving Lydia a keen look as he passed her a rum and Coke.

'But he's head over heels in love with you!' Annabel wailed. 'The way he looked at you, the way he touched you—I've never seen a man more obviously in love. He *couldn't* have broken up with you!'

'He didn't. I *did*,' Lydia said defiantly.

Annabel grabbed the nearest stool and hoisted herself up on it. 'Hurry up with my drink, Malcolm,' she ordered. 'We're going to get to the bottom of this.'

Her lip was stuck out; she looked very determined. 'Where's Nicolas?' Lydia asked.

'Sleeping on the chesterfield. Little wonder, he was up at six o'clock this morning. So Nicolas isn't coming to your rescue, Lydia, and you can tell us *exactly* what this is all about. *I* even thought you might get engaged last night.'

'We went to the wrong restaurant,' Lydia said flippantly.

Before Annabel could explode, Malcolm said quickly, 'Maybe Lydia doesn't want to talk about it.'

'I suppose I do,' Lydia said glumly, 'or why else did I come here?' She had come, if she were to be totally honest, to get approval for what she had done, reassurance that she had behaved correctly. 'Let me explain. James is in love with me, you're quite right, Annabel. And he wants to marry me. I told him right from the start I didn't want commitment or marriage. So I broke up with him.'

Annabel narrowed her eyes. 'James Connelly was the best thing that ever happened to you.'

'No, he——'

'I said to Malcolm, thank heavens Lydia has finally given up on those deadly dull men, those *safe* men, and is going out with someone who'll shake her up a bit and turn her into a normal woman who——'

'I *am* a normal woman,' Lydia interrupted, stung.

'No, you're not! You're the original ice maiden. How much longer are you planning to be a martyr to your parents? Sure, they were dreadful. Your mother's an alcoholic, poor soul, there's no getting around that, and your father's the typical executive who can only see people in terms of money and power. So you had a rotten childhood. OK. So are you going to carry it around for the rest of your life? Poor Lydia Winsby, her parents were cruel to her, so she's going to turn herself into a dried-up old spinster who's scared to love anything more alive than a *fig* tree—is *that* the real you, Lydia?'

Malcolm said levelly, 'You're coming on too strong, Annabel.'

'No, I'm *not*!' Annabel's eyes were suddenly awash in tears. 'I love you, Lydia; apart from Malcolm you're my best friend, I can't bear to see you do this to yourself. Oh damn, *why* am I crying?'

Malcolm passed her a box of tissues. Annabel blew her nose vigorously, used a second one to sop at her eyes, and said aggressively, 'Well—what have you got to say for yourself?'

Lydia looked as blank as James had looked twelve hours earlier. 'Nothing,' she said.

'Good. At least that shows you're thinking. Malcolm, you

agree with me, don't you?'

Malcolm smiled at Lydia and said calmly, 'Essentially, yes. Annabel and I have talked about you, Lydia, and even considered outright interference when you started going out with George. As you know, we didn't interfere, we thought nature had to take its course and when you were ready you'd expand your horizons. Male Horizons, that is. Consequently, when we met James, we were delighted. Annabel even went so far as to wonder which dress she'd wear to the wedding.'

'A maternity dress,' Annabel put in, her irrepressible smile reappearing like sun after rain.

'So your news this morning is discouraging,' Malcolm went on. 'I agree with Annabel: at some point you've got to come to terms with your childhood. I wonder how much your mother's illness and your father's visit have to do with all this?'

Thoroughly confused, Lydia sat in silence. She had sought approbation for her decision last night, and had instead been thoroughly scolded. Moreover, Annabel and Malcolm had said nothing that James had not already said.

Annabel looked at the kitchen clock. 'Is it *that* late?' she exclaimed. 'We're invited out for brunch today, what a barbaric custom, brunch when you've got a hangover, all those eggs. But we've got to go, it's Malcolm's boss and you know what *that* means, Lydia. *What* am I going to do about my face?'

'Lots of eyeshadow,' Malcolm said comfortingly.

'And that blouse with the low neck, that'll distract them,' Annabel said decisively. 'I'd better start getting ready, it's going to take longer than usual today. Lydia, I hope I haven't been too blunt, but I do believe every word I said, and if there's *anything* I can do to help, I'll do it.' She put her head to one side. 'Kidnap both of you and lock you up in a bedroom?'

'*That's* not the problem,' said Lydia.

'Then you're on the right track, darling.'

Lydia put her unfinished drink down on the counter. 'I don't think I want this, after all. Enjoy the brunch, both of you—and thank you for your concern. I——' She took a deep breath. 'I love you both,' she said in a rush. 'You're my best friends.'

Annabel's eyes filled with tears again. 'You've never told us that before.'

'No.' Lydia was almost crying herself. 'It's long overdue.'

They exchanged a clumsy three-way hug in the middle of the kitchen, then Lydia left. She went for a long walk before she went home, a walk on which she did not really feel alone, for Judith and Maxwell, James, Annabel and Malcolm walked along with her. Five different voices and she, twenty-nine-year-old Lydia, had to decide how to respond to them.

That afternoon she visited her mother. A very large bouquet of orchids had joined the carnations on the dressing-table. But Judith was tired and didn't want to talk about Maxwell's visit.

The next day Lydia was glad to get back to work. At the weekend she went to a delightful inn north of Toronto, went cross-country skiing, read a lot, and forced herself to examine objectively the course her life was taking. Unexpectedly, on the Monday, Judith helped this process.

Judith was nearing the end of her stay in hospital, and was sitting up in bed when Lydia got there; she was redolent with Scheherazade.

'You look well, Mother.'

Judith was gratified. 'I managed to persuade one of the aides to do my hair. It hadn't been touched since your father was here.'

So Judith had brought the subject of Maxwell into the open. 'I haven't heard from him since he left,' Lydia remarked.

'You know that he's remarried.'

'Yes, I know,' Lydia said cautiously.

'It came a great shock to me.'

'I was afraid it would.'

Judith said abruptly, 'I want you to do something for me, Lydia.'

'Of course I will.'

'Your father's letters are in that drawer.' Judith indicated the bedside stand. 'I want you to throw them out.'

'Mother!'

'Just do it,' Judith said irritably. 'Right now.'

Lydia opened the drawer, took out the small, beribboned bundle and crossed the room to drop it into the wastebasket. It hit with a small, metallic thud. Then she turned back to the bed.

Judith was crying, slow difficult tears that coursed down the wrinkles in her cheeks. 'Thank you,' she whispered. 'I couldn't have done it myself.'

Inarticulate with pity and love, Lydia gathered her mother into her arms and rocked her back and forth, and heard the thin little voice mutter, 'I do love you, Lydia. I always did. But somehow Maxwell always got in the way.'

It was the closest Judith could come to an apology for the long, silent years. Lydia said softly, 'I know he did—I understand. I love you, too, Mother.'

Judith being Judith, the embrace did not last long. She got Lydia to adjust her pillows, brush her hair and water the carnations, and when visiting hours were over said acerbically, 'When are you bringing that nice man back to visit me?'

'James? I stopped seeing him, Mother.'

'Then start seeing him again.'

And Lydia heard herself say meekly, 'Yes, Mother.'

Lydia went home, worked all week and thought about James incessantly, remembering every facet of his personality, rigorously comparing him to her father. A man more different from her father could not be found, was her conclusion. James was sensitive, generous and loving. He was an oak tree; Maxwell a particularly tough alder.

By Friday evening she was fully aware of the enormity of her mistake. Mistakes, she amended ruefully. Although she had left home at eighteen, Maxwell and Judith had been running her life ever since. Mistake number one. Number two was, of course, that she had treated James as if he were Maxwell. Number three was equally obvious, she decided, gazing into the glowing heart of the fire as she sat curled up on the chesterfield in her jeans. She had allowed fear to rule her. Fear, not love. She loved James. That was why she had been, underneath everything else, so unhappy ever since New Year's Eve. That was why she had worked so hard the last few days to understand herself and the pattern of her life. That was why she had made love to him: the only way she could express her love. The only safe way.

Now I can tell him I love him, she thought exultantly. I'm not afraid any more. I've freed myself of the past enough to understand how much I need him . . . how deeply I love him. A week was not very long for such a turnaround. But James had already begun the process, her mother's heart attack and Maxwell's remarriage had further disturbed her, and Annabel's anger had added the final impetus.

The coals pulsed orange and gold; the fire whickered and snapped. I love you, James, she said to herself. Then she said the words aloud. 'James, I love you.'

They acted like a catalyst. She got up from the chesterfield, hurrried to her bedroom and dialled his number. Her heart racing, she waited while it rang, rang again, and again.

Disappointment congealed in her heart. I need you, she cried silently into the mouthpiece, and in mocking reply the empty ringing continued in her ear.

She tried again at ten and eleven, and the next morning she started at eight-thirty. By afternoon she had decided he was away, and with a horrible stab of jealousy wondered if he were alone.

Of course he's alone, the new Lydia said stoutly. Maxwell always had other women, but James isn't Maxwell. James loves me. James would be faithful.

James doesn't know you want him back, a nasty little voice whispered in her ear. So why should he be faithful?

Because he's James, she snapped, and resolutely smothered the ugly thoughts of another woman in his arms.

She could have spoken to Betty in Scranton, but the explanation for her call if James were not there was more than she could face. She had waited a lifetime for James; she could surely wait another twenty-four hours?

But he didn't answer his telephone Sunday evening or Monday morning, by which time her imagination was having a field day. He was dead. Or in hospital. He'd been hurt on an oil rig. He'd left the country. At nine-thirty she phoned Finlay and Madson and asked for James Connelly.

'Mr Connelly is on vacation, madam.'

'Do you know when he'll be back?'

'We expect him next Monday. Would you like to leave a message?'

'No. No message, thank you.'

So that was that. She had a week to wait.

A week isn't long, Lydia.

A week is for ever.

And so it seemed. She jumped every time the phone rang, convinced it must be James, and of course the phone rang a great deal because Torrington's exotic plants were much in demand. Her body was in turmoil all week, and she had two quite startlingly erotic dreams, which made her blush when she remembered them in the sober light of day. And her spirits were much tried. On Friday she delivered some *Schlefflera* plants to a tourist bureau whose walls were adorned with posters of bikini-clad beauties on long white beaches, and was once again attacked by jealousy. Perhaps James had gone to the Bahamas. Perhaps he had met someone there. Perhaps even now he was splashing into the turquoise sea with his arm around a lissom, tanned blonde, or sitting in a bar, gazing into her sea-blue eyes. She could see James and the blonde quite clearly. James's hair was wet from the sea; he was wearing a loose tropical shirt, unbuttoned to his waist, while the blonde, in what appeared to be a black leather bikini, was running her scarlet-nailed fingers down his chest . . .

'You'll send us your invoice, Ms Winsby?'

Lydia gaped at the manager. 'Oh. Oh, yes. Next week,' she stammered, knowing she must look and sound like an idiot. Clutching the remnants of her dignity, she scurried out of the tourist bureau. Jealousy was a horrible emotion, she decided, standing in the doorway and searching for the keys to the van. Or, more accurately, a horrible mixture of emotions: fear, anger, pain, love and hate. If jealousy was any measure of love, then she loved James a great deal. And hated the blonde, she added darkly.

After a relatively mild day, the temperature had plunged, so that the sidewalk was like glass. The entire population of Toronto should be in the Bahamas, Lydia thought crossly, peering into the back of the van. She had two kangaroo vines and a *Dieffenbachia* for delivery to a newly opened wallpaper store five blocks east, and then she was through for the day. Her mind more on James than on her driving, she set out.

She came to a four-way stop sign. Only when she braked did she notice that the roadway was a sheet of ice. As if it were happening to someone else she felt the van slide across the street and turn in an elegantly inscribed circle; like a skater doing a pirouette, she thought, instinctively taking her foot from the brake and swinging the wheel to control the skid.

She caught a blur of movement to her left, heard the screech of metal colliding with metal and crumpling like paper, and felt her whole left side explode into pain. The seat belt cut into her body. Her nose banged against the windscreen. Then the van shuddered to stillness and there was silence, deafening in its intensity.

Her door wrenched open. 'My God, she's bleeding!' a man's voice exclaimed.

She looked into the bulging eyes of a moustachioed, red-faced man in a navy blue coat. 'I bumped my nose,' she said distinctly, and fainted.

Afterwards Lydia was very glad she had fainted, for the policeman who visited her in the emergency department of the nearest hospital allowed that the red-haired gentleman, whose black Mercedes had crashed into the side of the van, had been somewhat irate. 'Doesn't think much of women drivers,' said the policeman. 'But we got tyre marks, and he skidded across the intersection, too. There were accidents all across the city until the salt trucks got out.'

He took down the particulars that he required for his report, told her to get in touch with her insurance company, and departed. She was sorry to see him go, because he had been large and imperturbable, and consequently comforting. The emergency department was very busy; after a rapid assessment by an intern, she had been told Dr Wiseman would see her in twenty minutes.

A public telephone was on the wall near her seat. She

found a quarter in her wallet and dialled Finlay and Madson. The same receptionist answered. Mr Connelly was still on vacation.

Lydia had no pride left. She said, 'This is Lydia Winsby speaking. Please will you leave a message for him? Tell him that I *need* to see him. Please use the word need. He'll understand.'

Her knees were trembling as if she'd run a marathon. Gritting her teeth, she phoned the sales clerk in the wallpaper store to explain why the *Dieffenbachia* would not be arriving, then rang James's home number. She was not really expecting him to answer, nor did he. She would have given anything she owned to have him appear in front of her with his untidy blond hair and his blue eyes that from the beginning had seen through her façade to the isolated woman within.

When a nurse touched her on the arm, she jumped. 'Dr Wiseman will see you now. This way, please.'

Dr Wiseman was female, red-haired, and not a day older than Lydia. Her examination was thorough and of necessity painful enough to bring tears to Lydia's eyes. 'Nothing's broken,' the doctor said briskly. 'You're very fortunate. You do have quite bad bruising on that arm, superficial lesions on your nose, and by tomorrow, I'm afraid, you'll feel as if you've been run over by a tank. Lots of hot baths, I'll give you a prescription for a painkiller, no alcohol for twenty-four hours. Will someone be at home with you?'

'I'll call a friend.' Annabel would stay with her.

'I'd do that if I were you. An accident is a shock to the system, just as well not to be alone. I'd also get in touch with your local doctor on Monday, just to have a follow-up. Any questions?' She waited, smiling, her head to one side.

'My only question is how is all happened so fast,' Lydia

said wryly, 'and you can't answer that. Thank you, Dr Wiseman.'

'There are taxis at the side door. Here's your prescription, get it filled on the way home or have your friend pick it up this evening.' Another friendly smile, then she whisked out of the room.

A nurse's aide helped Lydia get her coat on, another painful process, then walked with her to the side door. The cab driver was happy to wait for her, with his meter ticking, while she picked up the prescription at the drug store nearest her home, and was solicitous enough to accompany her to the front door of her house and to wait while she unlocked the door. She gave him a wobbly smile and a generous tip and went indoors.

Taking off her boots and hanging up her coat seemed to take a very long time. Clutching her bag and the paper bag containing the pills, she toiled up the two flights of stairs to her bedroom. When she saw herself in the mirror she understood why the taxi driver had accompanied her to the door: her face was dead-white, except for a red scrape across her nose, and there was blood on the collar of her blouse. She looked as if she had been in a bar-room brawl.

She sat down gingerly on the edge of the bed and reached for the telephone. My entire life revolves around the telephone, she thought hazily, and rang Annabel's number.

There was no answer. They were probably out grocery shopping, a weekly ritual that Nicholas enjoyed far more than Annabel or Malcolm. They would be home soon, she told herself firmly, for the town house seemed very empty and she badly needed the company of another human being. She couldn't risk upsetting her mother with news of an accident, and while she could try her tennis partner or her friend Janice with whom she occasionally went to the theatre, they were acquaintances rather than close friends, and this was a time for close friends. Like Annabel. Or

James. She quailed from calling George.

What a disservice I've done to myself, she thought, her cold finger curled around the telephone. I've deliberately kept people at a distance all these years ... and now I'm paying for it. But at least I can admit now that I need people, and that's the first step.

She could not bear to try James's number again and be subjected to the repetitive unanswered ring, the loneliest sound in the world, she thought with a shiver.

Moving very slowly, she turned on the bathtub and undressed, dropping her blouse in the clothes hamper with a shudder of distaste. She used lots of bath oil and soaked in the steaming hot water for ten or fifteen minutes. The nightdress that was easiest to put on had very thin straps and no sleeves; over it she wore her red velour robe.

Still no answer at Annabel's. Maybe they'd gone away for the weekend, she thought, again assailed by the quietness of the house, by the sensation of empty rooms and of her own solitude in their midst. The hyacinths were dying, their scent unpleasantly cloying; even the bright colours of the cyclamen and begonias in the living-room did not cheer her up. Annabel was right. Plants were no substitute for people.

As if it were a magnet, her eyes were dragged over to the fireplace. She remembered the strain in James's face as he had leaned against the mantel on New Year's Eve, and wondered how she could have been so stupid, so blind as to send him away. James, I need you, she cried inwardly. Please come home.

The silence pressed against her ears; the walls seemed to echo with it. She said defiantly, 'I love you, James.' The words were swallowed by the silence as if they had never been.

I'm going crazy, she thought. This is what happens to people who are lonely—they start talking to themselves, carrying on conversations with the walls, speaking to people who aren't there.

She found she was shivering again, yet she lacked the energy to carry logs up from the garage to light the fire. A manageable alternative was to bring some cheese and crackers and a glass of milk upstairs from the kitchen, to drag her duvet off the bed and to swallow two pills. Huddled in the duvet on the chesterfield, she munched on the crackers. Gradually the soft folds of down hoarded the warmth of her body, and the drugs eased the pain of her bruised side and the dull ache in her nose. Her head drooped against the pillows and she dozed off.

Lydia awoke with a start. The doorbell was ringing; she had the feeling it had been ringing for some time. She untangled her legs from the duvet and got to her feet. The floor dipped up and down, as if she were on the deck of a ship in a rough sea. Resting her palm against the wall she stumbled to the head of the stairs, and laboriously began descending them. It would be just her luck if whoever was there had gone by the time she got to the door. She tried to yell, 'Coming!' and heard her voice waver like an ill-played violin.

The bell rang again as she reached the hall downstairs. Neglecting to check the peephole or turn on any lights, she opened the door, saw who was there and said blankly, 'I'm dreaming. You're away.'

'No, I'm not,' said James.

'Wish-fulfilment, they call it.'

'Are you going to ask me in?'

She stepped back, quavered, 'You're real,' and burst into tears.

James stepped inside, closed the door and took her into his arms, upon which she yelped with pain and sobbed all the louder. 'Lydia, what's wrong? Are you hurt? Where the *hell's* the light switch?'

'By the door,' she wept. 'Don't t-turn it on, I look awful.'

James reached behind him with one arm and turned on the light. He looked at her red-blotched nose and her paper-white face and said in a voice she had never heard him use before, 'Who hit you? I'll kill the bastard.'

Her breath caught in a hysterical giggle. 'I'd much rather you carried me upstairs,' she hiccuped, then let herself sag against his chest, her eyes closed. 'That's the third time I've wept all over you. It's g-got to stop. Oh James, I do love you.'

He was silent for a full ten seconds. Then he said, 'I think I must be the one who's dreaming ... *what* did you say, Lydia?'

She nuzzled her cheek into his jacket. 'I love you. I need you. And I've got to stop crying all over your jacket, it's ridiculous, I never used to c-cry. You'll have to send me the dry-cleaning bills.'

As usual James went for the essentials. 'I love you, too,' he said. 'Lydia, will you marry me?'

'Yes, please. Provided I can put some plants in your house.'

'You can fill it with plants,' he said dazedly. 'Can we have a couple of children as well?'

'Oh, yes,' she said dreamily. 'And you'll help me look after them, won't you?'

'Of course I will. Lydia, my love, I could stand here and discuss when we're going to get married—very soon, I hope—and the names of our future offspring, and the kinds of plants you're going to put in the living-room, but I have the feeling you could collapse any minute.'

'You're absolutely right,' Lydia said contentedly. 'If you carry me upstairs, be careful of my left side, it hurts ... I need to go to bed.'

'Wonderful idea,' he said, picking her up with considerable care. 'May I join you?'

He was holding her against his chest. She looked into his blue eyes, which were burning with tenderness, and said, 'I must look about as unsexy as a woman can look.'

He began climbing the stairs. 'To me, darling Lydia, you will always be sexy,' he said with great gallantry. 'Even when you look as if someone's wiped the floor with your face. What *did* happen?'

'I was in an accident with the van. This afternoon.' The heavyset policeman and the elegant Dr Wiseman seemed light-years away, and her loneliness that of a woman from another planet. She giggled again, light-headed from love and pain-killers. 'I collided with a black Mercedes. Nothing but the best.'

James put her down in her room and went to get the duvet, which he spread over the bed. She was still standing exactly where he had put her. He untied her belt and slid her robe carefully down her body, looking at her with mixed passion and concern. 'That's a very minimal nightdress,' he said, then ran his fingers lightly down her left arm. 'Did you get hit on the driver's side?'

She nodded. 'It was icy and I skidded through a stop sign.'

'You could have been killed,' James said roughly.

She gave him a dazzling smile. 'No, I couldn't. Because I had to tell you I love you. I was safe as I could be.'

'Did you have to crash into a black Mercedes to decide that you loved me?' he asked, and started taking off his clothes, folding them neatly on the chair. When he was naked, he eased her down on the bed beside him and covered them both with the duvet.

The answer to his question seemed much too complicated. Lydia put her good arm around his neck. 'Kiss me,' she said.

'Sweetheart, I'm scared to death to touch you,' he

protested. 'You must be in pain. One of these days we must try making love when neither one of us has been involved in an accident.'

'I don't know whether it's the pills I took or because I'm in love, but I feel wonderful,' Lydia said, curving her lips in a provocative smile.

'When you look at me like that, how can I refuse?' Leaning on one elbow, he bent over her and kissed her lingeringly on the mouth.

When he eventualy raised his head she said with desperate seriousness, 'James, make love to me . . . please.'

With infinite sensuality he caressed the white curves of her body until her breasts were swollen and aching, and her thighs opened to him; and the whole time his gentleness was exquisite, his concentration absolute: a testament to his love for her. When he entered her, she shuddered in ecstasy, her heart racing, her eyes locked with his in the greatest intimacy that exists, and the pulsing rhythms of her body drove him beyond control to his own deep release.

Lydia lay very still, tears of sheer happiness flooding her eyes. 'James, I have never felt so well loved in my life,' she whispered. 'You were wonderful to me . . . I love you so much.'

He eased himself free of her and lay down, gathering her into the curve of his arm so that their two heads lay on one pillow. 'Surely no more than I love you,' he murmured. 'It's not possible.'

'I'm so sorry I sent you away. I was wrong to do so.'

'Almost worth it when you welcome me back so beautifully. What made you change your mind, Lydia? Was it the accident? When I dropped into the office on my way home to see if there were any messages, there was one from you, from this afternoon.' He gave a twisted smile. 'The receptionist had underlined the word *need*. As soon as I saw that, I came straight here. I know you wouldn't have used that word if something pretty catastrophic hadn't happened.'

'I've been trying to reach you for the last week and a half,' Lydia confessed. Fumbling a little in her effort to be totally honest, she told him about Annabel's and Malcolm's reaction to the break-up, about Judith's admission of love and about her own painful reassessment of the course her life had taken. 'It was a watershed,' she said slowly, 'one of those times in your life when you know that the decision you make is crucial to all that will follow. You had laid the groundwork for that decision, James, and so I was finally able to admit that I needed your love, that I could trust in it as I had never trusted in my parents' love ... and that I loved you.' She grimaced at him. 'By which time, of course, you'd gone away. Did you go to the Bahamas?'

'Goodness, no. I went skiing in the Laurentians. By myself. Couldn't stand to have anyone else around.'

'Oh. *I* had decided you were with a beautiful blonde on the beach,' Lydia said. 'She had long hair and looked gorgeous in a bikini. Black leather.'

James began to laugh. 'Lydia my love, how could I possibly be with a blonde, however beautiful, when all I could think about was you? With your black hair and your stubborn chin and your total lack of co-operation ... I'd planned to stay in the Laurentians until Sunday, but when I got up today I knew I'd had enough—that I had to head home. If you hadn't left a message, I'd have been pounding at your door anyway to renew the assault.' Briefly he frowned, his eyes darkening with remembered bleakness. 'But, God, I was afraid I'd lost you! That I'd been too impatient, that I shouldn't have taken you to bed, that I'd pressured you too much and too soon.'

'I don't think you did. I was in a rut, James—sledgehammer tactics were called for. Subtlety would have been wasted on me.'

'So all *was* fair in love and war?' he said quizzically.

'We can concentrate on love now,' Lydia said happily, stroking his cheek. 'The war's over.'

He kissed her. 'And we've both won,' he said.

Harlequin Presents

Coming Next Month

1039 THE SHADOW OF MOONLIGHT Lindsay Armstrong
Meredith Sommerville's marriage was sudden, short and secret from her husband's wealthy family. After his death, the family accept her warmly—all except Evan, the eldest son. He is convinced that Meredith was just an unfaithful fortune hunter!

1040 COUNTRY OF THE HEART Robyn Donald
Finley was bound to recover from the pneumonia that prompted her vacation. Getting over a man like Blake Caird is another matter. Living together seems impossible—but living apart is infinitely worse. Yet she can't share Blake's island paradise forever!

1041 A REASON FOR MARRIAGE Penny Jordan
Jamie tells herself she'll never submit to physically becoming Jake's wife. And yet she knows, even as she makes the bitter claim, that she's already given him her heart. Even after six years he still holds it....

1042 KISS OF FIRE Charlotte Lamb
Impulsively buying race driver Liam Moor's book brings him back into Suzy's life. They share a guilty secret and Liam blames her entirely. He still hates her. She ought to hate him, but underneath is a totally different emotion.

1043 TOO BAD TO BE TRUE Roberta Leigh
In Leslie's mind, the huge settlement extracted by divorce lawyer Dane Jordan had caused her beloved stepfather's death—and she plans an appropriate revenge. All she has to do is stay out of Dane's arms and keep her heart out of the whole affair....

1044 BURNING INHERITANCE Anne Mather
Alex has always believed that Isabel's now ended marriage to his cousin was for money, so when she inherits shares in the family company he is delegated to persuade her to sell. Isabel bitterly resents his interference but can't resist the pull of his attraction.

1045 SAVAGE AFFAIR Margaret Mayo
Tired of fighting off fortune hunters, Rhiannon happily operates an elegant little hotel in the Canary Islands. A mysterious stranger arrives who makes her aware of the passion within her, but when Pasqual's true identity is revealed, her aching love turns to cold hate.

1046 PASSIONATE REVENGE Sally Wentworth
Seven years has only added to the legacy of bitterness Zara feels at Heath Masterson's rejection. Now she is in a position to extract anything she wants from him. Her head says revenge—but she can't get her heart to agree

He could torment her days with doubts
and her nights with desires that fired her soul.

Ride the Eagle

VITA VENDRESHA

He was everything she ever wanted. But they were opponents in
a labor dispute, each fighting to win. Would she risk her brilliant
career for the promise of love?

Six exciting series for you every month... from Harlequin

Harlequin Romance·
The series that started it all

Tender, captivating and heartwarming...
love stories that sweep you off to faraway places
and delight you with the magic of love.

◆

Harlequin Presents·
Powerful contemporary love stories...as individual as the women who read them

The No. 1 romance series...
exciting love stories for you, the woman of today...
a rare blend of passion and dramatic realism.

◆

Harlequin Superromance®
It's more than romance...
it's Harlequin Superromance

A sophisticated, contemporary romance-fiction
series, providing you with a longer,
more involving read...a richer mix of complex plots,
realism and adventure.

Harlequin
American Romance™
Harlequin celebrates the
American woman...

...by offering you romance stories written
about American women, by American women
for American women. This series offers you
contemporary romances uniquely North American
in flavor and appeal.

◆

Harlequin Temptation™
Passionate stories for
today's woman

An exciting series of sensual, mature stories of
love...dilemmas, choices, resolutions...
all contemporary issues dealt with in a true-to-life
fashion by some of your favorite authors.

◆

Harlequin Intrigue
Because romance can be quite
an adventure

Harlequin Intrigue, an innovative series that
blends the romance you expect...
with the unexpected. Each story has an added
element of intrigue that provides a new twist to
the Harlequin tradition of romance excellence.

Harlequin Books™

PROD-A-2

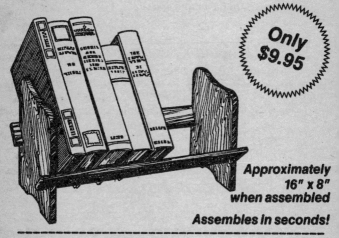

mond, a Republican from South Carolina, who became chairman of the Senate Judiciary Committee after the Republicans gained control of the Senate in 1980, and who sat on the board of trustees of Bob Jones University.[22] Like the President, Thurmond and Lott were foes of "judicial activism." In the words of a Justice Department memo prompted by Lott's letter, any court that read the law in a way that was not "clearly mandated by statute or the Constitution" had engaged in "judicial activism and policy-making."[23]

The group within the Justice Department that rallied to reverse Wallace's position on the merits became known as "the Bob Jones team." The senior member was Edward Schmults, the Deputy Attorney General and the department's second-ranking official. The team included William Bradford Reynolds, Assistant Attorney General for Civil Rights; Charles Cooper, his assistant; Carolyn Kuhl, an aide to Attorney General William French Smith; and Bruce Fein, an aide to Schmults.

The Reagan Administration's interest in the case bubbled up from the middle ranks. After Wallace took his stance, Fein wrote a paper arguing that the case deserved the Attorney General's special attention. In his words, "The IRS did not have the authority under the law to promulgate those regulations, and the obligation of the [Justice] Department was to go by what the law actually says instead of going the other way because it makes us feel good. One of the problems we've had in the last twenty years is 'feel good law.'" Kuhl found some campaign material saying that candidate Reagan had opposed "the IRS's attempt to remove the tax-exempt status of private schools by administrative fiat"[24] and that the 1980 Republican platform pledged to "halt the unconstitutional regulatory vendetta launched by Mr. Carter's IRS Commissioner against independent schools"—even though it was President Nixon's commissioner who, with Nixon's approval, had begun what the platform called a vendetta.

Reynolds might have been expected to show concern about the reaction of blacks to the Fein position, since, as head of the Civil Rights Division, he was responsible for enforcing laws passed to protect the rights of minorities. Instead, he agreed there was nothing in the tax code to deny tax-exempt status to Bob Jones University. During the first year of the Reagan Administration, the Justice Department had been criticized in the right-wing press for showing disloyalty to the President's social program by not pressing it hard enough. To senior officials like Reynolds and Schmults, other lawyers in the department observed, the Bob Jones case seemed to present a chance to improve the record.[25]

Trent Lott's letter was summarized in the President's log of congressional mail as urging the President "to intervene in this particular case." President Reagan scrawled in the margin, "I think we should." Some of the President's advisers believed the shift contemplated by the Bob Jones team was no more than an about-face on a policy of the Carter Administration, and they approved. Not long afterward, Michael Deaver, one of the President's initial triumvirate of senior advisers, said, "I just heard that it was a reversal of Carter policy and at that point I tuned out."[26] The Bob Jones team held a series of meetings about the case, excluded Wallace from them, and encouraged him to continue drafting a brief for the government as he saw fit; by the time Wallace was invited to take part in a review of the Justice Department's options, the team had already convinced Attorney General William French Smith to overrule the Acting Solicitor General.[27]

To lawyers in the SG's office, which sometimes displays its skills by presenting conflicting sides of a case with equal weight, the Bob Jones team's position was indefensible. First, they believed that it was wrong on the law. For a decade, the IRS had applied the tax law in keeping with the commitment to halt discrimination. Congress had considered amending the tax code thirteen times since then, each time deciding it was not necessary to clarify the law because the IRS was already reading it properly. The Supreme Court summarily upheld this position in 1971.[28]

Next, the change didn't appear to serve the Administration's interests. If the President's followers wanted to make a statement about the appropriate division of responsibility under the Constitution for making, enforcing, and interpreting the law, a case that required the Administration to endorse racism while doing so was an ill-chosen vehicle. Bradford Reynolds defended himself in 1985 by declaring that "neither I nor the Administration ever favored granting tax-exempt status to racially discriminatory private schools,"[29] but that was the instant effect of their judgment that the statute in question permitted no other reading. Though the crux of the Administration's theory may have been based on an earnestly held principle—that the doctrine on which the IRS based its decision to revoke tax exemptions in 1970 had no obvious limits—it was not convincing. The Administration asked: If Bob Jones no longer qualifies for an exemption because its exclusion of blacks violates public policy to end racial discrimination, what about schools that admit only women? Can't they be said to violate public policy against discrimination based on sex?[30] But the IRS had made no move to expand the doctrine along these lines, and there was solid evidence that Congress had approved the agency's special concern about race. Tied to this divisive issue, the Administration's position came off as a construction of lawyers whose insensitivity seemed willful.

Finally, the reversal took no account of the perspective of the Supreme Court. Reagan aides treated the flip-flop in position, from the brief acquiescing to the brief on the merits, as if it were a natural course of events. Yet the move had no serious precedent. The credibility of the Solicitor General had been built up, among other ways, by close inquiry into the case at hand and then by maintaining a consistent position about it before the Justices.[31] The Attorney General's decision meant a rejection of the brief that Wallace had submitted four months before, when he recommended that the Justices take the case. "I had the responsibility to represent the United States in the Supreme Court," Wallace said. "It was my case. I can't remember another occasion during my 14 years in office when we've changed position in a case after taking a position with the Supreme Court."[32]

After the Administration's new stance was announced, the views of the Reagan Administration were widely seen as an endorsement of racism. "THE REWARDING OF BIAS," the Los Angeles *Times* called the government's new stance. "HYPOCRITICAL TAX CHANGE MEANS RACISM WILL PAY," judged the Tallahassee *Democrat*. "TAX-EXEMPT HATE," *The New York Times* summed up.[33] White House aides tried to convince reporters that the President had not guided the decision to overrule IRS policy in the case,[34] but at a press conference President Reagan rejected this cover. He was asked by ABC's Sam Donaldson, "Are you responsible for the original decision, or did your staff put something over on you?" The President replied, "Sam, no one put anything over on me. No, Sam, the buck stops at my desk." He requested, "Judge us [by] how well we recover and solve the situation." [35]

In the wake of the public outcry, the President's aides tried to make their judgment sound coherent, and declared that Congress should take responsibility by amending the IRS code to forbid tax exemptions to schools like Bob Jones. Backpedaling from Southerners like Strom Thurmond, who argued that the case had to do with "religious and private civil rights," the President repeated the logic of his 1980 platform: the only reason for his Administration's new policy was to keep the IRS from governing by "administrative fiat." As the President summed up the extreme position of his lawyers, "There was no basis in the law for what they"—that is, the IRS—"were doing." [36] Under the heading "Just a Little More Tax-Exempt Hate," the *Times* articulated a common response in an editorial: "Until Congress passes the law, Mr. Reagan insists that the Internal Revenue Service begin granting such exemptions. Whatever his preference in this case, therefore, he persists in signaling that his Administration will acquiesce in discrimination wherever and for as long as it can." [37]

The proposal for Congress to provide a bailout and settle the issue went nowhere, because many members appeared to believe there was no "problem" to fix. Under other circumstances, they might have taken the opportunity to clear up an ambiguous detail of the tax code. Now they felt manipulated by a government trying to get Congress to cover up the Executive Branch's gaffe. William Brodhead, a Democratic Congressman from Michigan, told witnesses for the Administration that testimony they had given about their proposal was "the shabbiest, most unbelievable bunch of crap I've heard since I've been here." [38]

The Acting SG's role in the case sparked a final bit of drama over submission of the Administration's brief. The Bob Jones team wanted Wallace to sign it, making it look like business as usual; Bruce Fein threatened to have Wallace disciplined [39]—lawyers in the SG's office say fired—if Wallace did not cooperate; Wallace proposed that Edward Schmults, the Deputy AG, sign the brief on behalf of the Attorney General; and Schmults called Rex Lee, who was out in Utah giving a legal seminar, to get Wallace to sign the brief. Lee calmed everyone down ("The Bob Jones team realized they couldn't chop off the head of the senior Deputy Solicitor and not have the Washington *Post* on their backs for weeks after," observed a lawyer involved with the case),[40] and urged a compromise. Wallace signed, and "dropped" his footnote.

Around this time, Wallace received a personal letter from Marvin Frankel, a former federal judge who is now a lawyer in private practice. It was one of a dozen well-wishing notes or calls that the deputy received in response to his footnote.[41] "With the semi-proprietary interest of an SG alumnus (1952–1956)," the judge wrote,[42] "I have watched your career from afar with approval and admiration. Not being a writer of fan letters, I haven't found occasion to share these sentiments with you. Now, however, I'm prompted to report directly my special applause for your sound and courageous stance on the IRS-racial discrimination business. I'm sure the decision to take this position was not reached lightly or without anguish. Recognizing the personal cost to you, I want you to know that some of us out here appreciate your contribution to principle and public decency."

A year and a quarter later, the Supreme Court gave Wallace a public vindication. "Given the stress and anguish of the history and efforts to escape from the shackles of the 'separate but equal' doctrine of Plessy v. Ferguson," the Court stated about the 1896 decision, "it cannot be said that educational institutions that, for whatever reason, practice racial discrimination, are institutions exercising 'beneficial and stabilizing influences in community life,' or should be encouraged by having all taxpayers share in their support by way of special tax status." The Executive, Legislative, and Judicial Branches had long agreed on this interpretation of public policy, a majority of the Court went on, and the IRS couldn't "blissfully ignore what all three branches of the federal government had declared." Signed by Chief Justice Warren Burger, a consistent conservative, the Court's opinion stated that "there can no longer be any doubt that racial discrimination in education violates deeply accepted views of elementary justice."[43]

With William Rehnquist dissenting, the Justices ruled eight to one in favor of the IRS.

After the Bob Jones decision was handed down, the White House adopted the view that the media were responsible for damage to the Administration caused by its handling of the case because reporters had misrepresented the story. Bradford Reynolds assigned blame to the Supreme Court and to blacks as well. Taking the Court's reference to the Plessy case out of context, he said, "I believe that one factor in their decisional process was that this was an extremely controversial issue that had been played in the media and understood by the public only in terms of the segregation of schools. The Court, I think, wanted to be sure whichever way they decided it, that this wasn't going to be pinned on them as another Plessy v. Ferguson." Reynolds also commented, "Bob Jones was and will remain an albatross for us, particularly out in the black community. When the press blatantly labeled our actions as racist, the large majority of the black community—which don't have the kind of education that would permit them to sort through the legal issues—came away with the attitude, 'Gee, they must have people in there that really are racist!' " [44]

A summary of the Administration's views was included in a study of the event by the Kennedy School of Government at Harvard University. The chronicle of the Bob Jones case concluded that, despite "widespread unhappiness over the way the case had been handled, the controversy was not of serious personal consequence for any official. No one got fired, transferred or disciplined because of Bob Jones; indeed a number of officials who played leading roles in the drama were promoted." [45]

Lawrence Wallace became an unrecorded casualty of the case. He had for many years handled the government's civil-rights cases. It was known as a controversial area, but he had an idea how to keep in-house disagreements in check. He expressed it with a nautical metaphor. When the government's opinions heeled to the left, as they had during the Carter Administration, the SG's recommendations should shift to the right, like ballast against the keel of a boat. And when the prevailing views went off on the opposite tack, the SG's recommendations should move accordingly, to provide balance, maintain continuity, and keep the government as upright as possible. [46]

During his fourteen-year tenure, Wallace had worked for four SGs and five Administrations, with the Republicans outnumbering the Democrats three to one (the SGs) and three to two (the Administrations). He considered himself a civil servant with a duty to the government, and although he regularly miffed both Democratic and Republican political appointees by toning down their partisan contentions, he had succeeded until the Reagan Administration by employing this notion of counterpoise. "Larry was right about every major civil-rights case in which he participated, from the day he arrived in the Justice Department," said Brian Landsberg, who until 1986 was the senior career attorney in the appellate section of the Civil Rights Division, "and he is an awesomely talented lawyer." [47]

In his letter to Wallace, Marvin Frankel had concluded, "I would hope that neither this good action or anything else will require you to need specific support from colleagues like me. But I ask you to record my availability if and when you think I might be of any use. Meanwhile, accept my respectful cheers and gratitude. And my confident wishes and expectations for your continued distinction at the top of our shared profession." Wallace didn't call on Frankel for assistance, but he might have. After the Bob Jones case, Wallace was relieved of all responsibility for civil-rights cases. [48] Though he remained a Deputy Solicitor, he was treated by Reagan loyalists like a whistle-blower who had to be kept away from any sensitive assignment.

The support of Warren Burger in the Bob Jones decision actually hurt Wallace in the eyes of the Reagan team. By the time the Chief Justice handed down his opinion for the Court, Wallace had been singled out by top appointees at the Justice Department as the cause of things gone wrong in the case. If it hadn't been for Wallace's footnote, the case would have come out differently [49]— and, for them, the judgment of the Supreme Court confirmed this. Though Wallace considered it his duty to protect the President from the zeal of his political appointees, he was accused of disloyalty. The lesson of the Bob Jones case for the Bob Jones team was that if other cases arose in which the Solicitor General had to disqualify himself, the President would not be able to tolerate having Wallace in charge. [50] Toward the end of the Carter Administration, the day Benjamin Civiletti was sworn in as Attorney

General to replace Griffin Bell at the Justice Department, a young lawyer had found Wallace in his office instead of at the ceremony. "I've seen Administrations come and go," the Deputy Solicitor General told her with misplaced confidence, "and they've never made much difference to my work." [51]

Wallace's ouster was consistent with the theory that the Bob Jones dispute resulted from his inability to get along with Bradford Reynolds and other top civil-rights attorneys appointed by the Reagan Administration. Since Wallace is a large man, with a habit of flicking his hands in the air like a conductor, he brings out the mimic in many lawyers at the Justice Department who have dealt with him. The aping is sometimes meant as affection, but Wallace's manner can be fussy and he may have simply rubbed Reynolds the wrong way. "Larry put himself in the way of a lot of trouble," said one of his colleagues in the SG's office. [52]

The nature and timing of Wallace's replacement suggested why another analysis of Bob Jones was more accurate: a political appointee took his place at the start of 1983, five months before the Supreme Court ruled on the case. For the first time in the history of the SG's office, the Reagan Administration appointed a Counselor to the Solicitor General and Deputy Solicitor General, who became known as the political deputy. The reason given for the new post was plausible: the SG should be backed up by a second lieutenant of the President's so that when the Solicitor had to remove himself from a case, as Rex Lee did in Bob Jones, he could defer to a manager whom the Administration trusted. [53] But the appointment of the political deputy was the first hard evidence of how the relationships, first, between the SG's office and the rest of the Justice Department, and then between the SG's office and the Supreme Court, were being transformed by the Reagan Administration.

The new man was Paul Bator, a conservative legal scholar from Harvard Law School. A *summa cum laude* graduate of Princeton and of Harvard Law School, where he presided at the *Law Review*, he had clerked for Justice John Harlan, an outstanding conservative jurist. Bator was widely respected as a co-author of the second edition of a definitive volume about the workings of federal law known as Hart and Wechsler, after the two original authors who created a new field of legal study in the nineteen-fifties and who also served in the SG's office. Bator's finicky style challenged the mandarins in the SG's office to meet a new standard. "Once you've served in the office," he said, "you're hooked. It's like opera singers who perform at La Scala."[54]

In keeping with the Reagan Administration, one of Bator's favorite themes was judicial restraint. "More precisely," he instructed, "we want our federal judges to do *two* things—both hard. We want them to be bold, to be fearless, in exercising the power they legitimately possess, to rule without timidity where the law requires them to rule, and damn the consequences. But we ask another thing, too, one that may be harder. We ask that they be scrupulous *not* to rule, *not* to act, to leave the exercise of power to others, where the law does not justify judicial intervention." Bator illustrated his understanding of the choice by quoting Romantic poetry. He said, "Shelley's 'Adonais' asks: 'Of what scene are we actors, of what the spectators?' To intervene everywhere is bad; never to intervene is bad; is there a concept of the judge's role that solves—or, more accurately, dissolves—the antinomy?" He found it in *"interpretation,"* and, comparing a judge to Arturo Toscanini conducting Beethoven, or Vladimir Horowitz playing Brahms, he declared that the judge's responsibility was to interpret the law in a "spirit of obedience."[55]

Bator had his own views about what he was meant to do as political deputy. He said in 1985, "It was rather clear from the situation what was needed. They were not looking for someone who would give the office a political trashing. If someone was put in there whom the office regarded as incompetent or as merely political, who was not a fine lawyer or a person of distinction— that would have been inappropriate. I think that the office and the Solicitor General himself thought that I was an ideal solution. In a soft and general way, I was sympathetic to the Administration, certainly in the area of constitutional law. But basically I'm an apolitical person. I'm a professor, I'm an academic, I believe in academic integrity. I've always stood for very severe professional standards. The SG's lawyers felt that I would have credibility vis-à-vis the political people, while being sensitive to concerns of tradition, continuity, and integrity, and the Administration types felt that I would be a more sympathetic ear to their concerns than Larry and some of the others."[56]

Arguing like lawyers to soften the impact of their decision reorganizing the SG's office, Reagan officials cited the precedent of a political appointment made during the Nixon Administration.[57] Jewel Lafontant had made a speech to second the nomination of Richard Nixon at the 1960 Republican Convention, the year that Kennedy defeated Nixon, and she eventually served as a representative to the United Nations during the first Nixon term.[58] As a "three-fer" (she was young, female, and black—a symbol of Nixon's needed support from three groups), she was then named a Deputy Solicitor in the SG's office.[59]

Paul Bator bore no resemblance to Lafontant, and his mission was completely different. Whereas Lafontant was expected to perform like other lawyers in the SG's office, Bator had a new charter. He was brought in as a monitor, by an Administration that did not trust the counsel of the Solicitor General's career attorneys.

"You must remember that the tradition of independence has always been within the context of an underlying responsibility running from the Solicitor General to the Attorney General, and from the Attorney General to the President," Bator explained in 1985, oversimplifying and, by emphasis, contradicting the understanding of the Solicitor Generalship expressed by the Office of Legal Counsel at the time of Bakke. "It has never been *real* independence."[60]

VI

Judicial Restraint

DURING THE SUMMER of 1913, when William Howard Taft left the Presidency and moved to Connecticut to teach constitutional law at Yale Law School, he read every case in which the Supreme Court had interpreted the Constitution.[1] Today, even a scholar whose energy and talents matched Taft's couldn't begin to make his way in a summer's time through the volumes of Supreme Court decisions on constitutional law. Professors say the law has been "constitutionalized,"[2] meaning that many aspects of social life once the province of politics, like abortion and school prayer, have been dealt with by the Supreme Court as matters of constitutional law.

This phenomenon is part of a broader change in the role of courts in the United States. During the Carter Administration, the Justice Department commissioned a bipartisan group of lawyers, judges, and scholars to prepare a report on the topic.[3] This 1984 study confirmed that in the past generation the number of cases in federal courts had dramatically increased. The number in state courts dwarfed those in federal courts—roughly, 100 million a year versus 250,000—but on the basis of cases per capita both showed a significant increase. At the turn of the century, there were 19 cases filed in federal court for every 100,000 people; in 1980, there were 80, or more than four times as many.[4]

The most prominent change noted by the study was in "major constitutional reform." Beginning with the Supreme Court's landmark opinion in Brown v. Board of Education, in 1954, the Justices "taught in a dramatic and visible way that when other institutions fail to respond, constitutional claims can be vindicated in American courts." Congress contributed to this change by being "prolific in recognizing new claims and entitlements" and passing "dozens of major statutes" to protect civil rights, the environment, and a wide range of other social interests. The change in courts that caused the most concern was the redefinition by judges of the role of federal courts. [5]

The controversy centered mainly on the courts' treatment of lawsuits brought to reform public institutions like schools, prisons, hospitals, and police departments. Instead of simply forbidding unlawful actions or awarding damages for wrongs, which was their historical function, the courts gradually took to telling the Executive Branch, states, and local governments what to do and how—what Archibald Cox called "an unprecedented judicial undertaking." The traditional notion that judges should serve as referees in disputes between parties was challenged by a new breed of activist lawyer and a new concept of the activist judge, in which courts guided the parties to shape a solution to a problem—as the study on the role of courts described it, "to take on social grievances left festering by indecisive political institutions." This idea had not always worked well, the commission acknowledged, but it was successful enough to warrant serious discussion. Contrary to the view that courts had usurped power from other branches of government, for example, the report judged that they had "helped to energize them." Instead of weakening public confidence in courts, "judicial decrees ha[d] arguably increased respect for the judiciary in general." In fact, the report concluded with a flourish, courts had stirred a "deep and durable demand for justice in our society." They assured the vindication of rights that otherwise would have gone unprotected. [6]

When the Reagan Administration came to power, it expressed a much less tolerant view of this expansion in the role of courts. Among lawyers who once brought suits to reform institutions like schools and prisons, there was a growing nucleus who recognized problems associated with policymaking by courts. [7] Was it fair that a small group of attorneys could take it on themselves to direct social change simply by filing a lawsuit? Was it right that the prospects for change could turn on whether the attorneys drew a sympathetic judge? Even if they did, and the judge, through the cumbersome mechanism of a trial, was able to learn what he needed to know to order reforms, could he manage alone something as complex as a school system or a prison?

The Reagan Administration explored none of these questions in detail. Its conclusions about the expanding role of courts were categorical and wholly negative. In remarks before the Federal Legal Council in October of 1981, Attorney General William French Smith declared, "We believe that the groundswell of conservatism evidenced by the 1980 election makes this an especially appropriate time to urge upon the courts more principled bases that would diminish judicial activism. History teaches us that the courts are not unaffected by major public change in political attitudes."[8]

The Attorney General went on to identify three ways the Administration would press the courts to retreat from "policymaking": by limiting the matters they considered to narrowly defined cases or controversies as opposed to cases that raised general problems; by resisting the "multiplication" of constitutional rights; and by cutting back on the "extravagant use" of injunctions and remedies to right social wrongs. Smith called this agenda a commitment to "judicial restraint"—what he termed "the importance of judicial restraint to the constitutional principle of separation of powers." Having said what the Administration would do, Smith then tried to dampen criticism before it arose. He assured his audience that although the Administration would lobby the courts to be constrained, it would not fail to enforce the law of the land, even if the new officials "disagreed" with the statutes or court rulings in question. He said, "No one should doubt that this Administration's adherence to the Constitutional principle of separation of powers will exact from us the same degree of obedience and moderation that we will urge upon the courts."[9]

Smith made a point of emphasizing that the Administration would take its legal views "all the way to the Supreme Court,"[10] and that the Solicitor General was already looking for cases that would be good vehicles for the trip. The Administration had tried to select a man who was right for the job, and from its point of view Rex Lee appeared to be a fitting choice as Solicitor General. The dean of Brigham Young University's J. Reuben Clark Law

School and a Mormon, Lee had graduated first in his class from the University of Chicago Law School, clerked for Justice Byron White, and served in the Ford Administration as Assistant Attorney General in charge of the Civil Division.[11] In two compact volumes (*A Lawyer Looks at the Constitution* and *A Lawyer Looks at the Equal Rights Amendment*),[12] he had shown an ability to articulate conservative legal ideas in plain terms.

The first book made some lawyers in the SG's office nervous, because its survey of constitutional law struck them as simplistic.[13] (Chapter 1, paragraph 1: "The Philadelphia summer of 1787 was unusually hot and humid. For the fifty-five delegates gathered to deliberate as a Constitutional Convention, there were problems more serious than the unpleasant weather.")[14] They wondered how a mind tuned to this level would deal with the nuances of Supreme Court practice.

The second provoked another concern. No one knew what the Equal Rights Amendment would mean for constitutional law, the author argued, but, whatever its impact, the objective could be reached in better, more flexible ways than amending the Constitution. (The ERA was defeated in 1982. It had been a divisive subject since it was proposed in 1972.) At Lee's confirmation hearings before the Senate Judiciary Committee, Eleanor Smeal, president of the National Organization for Women, described his ERA writing as "a mass of error, omission, and distortion unworthy of a candidate for the position of Solicitor General of the United States."[15] She tied his "significant bias" against, or "extreme insensitivity" to, equal rights for women to his "close association" with a conservative public-interest law group called the Mountain States Legal Foundation and to some of his actions as dean at the Brigham Young law school which Smeal found objectionable. As a board member of the foundation when it was directed by James Watt (who later became Ronald Reagan's first and often combative Secretary of the Interior), Lee had supported lawsuits that were, in the words of Joseph Coors, its onetime chairman, designed to "meet the challenges made by the extreme environmentalists, no-growth advocates, and excessive government." The group had also opposed the latest congressional extension of the period for ratifying the ERA. Until his nomination, Lee had also been the founding and only dean of the law school. "During his tenure," Smeal contended, "he demonstrated no serious commitment to (or concern with) the involvement or advancement of women in his profession."[16] Only 16 percent of the students at J. Reuben Clark Law School were women, as opposed to the national average of 33 percent; there was only one woman member on the twenty-five-person faculty, for 4 percent of the total, versus 10 percent on average at law faculties across the country. The opposition from liberal lawyers and feminists that was stirred by Lee's background and books endeared him to Reagan supporters.

A lawyer who worked for him in the SG's office observed, "You meet Rex Lee, and you think, Huck Finn."[17] Lee is a tall, slim, boyish-looking man, with slick brown hair and a slight stutter. His manner is open and winning. He was forty-six when the Reagan Administration chose him to be SG. "I had heard they had a list of candidates for the job," Lee recalled in 1985, "and after I had an interview in March of 1981, the phone call came that April, two days after the Boston Marathon. I was about to go back home, after running pretty well—three hours and seven and a half minutes, which is a good time for me. I will remember Mr. Smith's sentence throughout this life and the next. He simply said, 'We would like to have you come and join this Administration as the Solicitor General.' "[18]

If one goes by the numbers, Lee's four years as SG were extremely successful. In one year, the government won a higher percentage of its cases in the Supreme Court than in any Term since the Justice Department began keeping modern statistics, in 1955,[19] and in the other three it did almost as well; it consistently persuaded the Court to review a high share of the government's lower-court losses; and, as a friend of the Court, it played a part in helping resolve major cases to which it was not a party. During one of those four years, Lee's record in persuading the Supreme Court to overturn the Ninth Circuit, which is now considered the country's most liberal Court of Appeals, was phenomenal. In the 1983 Term, the Supreme Court reversed the Ninth Circuit in twenty-seven out of twenty-nine cases. The Justices reviewed fourteen of those cases in part because Lee asked them to—he had filed twice as many petitions from rulings of that circuit as he had from the next highest circuit on the list.[20]

As things turned out, this record of accomplishment was not

Lee's legacy. In the SG's office, the cases that marked his tenure were like Bob Jones. They were known as "agenda cases."[21] Whether they were the vehicles William French Smith had in mind when he outlined the Reagan Administration's campaign for judicial restraint, they came to represent the President's efforts in the Supreme Court while Lee was SG. The core of the President's social agenda was identified in his speeches and in key planks of the Republican National Platform: against mandatory busing as a tool of school desegregation; in favor of voluntary prayer in public schools; against the constitutional right to abortion; against affirmative action for admission to schools or hiring in jobs to remedy past discrimination against minorities; in favor of cutting back on the legal rights of individuals accused of committing crimes.[22]

In his writings before he became Solicitor General, Lee had adopted each of these positions; and in his early days as SG he spread the word that too many people with too many causes had access to the federal courts, and too many fundamental rights were available for them to assert.[23] At the end of his second year as SG, Rex Lee viewed the Reagan agenda in a new light: he described it to the Los Angeles Times as "an albatross around my neck."[24]

Lee's unhappiness with what he called the "enormous pressure" on him to push the Supreme Court "too far too fast"[25] had a lot to do with the difference between his concept of the law and the one prevailing within the Reagan Administration. A key part of the disagreement focused on the meaning of judicial restraint. Since the start of the Republic, the great debate in American law has centered on the proper scope of the power of unelected federal judges. The Constitution makes no mention of the Supreme Court's power to rule on the lawfulness of acts of Congress and the President, but legal scholars and Congress have long agreed that the Court must have that authority, which is ultimately derived from the Constitution. In his starched, imperious style, Learned Hand once lectured that the power of judicial review was "not a logical deduction from the structure of the Constitution but only a practical condition upon its successful operation." He went on, "Without some arbiter whose decision should be final the whole system would have collapsed."[26] Alexander Hamilton expressed the same idea in Number 78 of the *Federalist Papers*, and this power of review has been a tenet of the American system of law since 1803, when Chief Justice John Marshall, in Marbury v. Madison, declared, "It is emphatically the province and duty of the judicial department to say what the law is." [27]

Yet many disagree about the proper bounds of judges' review, and the main opposing views among legal theorists reflect a deep conflict about the role of courts in the American version of democracy. One side sees judicial review as a simple but crucial part of a system of checks and balances whose distinction comes from its ability to protect the freedom of minorities from the tyranny of the majority. Adherents of this notion, sometimes known as "political jurisprudence," have won wide support for the idea that courts are inevitably engaged in politics, and that judicial review is a basic function of a democratic government. [28] ("Few accusations against the Supreme Court are made with more heat and answered with less candor than that it makes political decisions," Robert Jackson once wrote. "Of course, the line between political science and legal science is not fixed and varies with one's definition of his terms. Any decision that declares the law under which a people must live or which affects the powers of their institutions is in a very real sense political.") [29]

The other side sees review by judges as what Alexander Bickel called "a deviant institution" whose existence contradicts the "distinguishing characteristic" [30] of American government—rule by the majority. From this vantage, judicial review—hardly a democratic process—appears to undermine the ultimate freedom, the freedom of the majority to govern. Its scope must be sharply limited.

To ease the tension between the fact of judicial review and the majoritarian roots of American government, lawyers and judges from the second school have promoted a philosophy of judicial restraint. A classic scholarly statement of the philosophy was made in 1893 by James Bradley Thayer, a Harvard Law School professor. [31] He used the notion that judicial review is undemocratic to create a guiding stricture, urging that judges restrict their findings of unconstitutionality to laws that can't fulfill any legitimate purpose. He translated a theory about the Constitution's limits on the role of courts into a practical rule.

In the first decades of this century, Justices Oliver Wendell Holmes and Louis Brandeis articulated this theme when they dissented from Supreme Court rulings that struck down social legislation viewed by the conservative majority as anti-business. A generation later, Justices Felix Frankfurter and John Harlan and federal judges like Learned Hand built on the theories of Thayer, Holmes, and others, with memorable lines of explanation: "The Constitution is not a panacea of every blot on the public welfare, nor should this Court, ordained as a judicial body, be thought of as a general haven for reform movements," Harlan maintained. [32] Courts shouldn't serve as "superlegislatures" nor judges as "a bevy of Platonic Guardians," wrote Hand. [33] "There is not under our Constitution a judicial remedy for every political mischief, for every undesirable exercise of legislative power," Frankfurter declared. "The Framers carefully and with deliberate forethought refused so to enthrone the judiciary." [34]

The judges who best articulated the philosophy of restraint were also gifted legal craftsmen, and they constructed modern canons for the courts to follow, to limit the scope of judicial review. The Supreme Court and other federal courts should defer when possible, they said, to the judgments of democratically elected bodies, from the Congress down to local school boards. Since the states are the foundation of the Union, and the Constitution draws its power from them, the courts should defer to state and local over federal authority. Exercising passive virtues, the judges went on, courts should decide no case unnecessarily. When they do rule, they should do it on the narrowest possible grounds. Except in unusual instances, they should keep the law consistent and avoid rash decisions by closely following precedent. Judges should carefully interpret all sources of law, including cases, statutes, and the Constitution itself, and they should not read into a case or law provisions that are not there. With these canons, the theory of judicial restraint became a force for legal conservatism— helping judges conserve their authority for use in the gradual evolution of the law. [35]

Legal doctrine is shaped by circumstances, and judicial restraint became a preoccupation in the law during the constitutional crisis of the nineteen-thirties. When Franklin Roosevelt came to the Presidency, [36] the Supreme Court was controlled by

Willis Van Devanter, James McReynolds, George Sutherland, and Pierce Butler, a quartet of conservative Justices known as the Four Horsemen. While Roosevelt's government was likely to win the backing of Louis Brandeis, Harlan Stone, and Benjamin Cardozo in Court arguments, losing the vote of either Owen Roberts or Charles Evans Hughes (whose son gave up the Solicitor Generalship after only a year, so his father could become Chief Justice) [37] had instant consequences: it meant that whatever statute in the President's program of social and economic revival was under examination would be overturned. In the spring of 1935, when the Depression remained severe, Roberts joined the conservatives to strike down several pieces of important New Deal legislation. And on a day known by historians as Black Monday, the Justices unanimously outlawed a key piece of legislation called the National Industrial Recovery Act. The pattern continued through the next year. Justice Stone wrote, "We finished the Term of Court yesterday, I think in many ways one of the most disastrous in its history." [38]

In retrospect, most scholars agree that the Supreme Court overreached itself to break down the legal foundations of the New Deal. With no other recourse at the time, Roosevelt proposed his audacious Court-packing scheme to remake the courts and overcome this roadblock. If a judge or Justice did not retire or resign within six months after his seventieth birthday, the President proposed to add a new judge to the same bench. He could appoint up to forty-four new lower-court judges. Since there were six Justices near or over seventy, the plan would also give Roosevelt the authority to choose a half-dozen new ones almost immediately and control the High Court.

For half a year, the proposal caused a national furor. The President was accused of perverting the Constitution, showing disrespect for the Judiciary, and pretending that his scheme was prompted by an aging bench of Justices when it was really motivated by their judgments against the New Deal. In Congress, where the President had strong allies, there was also a sustained debate about Roosevelt's plan. When the plan was officially presented to the members in February 1937, Vice-President John Nance Garner held his nose and pointed thumbs down. [39]

The next month, Owen Roberts settled the question. Perhaps

responding to the Court-packing threat, he voted for a minimum-wage law that was hard to distinguish from one he had voted against not long before, and swung the Court in favor of the Roosevelt-backed law. The Court never overturned another piece of New Deal business regulation, and the Roosevelt scheme died in Congress. By 1941, Roosevelt had appointed seven Supreme Court Justices to fill vacancies that occurred naturally over time,[40] and any need for his questionable scheme was past.

To prevent a reprise of the crisis and to keep their power in check, judges who were sympathetic to the liberal aims of the New Deal embraced the conservative doctrine of restraint. Because of the eminence of the judges who led this movement, the canons of restraint that they developed came to be associated with objective standards of good lawyering more than with a particular philosophy. The craftsmanship of these judges provided a ready and persuasive answer to the charge made by members of another compelling movement, known as Legal Realism, which developed during the twenties and thirties. The realists contended that court-made law was based only on the personal views of judges and not on any neutral principles of law.

Possibly the most influential contribution to legal scholarship after the critique of realism or the canons of restraint was another attempt to state neutral principles for lawyers and judges. It consisted of a set of teaching materials for law students, and its conclusions were so quickly accepted as common wisdom that lawyers usually fail to credit them at all. Called "The Legal Process: Basic Problems in the Making and Application of Law," the materials were put together by Henry Hart, the onetime assistant to the Solicitor General who is better known for co-authoring the innovative volume on federal courts referred to as Hart and Wechsler, and by a young Harvard Law School colleague of his named Albert Sacks, who later became the law school's dean. They were assembled in the fifties, distributed to students at Harvard and other major law schools in mimeographed form, and never published as a book.[41] Though the 1,417 pages of legal-process materials can't be reduced to a nutshell, and they summarized generally held notions as much as presenting new ideas, they did better than any law-school casebook in telling what it meant to "think like a lawyer." Karl Llewellyn, of the University of Chicago Law School, said the cardinal mistake made by law students was to think that because there is no right answer in the law, every answer is equally correct. [42] Dealing almost exclusively with court decisions interpreting statutes rather than the Constitution, the legal-process materials gave lawyers guidelines for addressing legal problems when the law itself dictated no answers.

Instead of worrying about the outcome of cases, the materials focused heavily on "process"—which institutions in the law are most competent to decide what. Is a controversy about fact or law, and should a jury or a judge resolve it? If a court is faced with a question about the meaning of a statute, should it require evidence of individual legislators' intentions to clear up the ambiguity, or should it look at the purpose of the law and interpret it by making sure the application in the case at hand squares with that general purpose? The materials were criticized for overemphasizing process at the expense of substance, and for ignoring the outcome of cases, on the theory that big corporations and others with money and status are more likely to control the process than the poor and the powerless, and to get what they want. The authors were chastised for operating on unreal assumptions—for instance, that laws passed by legislatures reflect a consensus from which a common purpose can be gleaned, instead of compromises between antagonistic groups that defy neat understanding by a judge.

Yet, like the writings of Frankfurter and the other respected promoters of judicial restraint, the legal-process materials came to stand for the essence of good lawyering. They called for a mixture of close analysis and common sense, and favored careful argument, attention to facts and to precedent, and written documentation. They put a premium on step-by-step decisions and intellectual honesty—on gradualism, continuity, and measured change in the law. These are the qualities singled out by lawyers when they describe the virtues of the SG's office. In the paradoxical ways of the law, they make far more persuasive the government's occasional calls for novel legal doctrine to accommodate sweeping social change.

When Rex Lee was Solicitor General, he used the word "restraint" in two senses. [43] On the one hand, like supporters of judicial restraint who hailed from previous generations, he believed that the philosophy of a limited role for the courts was best fulfilled by observing the canons that had been constructed. He concurred with the understanding of separation of powers expressed by William French Smith, but he thought the philosophy only took on life through conservative legal practices. On the other hand, he admired the careful and intelligent craftsmanship of the lawyers in the SG's office, and recognized how much they relied on restraint in their lawyering before the Supreme Court. He believed in the principles that they followed. The government should only raise issues that are ready for decision by the Court. If it appears as a friend of the Court, it should not raise issues that no party to the suit has brought up. If it discovers a precedent cutting against the argument it is making to the Justices, the government has a duty to let the Court know about the case. The "restraint traditionally exercised by Solicitors General" had a measurable value, Lee judged, because "the single most important factor contributing to the success of a President's litigating objectives is the preservation of the Solicitor General's unique standing with the Supreme Court."[44] As he told the Los Angeles Times, "the positions taken by the Solicitor General for years have carried special weight with the Supreme Court because they are regarded as representing not merely the political views of the Administration but the broad interests of the nation. One of the most important jobs I have is protecting the tradition of John W. Davis, Robert H. Jackson, Charles Fahy, and Thurgood Marshall."[45]

The idea of judicial restraint embraced by the Reagan Administration was notably different from the traditional view adopted by Lee and others. It was distilled by Judge Richard Posner, of the U.S. Court of Appeals for the Seventh Circuit in Chicago. "I believe judicial restraint refers to a policy of reducing the power of the federal courts vis-à-vis the other branches of government," he stated in 1985 at a symposium on the courts sponsored by a conservative organization called the Manhattan Institute for Policy Research. "It is not a policy of standing by whatever has been done. If it is that, it would constitute an irresistible engine of judicial activism."[46] By Posner's logic, if believers in the new substantive version of restraint applied the old-style standards, they would end up extending decisions of the "activist"—that is, liberal—judges they opposed. To undo the damage of these judges, Reagan's judicial appointees had to be unrestrained in the traditional sense and his lawyers had to urge unrestrained positions. Posner distinguished between his philosophy of judicial restraint and the techniques of judging that should be used to enact it; he argued that judges had to abandon restraint in the latter to put the former into practice. Frankfurter and others had warned that judges should be reluctant to expand their power. Posner urged that judges dramatically cut it back. In place of restraint, he counseled what might be called "judicial retrenchment," and, along with other Reagan judicial appointees like Robert Bork and Antonin Scalia, he acted on that philosophy.

In a 1985 book called *The Federal Courts,* Posner recognized an astonishing implication of his theory. He volunteered that his definition would make it "restrained" to overturn one of the most important precedents in American law. In Marbury v. Madison, Chief Justice Marshall affirmed the power of the Supreme Court to hold acts of Congress unconstitutional. He set forth a rationale for an essential aspect of judicial review. "A decision overruling Marbury v. Madison would be pretty wild stuff," Posner wrote, "but it would be self-restrained in my terminology because it would reduce the power of the federal courts vis-à-vis the other organs of government." [47] Rarely has the term "restraint" been used to signify anything so far from its standard legal meaning.

As one step in his first-rank training (Yale College, *summa cum laude;* Harvard Law School, where he was president of the *Law Review;* a clerkship for Justice William Brennan), Posner, too, had worked as a young lawyer in the SG's office. [48] He was a favorite of the Reagan Administration years before he provided it with a rationale for its new notion of judicial restraint. The most controversial legal scholar of the late seventies and early eighties, he has done more than anyone to create the movement known as Law and Economics. Building on the work of Robert Bork and others at the University of Chicago, the movement holds that the conservative free-market economics promoted by Adam Smith and current followers of his like Milton Friedman, is the best guide to human behavior under law, and to prescribing what the law should be. Law and Economics is considered by many (overlooking the contribution of "The Legal Process") the most influential legal movement in the past half-century. It directly squares with the Reagan vision of economics. [49]

In over a hundred articles, fourteen textbooks, book reviews, testimony before Congress and federal agencies, speeches, law-school classes at the University of Chicago, where Posner taught, and, eventually, in appellate opinions after President Reagan appointed him to the Court of Appeals in 1981, the prolific Posner has urged to a widening audience that the life of the law is really economics. As George Priest, of the Yale Law School, put it, "Posner achieved for the law Einstein's dream for physics: a unified theory." [50] One of Posner's recommendations, formulated in collaboration with an associate, Elisabeth Landes, was to abolish adoption agencies and legalize the sale of babies to the highest bidder. He argued that the high cost of foster care and the growth of a black market in healthy infants demonstrated both the failure of government regulation and the promise of unfettered exchange. [51]

That particular idea has not been accepted, but Posner's Law and Economics views have helped to change how many lawyers do their work. Instead of concentrating on the reasoning that defines a legal doctrine, many lawyers and legal scholars now analyze a law's purpose and impact in terms of economics. Where almost any law does not follow the logic of economics, they insist it should. The wide popularity of this view has helped ease the impact of the Reagan Administration's approach to the law: it has given new currency to a focus on social results instead of legal reasoning. Posner has a gift for provocation and he once sharpened the edge of his radical ideas by delivering them with a paraphrase of Oliver Wendell Holmes. "I hate 'justice,'" Posner said. "The word is meaningless. If it's used in a judicial opinion, it's used to obscure the grounds. I think we could do without it." [52]

The Administration's notion of judicial restraint has often been presented as a call for results, and not for a shift in legal philosophy. In an interview in the Los Angeles *Times* in June of 1986, for example, President Reagan seemed to turn the definition of judicial restraint upside down once again, when he explained that "restraint" meant achieving in the courts what Congress had refused to do for the Administration. "Well," said the President, "you have found that Congress has been unwilling to deal with these problems that we brought up." A reporter told the President that one of his senior aides, Patrick Buchanan, had said, "If you got two appointments to the Supreme Court it could make more difference on your social agenda in achieving it than twenty years in Congress." The reporter asked, "Do you agree with that?" The President replied, "Yes."[53] In a speech to the Knights of Columbus not long afterward, he made a similar point. He predicted, "In many areas—abortion, crime, pornography, and others—progress will take place when the federal judiciary is made up of judges who believe in law and order and a strict interpretation of the Constitution."[54]

Ronald Reagan equated support for his social agenda with support for judicial restraint, and so did his advocates. Bruce Fein, the member of the Bob Jones team who often wrote articles and appeared on TV to popularize the Administration's legal views, contended that "judges wedded to the doctrine of judicial restraint" were judges "who reject the idea underlying the Supreme Court's decrees on abortion, school prayer, civil rights and criminal law: that the judicial power of interpretation is not confined to carrying out the intent of our constitutional authors."[55] According to *Benchmark*, a New Right journal, the principle of "restraint" demanded that judges not "impose alien values upon the American people, enlarge the rights of criminals, impede Federalism and the restoration of States' Rights, or further the cause of abortion."[56]

The Fein and *Benchmark* lists strayed from the line laid down by Richard Posner, and they had little to do with the tenets established by Frankfurter, Harlan, and others. They also identified the cases in which Rex Lee encountered what he called "enormous pressure" to forsake his commitment to the canons of restraint and the traditional restrained practices of the SG's office, and to campaign for the Administration's agenda in the Supreme Court.[57] During the first year of the Reagan Administration, Lee sometimes brushed aside initiatives from low- and middle-level political officials at various government agencies who were eager for the SG to append an idea to a government brief, even if it had little bearing on the case at hand. ("Rex rarely entertained these juvenile right-wing fantasies," said one former lawyer in the SG's office.)[58]

When, however, the Administration began to press for legal

changes that would enact the beliefs at the core of the President's social agenda, the story changed dramatically. Contradicting Lee's sense of his responsibilities, Bruce Fein told the *Wall Street Journal* that the SG "shouldn't be abashed about urging the Court to overrule decisions and making speeches criticizing the Court." For the sake of a version of judicial restraint that was unrestrained, Fein urged the SG to proceed aggressively as well. Dismissing the idea of an independent SG, he insisted, "My conception of the office of Solicitor General is that it should be a foremost promoter of the policies of the President before the Court." The *Journal* made clear its understanding that Fein was speaking for the Administration.[59]

Besides recasting the idea of judicial restraint without admitting the liberties they were taking, the President's lawyers based their radical legal strategy on an unsupported premise. Like William French Smith, the lawyers used the President's victory at the polls in 1980 as a mandate for the Reagan social agenda. In fact, as Thomas Ferguson and Joel Rogers pointed out in the *Atlantic Monthly* in 1986,[60] the American public was steadfast in rejecting central parts of the Reagan agenda. Only a third of those who originally voted for the President agreed with his views about abortion, according to a Los Angeles *Times* poll. By 1984, NBC News reported that two-thirds of the voters believed abortion should be legal and that the decision should be "left to the woman and her physician." At the end of the Carter Administration, Louis Harris found, only 45 percent of the public agreed that affirmative-action programs were necessary if women and minorities were to get their share of jobs and higher education and break the historic cycle of discrimination against them. By the second year of the Reagan Administration, the number had jumped to 57 percent, and by 1985, 71 percent. As Ferguson and Rogers reported, "Here, too, the movement of public opinion has been directly opposite to the movement in public policy." The numbers revealed that the campaign to turn the President's agenda into law was fueled not by a wave of American opinion but by the personal beliefs of the President and his followers.

VII

The Shadow
Solicitor

THE PRESSURE ON Rex Lee to promote the Reagan agenda came mostly from William Bradford Reynolds, Assistant Attorney General for Civil Rights. At first glance, he seemed an unlikely antagonist. Reynolds is an ascetic-looking man, with thinning blond hair, a well-defined forehead, and rimless glasses that frame his clear gray eyes. A graduate of Yale College and Vanderbilt School of Law, where he was second in his class and editor-in-chief of the *Law Review*, he had practiced law with a conventional Washington firm;[1] though he later downplayed the overture,[2] his moderate leanings were suggested when he expressed a serious interest, never realized, in running the Antitrust Division of the Justice Department during the Carter Administration.[3] Reynolds had also worked for three and a half years as an assistant to the Solicitor General under the Nixon Administration. While at the SG's office, he argued eleven cases before the Supreme Court and wrote the briefs in forty.[4] He was known as a good soldier.

Reynolds had no special preparation for the post of Assistant Attorney General for Civil Rights. As the Reagan Administration began to make its appointments, Reynolds's first job choice was the post of chief of the Attorney General's Office of Legal Counsel,[5] which had issued the paper about the role of the Solicitor General. When, however, other candidates for the civil-rights job proved too controversial,[6] Reynolds was named to the position because he had good credentials and the unblemished appeal of a moderate. It was the understanding of lawyers in the Civil Rights Division that he secured the appointment by promising to lead the Reagan Administration's attack on school busing and affirmative action,[7] but his prior record gave no hint of his future zeal as a promoter of the President's agenda.

Soon after the Administration took office, Reynolds made good his pledge about busing.[8] The case involved the schools in Seattle. The city's school board had taken a lead from the Supreme Court in an earlier case, and had voluntarily approved a plan to use mandatory busing as part of a remedy for segregation in the schools. When the voters of Washington passed a referendum to ban busing, the school board challenged the legality of the referendum. Under the Carter Administration, the Justice Department had supported the school board's successful defense of the plan. The Reagan team arrived the year the case rose to the Supreme Court, and Reynolds recommended that the Administration switch sides. Rex Lee concurred. The Justices, however, rebuffed the government's new position and upheld the busing plan.

Reynolds appeared to overlook some basic facts about busing. Like others in the Reagan Administration, he seemed to treat mandatory busing as a social menace that had to be stopped before it touched many more communities. In reality, in the United States at the time half the children went to school by bus, and less than 7 percent were bused as part of a desegregation plan. While busing indirectly helped increase segregation rather than diminish it in cities like Boston where whites fled to the suburbs, more students were bused to segregated schools (public, private, and parochial) than to integrated ones, and most of this busing was done at public expense.[9]

Even in the places where mandatory busing was used to help desegregate schools, the story was different from that told by the Reagan Administration. In a speech in Charlotte, North Carolina, President Reagan declared that the Democrats "favor busing that takes innocent children out of the neighborhood school and makes them pawns in a social experiment that nobody wants. And we've found out that it failed."[10] The President picked the wrong audience for this comment.[11] The schools in the area known as Charlotte-Mecklenburg were the first in the nation to be integrated under a court order for busing. According to the Charlotte *Observer*, the area's "proudest achievement" in the previous twenty years was its "fully integrated school system." An editorial directed at the President said, "It would have been quite appropriate and very much appreciated if you had noted that accomplishment, which any president might hold up as a model to the rest of the country. Instead, you said something quite different, an unwelcome reminder of some ugly emotions and unfounded fears that this community confronted and conquered more than a decade ago." [12]

Not long after the Supreme Court decided the Seattle case, Reynolds went to Capitol Hill to testify on the Administration's civil-rights policies. He was asked by Carl Stern of NBC News whether the White House had applied any pressure on the Justice Department to drop its support of school busing in Seattle. Reynolds said no. [13]

"No pressure from the White House as to the Administration's view?" Stern continued.

"Absolutely none," Reynolds answered.

Stern then showed Reynolds a copy of a memo he had obtained that had gone from Lyn Nofziger, a political aide in the White House, to Reynolds and three others.

"I enclose for your perusal a letter to me of August 4 from Ken Eikenberry, the Attorney General for the State of Washington, and a longtime Reagan worker and supporter," Nofziger had written.

"Not surprisingly, he, like 99.9 percent of the people who have supported Ronald Reagan in the past, is at odds with mandatory school busing—as I think we all are. Surely, if we are going to change the direction of this country, mandatory school busing is a good place to make changes—as I thought we would do because I thought that was what the President wanted.

"I do hope we can give Mr. Eikenberry's problems a careful look."

Stern asked Reynolds about the memo: "You believe it doesn't contain a White House view?"

"It may contain Lyn Nofziger's view. I don't think I read it as a . . ."

"What does it say on the top of this letter?"

"You can read the letter."

"It says 'The White House.' "

The letter confirmed what lawyers at the Justice Department and in the civil-rights community had suspected: in major cases like those on the Reagan agenda, Reynolds formed his legal opinions with the President's political goals in mind. He took his cues from the White House, and was rewarded with its strong support.

One lawyer, who dealt with Reynolds on behalf of the SG's office and who was sympathetic to his aims, observed, "Brad, whom I like and admire in many ways, is also very fearsome because he is so rigid. Once he takes a position, he is a bit of a bully and very hard to deal with. He's incredibly willful. Sometimes he's the most charming, delightful, sophisticated person, and then, when he gets into the mode of someone who's got to have his way, he's impossible. He's totally domineering. The most important thing about Brad Reynolds is not to think of him as political. He isn't even an ideologue, though many people think so. In some ways, he's a seventeenth-century lawyer. He gets ideas into his head that this is the way the law is, and then, by God, it's like that. He thinks of the law as a very formal set of syllogisms."[14]

An early incident at the Civil Rights Division showed that Reynolds's dealings with lawyers who challenged him were sometimes as rigid as his thinking about the law. In July 1981, he received a memo from Robert D'Agostino, one of his aides. It was about a desegregation case in Yonkers, New York. D'Agostino offered a critique of a letter from the Justice Department to the Superintendent of Schools in Yonkers detailing why the department had sued the school system.[15] "Paragraph four," he wrote, "states that blacks were 'improperly classified as emotionally disturbed.' Why improperly? And by what evidence does Justice presume to impose their views on who is or who is not emotionally disturbed (presumably disruptive in the classroom)? Justice's position is that unless equal proportions of blacks and whites are classified as emotionally disturbed, the law violates the civil rights statutes or the Constitution. What hogwash. *Blacks, because of their family, cultural and economic background, are more disruptive in the classroom on the average.*" (Italics added.)

Not long after, over a hundred government civil-rights lawyers—more than half of those working for him—sent Reynolds a petition: "The undersigned Civil Rights Division attorneys wish to express our profound concern with the unsupported assumptions and sweeping generalizations" in the D'Agostino memo. "We believe that those assumptions and generalizations—particularly those regarding the impact of family, cultural and economic background on the behavior of black children—as well as the pejorative use of historically emotional code words such as 'racial mixing' are antithetical to the recent pronouncement of Attorney General Smith that the Justice Department 'will not permit any of our citizens to be stigmatized by government as the result of their race,' and reflect a shocking insensitivity to and lack of understanding of the principles which form the very basis for this Division's existence. As attorneys who share the Attorney General's stated commitment to 'vigorously enforce the Nation's civil rights laws,' we petition the leadership of this Department to repudiate the racially offensive statements" in the memo.[16]

Reynolds called a meeting of the lawyers who had signed the petition. Instead of disavowing or downplaying the words of his aide, however, he angrily scolded those who had circulated the petition and called them "unprofessional"[17] for taking the matter public. Minor as it may seem, this clash between Reynolds and the career attorneys in the Civil Rights Division over the D'Agostino memo was a forewarning of the Assistant Attorney General's frequent and explosive disputes with the office of the Solicitor General. The fights that Reynolds picked with the SG's office about the Administration's filings in the Supreme Court unleashed considerably more of his fury because so much was at stake.[18]

Reynolds exercised his will in a wide range of cases, but those dealing with affirmative action provided model examples.[19]

The day Ronald Reagan replaced Jimmy Carter as President, the status of blacks and other minorities in America was not instantly transformed. The discriminatory conditions that Carter Administration lawyers for and against affirmative action had agreed were the backdrop for the Bakke case could be found in other cases. Once the overarching challenge of establishing legal equality among people of different races was met during the sixties, every President from Lyndon Johnson through Jimmy Carter recognized that legal equality for people of different races did not assure them equality of opportunity. In executive orders of the President, in statutes passed by Congress, and in decisions of the Supreme Court, each branch of the government reached a conclusion stated by Justice Harry Blackmun in the Bakke case. "In order to get beyond racism, we must first take account of race," the Justice wrote. "There is no other way. And in order to treat some persons equally, we must treat them differently." [20]

In recent years, there has been caustic disagreement among scholars about the meaning of social data on blacks and other minorities. [21] Some believe that the gap between white and black prosperity is closing, and, measured over several generations, it is certainly true. Others see a drop in discrimination by whites against blacks, yet no real progress in closing the prosperity gap, and they worry that many blacks lack the ability to compete with whites. They hold that blacks must escape from dependence on special favors, like public subsidies and affirmative action, and prove their worth in the working world. In either case, disparities exist that lead some people to consider affirmative action necessary.

According to a National Urban League report titled "The State of Black America 1986," as the American economy marched briskly on during the middle years of the Reagan Administration, "black Americans slipped further and further to the rear of the parade." [22] The black unemployment rate held steady at three times the white, the proportion of blacks living in poverty was three times the proportion of whites (and four times for children), and, as the Census Bureau reported, blacks owned on average less than one-tenth the property and material wealth that whites did. The facts that had for a generation buttressed laws in favor of affirmative action were, if anything, more dispiriting in the Reagan Administration, because the country had failed to improve them in any dramatic way. [23]

Reynolds claimed to follow a simple principle: not only should society be color-blind, but the Constitution is color-blind as well, and, with the federal civil-rights laws, it requires "individual equality of opportunity." [24] Where individuals prove they have been victims of discrimination, the wrongs should be righted. The vic-

tims should be made whole, one at a time. Whatever the burdens of race handed down to current generations from the past, the Constitution does not allow favoring people of one race over another, even if the purpose is to help them achieve the same opportunities as others in society. To Reynolds, this philosophy represented an alternative to civil-rights "orthodoxy." In the old days, government and other lawyers had sought and courts had permitted what Reynolds called "mandatory busing to achieve racial balance in schools; hiring, promotion, and even layoff quotas to guarantee equal race and sex proportionality in the work place; and manipulation of electoral systems to assure racially proportionate success in elections." Reynolds referred to the goal of this orthodoxy as "equal results," not "equal opportunity," and observed that its supporters believed in treating people as "fungible representatives of some group" instead of "unique individuals." He compared using affirmative action for blacks to treating people suffering from alcoholism with liquor.[25] He described the results of the traditional approach to civil rights as a "racial spoils system."[26]

To make sure his version of affirmative action would be presented, Reynolds often chose to disagree with the Solicitor General about tactics when he had no difference of opinion over the desirable outcome of a case.[27] Reynolds was consulted by the SG just as prior civil-rights chiefs had been by previous Solicitors, but that did not satisfy him. He tried to usurp the role of the SG. In a 1983 case about layoffs from the Boston Fire Department, the question was whether, when layoffs were necessary, the Civil Rights Act of 1964 allowed the department to retain blacks hired in an affirmative-action program and lay off white firemen with seniority.[28] The assistant to the SG who worked on the case was a young former law professor named Carter Phillips, who had once clerked for Chief Justice Warren Burger. "I'm not a flaming liberal" is how Phillips described himself.[29] He agreed with Reynolds that Title VII, the part of the Civil Rights Act at issue, protected the white firemen with seniority. As a sports-minded lawyer in the office remembered, "The only question for the SG to decide, in Rex's words, was, 'Do you go for a touchdown, and make the case for seniority over affirmative action?' Or, 'Is this the case where the government should seek a big victory in cutting back affirmative action, so you go for the Super Bowl?' "[30]

According to Phillips's reading, the legislative history of Title VII indicated that the law permitted no affirmative action when a public agency like the fire department was deciding who should get laid off. Retaining less senior blacks when layoffs were required would amount to applying an illegal quota, because all the firefighters whose jobs were in jeopardy had proved themselves and the fairest basis for distinction among them was seniority. Affirmative action in promotions, on the other hand, was easier to justify as a tool of opportunity, and, in hiring, easier still. Since one section of the statute dealt with layoffs and another with hiring and promotions, it seemed sensible to devote the government's brief to the question about layoffs, which was now before the Court, and leave aside any discussion of affirmative action in hiring, which wasn't. "One of the traditions in the SG's office," said the lawyer familiar with the case, "is that we don't hide the ball. We try to be full and frank in making our arguments, to give the whole picture, and we didn't have room to do that about affirmative action in general."[31]

Reynolds would not accept Phillips's view. He insisted that his own deputy, Charles Cooper, from the Bob Jones team, write an alternative brief.[32] For ten days, Reynolds led a move to transform the SG's brief into a broadside on quotas as a form of affirmative action. When Rex Lee sided with his assistant, Reynolds went over Lee's head to Attorney General William French Smith. (This was a tactic known to lawyers in the Justice Department as "running to the AG," which Reynolds often used and which, to some government lawyers, reflected his disdain for the SG's independence.) As if Phillips's decision not to submit a brief that argued against *all* quotas were a sign of weakness, Reynolds called him "that quota lover!" in a meeting with the Attorney General.[33] Smith told Lee and Reynolds to resolve their differences. At Lee's instruction, Phillips did his best to incorporate the Reynolds point of view in a rewritten brief. Not long afterward, the case became moot when the Massachusetts legislature passed a law reinstating all the firefighters who had been laid off, but the effort to protect the SG's diminished independence still had costs.[34]

The struggle over the Boston affair went unnoticed outside the Justice Department, but a case much like it the next Term drew wide attention.[35] Carl Stotts was a middle-aged black firefighter who had been one of the original dozen blacks hired by the Memphis Fire Department in 1955. Memphis has a population of 650,000 people, about half white and half black. By 1976, the city had hired 1,863 white firefighters and 94 blacks: the ratio was about eighteen to one. Blacks were rarely promoted, and after years of being passed over, Carl Stotts decided to do something about it. He brought a lawsuit in 1977, and he won. The city of Memphis settled out of court. Until the racial makeup of the fire department reflected the balance of whites and blacks in Memphis, the city agreed to a goal of making blacks 50 percent of new firefighters hired, and 20 percent of those promoted.

A second Stotts case was before the Supreme Court in 1984.[36] It arose out of unexpected circumstances. In 1981, a year after the settlement in the first case, cutbacks in the federal budget forced Memphis to lay off firefighters.[37] Twenty-two drivers of firetrucks had to be furloughed; nine of them were black. Seventeen lieutenants had to be demoted; fifteen of them were black. Three captains had to be stripped of their rank; two of them were black. The contract between the city and the firefighters' union ordained that last hired should be first fired. Even though officers had not been promoted solely according to seniority (otherwise more blacks would have been officers), the union insisted that the city protect the "senior" firefighters when it decided whom to lay off. Carl Stotts filed suit and won the early rounds of his second lawsuit against this policy.

Although the Memphis case raised the same issues as the one from Boston, which Rex Lee had steered Carter Phillips to resolve by focusing on the issue of affirmative action in layoffs, Reynolds insisted on reopening the question in the Memphis brief. He tried again to have the SG make a more general case against affirmative action. Reynolds and Phillips ended up in shouting matches along the corridor between the Civil Rights Division and the SG's office. One of the Solicitor's assistants familiar with the case said, "Working on an agenda case, you knew life would be pretty unpleasant." He added, "If Brad had shown the same enthusiasm in defending the civil rights of minorities as he did in attacking them, I would have no problem with him. But even in the instances when he came out on the side of the minority communities, he did it grudgingly, and he was always looking for a way out."[38] The Supreme Court ruled against Stotts on the question of layoffs, but the Justices made no ruling on the original settlement between Memphis and Stotts for hiring and promoting black firefighters, and it remained in effect with the force of law.[39]

In these and other disagreements between Reynolds and the Solicitor General's office, the issues at stake were often the sort of technicalities that cause passionate divisions among lawyers and bafflement for almost everyone else. To civil-rights lawyers, no struggle is more important than convincing a court to use an "effects" standard, as opposed to "intent," when interpreting a law that requires an individual to prove his rights have been violated.[40] It can spell the difference between winning and losing. If the court finds that the law calls for an intent test, it is unusually difficult to prove that a defendant has discriminated, because motives are hard to pin down. In some suits brought by blacks, this is tantamount to proving the charge that a defendant is a racist. To Reynolds, urging an intent test was consistent with his philosophy of equal opportunity: an individual who had been wronged ought to be able to prove his antagonist's intent to discriminate.[41] An effects test would let a class of people recover even if no one had consciously meant to injure them, so it would confer benefits on individuals who could not show they had been personally discriminated against.

Reynolds weighed in heavily on an intent/effects case called Guardians Association v. Civil Service Commission (best known as Guardians), which went to the Supreme Court in 1983.[42] It posed the question whether in the Civil Rights Act of 1964 the ban on discrimination by any institution receiving funds from the government required the plaintiffs to prove the defendants intended to discriminate, or simply to prove the effects of the defendants' actions. The plaintiffs were blacks and Hispanics on the New York City police force who claimed that written exams used to make appointments to the force discriminated against minorities. Applicants were appointed in order of their test results, and the plaintiffs had been hired after whites who scored higher.

Congress had not chosen between the two tests, and had delegated to federal agencies the power to interpret the section of Title VI of the Civil Rights Act, the law at issue. Lawyers in the SG's office wondered how the government could argue that it favored an intent test. [43] The standard was difficult to meet, it violated the law's spirit, and it contradicted hundreds of long-standing rules made by federal agencies, which almost uniformly relied on an effects test. It contradicted the standard designated by many other laws that were modeled on Title VI as well, and it was not practical. Government inspectors could rarely put witnesses under oath to increase the reliability of statements about intent. Even if they could, an inspector who might find evidence of discrimination under the less stringent effects test was likely to doubt whether the evidence met the more demanding test of intent.

Without consulting any of the agencies whose inspection procedures would be implicated—a breach of tradition for the Civil Rights Division—Reynolds pressured the SG to back the intent test. He was vehement, and he transformed the government's choice between favoring the effects test or the intent test into a choice between backing the intent test or filing no brief at all. [44]

"In Guardians," explained a veteran in the SG's office, "Reynolds pressed a line that showed the Administration's lack of commitment to the rule of law. In that case, rules of every federal agency were implicated. Reynolds and other Reagan folks urged a view that would have had a huge impact on all these rules, because they wanted the Court to hold that the law dealt only with intentional discrimination, all else being innocent. Reynolds refused to talk with the affected agencies, and he disregarded the canon saying that an entrenched interpretation of the law by agencies—a long-standing practice—is what federal courts defer to unless they have a very compelling reason not to. In this case, the canon was supported by the fact that Congress had approved the government's understanding of the law through subsequent decisions to fund the fight against discrimination. The Supreme Court rejected the line that Reynolds pushed, but there were four dissenters who went with his view and said the law should be interpreted more narrowly. What was disturbing about the dissent is that the Court never got the impression from the SG's office of how deeply entrenched the broader interpretation of the law really was throughout the government—the five-to-four vote, inviting challenge, might have been six to three, or even seven to two, if the Solicitor General had been allowed to play his usual role and inform the Justices about the workings of the law. Guardians was the only major civil-rights case in the last ten years where the Department of Justice sat out. Guardians was as big a scandal as Bob Jones, and no one outside the government noticed." [45]

In the roster of cases where Reynolds squared off against the SG's office, the fight in 1985 over Vasquez v. Hillery was especially instructive of how Reynolds pursued policy at the cost of lawyerly restraint. [46] On the surface, nothing happened. Inside the government, however, dealings about the case between the SG's office and Reynolds became a stressful trial. [47]

The case arose from the following events. In 1962, a black man, Booker T. Hillery, was indicted for murder by a grand jury in Kings County, California. [48] ("Did I understand you to say that this crime occurred in *1962*?" Chief Justice Warren Burger asked when the case was argued before the Supreme Court in 1985.) [49] Hillery asked the local court to quash his indictment, on grounds that blacks had been systematically excluded from the grand jury. Even though the judge responsible for impaneling the jury, Meredith Wingrove, admitted he had never appointed a black to a grand jury in the six years he had been on the bench, and that, in looking for "the better type of our citizens" for the jury, he had never found a black "that the court feels would make a proper Grand Juror," he also said that he had once tried to find a black for a jury but recalled that the number of blacks in Kings County in 1962 was only around 5 percent of the total population.

After the defendant was convicted and sentenced to death, his case followed many steps. They took sixteen years, which the defendant spent in prison. In May of 1978, after Hillery's appeals in state court ran out, he filed a petition for habeas corpus in federal court. (Habeas corpus is a writ used by prisoners who believe they are illegally confined, and often goes to a federal judge with a claim that the prisoner has been wronged in state court.) Hillery claimed that he had been denied equal protection of the law because blacks had been systematically excluded from the Kings County grand jury. Another five years, and the court granted Hillery's petition, overturning his twenty-one-year-old conviction for murder.

"For over 100 years," the district court observed, "it has been held that a criminal conviction cannot stand if it is based on an indictment returned by a grand jury from which members of an identifiable group to which [the defendant] belongs have been excluded because of their race." [50]

Among evidence heard by the judge, an expert on statistics testified that if the grand juries empaneled in Kings County between 1900 and 1962 had been picked by chance, the probability that no black would have been included was fifty-seven in a hundred billion. The judge thought this analysis might be too sweeping, so he narrowed his sights to the by now seven-year period when Judge Wingrove, the only superior court judge in the county, selected juries. The chance that no black would ever be selected was two in a thousand. [51] The Court of Appeals upheld the ruling.

In the Civil Rights Division at the Justice Department, Walter Barnett, a career attorney then in charge of the appellate section, recommended to Reynolds that the government stay out of the case in the Supreme Court. The main question for the Justices, he wrote, was "whether racial discrimination in state grand jury selection can be challenged on federal habeas corpus where there were no infirmities, in jury selection or otherwise, at the trial." [52] Since the Court had considered the same question in 1979, not many years before, and five current Justices, or a majority of the Court, had accepted the position that the government urged as a friend of the Court in that case, Barnett argued that the "repetition of our previous argument would be superfluous." The Criminal Division of the Justice Department, with the main responsibility for the new case, agreed, because a recent statute called the Jury Selection and Service Act had virtually eliminated the central issue in the Hillery case by outlawing the sort of discrimination under review by the Supreme Court. [53] Even if the constitutional basis for the Hillery decision was reversed, the statute left ample grounds for similar lawsuits. As a prosecutor, the United States had nothing to gain by taking part in the case.

Reynolds disagreed, and presented the Hillery case as a paradigm of the kind the Reagan Administration should pursue, to cut back on the use of the "dramatically and unduly expanded"[54] doctrine of habeas corpus, preserve the "finality" of state criminal judgments, and limit access to the federal courts. He wrote, "Even if we would otherwise be inclined to stay out of this case, I believe we have a special responsibility to the Court to participate." The brief filed by the government in the previous case "contained the same fundamental analytical flaws as the decision ultimately rendered" and the government was "obliged to correct this mistake by now urging the Court to adopt a rational approach to the problem of grand jury discrimination." He went on, "I do not believe that we properly carry out our responsibilities to either the judicial or executive branch of government by automatically giving preclusive effect to the analysis contained in our earlier filings. *This is particularly true in the civil rights context where, to say the least, we have not slavishly adhered to the constitutional reasoning advanced by prior Administrations.*" (Italics added.)

"This is the way this guy thinks with mirrors," said a lawyer in the SG's office who was familiar with the case. "He takes the standard logic of government lawyers before the Supreme Court and reverses it."[55]

Joshua Schwartz was the assistant to the SG on the case. "While it is undoubtedly necessary and proper for the government to alter its position on important issues of law from time to time in a democratic nation," Schwartz conceded in a memo to the SG, "the Supreme Court's willingness to allow us to do this freely is intimately related to its conviction that we exercise a very high level of self-restraint in our dealings with the Court." He cited a Supreme Court opinion praising this trait of the Solicitor General's, and continued, "The government as a whole accordingly has a vital interest in reserving the kind of change of position that would be involved here for cases in which there are compelling federal governmental interests that must be served and where no other party can be counted upon to make the arguments that we could make. This is not such a case." With drama and a touch of deadpan, he closed, "I think it important to note that the argument on the merits simply isn't as open and shut as the memos from OLP"—a division of the Justice Department called the Office of Legal Policy, which was known for its New Right political cast

and had concurred with Reynolds—"and Civil Rights suggest. To file a brief supporting the state would be to ask the Court to discard 100 years of precedent regarding practices that have been thought by Justices adhering to a wide variety of viewpoints to impair the integrity of the judicial process. I do not see a sufficient justification for the United States to file such a brief." [56]

The precedent Schwartz had in mind was an 1880 case in which the Supreme Court said that deliberate exclusion of blacks from a grand jury "is practically a brand upon them, affixed by the law, an assertion of their inferiority, and a stimulant to that race prejudice which is an impediment to securing to individuals of the race that equal justice which the law aims to secure to all others." [57] In more than a dozen cases since then, the Justices had rejected the Reynolds notion that a conviction should stand despite racial discrimination in the selection of a grand jury, and Rex Lee agreed with his assistant that the government should not challenge this line of precedent. Lee couched his judgment in terms that radiated sympathy to the President's agenda. "The most significant issues the Court will consider next term involve some aspect of racial discrimination," he wrote, "and all of these cases are central to the Administration's objectives. The Court is likely to be closely divided on all these issues. In the interest of success in these cases we must not do anything to imply that we are opposed to elimination of racial discrimination in jury selection or broader contexts." [58] Reynolds asked the Attorney General to overrule Lee, but the recently sworn-in Edwin Meese did not. In January of 1986, for a majority of the Supreme Court, Justice Thurgood Marshall wrote an opinion supporting the SG's judgment. About the view urged by Reynolds and argued in the Court by lawyers for the warden of a prison in California, Marshall echoed the lower-court judge and sounded the theme struck by Joshua Schwartz. "Our acceptance of this theory would require abandonment of more than a century of consistent precedent," Marshall wrote, and he concluded, "the need for such a rule is as compelling today as it was at its inception." [59]

THE FIGHT OVER Vasquez v. Hillery was one of the many disputes between Reynolds and the SG's office that stayed private during Rex Lee's tenure, and spared Reynolds the burden of public scrutiny. Though Reynolds regularly brought pressure to bear on Lee and the SG's office, the only dispute between Reynolds and Lee that went public was about one of a series of appeals known as the religion cases. It was this dispute that led ultimately to Lee's resignation as SG. [60]

The religion cases took on the urgency of the President's agenda when one (Lynch v. Donnelly) raised the question whether the city of Pawtucket, Rhode Island, had violated the Establishment Clause of the First Amendment by sponsoring a nativity scene as part of its annual Christmas display. [61] At Lee's request, Paul Bator took charge of the case. Bator's junior partner was Michael McConnell, a young lawyer in the SG's office who now teaches at the University of Chicago Law School. [62] Bator and McConnell saw it as an opportunity to challenge the wisdom of the Supreme Court's three-part test for determining whether government involvement with religion was constitutional. According to Lemon v. Kurtzman, decided in 1971, government involvement with religion is permissible only if it has: a secular purpose; a primary effect that neither enhances nor inhibits religion; and no entanglement between the institutions of government and religion. [63] To the lower courts, sponsoring a crèche as part of Pawtucket's Christmas celebration enhanced religion by giving it the city's seal of approval, so it was unconstitutional. [64] To Bator, this was a wooden reading of the First Amendment.

The core of the government's brief was a recommendation that the Supreme Court reconsider the Lemon test. "We suggest," it said, "that the three-part test . . . results in analytic overkill when applied to the type of government action under consideration here." Applying it to the annual sponsorship of a crèche by a city "tempts courts to engage in hypocrisy." "It should not be necessary," the brief observed, "for a court to assert that the traditional religious references that fill American official life have lost all religious significance in order to uphold them. This Court's sessions are opened by the traditional cry, 'God save the United States and this honorable Court.' Are we to say that the constitutional *validity* of this plea *depends* on it being wholly perfunctory, a piece of meaningless boilerplate?" The crux of the Bator-

McConnell idea was accommodation of religion—and accommodation between the conflicting injunctions of the First Amendment's Establishment Clause ("Congress shall make no law respecting an establishment of religion") and its Free Exercise Clause ("or prohibiting the free exercise thereof"). They urged that Pawtucket be allowed to include "a small nativity scene as part of an elaborate annual display connected with the celebration of Christmas."[65] To the consternation of old-line civil libertarians and the satisfaction of the Reagan Administration, the Supreme Court agreed.[66]

Some lawyers in the Justice Department considered the "accommodation" theory quite radical,[67] since it rejected the ideal of a separation between church and state celebrated by decades of active Supreme Court precedents.[68] These lawyers considered the theory more useful as a symbol of the Reagan Administration's commitment to promoting religion in American life than as a tool of law, because it appeared to justify almost any government support of religion that stopped short of outright endorsement of a specific sect. The Supreme Court had not in fact endorsed the concept. To reach the result favored by the government, it applied the Lemon test.

But the "accommodation" theory did not represent the most extreme point of view in the debate on this issue. A New Right organization called the Center for Judicial Studies gathered some of the more vociferous extremists and published their views in *Benchmark*, a bimonthly journal.

The masthead of *Benchmark* provided a key for understanding its influence during the Reagan Administration.[69] In 1984, the journal's book-review editor was Gary McDowell, who then took a leave of absence to join the Justice Department and run the staff that drafted the Attorney General's speeches. In 1985, the journal's Supreme Court editor was Bruce Fein, the former Associate Deputy Attorney General and member of the Bob Jones team. A dozen other editors and contributors either worked for the Reagan Justice Department or, when its point of view was considered too far out for a government official to present, carried its message to the public as friends of the Administration.[70]

The journal and the center were founded by James McClellan,

a former aide to Senator Jesse Helms, the Republican from North Carolina, and a former chief counsel to the Senate Judiciary Committee. McClellan also edited *Benchmark*. According to him, the purpose of the center and the journal was to counter the "liberal" views that prevailed in the American Bar Association and American law schools, and to rein in the "liberal" and "activist" judges who dominated the federal bench.[71] His own writing about the crèche case showed how he planned to do it.[72]

In the Pawtucket brief, McClellan found a weak rehearsal of the "confused and inconsistent" ideas of the Justices. He wrote, "Because the Solicitor General's brief did not question any of the Court's prior interpretations of the Establishment Clause, which emerged unscathed to haunt future generations, the Justices were not compelled to reexamine their holdings or defend their position."[73] That McClellan's comments could not be written off as crank became clear when another religion case came along, this time dealing with a prime item on the President's agenda.

As McClellan told the story of Wallace v. Jaffree, which addressed the constitutionality of an Alabama law permitting silent prayer in public schools and raised the question of spoken prayer, "Federal District Judge Brevard Hand, after meticulously examining the historical record, including countless new documents never before mentioned in any Supreme Court opinion, lifted his own earlier injunction against Alabama authorities and came to the startling yet compelling conclusion that the Supreme Court had been misinterpreting the Establishment Clause since 1947. Exposing in stark relief the constitutional flaws of the Supreme Court's wall of separation doctrine"—the doctrine about separation between church and state—"Hand also argued convincingly that the Federal courts do not even have jurisdiction over cases involving prayer in the public schools. Going one step further, Hand even challenged the Supreme Court's doctrine of incorporation, relying again on original sources to demonstrate the unassailable fact that the Framers and backers of the Fourteenth Amendment never intended to apply the Bill of Rights to the States or give Federal courts jurisdiction over disputes between States and their citizens where freedoms in the Bill of Rights were at issue."[74]

Approving Judge Hand's opinion, McClellan treated Hand's

series of "startling" conclusions as belated advances in legal reasoning rather than as judgments flying brazenly in the face of thirty-five years of constitutional law. In his rendition, McClellan failed to mention that it was his own research and thinking on which Judge Hand had relied as authority for his assault on Supreme Court doctrine. (A footnote in the judge's opinion expressed "indebtedness" for McClellan's "vision"; and, according to Forrest McDonald, a University of Alabama historian who followed the case, McClellan also drafted Hand's opinion.)[75] McClellan did comment about the background of one of the basic ideas attacked by Hand.

In *A Lawyer Looks at the Constitution,* Rex Lee called the First and the Fourteenth Amendments the two constitutional amendments most important to the country's fundamental law.[76] Many hold this view. The latter was adopted in the aftermath of the Civil War, and since 1925 the Supreme Court has understood it to mean that a phrase called the Due Process Clause ("nor shall any State deprive any person of life, liberty, or property, without due process of law") incorporates most of the guarantees of the Bill of Rights and applies them to the states. To many historians, this step of incorporation assured that all citizens would benefit from basic protections: against unreasonable searches and seizures by police, against government encroachments on private religious worship, and the like. To McClellan, however, the Court had used the doctrine "to acquire jurisdiction over civil rights disputes that were originally intended to remain under the exclusive control of the States." Giving his radical idea some mainstream polish by tying it to an insistent theme of legal conservatives, McClellan announced that incorporation was "the great seedbed of judicial power in the modern Court."[77]

McClellan's ideas became more fashionable than Judge Hand had made them when Bradford Reynolds decided to sponsor them as well. Paul Bator recalled,[78] "The prayer story is the most continuous single story involving the tension between the legal and the political, and the complexity that arises from the fact that the SG's office has a relationship with both the Administration and the Court. The first time I heard about the Alabama school-prayer case was when memos started floating around as the case was going from the district court to the Court of Appeals. Brevard Hand had issued an extraordinary opinion, saying that the Fourteenth Amendment didn't incorporate the First and therefore that the First Amendment does not prohibit a state from establishing a religion and therefore that Alabama is free to allow prayer in schools. A district judge was repudiating Supreme Court precedent! Brad Reynolds and other people in the Administration pressed us to file an amicus brief in the Court of Appeals arguing that Judge Hand had gotten the thing right. We were being urged to do this because the President had said the same in speeches and otherwise that it was his policy to restore prayer in the public schools. This came into the office very shortly after we had decided to go into the Pawtucket crèche case with my enthusiastic support. I was of the view that our office could be helpful and influential in that case. But when I heard about the prayer case, it made me very nervous. We couldn't do anything but insist on a reversal of Judge Hand. As a lower-court judge, he was bound by Supreme Court precedent. If not, what is the rule of law? The Justice Department cannot encourage lawlessness on the part of lower-court judges, and that's what we were being told to do. The question was a major one during the fifties, when desegregation cases came up and some federal judges refused to enforce the Justices' holding in Brown v. Board of Education. The principle that district-court judges must obey the Supreme Court is one that every lawyer ought to be clear on. In the Justice Department, the issue was up for grabs in the Jaffree case, but there was no doubt what the correct opinion should be."

Bator and Rex Lee agreed that the Solicitor General should not file an amicus brief supporting Judge Hand's opinion in the Court of Appeals,[79] and they persuaded Reynolds to back off. When the court overturned Hand, Reynolds again took up the fight. According to the *Wall Street Journal*, Reynolds had the support of the White House.[80] "As you know," he wrote to the Solicitor General, "at the time we discussed our participation in this case in the Court of Appeals, there was general discomfort with the Government filing a brief that would effectively ask the Eleventh Circuit to overrule" major precedents.[81] "The consensus was, as argued by both you and Paul, that such a position should be advanced only in the Supreme Court, and that the government would be acting irresponsibly were it to urge a lower federal court to disregard Supreme Court rulings. There was the added concern that the district court's rejection of the 'incorporation doctrine' opened a Pandora's box with which we were not prepared to deal. We are now in the Supreme Court," he pointed out, and he contended that the government should urge the Justices to overturn the precedents forbidding school prayer.

The primary issue of dispute between Reynolds and the Solicitor General was the appropriate extent of the government's call for reversal of the Court of Appeals. As Reynolds put it, referring to the Supreme Court's major precedents in this area of law, which prohibited spoken prayer in public schools, "It would be counterproductive for the Government to argue strenuously for a narrow exception to the Schempp and Engel doctrine . . . if, in so doing, we effectively endorsed the existing school prayer precedents." He wrote, "Our position in the Supreme Court must be crafted in such a way as to make abundantly clear that we view Schempp and Engel as wrong and unworthy of respect." [82]

When Rex Lee opposed the Reynolds line, Attorney General William French Smith asked, "What am I going to tell the White House?" [83] Paul Bator again took charge of the government's brief and provided the Attorney General with an acceptable explanation to give to the President's aides. He framed the choice differently than Reynolds. "The important question," Bator said, [84] "was whether we should ask the Court to uphold the part of the Alabama statute that would allow a teacher to recite a verbal prayer, which would have required the Solicitor General to tell the Court that Schempp and Engel were based on an erroneous principle. There's nothing wrong with the government doing that. The 'independent' judgment of the SG at this juncture—that is, our professional judgment—was that going to the Supreme Court on the spoken-prayer issue was a kamikaze mission, that we would not get a single vote on it, that we would receive a stinging rebuff, that it would be unprofessional in a more subtle sense. It would put to the Court an issue for which the intellectual preparation had not been done. You go to the Court when there are lower-court decisions and law-review articles and other expressions in the legal culture showing serious and thoughtful controversy about a matter. In the case of the prayer decisions, the intellectual preparation had not been done, and more work was still required to make that a question worth bringing to the Court. I had a strong feeling that we would jeopardize our other religion cases if we just said to the Court, 'Throw out your jurisprudence about the wall of separation between church and state.' We would have lost nine to zip. Instead, I believed the SG should go in on the silent-prayer issue, and everyone finally agreed. Our view was that it was perfectly legitimate for the government to say that the major precedents did not bar a moment of silent prayer. The theme I wanted to stress was that of tolerance, including tolerance for those who are under a claim of conscience to make religious observance a part of daily life. My thought was that intolerant secularism is as out of harmony with the religion clauses of the Constitution as an official religion would be."

A majority of the Supreme Court treated Bator's thought that a moment of silent prayer could be "an instrument of toleration and pluralism, not of coercion or indoctrination" as a generalization that didn't apply to the case. The state senator who sponsored the law permitting a moment of silence in Alabama had stated that he intended to give children the chance to share in the spiritual heritage of their state and country. His purpose was obviously religious, not secular. It was "to return voluntary prayer to our public schools," he said. The law was "a beginning and a step in the right direction." Writing for a majority of the Justices, John Paul Stevens reminded that this purpose conflicted with the "freedom of conscience protected by the First Amendment"—what he called "the right to select any religious faith or none at all."[85] Religious beliefs "worthy of respect," he pointed out, are "the product of free and voluntary choice by the faithful," and "the political interest in forestalling intolerance extends beyond intolerance among Christian sects—or even intolerance among 'religions'—to encompass intolerance of the disbeliever and the uncertain." There was no more poignant expression of intolerance than the ostracism by other students of a couple of second-graders and of a single child in kindergarten—in this case, the Jaffree children, whose father brought the lawsuit—when they refused to take part in various acts of religious worship led every day by their teachers.

Answering the argument favored by Reynolds, Justice Stevens also referred to Judge Hand's "remarkable conclusion that the Federal Constitution imposes no obstacle to Alabama's establishment of a state religion." [86] The Justice went on, "Until the Fourteenth Amendment was added to the Constitution, the First Amendment's restraints on the exercise of federal power simply did not apply to the States. But when the Constitution was amended to prohibit any State from depriving any person of liberty without due process of law, that Amendment imposed the same substantive limitations on the States' power to legislate that the First Amendment had always imposed on the Congress's power." The Justice declared, "This Court has confirmed and endorsed this elementary proposition of law time and time again."

The government's brief drew a compliment from a concurring opinion by Justice Sandra Day O'Connor, who agreed that "moment of silence laws in many States should pass Establishment Clause scrutiny because they do not favor the child who chooses to pray during a moment of silence over the child who chooses to meditate or reflect." [87] But this endorsement did not quiet the noise from the right. In *Benchmark*, James McClellan complained about the school-prayer case, "Here was an historic occasion for the Solicitor General to lay the foundation for a conservative constitutional revolution." [88] Instead, the SG filed a brief about a moment of silence—"a secondary issue of the case"—and bowed to precedent.

McClellan's writing appeared under the title "A Lawyer Looks at Rex Lee," a takeoff on the titles of Lee's books. It singled out the SG as he had never been before, but Lee did not benefit from this attention. The piece called for Rex Lee's "prompt removal" as Solicitor General, and it was a cutting and inaccurate polemic. McClellan twisted Lee's personal history to improve the sound of the case against him. Soon after Lee's Supreme Court clerkship in the early sixties, for example, he had been asked for legal advice by the American Civil Liberties Union. McClellan turned this into an insinuating pejorative, calling it Lee's "ACLU Connection." He criticized Lee for failing to follow what McClellan said was the tradition of Robert Jackson, SG from 1938 to 1940, claiming that Jackson had been blunt about pointing out the errors of the Supreme Court's ways during the Roosevelt era and that in one year he had been willing to lose two-thirds of his cases rather than follow mistaken doctrine. [89]

On both points, McClellan was telling half-truths. In political speeches outside the Court before and during his tenure as SG, Jackson did criticize some Court decisions; and in the 1935 Term, under Jackson's predecessor, Stanley Reed, the government did lose the lion's share of its cases. But by the time Jackson assumed the office, in March 1938, the Court had already swung in favor of the New Deal. In his own appearances before the Court, he proved to be both a respectful and a successful advocate. As annual reports of the Justice Department indicate, under Jackson the government's record in the Court was better than at any time in the previous decade. [90] Far from being at odds with the Court as SG, Jackson maintained cordial relations with most of the Justices and even called on the Chief Justice in his chambers to obtain special dispensation for the scheduling of an argument. [91]

In the categories of abortion, religion, states' rights, labor law, and the interpretation of statutes, McClellan faulted Lee's management of government litigation in the Supreme Court. This judgment rested on a redefinition of the SG's mandate rather than on twisting the facts, though McClellan did both. He complained that Lee had not urged the Court to overrule "a single prior decision," and that the SG had "opposed the idea that his primary responsibility as Solicitor General was to advocate the Administration's policies, insisting instead that he had an independent relationship with the Court based on trust between the Justices and the Solicitor General's office." McClellan accused Lee of "orthodox liberalism," and of "slavish submission" to prior rulings of the Supreme Court: "Lee ha[d] consistently addressed the Court as a dutiful and fawning serf might approach the Czar." [92]

McClellan seemed especially irked by the interview Lee had given to the Los Angeles *Times*. "In that same interview," McClellan went on, "Lee also remarked that such social issues as prayer in the public schools and abortion were 'an albatross around my neck,' and asserted that he would resist the 'enormous pressure' he was under to take stronger positions on those issues. Lee has, in fact, stoutly resisted not only the so-called social or children's issues, but also basic principles of limited constitutional government and many of the policies of the Administration he was appointed to serve. Upon a close examination of actions taken by Lee before the Supreme Court, we find that he has repeatedly taken positions that are directly at odds with the President's program, and has regularly advanced points of law that are calculated to preserve intact existing case law and the doctrines of the Supreme Court."[93]

To any Court-watchers but those on the Solicitor General's right flank, Lee's opposition to the President's program was news. In an unpublished essay called "Another Lawyer Looks at Rex E. Lee: A Reply to James McClellan," Richard Wilkins, who had worked as an assistant to Lee in the SG's office and was now an assistant professor of law at Brigham Young University, wrote that the SG understood "what some of his conservative critics do not; that is, that the law moves in careful modulations rather than great leaps. It has taken a number of years and some patience, but because of Rex Lee's careful persistence and craftsmanlike presentation of the government's position, the Administration's views on a number of important social issues are—for the first time—beginning to bear substantial fruit in the Supreme Court. And when that occurs, Rex Lee is not the only winner. President Reagan wins too."[94]

Lee was caught between the New Right's impatient call for change and his own sense of the limits required by the law's "careful modulations." It was not surprising that his performance drew irreconcilable reviews, as it did in a prominent case about abortion. Instead of being marked by "servile deference to recent judicial precedents,"[95] as McClellan contended, Lee's role in 1982 in a pair of abortion cases out of Ohio and Missouri known as the Akron case led some observers to think he'd pushed the bounds of government advocacy farther than any SG before him. Under the heading "No Friend of the Court," *The New York Times* ran a lead editorial about his brief: "The Reagan Justice Department filed a curious document with the Supreme Court last week in connection with pending abortion cases. Though called a brief for the United States as a friend of the court, it is in fact a 20-page lecture. 'The time has come to call a halt,' it says, to the way the Court has been dealing with abortion disputes. The document goes out of its way to disparage the Court's famous 1973 abortion decision, Roe v. Wade. Then it goes on to urge the Court to uphold some of the nation's most restrictive abortion regulations.

"We trust that the Court, which needs no such lecture, will ignore this political tract, for it is of scant help in deciding the complex cases to be heard in the fall term. The brief is better suited to the partisan purposes of an Administration eager to appease its disgruntled right wing." The editorial went on, "With this brief, Solicitor General Rex Lee has vented his deep personal quarrel with most of the Court's abortion decisions while distorting the function of his respected office." [96]

When Lee argued the case before the Supreme Court, Justice Harry Blackmun, who had written the majority opinion nine years before in Roe v. Wade, said he could not understand the government's position. Was the Solicitor General asking the Court to overrule Roe? Distinguishing himself from McClellan, Lee replied, "I am not, Mr. Justice Blackmun." [97] Though the SG viewed the abortion case as one of the few in which he was willing to risk irritating the Court by promoting the President's policy when restraint told him not to ("There is the point of view that the election results give you the four-year right to drive the engine of government," Rex Lee said about the agenda cases, in the Los Angeles Times. "There's no sense in leaving the car in the garage."), [98] he stopped short of doing what he considered disrespectful.

Justice Lewis Powell, whose caution and pragmatism made him the Court's leading promoter of traditional judicial restraint, wrote the opinion about the abortion case, and he suggested that Lee's amicus brief had still gone too far. Powell lectured about the legal doctrine of stare decisis—that is, abiding by precedent. According to the Justice, following a principle laid down in a previous case that is like the new one before the Court "is a doctrine that demands respect in a society governed by the rule of law." [99] Though no precedent is shielded from scrutiny about its continuing vitality in the law, the Justice found "especially compelling reasons for adhering to *stare decisis* in applying the principles of Roe v. Wade." The case had been "considered with special care"—it had been argued and then reargued before the Justices were ready to decide it. After the 1973 ruling, the Court "repeatedly and consistently" had "accepted and applied the basic principle that a woman has a fundamental right to make the highly personal choice whether or not to terminate her pregnancy." For a six-to-three majority, Powell reaffirmed a woman's right to abortion.

In June 1985, Rex Lee resigned after four years as Solicitor General. "My wife and I were shopping," he reported, "and she reached for some English muffins. They were the Thomas's brand, and I said to her, 'We can't afford those.' I don't want to dwell on this, but I can't afford to send three kids to college and support four others on a government salary. That's the immediate reason why I'm leaving." Lee added, "It seems that this is the right time to move on." [100]

Lee also, however, spoke to what most observers of the SG's office believed was the true reason for his departure. It was the constant hounding from the Reagan Right, from critics outside the Administration like James McClellan and from lobbyists inside like Bradford Reynolds, that drove him from the post he considered the best job for a lawyer in America. "Stare decisis is an important part of American law," Lee said. "I know that. Even though I might have some misgivings about certain precedents, where they are well established and it's obvious the Court isn't going to depart from them, it isn't smart to lecture the Justices about where they went wrong. It accomplishes nothing. I have no qualms about taking a position that might not be immediately persuasive, but which might bear fruit down the road. That's not what we're talking about. If I had done what was urged on me in a lot of cases, I would have lost those cases and the Justices wouldn't have taken me seriously in others. There has been this notion that my job is to press the Administration's policies at every turn and announce true conservative principles through the pages of my briefs. It is not. I'm the Solicitor General, not the Pamphleteer General." [101]

BY COINCIDENCE, the same week that Lee resigned the Senate Judiciary Committee opened hearings on the nomination of William Bradford Reynolds to serve as Associate Attorney

General. The hearings revealed much about the nature of the pressure Lee had faced as Solicitor General. The insights had to do with the question of Reynolds's attitude about the law. Events recounted to the senators showed him to be a lawyer whose dedication to the ends of the Reagan agenda made him headstrong and, often, insensitive about his choice of means. The Judiciary Committee documented the performance of a radical conservative whose impatience for results made him deaf to the appeals for craftsmanship made by lawyers in the Civil Rights Division and the SG's office. The senators also heard substantial testimony that went to the issue of character. From a considerable record—the report on the Reynolds hearings filled 1,037 pages—it appeared to some senators that Reynolds pressed to have his way as expeditiously as possible and that at times he overlooked or hid the truth to get it. [102]

A group called the Lawyers' Committee for Civil Rights Under Law submitted to the senators a detailed account of Reynolds's record. [103] The committee was organized in 1963 at the request of President Kennedy, who wanted private attorneys to help in the effort to assure civil rights for all Americans, and it had continued its work with the encouragement of every President until Ronald Reagan. It was composed of liberals and conservatives, and Democrats, independents, and Republicans, and for the first time in the committee's history, they felt compelled to oppose a Presidential nomination. The main author of the committee's report was Thomas Barr, [104] a senior partner in the prestigious New York law firm of Cravath, Swaine & Moore and as weighty a figure as the American legal establishment could offer to criticize Reynolds.

Barr wrote that Reynolds's performance on behalf of the Reagan Administration represented "a sharp break with the past." For twenty-four years, under every head of the Civil Rights Division since it was founded in 1957, the Justice Department had followed a steady, moderate course in enlarging and defending the rights of minorities. Under Reynolds, the Civil Rights Division had abruptly and dramatically "undercut" those rights. "As a result of those policies," Barr stated, "the Lawyers' Committee and lawyers affiliated with it now find themselves in a novel and regrettable position. In increasing numbers of civil rights cases throughout the country, where we represent the interests of minorities and women, we are encountering for the first time the fervent and vigorous opposition of the federal government." [105]

The Lawyers' Committee divided their conclusions into three sections: areas where Reynolds had violated the "obligation faithfully to execute the law," [106] by ignoring or overriding "clear and well-established law"; where he had tried to weaken the law in a way that would "impede the progress of minorities toward equality under law"; and where enforcement of the law had been "lax or virtually non-existent."

Barr summed up: "Our concern over the policies of the Civil Rights Division under Mr. Reynolds runs far deeper than any differences of opinion in a few isolated cases; it runs deeper than any simple dispute over Administration policy. The record of the present Administration in civil rights—Mr. Reynolds's record— reflects an abdication of responsibility for the enforcement of civil rights and, even more disturbing, a disregard for the rule of law as it governs those rights." [107]

To career attorneys at the Civil Rights Division, the report refuted what they called "the big lie." [108] The main form of the "lie" was that the Reagan Administration and especially Bradford Reynolds had vigorously enforced civil-rights laws. The report contradicted this claim. Reynolds's determination to prosecute whites who had violated federal laws that were passed to punish severe abusers of civil rights (for example, some police officers and members of the Ku Klux Klan) made it difficult to write him off as a racist, but, criminal cases aside, the Lawyers' Committee noted that he often advised the United States to support whites contesting blacks.

A second version of the "lie" was that the only major differences between the views of past administrations and the current one came in the areas of school busing and affirmative action, on grounds of policy and not law. Among those convinced this was true was Griffin Bell, the former Attorney General to President Carter. "Mr. William Bradford Reynolds has been under sharp attack recently because of the Department of Justice's policies on quotas and school busing," [109] Bell wrote to the members of the

Judiciary Committee in a letter endorsing Reynolds, as if that were the whole story. As the Lawyers' Committee reviewed the record, it was not.

Reynolds had led the Reagan Administration to make obvious changes in policy as well as law, in the areas of housing, voting rights, the rights of the handicapped, and all other areas for which the Civil Rights Division was responsible. To the Lawyers' Committee, the Reagan Justice Department went beyond reversing the practices of previous administrations. It went beyond favoring whites over minorities whom the civil-rights laws were passed to protect. With Reynolds as the leader of the Civil Rights Division, the department had turned its back on the judgments of Congress and the Supreme Court about the dictates of the law.

Some of the examples considered during the Senate hearings concerned Reynolds's dealings with the Solicitor General's office. After the Supreme Court ruled in favor of the government's position about layoffs in the Stotts case, for example, Reynolds treated the holding as the deep blow to affirmative action in hiring and promotions that he had wanted the Justices to strike. All the Courts of Appeals that interpreted the Court's opinion disagreed, and treated it only as a ruling on the narrow question about layoffs. Reynolds spurned this uniform reading, and sent what became known as "the Stotts letter" to fifty-one state and local governments across the country. Disregarding the government's "legal obligation" [110] to defend lower-court decrees previously worked out by elected officials and judges, and signed by the government, he pressed the local governments to effectively end their affirmative-action programs in hiring.

Arlen Specter, a Republican from Pennsylvania, asked Reynolds about "what appears to be a pattern of elevating your own legal judgments over the judgments of the courts—stated differently, in disregarding the established law." [111] Referring to Reynolds's refusal to read the Stotts decision as the federal courts had done, Specter said, "We are all obliged to follow the law as it is finally interpreted by the courts."

Specter also rebuked Reynolds for misleading him at a hearing in 1982. The topic had been certain election laws in Burke County, Georgia, which the Supreme Court eventually struck down on the

grounds that they discriminated against blacks. The Assistant Attorney General had told the senator that he would not challenge the laws because he lacked the resources. A federal statute required the county government to justify the new election laws when challenged, and Reynolds had given Specter the impression he was sympathetic to the suit that had been brought against the laws. But two months earlier, in a memo to the Solicitor General, Reynolds had taken the opposite position. He had argued that if the government entered the case, it should go in against the blacks on the side of the all-white county government. Despite the specifications of the federal statute, Reynolds would have preferred to shift the burden of proof to the people challenging the changes. Specter learned about what he considered Reynolds's dissembling when the Justice Department complied with the Judiciary Committee's request for documents. He was upset by the news.

"Wasn't your response to me deceptive?" Specter asked. Reynolds said, "I apologize to you, Senator, for leaving that impression," and explained that he had not wanted to discuss an internal memo. "Well, Mr. Reynolds," Specter commented, "I find that hard to accept." [112]

Charles Mathias, a Republican from Maryland, also focused on Reynolds's part in a case involving the Solicitor General. Earlier in the hearings, Reynolds had been asked whether there had been any controversial cases where the result pleased civil-rights groups. (The question went "Name me a close call where those folks thought, 'Doggone that Bradford Reynolds, he got it right this time.'") Reynolds had answered, "Havens Realty," a Supreme Court case where the question was who had the right to sue a landlord for discrimination. In the past, people known as testers had played a part in suits against housing discrimination. When a black was turned down by a person renting a place to live, a white tester with similar credentials would come along to look at the same house. If the white was told he could have it, there was strong proof of discrimination against the black to use in a lawsuit. Blacks sometimes lacked the resources to take on the landlord. Testers representing public-interest groups could sue in their stead and have the same impact. Havens Realty, Reynolds said, where "the Supreme Court accepted our argument is another one that I would say the civil rights groups ought to be extremely happy with." [113]

In fact, while Rex Lee had urged the Justices to uphold the right of testers to bring suits, Reynolds had opposed that position. "My preference is to stay on the sidelines and quietly watch," [114] he wrote Lee in a lengthy memo telling the SG why to leave the case alone. As Mathias put it, ". . . the result was the opposite of the way you started." [115] Although it had not come out at the original hearing, Reynolds took credit for a victory the government had a hand in only after it overruled his objection to entering the case.

Reynolds had begun his tenure as Assistant Attorney General by refusing to enforce laws with which he disagreed, and he had compounded this show of contempt by trying to alter the spirit of the law where the letter did not explicitly prevent him from doing it. When Dennis DeConcini, a Democrat from Arizona and a member of the Judiciary Committee, explained why he had decided to vote against Reynolds, he said that the Assistant Attorney General hadn't "told the truth here." Reynolds had a "tendency to uphold the laws and decisions he like[d] and ignoring or refusing to follow or enforce the ones he [didn't]"; and "he altered the truth to suit his own purposes." [116]

The Senate Judiciary Committee voted ten to eight against Reynolds's confirmation, with Republicans Specter and Mathias joining the unanimous Democratic minority. As of July 1987, Reynolds's was the only nomination for a presidential appointment in the Executive Branch voted down by the committee during the Reagan Administration. [117]

When Rex Lee left the Solicitorship, he suggested that the main difference of opinion between himself and his critics on the right appeared to be about a matter of degree: how hard should a Solicitor press the Administration's policies? [118] In light of the Reynolds hearings, Lee's idea seemed naive. As a result of Reynolds's attitude, which, for want of a better phrase, amounted to disrespect for the law, and his authority within the Reagan Administration, Reynolds had managed to reverse the traditional relationship between the Solicitor General and the other senior political officials in the Justice Department.

"If the independent legal advice of the Solicitor General is to be preserved," the memorandum by the Office of Legal Counsel about the role of the SG had concluded, "it should normally be the Solicitor General who decides when to seek the advice of the Attorney General or the President in a given case."[119]

Rarely, however, had Reynolds waited for Rex Lee to call on him for counsel. As point man for the White House at the Justice Department, Reynolds had pressured the SG's office as hard as he had campaigned for the Reagan agenda in other forums. When it appeared that career civil-rights lawyers, who worked down the hall from the SG's office, were undercutting Reynolds by kibitzing about cases with Rex Lee's aides, Reynolds forbade his staff to talk to the Solicitor General's assistants until they cleared it with the front office in the Civil Rights Division. When assistants to the SG resisted his arguments, he effectively blackballed them from working on civil-rights cases and made sure that only lawyers he considered acceptable were assigned to work on later cases.[120]

It was a steady, driving, effective performance. Dealing with the Reynolds whose radical practices were copiously recorded by the Judiciary Committee, and with other senior Justice Department officials for whom Reynolds established a precedent by lobbying the Solicitor General,[121] Rex Lee was handicapped by the standards of restraint he thought he should maintain. At the end of his tenure, Lee reported that Reynolds had never bested him in an argument about which side the government should take in a Supreme Court case. But Reynolds prevailed in other ways.[122] He kept the SG from entering cases he otherwise would have, he changed the terms on which the SG presented cases, and in general, he played a major part in altering the SG's role. Lee tried to fulfill what he called "my obligations to the Court and to my office,"[123] but he was inevitably worn down.

In the spring of 1985, a memo that circulated at the Justice Department explained how the promotion of Reynolds to the third-highest post in the department was intended to have direct consequences for the SG's office.[124] Since the permanent establishment of this post in 1977, the Associate Attorney General had been in charge of either civil or criminal matters in the department. The chain of command had been revised again, so that for the first time since 1870, when the office of the Solicitor General was established, an official besides the Attorney General—in this case, Reynolds— was to be given authority to oversee the SG's business.

The memo confirmed what Reynolds had achieved in his regular sorties against Rex Lee in civil-rights cases and a widening circle of other matters. [125] By 1985, the SG's independence had been officially and markedly cut back. Even without becoming Associate Attorney General, William Bradford Reynolds was already a Shadow Solicitor.

VIII

Meese's Law

DESPITE THE POWER of Bradford Reynolds over the Solicitor General in the Reagan Administration, his influence was only derivative. From the outset, Reynolds's authority stemmed from the Administration's dominant legal figure, Edwin Meese.

Meese first caught Ronald Reagan's attention as a deputy district attorney in California, where, in the sixties, he prosecuted students protesting at Berkeley as part of the free-speech movement.[1] As a prosecutor, Meese showed little interest in balancing the state's desire for public safety with the rights of individuals, and his views squared with Reagan's. He was appointed legal-affairs secretary to Governor Reagan, and later, moving with Reagan to the White House, he became the President's most powerful adviser.[2] Meese repeatedly expressed his legal views in recommendations on public policy. He was instrumental in the Administration's decision to concentrate its law-enforcement efforts on prosecuting criminals rather than vigorously protecting civil rights and liberties. (In a speech to a convention of policemen in California, he called the American Civil Liberties Union "a criminals' lobby.") He persuaded President Reagan to back the Administration's decision favoring tax exemptions for segregated schools in the Bob Jones case, called for abolition of the Legal Services Corporation, and approved lax enforcement of environmental, antitrust, and occupational health and safety laws.[3] When lawyers at the Justice Department said they felt pressure from the White House to take a position in a case, they invariably meant from Meese.[4]

Edwin Meese's attitude about the law was revealed in detail in the report of an independent counsel issued in September 1984 after questions had arisen about Meese's personal business affairs.[5] The report dealt with allegations of wrongdoing that led the Senate to postpone for eleven months a vote on Meese's nomination to serve as Attorney General. President Reagan called the 385-page report a "vindication," Meese said he was "very happy" with it, and his lawyers claimed that the independent counsel exonerated their client when he found "no basis with respect to any of the 11 allegations for the bringing of a prosecution against Mr. Meese for the violation of a federal criminal statute."[6] (In fact, while the independent counsel found no basis for prosecuting Meese on most of the charges that had been leveled, in some instances he did find a basis for prosecution but chose not to bring charges.)[7] Yet among the events that the report chronicled, a handful had the impact of a hard slap.

Meese cashed a check made out to him by the Presidential Transition Trust for his "moving expenses" from California not long before he came East to join the Administration in 1981.[8] He learned from the Justice Department that it was illegal for the trust to pay moving expenses for people taking government jobs, and after he cashed the check for its intended purpose, he had the record changed so that the check would be passed off instead as payment of a "consulting fee." Then he told the Senate Judiciary Committee that he had paid all the expenses when he and his family moved from California to Washington.

Meese sat on the White House Senior Staff Personnel Committee that approved a job as an Assistant Secretary of Commerce for Thomas Barrack, a real-estate developer who had helped Meese sell his house in California. Barrack had used $70,000 of his own money to cover the down payment for a buyer of the house and another $13,000 for general expenses related to the sale. Meese did not tell his colleagues on the committee about this help.[9] He also sat on the committee that approved an appointment to the Postal Board of Governors for John McKean, who loaned Meese $60,000, and did not reveal to the committee that McKean loaned him the money. And Meese approved government jobs for three officers and a director of the Great American First Savings Bank in San Diego, from which he had borrowed $423,000 to buy the house that he eventually sold in California and, later, a house in Virginia.

As chairman of Common Cause, former Solicitor General Archibald Cox wrote what was echoed by dozens of editorial pages across the country: "The Attorney General must symbolize the highest standards of honor, integrity, and freedom from self-interest in the performance of public office."[10] In the dealings chronicled by the report of the independent counsel, Cox concluded, Meese showed himself either contemptuous of these standards or oblivious to them.[11]

A rumor circulated in Washington during the Meese inquiry that his fellow presidential aides, James Baker and Michael Deaver, were tired of his bumbling, disorganization, and rigid ideology, and saw William French Smith's decision to leave the Attorney General's office as a chance to move Meese out of the White House and into the Justice Department.[12] The right-wing press (*Human Events*, the Washington *Times*, and other publications) portrayed Meese as a pillar of principle who was a victim of leaks, slurs, and innuendoes from moderates trying to banish him from the President's inner circle.[13]

In any case, the month after the Senate Judiciary Committee voted against the Reynolds nomination in 1985, and six months after it confirmed Meese as Attorney General, Meese began a series of speeches that confirmed which side he took in the fight between traditionalists at the SG's office and their antagonists, like Bradford Reynolds and James McClellan. Written by *Benchmark* contributors,[14] the Attorney General's first major speeches were delivered in Washington and then in London to the annual convention of the American Bar Association. His subject was the role of judges in the American system of government, and the proper limits on their reading of the Constitution.

Dwelling on certain opinions of the previous Term (like Wallace v. Jaffree, in which the Justices had rejected the Administration's call for change and had relied on a traditional analysis of the First Amendment's religion clauses), the Attorney General accused the Court of overstepping its constitutional bounds. In his words, ". . . far too many of the court's opinions were, on the whole, more policy choices than articulations of constitutional principle." The Justices' "voting blocs, the arguments, all reveal a greater allegiance to what the court thinks constitutes sound public policy than a deference to what the Constitution—its text and intention—may demand."[15]

Meese proposed that courts use what he termed a Jurisprudence of Original Intention. The way to assure that Supreme Court Justices and other federal judges did not jeopardize the separation of powers distinguishing American democracy was to have them "resurrect the original meaning of constitutional provisions and statutes as the only reliable guide for judgment." As he put it, "To make certain the ideal of the rule of law is given practical effect, the law must be fixed and known." By Meese's lights, the widely shared view of the Constitution as a living testament that takes "meaning from the circumstances of each age" was mere "chronological snobbery."[16]

Although these remarks were general enough to be construed in different ways, and they appealed to students of the Constitution who believed that, in the past generation, the Supreme Court has not been sufficiently mindful of the limits on judicial power inherent in that document, what Meese said went far beyond the bounds of mainstream thinking. Over the years, liberal and conservative scholars have agreed that the Framers of the Constitution deliberately chose ambiguous language as a form of compromise on many important questions. "No Constitution is the same on Paper and in Life," wrote Gouverneur Morris, one of the authors of the text, and, along with other Framers, he began to debate its meaning almost as soon as it was adopted.[17] Liberal and conservative Justices alike have declared that the words of the Constitution are capable of well-tempered growth, and that the Supreme Court must continually reinterpret the document, with its ambiguities, compromises, and internal tensions, in the light of new conditions. (In one glaring respect, Justice Thurgood Marshall has pointed out, the imperfections of the Constitution could not be fixed by interpretation. Its sanctioning of slavery had to be expunged, and women's suffrage added, by major amendments before the fundamental American law guaranteed equality to all citizens.) The most honored declaration about the idea of a living charter—John Marshall's warning that "we must never forget that it is *a constitution* we are expounding"—has been taken as given since at least

1819. (The Constitution, Marshall explained, was "intended to endure for ages to come and, consequently, to be adapted to the various *crises* of human affairs.")[18] Meese interpreted Marshall to mean the opposite, and said that kind of thinking "suffers the defect of pouring new meaning into old words, thus creating new powers and new rights totally at odds with the logic of our Constitution and its commitment to the rule of law."[19]

It took awhile for the legal community to recognize the breadth and depth of Meese's attack on conventional notions about constitutional law; but by the late summer of 1985, Meese found himself the center of attention from students of the Constitution. He regularly took advantage of the spotlight to promote his views. Instead of speaking in the measured tones of authority, of a powerful figure who felt accountable for the actions of a government which had held sway for a number of years, Meese addressed his audiences with the vigor of a young Turk challenging the old order.

"The past several decades of American life have been influenced by an aggressively secular liberalism often driven by an expansive egalitarian impulse," he told a gathering at the American Enterprise Institute. "The result has been nothing less than an abandonment of many of the traditional political and social values the great majority of Americans embrace." Meese's anchor against this drift was the "restoration of fundamental Constitutional values"[20]—that is, his Jurisprudence of Original Intention.

This included removing from the federal courts jurisdiction over social issues like abortion and school prayer. It meant questioning whether the independent agencies that for years had been operating as a wing of the government, with commissioners appointed by the President and a mandate directly from Congress, were constitutional. It meant giving up the form of affirmative action used by every Administration since Lyndon Johnson's in the nineteen-sixties. "A new version of the Separate but Equal doctrine,"[21] Meese labeled affirmative action.

Finally, Meese redoubled his effort to cut back on the protections afforded by the Supreme Court to individuals suspected of crimes. "Miranda only helps guilty defendants,"[22] he said about Miranda v. Arizona, the Supreme Court's landmark decision requiring the police to advise suspects of their rights to remain silent, to know that anything they say can be used against them, and to request the presence of an attorney for whom the state will pay if the suspects could not afford one, before they are interrogated. He finished, "Most innocent people are glad to talk to the police." (After the Attorney General's comment drew criticism, he said he had made "a poor choice of words,"[23] but stood by the substance of his remarks.)

The attack on Miranda was particularly odd because it was aimed at a target whose allegedly pernicious effect had already been greatly reduced since it was created by the 1966 ruling.[24] The purpose of the holding was to protect suspects' rights against self-incrimination under the Fifth Amendment and to guarantee them their right to counsel under the Sixth. Until Miranda, as long as a defendant's statement to the police was "voluntary," it could be admitted into evidence in court. By then, however, a double standard about criminal rights (one in the privacy of a police station, where a confession may have been coerced; the other in the public forum of a court, where due process usually prevailed) meant that a statement may have been voluntary only in the sense that a defendant had offered it to protect himself from a beating. The police often acted as if they had a right to hear a confession, regardless of how they obtained it, and Miranda dispelled that misimpression.[25]

A study published by the *Yale Law Journal* in 1967, a year after the Miranda decision, when the police still considered the landmark a rebuke, found that "not much" actually changed because of it. As subsequent rulings made clear, the landmark decision had balanced the interests of the police in convicting criminals and of individuals in maintaining their dignity,[26] and that is how it was applied. While law-enforcement officials had feared that Miranda meant they couldn't ever question a suspect unless they gave him the full warnings, the Justices said that the warnings were only required when the police took someone into custody. The Justices also decided that while the police could not use an illegally obtained confession in court, they could do something almost as good: they could use the confession to impeach the testimony of a defendant who contradicted it on the stand.[27] The Miranda decision proved not to hamper the police, and increasingly law enforcement officials came to believe that it actually helped: only a small percentage of convictions had depended on confessions and, despite getting their warnings, the same percentage of suspects confessed after the Miranda decision as before.[28] The warnings also raised the number of valid confessions. They were easy to give, and they helped the police avoid claims by defendants that their constitutional rights had been violated. Many law-enforcement officials decided they were better off with Miranda than without it.[29]

Meese's ideas eventually provoked an extraordinary response. For the first time since the drama caused by Roosevelt's Court-packing scheme in the thirties, when Chief Justice Charles Evans Hughes informed the Senate that the Supreme Court had no need for the six new Justices proposed by the President, members of that bench entered into debate with a senior figure from the Executive Branch. The Attorney General's speeches drew scholarly rebuttals from Justices William Brennan and John Paul Stevens.

Brennan has served since President Eisenhower appointed him in 1956, when he was fifty, and he is the Supreme Court's leading liberal. The Justice spoke a couple of months after the Attorney General, and appeared to respond to him point by point.

At a Georgetown University symposium about interpreting texts as different as the Constitution and the Bible, the Justice opened his remarks with a confession. He said, "The encounter with the Constitutional text has been, in many senses, my life's work."[30] To Brennan, the discussion sparked by Meese was "really a debate about how to read the text, about constraints on what is legitimate interpretation."

"There are those who find legitimacy in fidelity to what they call 'the intentions of the Framers,'" Brennan said. "In its most doctrinaire incarnation, this view demands that Justices discern exactly what the Framers thought about the question under consideration and simply follow that intention in resolving the case before them. It is a view that feigns self-effacing deference to the specific judgments of those who forged our original social compact.

"But in truth," Brennan continued, "it is little more than arrogance cloaked as humility. It is arrogant to pretend that from our vantage we can gauge accurately the intent of the Framers on application of principle to specific, contemporary questions. All too often, sources of potential enlightenment such as records of the ratification debates provide sparse or ambiguous evidence of the original intention." [31]

He went on, "One cannot help but speculate that the chorus of lamentations calling for interpretation faithful to 'original intention'—and proposing nullification of interpretations that fail this quick litmus test—must inevitably come from persons who have no familiarity with the historical record."

Brennan concluded, "We current Justices read the Constitution in the only way that we can: as Twentieth Century Americans. We look to the history of the time of the framing and to the intervening history of interpretation. But the ultimate question must be, what do the words of the text mean in our time." [32]

In remarks to the Federal Bar Association in Chicago, Justice Stevens also responded to the Attorney General's promotion of his Jurisprudence of Original Intention. Stevens was appointed to the bench in 1975 by President Ford, and he is known for either his independence of mind or his quirky, unpredictable opinions, depending on who is commenting. Stevens takes a centrist's approach to the law, and in his speech he criticized Meese for failing to evaluate "subsequent developments in the law as well as the original intent of the Framers" [33] when he offered judgments about the Supreme Court.

While the Justices' words were fresh in the public mind, Meese answered no questions about the responses from the Court to his speeches. He said only that he thought it was "a very good thing" [34] they had joined the debate: the rejoinders from the members of the Court brought Meese's ideas to wide public attention. Even though the "jurisprudence" was eventually dismissed by many in the legal commuity—including Justice Byron White, who has otherwise endorsed some of the Administration's most controversial positions, but who called Meese's notion "simplistic"—the Attorney General and his aides were pleased by the clamor. [35]

A few months later, in the winter of 1986, Meese changed his tactics. In a journal called *Policy Review,* published by a New Right think tank called the Heritage Foundation, Meese replied with an article called "The Battle for the Constitution." "In the main," he wrote, "a jurisprudence that seeks to be faithful to our

Constitution—a jurisprudence of original intention, as I have called it—is not difficult to describe. Where the language of the Constitution is specific, it must be obeyed. Where there is a demonstrable consensus among the Framers and ratifiers as to a principle stated or implied by the Constitution, it should be followed. Where there is ambiguity as to the precise meaning or reach of a constitutional provision, it should be interpreted and applied in a manner so as to at least not contradict the text of the Constitution itself." [36] These guidelines presented a mainstream view of constitutional review, and marked a retreat from some of Meese's earlier comments. Though his new statement addressed none of the hard questions about interpreting constitutional ambiguities, it was uncontroversial.

Now, instead of quarreling with Brennan and company on grounds of theory, Meese attacked their application of the law. If not *ad hominem*, Meese's strikes were unmistakably barbed. "Sadly," Meese continued, "while almost everyone participating in the current constitutional debate would give assent to these propositions, the techniques and conclusions of some of the debaters do violence to them. What is the source of this violence? In large part, I believe that it is the misuse of history stemming from the neglect of the idea of a written constitution." Invoking the spirit rather than the letter of America's basic law, Meese argued in response to Brennan, the Supreme Court had done lasting harm to the nation. It "read blacks out of the Constitution" in the Dred Scott decision, by holding that slaves were not citizens, and brought on the Civil War. [37] It "contrived a theory" to "support the charade of 'separate but equal' discrimination" in Plessy v. Ferguson. [38]

Making his argument, Meese seemed to misuse history. The Dred Scott case stands mostly for the proposition that racial prejudice runs deep in American experience and that institutions like the Supreme Court, which are capable of great deeds, can also inflict grievous wounds on themselves and the country. As to Plessy, according to Alexander Bickel, the idea of "separate but equal" flourished when the Civil War amendments, including the Fourteenth Amendment, were adopted as part of the Constitution—it was Brown v. Board of Education that, to use Meese's word, "contrived" a theory of equal opportunity to overturn

Plessy and call for desegregation of public schools, in a unanimous opinion widely cited as the worthiest precedent for judicial activism. [39]

Meese went a calculated step further. Without an acknowledgment that he was yoking one of the Court's champions of equality to its most notorious decisions endorsing racism, he suggested that those cases fairly represented the contribution of Brennan-type judges. "It is amazing how so much of what passes for social and political justice is really the undoing of old judicial mistakes," [40] he observed—and warned that the only way to protect the law from future Dred Scotts and Plessys was to apply it as Meese did, and not Brennan.

DURING THE WEEK that the Attorney General began riding circuit to air his views in the summer of 1985, the government filed a Supreme Court brief marking the official start of the Meese era for the office of the Solicitor General. [41] The subject was a pair of cases from Illinois and Pennsylvania dealing with the constitutionality of state laws regulating abortion. "In America," Meese told his London audience, "we face the difficult question of abortion. It is a question made more difficult by the entry of the federal judiciary into an area once clearly reserved, under our Constitution, for the states themselves to decide. We know there are fervently held opposing views about abortion. It is our responsibility and practical task to dedicate ourselves to the principles and purposes of our Constitution, particularly in areas of great controversy. This week the United States filed as amicus in the Supreme Court a brief arguing that the Court should return the law to the condition in which it was before the 1973 case, Roe v. Wade, was decided." The Attorney General declared, "The responsibility of the Justice Department to urge that constitutionally-wrong decisions be overruled is no less strong today in this case than it was in 1954 in Brown v. Board of Education." [42]

For the dozen years since the Supreme Court had struck down anti-abortion laws in forty-six states and had ruled by a seven-to-two vote that women have a constitutional right to abortion, the decision had troubled even constitutional scholars who agreed with the result. [43] According to John Hart Ely, the former dean of Stanford Law School, who was regularly cited as a legal authority by the Reagan Administration, "Roe v. Wade was the clearest example of noninterpretivist 'reasoning' on the part of the Court in four decades." Interpretivists, Ely wrote, hold that "judges deciding constitutional issues should confine themselves to enforcing norms that are stated or clearly implicit in the written Constitution," while noninterpretivists contend that "courts should go beyond that set of references and enforce norms that cannot be discovered within the four corners of the document." [44]

Writing for the majority in Roe v. Wade, Justice Harry Blackmun grounded the right to abortion in the Due Process Clause of the Fourteenth Amendment and the right to privacy staked out by the Supreme Court in a series of cases beginning in the late nineteenth century, in which the Justices had affirmed the right of individuals to decide whether and when to marry, whether to conceive and bear children, how to raise and educate them, and how much to disclose of their personal lives. Blackmun's critics, interpretivists and noninterpretivists alike, understood the Justice's conclusion, but they did not agree with his legal reasoning. The Constitution didn't "clearly reserve" regulation of abortion to the states, as Edwin Meese claimed, but, as John Hart Ely put it, there was nothing in the Constitution that marked the freedom to have an abortion as a special value. "A neutral and durable principle may be a thing of beauty and a joy forever," Ely wrote. "But if it lacks connection with any value the Constitution marks as special, it is not a constitutional principle and the Court has no business imposing it." [45]

The 1985 abortion case that Meese was describing raised a legal dilemma. Should the Court perpetuate a widely heralded constitutional right whose source was in dispute? Or should it remove from the books a troublesome holding, and wipe the slate clean? To Meese, the proper solution to this problem lay in the dramatic step of simply revoking the constitutional right to abortion. In making his proposal, Meese disregarded the opinion written only two years before, by Justice Lewis Powell, in the Akron decision affirming Roe v. Wade. (Justice Powell had reminded that stare decisis—abiding by precedent—"is a doctrine that demands respect in a society governed by the rule of law.")[46] Meese also seemed to ignore the workings of the law itself. Picking up on a theme of Justice Stevens, John Hart Ely explained what Meese was overlooking when the Attorney General supported the Reagan Administration's call for the Court to reverse its landmark decision about abortion.

"It's been almost a decade and a half since Roe v. Wade was decided,"[47] Ely said in 1986, "and it isn't sitting out there all by itself. The Justices have built a number of decisions on it, and the holding is now part of an elaborate system of legal doctrine. It's part of the law. I haven't changed my mind about the merits of the original judgment, and if the whole subject could come up fresh, I'd still be against the Court ruling as it did. But in this case that's no longer possible. If I were on the Court, I'd feel bound to uphold the decision." (Both Congress and the state legislatures seemed to assent to this development of the law by making no serious move to reverse the abortion ruling with an amendment to the Constitution.) Just as Meese's initial proposal for a Jurisprudence of Original Intention was based on the idea that the meaning of the Constitution was frozen in time, Meese appeared to think that rulings like Roe v. Wade marked legal moments that could be judged right or wrong no matter how far in the future, as if nothing in the interim counted for the law.

The abortion case drew special notice from lawyers because it was the first in which the Solicitor General had asked the Supreme Court to decide that a right the Justices had previously found in the Constitution was no longer there.[48] Important as this was, it paled in significance next to another insight that the case revealed about the Reagan Administration's view of the law. The Attorney General's statement in London about the right to abortion was the first of several in which he indicated the most radical belief that he and other Reagan officials seemed to hold: that their judgments about the law were as authoritative as those of the other two branches of government, if not more so.

Once again, Meese suggested that his idea was grounded in "original intention," but now it was found in the Constitution's provisions about the structure of government. As Meese put it, "Some of the chief problems of government today stem from the fact that how the federal government works in practice doesn't always resemble how it is supposed to work according to the Constitution." [49] But, while the Framers were deeply concerned about the government's structure, they never directly addressed the question of which branch would have ultimate responsibility for interpreting the Constitution, and certainly did not resolve it the way Meese claimed they had. By voting down a proposal for a body called the Council of Revision, which would have given the President a role in judging the constitutionality of federal statutes, the Framers explicitly rejected the very principle that Meese was now proposing centuries later. The Attorney General, however, was not deterred by history. He invented a new axiom of constitutional law: if the Supreme Court handed down decisions with which the Executive Branch disagreed, then officials in that branch of government should treat their own views as authority for the true meaning of the law.

The Attorney General developed his argument with an illustration from Cooper v. Aaron—the only opinion in the history of the Court that was individually signed by all the Justices. The Court's statement of unanimity was prompted by a dramatic series of events: the school board in Little Rock, Arkansas, sought to desegregate the city's public schools in 1957, under a plan approved by a federal court; after declaring his commitment to defending the Southern way of life, Arkansas's Governor Orval Faubus claimed he was not "bound" by the Supreme Court's call for desegregation in Brown v. Board of Education, and he ordered the National Guard to place Little Rock's Central High School "off limits" to blacks; the case rose quickly to the Supreme Court, which built on one of its venerable themes and declared, according to "the basic principle that the federal judiciary is supreme in the exposition of the law of the Constitution," [50] that Arkansas had to abide by the Brown decision.

Almost thirty years later, Meese disagreed and reopened the argument. He took Faubus's side in the debate. He insisted that while the decision in Cooper "was binding on the parties in the case," [51] it was not binding on anyone else. The error of his position was easy to show, because if the Attorney General was right, Brown v. Board of Education would have pertained only to the public schools in Topeka, Kansas. To force schools to desegregate throughout the rest of the country, children and their parents would have had to bring lawsuits in every single district, which was not how the law had worked before, not what the Supreme Court intended, not how lower-court judges eventually responded, and not what most Americans understood the law of the land to be after Brown.

Although the Attorney General attacked the Supreme Court's judgment in Cooper v. Aaron, which reaffirmed the long-settled duty of the states to obey federal law, he seemed primarily interested in the Court's relationship to Congress and the President. He skirted the question at the core of this subject—which branch of government the Constitution empowers to resolve disputes between them when, for example, the Congress passes a law the Supreme Court finds unconstitutional, or the President and the Supreme Court disagree in a case about the meaning of the Constitution. He overlooked the enduring answer provided in Marbury v. Madison, or in McCulloch v. Maryland, when Marshall wrote, "On the Supreme Court of the United States has the Constitution of our country devolved this important duty"[52]—namely, of deciding the law of the land. Instead, the Attorney General invoked the Dred Scott case once more.

Dred Scott dealt with the legality of slavery in a territory not yet part of the United States. Abraham Lincoln feared that the ruling was a step toward what he called "the nationalization of slavery," because since the Court had already decided that neither Congress nor the legislature of a territory could constitutionally outlaw slavery, the Justices could as easily rule the same about the states. Lincoln recognized that he couldn't challenge the Dred Scott case as it applied to the parties whose controversy had been resolved by the Court ("We offer no resistance to it," he emphasized), but, as he put it, "All I am doing is refusing to obey it as a political rule. If I were in Congress, and a vote should come up on a question whether slavery should be prohibited in a new territory, in spite of that Dred Scott decision, I would vote that it should."[53]

Meese interpreted this to mean that Abraham Lincoln, like Orval Faubus, had refused to honor the Court's holding because he believed that the Justices were wrong about the law.[54] He thought that the Reagan Administration could make a laudable contribution to the law by doing the same. While the Administration's legal logic was not completely wrong—the Constitution is different from constitutional case law; the Supreme Court isn't irreproachable, and it has regularly demonstrated its commitment to the Constitution by correcting what it considers errant decisions—Meese and the Reagan team never acknowledged some crucial facts.

Dred Scott was unlike any other legal case in American history. It is an irrefutable example of why the Supreme Court cannot claim to be infallible. If it had been resolved otherwise, the debate about the Court's authority as the supreme source of American law would have been very different. Rather than observing the tension between the lessons of Dred Scott and Cooper noted perennially by constitutional scholars (the Court is fallible, and yet it has the authority to state the law of the land), and noting that the tension can be partially resolved by understanding how the facts in each case explain their current significance in the law (Abraham Lincoln interpreted Dred Scott narrowly because the decision favored slavery and held that blacks were not citizens; the Justices in Cooper warned Governor Faubus and his cohorts about the need to comply with the Court's desegregation order handed down in Brown), Meese lectured about the dangers of equating judges and lawgivers, and of submitting to government by judiciary.

The Attorney General belittled the principle of judicial review, which the Justices in Cooper v. Aaron called "permanent and indispensable,"[55] and which Chief Justice William Rehnquist defended in 1987 by calling the Supreme Court "the final arbiter of questions of constitutional law."[56] Using the word "interpret" in a very active sense, Meese approved the notion that "each of the three coordinate branches of government created and empowered by the Constitution—the executive and legislative no less than the judicial—has a duty to interpret the Constitution in the performance of its official functions," and announced that the Supreme Court's interpretations of the Constitution do "not establish a 'supreme Law of the Land.' "[57]

Whether he meant to or not, Meese thereby licensed an attitude about the law that, if taken seriously, leads to conflict, chaos,

and lawlessness. That was the result in Little Rock after Governor
Faubus refused to integrate Central High. In an effort to restore
order, the federal district court granted a request from the school
board that the desegregation plan be postponed for many months.
The court explained that the "chaos, bedlam and turmoil" caused
by Faubus were "intolerable." [58] President Eisenhower sent in
troops to enforce the law, and Faubus backed down.

Examples abound of Meese's and the Reagan Administration's
inclination to read the law according to their own lights and to
reallocate power among the branches of the federal government—
above all, to increase the authority of the Executive Branch. Meese
castigated the Justices because, in his opinion, "far too many of the
Court's opinions were, on the whole, more policy choices than
articulations of constitutional principle." [59] Bradford Reynolds
broadly interpreted a narrow Supreme Court ruling about layoffs
and affirmative action, counter to every reading of the opinion by
Courts of Appeals. Roger Clegg, a young lawyer who held a
number of political jobs in the Justice Department before becoming an assistant to the Solicitor General, suggested how casually
the Administration did this in a memo criticizing a widely respected, three-decade-old precedent applying the Constitution's
Equal Protection Clause to the District of Columbia, just like any
state. He doubted it should apply. "I know the Supreme Court
thinks so," the lawyer wrote, "but that does not make it true." [60]
Clegg did not mention the consequence of his judgment, which
was as telling as his statement about the authority of the Court: if
the Equal Protection Clause was not applied to the District as the
Justices did in the decision the lawyer criticized, then because of
the District's odd status in American law, there would be no
apparent way to outlaw segregation in the District under the
Constitution. [61]

When Archibald Cox was Solicitor General, he warned that
"the very fabric of a free society is strained when criticism and
efforts to change the law slip over into efforts to frustrate or re-
vile the courts." [62] The Reagan team regularly strained that fabric,
and went beyond lack of respect for court rulings. They often
elevated legal judgments of the Executive Branch over those of
Congress as well. At its most dramatic, this took the form of
unlawful acts rationalized by patriotism: many students of the

Iran-Contra affair concluded that Ronald Reagan's aides violated the law to carry out a clandestine foreign policy. When Secretary of State George Shultz was asked by Congress about these operations, even he testified, "Some things took place that were illegal." [63] Once the President disclosed his knowledge and approval of some of the secret dealings, it became impossible not to ponder the degree of his complicity too. But in the present administration, these acts are distinguished mainly by their scale; they are not an aberration. Whether the subject was national security, the environment, on-the-job safety, labor, housing, or civil rights, the Administration regularly violated or failed to enforce statutes it disapproved of. [64] The attitude prevailing among many Reagan aides was described by an official who helped supervise the Administration's role in the Nicaraguan war: "Legality," he advised the Washington *Post*, "was viewed as an obstacle that had to be gotten around." [65]

The President's lawyers sought to alter the relationships between the branches of government in other ways as well, less publicized but just as revealing. The Meese Justice Department came up with a new technique for elevating the judgments of the Executive Branch to equal standing with those of Congress in cases raising statutory questions, where the Executive's were, by custom, essentially irrelevant. As if the President's understanding of the purpose of a statute were as important as the Legislature's in guiding interpretations of the law, the department decided to expand the statements made by the President at media events where he signed congressional bills into law. The department expressed a new view about separation of powers, and turned what had long been ceremonial speeches into Presidential proclamations about congressional intent.

Then the Attorney General arranged to have them published in the same volume as the official legislative histories of major statutes. [66] His reasons for doing so strayed far from standard legal thinking. The President's only choice about a bill forwarded to him for signature by Congress is to sign it or not, because the Chief Executive is to execute and enforce, not to make, the law: he has no constitutional role in stating the purpose of a law or the intent of its framers except when he proposes legislation. Even when he does, his comments are at best peripheral to understanding the history of a federal statute, since he is a secondary figure in the lawmaking process. The President does make a statement when he vetoes a bill, but the statement merely explains his decision to veto. It does not become the official history of the proposed law.

The Attorney General wrote to the president of West Publishing Company, a major publisher of official legal records, and insisted on "the importance of presidential signing statements as an aid to statutory interpretation."[67] Like many of Meese's statements, the letter appeared plausible on first reading, though it was in fact a distortion of the President's role in lawmaking. The publisher took his word for it. "We appreciate your suggestion," West's Dwight Opperman wrote back. "I am surprised nobody thought of it before."[68]

The Meese Justice Department adopted another policy that involved a deliberate encroachment by the Executive Branch on the authority of the Legislature. A statute called Public Law No. 96-132 requires that in any case where the Attorney General decides to refrain from enforcing a provision of a statute passed by Congress because he thinks the act is unconstitutional, he must report that decision to both Houses of Congress.[69] For many years, through the Carter Administration, the Attorney General closed his report to the Vice-President of the United States, in his role as President of the Senate, and to the Speaker of the House with a paragraph acknowledging the gravity of this judgment whenever he exercised it. "I should like to conclude by reiterating my belief that the Attorney General is obliged to defend the constitutionality of Acts of Congress in all but the most unusual circumstances,"[70] Attorneys General Griffin Bell and Benjamin Civiletti began their paragraph. In the Reagan Justice Department under William French Smith, the boilerplate was trimmed. "I believe that the action I am taking is consistent with my responsibility to support and defend the Constitution and at the same time will facilitate prompt judicial consideration of the constitutional issues,"[71] Smith wrote. And in the Justice Department under Edwin Meese, even though career attorneys in the Solicitor General's office continued to forward for his signature the old language about defending the Constitution,[72] the Attorney General cut it out altogether.[73]

In the Reagan Administration, then, the Executive Branch

decided it was empowered to judge the law as well as the Congress or the courts, and believed it had little obligation to show, through protocol or other means, deference to the other branches of government even as co-equals. To the Reagan team, separation of powers appeared to mean that the Executive Branch could decide which laws to enforce, that it owed no deference either to Congress or to the courts in determining how to interpret the law until the other branches of government recast it as the Reagan Administration wished them to.

One measure of the Administration's true interest in results instead of restraint—and of its cynicism about the process by which laws are made and interpreted—may lie in the clear willingness it showed to go counter to its own professed views on the proper role of the judiciary, when this suited its purposes. Thus, after failing to persuade Congress to enact into law various elements of the Reagan agenda, the Administration turned to the courts as the main forum for the pursuit of its domestic objectives. Perhaps most important, it sought to pack the courts with judges who appeared willing to put aside conservative canons of judging in order to fulfill the Administration agenda. According to Sheldon Goldman, a political scientist at the University of Massachusetts, during the first six years of the Reagan Administration, it relied on ideology as a primary test of a candidate's fitness for the bench more than any government since Franklin D. Roosevelt's and perhaps more than any in American history.[74] Largely rich, male, white, and Republican; younger on average than the judges appointed by the five previous Presidents; and, according to the American Bar Association, diminishing in quality as the pool of acceptable ideological candidates appeared to be drained[75]—the judges chosen by Ronald Reagan made up forty percent of the federal bench by 1986.

The last administration to draw attention to the law as Ronald Reagan's did was Richard Nixon's, during Watergate. But unlike the Nixon Administration, which became notorious for holding that it was *above* the law, the Reagan Administration in essence regularly proposed that it *was* the law. In doing so, the Administration encouraged a climate of lawlessness in its private dealings as well as in its public acts. Members of the Administration compiled a record of misdeeds, impropriety, and unlawful behavior that defies comparison with that of any of its predecessors. To take one measure: By the count of the Washington *Post,* between January 1981 and April 1986, one hundred and ten senior Reagan officials were accused or found guilty of unethical or illegal conduct. This was months before word of the Iran-Contra affair leaked out, adding names to the list like Oliver North, and before the Wedtech scandal implicated yet another group of top officials, including Edwin Meese. The Reagan record of ignominy dwarfs that of any other administration, including Nixon's.

By contravening the standard reading of the Constitution, the Reagan Administration flouted the will of Congress and chose not to execute laws with which it disagreed. In theory and practice, it sought to redefine the role of the judiciary, by claiming that judges lacked the authority that scholars had long agreed the Constitution gives them and, at the same time, packing the courts and turning to them (after failing in Congress) as a key instrument of change in social policy. But the Administration's elevation of the Executive Branch's judgments about the law to equal or greater status than those of the other two branches explains why the Reagan team could overlook the logic of the 1977 memorandum from the Office of Legal Counsel about the traditional role of the Solicitor General. To Griffin Bell's Justice Department, the major safeguard against errors of an independent Solicitor General was the Supreme Court. If the SG made a mistake, the Court could correct him. If the Justices upheld him, "then all the better, for his legal judgment and not that of his superiors was correct."[76] But if, as Edwin Meese made clear in his speeches on constitutional law, the Reagan Administration did not grant the Supreme Court this authority, then the SG's dual responsibility to the Court and the Executive Branch lost its point. There was no need for the Solicitor to defer to the Court if the Court's rulings did not establish what the law was any more than did the judgments of the Executive Branch, and the SG might then just as well carry to the Justices the policies of the Administration even where they conflicted with the law as previously expounded by the Court. In the abortion case, Acting Solicitor General Charles Fried served notice that this was what he intended to do.

IX

The Abortion Brief

CHARLES FRIED'S VIEWS about the law were an uncanny match for the Reagan Administration's. Born Karel Fried (pronounced Freed) in Prague, Czechoslovakia, he and his family fled the Nazis in 1939 and settled in Manhattan when he was almost six.[1] He once wrote that he "loves his country as a lover would, not as a child loves the parents he never chose."[2] Tall and sharp-nosed, Fried has deep lines etched in his forehead and a pliant mouth that stretches from a tight line, when he is watchful, to a broad grin. Like Paul Bator, whom he replaced in the winter of 1985, Fried had been a professor at Harvard Law School before joining the Reagan Administration as the political deputy in the SG's office. (Fried was political deputy for four months.) In fact, before the Administration brought in Bator, two years earlier, officials in the Justice Department got in touch with Fried about the job. Instead, Fried recommended his old friend and colleague as an expert in constitutional law. As a scholar in the philosophy of law and a teacher of subjects like contracts and torts, where judge-made rules comprise the heart of the law and the Constitution is not central, he had no special knowledge about the work of the Solicitor General, he explained.[3] Though he also taught criminal law, where the Constitution can figure prominently, he had no background in litigation or federal courts. But, as a member of Scholars and Educators for Reagan in 1980, co-chairman of Law Professors for Reagan-Bush in 1984, and a consultant to Edwin Meese in 1984 and 1985, Fried was eager to find a place in the Administration, and he eventually accepted one in the SG's office. In pictures of him taken not long before he left Harvard for Washington, Fried's glasses had thick black frames and his hair jutted out from the sides of his head in a windswept, bohemian look.[4] By the time he became Acting SG, in June of 1985, his frames were silver and streamlined, and his wiry graying hair was close-cropped, giving him the aura of an investment banker.

Fried had earlier showed his sympathy with the Reagan agenda by writing occasional Op Ed and magazine pieces,[5] on topics like "Curbing the Judiciary," "Questioning Quotas," and "The Trouble with Lawyers." The hallmark of a Fried piece was an argument rocketing along on the strength of its own self-evident truth: though federal judges have usurped power from the other branches of government, this is a symptom as well as a cause of problems; the legal theory in which many judges have been schooled—"that law is policy, and nothing but policy"—has bred a "corrosive cynicism" that explains why "judges feel there is little inherent in their role as expositors of the law to constrain them";[6] to relieve judges of this symptom, Fried proposed shrinking the power of courts over the daily business of government. Or: "The problem with lawyers, critics say, is the maldistribution of legal services," because only "big business and the very rich benefit from the legal system," but "this is nonsense," because the "rich and big corporations are more victims than beneficiaries of the legal system"; the law firms that serve the big corporations charge high fees, and the work done for a company by a firm can be handled more efficiently and just as well by in-house counsel. As for the middle class, wrote Fried, it "gets quite enough legal services," and "the poor need other things far more urgently than they need lawyers."[7] (In a commencement speech at Georgetown University Law Center, Justice Sandra Day O'Connor offered a different view about the need of the poor for legal services. "The gap between the need for legal assistance and the ability to pay for it seems to be widening," she said. "Costs of legal services have escalated beyond the means of many.")[8]

One of Fried's more memorable comments about law and society came at an unusual gathering about the curriculum at Harvard Law School, before he left the faculty to go to Washington. The school was intensely divided between the academic legal right and left, and the faculty was asked to attend an open meeting with the student body. One student complained that the school taught too much corporate law and too little poverty law. Fried lectured the student on the error of his views, and concluded that Harvard should teach more corporate law. An impulsive man who likes to cause a flap, Fried finished his remarks with an analogy. The Massachusetts Institute of Technology "teaches nuclear physics," he said, but it doesn't tell students "how to repair toasters." The room erupted in hisses and boos. [9]

Fried's 1976 law-review article, called "The Lawyer as Friend," [10] argued that an attorney who defends a big corporation has as much claim to being morally correct as a poverty lawyer. The piece contended that as long as they provide faithful counsel, lawyers should be free to live as they wish, because each individual has the freedom to choose, as well as the responsibility for, his own destiny. There is no sense living as if we are preparing for the Day of Judgment, Fried maintained, because what happens if it never comes? The article was treated by Fried's academic allies as a casual effort, and was greeted by students and a number of law teachers with scorn. "Many conservatives who see a bad or obnoxious or ugly practice in society have a recognition of grim reality for what it is," Robert Gordon, who is a professor at Stanford Law School, told the *National Law Journal*. "Charles is perversely determined to defend some of the obnoxious social practices as not only being tragically unavoidable but as somehow morally compelled." [11]

Fried's writing grew out of his background in the philosophy of law, and the core of it was a series of books about legal principles (*An Anatomy of Values, Right and Wrong,* and *Contract as Promise*) amounting to a grand declaration (not an argument, the philosopher Alasdair MacIntyre said about the second book, for "if we do not already agree with Fried's premises, so much the worse for us") [12] that absolute commands of right and wrong should take precedence over the dictates of utilitarianism—that is, doing the greatest good for the greatest number of people. From his early law-journal articles ("I propose to examine the foundations of the right of privacy—the reason why men feel that invasions of that right injure them in their humanity") [13] to his more widely known book about right and wrong ("This is a book about how a moral man lives his life: how he approaches choices between his own interests and those of others, what he should do if helping one person means hurting another, how far he must take on himself the burdens of the world's suffering"),[14] Fried made a spirited case for the autonomy of the individual. He made no great mark in the worlds of law or philosophy, but his work was respectfully reviewed by major journals. The *Yale Law Journal* wrote, "Fried is haunted by the nightmare of our being saddled with excessive personal responsibility for the state of the world."[15]

Fried had begun to express his belief in individual autonomy as early as the year he graduated from Columbia Law School (he already held degrees from Princeton and Oxford), when he clerked for Justice John Harlan. During the 1960 Term, the Supreme Court decided Poe v. Ullman, a case where the majority had chosen not to rule on the merits of a challenge to a Connecticut statute on birth control. Harlan dissented, and Fried worked with the Justice on his opinion. Harlan wrote, "I believe that a statute making it a criminal offense for *married couples* to use contraceptives is an intolerable and unjustifiable invasion of privacy in the conduct of the most intimate concerns of an individual's personal life."[16] Relying on the Due Process Clause of the Fourteenth Amendment, as Justice Blackmun would a dozen years later in Roe v. Wade, Harlan went on, "Due process has not been reduced to any formula; its content cannot be determined by reference to any code. The best that can be said is that through the course of this Court's decisions it has represented the balance which our Nation, built upon postulates of respect for the liberty of the individual, has struck between that liberty and the demands of organized society."

The value of privacy that Fried favored, as a law clerk to Harlan and as a young scholar, was embraced by the Supreme Court in its landmark decision about abortion, Roe v. Wade. Among his Harvard colleagues, Fried applauded this ruling and defended it from attack by others then on the faculty, including his colleague John Hart Ely.[17] To Fried's fortune as a prospect for political appointment in the Reagan Administration, he did not emphasize his support for Roe v. Wade in print. One of his law-school colleagues said, "Right before he went to Washington, we were together and someone asked him flat out: 'Does the Administration know your position on abortion?' He smiled and said,

'Well, I've never written it down.'" When a reporter for the Washington *Post* asked him about this in 1986, Fried answered, "You never know when you're 50—you have said a lot of things. I don't remember what I thought about the case in 1973." [18]

Not long after Fried filed the abortion brief as Acting SG, he said, "My passion is philosophy. Everything else is an excursion." He commented about himself, "I think a person who has lived life as a practicing lawyer is somehow restricted in what he sees in the law—that someone who has a larger, subtler view, as I inevitably do from my training, sees more issues." [19] Fried's commitment to his brand of philosophy explained why his approach to the Solicitor Generalship fit the legal view of the Reagan Administration. A friend of his, Philip Heymann, who is a professor at Harvard Law School and was the head of the Criminal Division at the Justice Department during the Carter Administration, noted the connection. Heymann clerked for Justice Harlan the same year as Fried and served as an assistant to the Solicitor General during the Kennedy Administration. He reflected, "When you get to the Reagan Administration, you find that the Solicitor General is in a different position. It is basically the view of this Administration that courts have misbehaved, including the Supreme Court, making law where they shouldn't, and doing social justice instead of law. They regard it as an important responsibility of the Department of Justice to straighten out the courts, both through judicial appointments and through declarations in briefs that they should stop what they've been doing. Charles Fried believes this, and he thinks that he does not have an obligation to the courts as much as to the law. He substitutes for a concern about the law as shaped by the courts a broad philosophical view. The law, whether in the Constitution or in statutes, is there to be interpreted by the Solicitor General; the law is not necessarily what the Supreme Court says it is. In fact, in his view courts regularly ignore the law or make it into something it isn't. Charles would say he's as committed to holding the Administration to the law as any of his predecessors, but for him the law is something that any right-minded lawyer can see." [20]

Fried's usual response when he was asked about the Reagan Administration's abortion brief after it became a legal event was

"You won't get a whisper of my views on abortion in that document. It's about the law." [21] Roe v. Wade should be overturned, Fried contended in the cases called Thornburgh v. American College of Obstetricians and Gynecologists and Diamond v. Charles, [22] because the decisions of the lower courts in the cases at hand had failed to balance the interests recognized in Roe v. Wade ("the state's interest in maternal health and in unborn and future life" versus "a woman's unfettered right to an abortion"). The Court's previous judgment about abortion, in the Akron case, had "expressed considerable impatience" with attempts by state legislatures to strike the proper balance. "To the extent this is so," Fried argued, "these cases and Akron itself are not just wrong turns on a generally propitious journey but indications of an erroneous point of departure. Indeed, the textual, doctrinal and historical basis for Roe v. Wade is so far flawed and, as these cases illustrate, is a source of such instability in the law that this Court should reconsider that decision and on reconsideration abandon it." [23]

The strongest language of the Acting Solicitor General's brief was directed at the courts below. "The courts of appeals betrayed unabashed hostility to state regulation of abortion and ill-disguised suspicion of state legislators' motives," [24] it read. Where the Court of Appeals for the Third Circuit, in Pennsylvania, found obstacles to abortion in the state legislature's regulations, the Acting Solicitor General found law that was constitutional. For example, the appeals court struck down requirements that: a pregnant minor be obliged to persuade a state judge she was mature enough to give her informed consent for an abortion; two doctors attend an abortion for a woman during the third trimester of her pregnancy, after the term of potential viability for a fetus; a woman's consent to an abortion be considered informed only if her doctor had told her in detail about the medical risks of the procedure; a doctor report to the state about each abortion he had performed, and why he determined "a child" was "not viable" from the pregnancy he ended. Charles Fried argued that these requirements were valid.

The last section of the government's brief made a general argument. The analysis in Roe v. Wade had "no moorings in the text of our Constitution or in familiar constitutional doctrine," the brief claimed, and it gave courts scant guidance for ruling on the lawfulness of statutes. "The result has been a set of judicially crafted rules that has become increasingly more intricate and complex, taking courts further away from what they do best and into the realm of what legislatures do best," it concluded. Roe v. Wade had divided pregnancy into trimesters, for example, and drawn an arbitrary line between them, on grounds that whenever the prospective childbirth posed a danger to the life of a pregnant woman, an abortion in the first trimester might be most defensible, and an abortion in the last, when an abortion might be more dangerous than childbirth, least defensible. But look at the confusion in the courts about the general meaning of the decision, Fried admonished: a state could require that information about abortions be given to a woman by a doctor and his assistant, but not by the doctor alone; a state could require that second-trimester abortions be performed in clinics, but not in hospitals. The Supreme Court's key standard for judging the lawfulness of an abortion was "viability" (the ability of the fetus to survive outside the womb), but in the words of the government's brief the notion of viability was "particularly unworkable" because the meaning of the term was changing with "advances in technology."[25]

More important than the practical problems caused by the Supreme Court's ruling, Fried observed, "There is no explicit textual warrant in the Constitution for a right to an abortion. It is true, of course, that words, and certainly the words of general constitutional provisions, do not interpret themselves. That being said, the further afield interpretation travels from its point of departure in the text, the greater the danger that constitutional adjudication will be like a picnic to which the framers bring the words and the judges the meaning." In Roe v. Wade, the Justices had brought along the conviction that "free access to abortion is a fundamental expression of individual freedom, and that such freedom is the first principle of a just society," but the conviction did "not constitute constitutional argument."[26]

On one level, Fried's brief presented an urbane version of a standard criticism of Roe v. Wade. Though he said that his brief presented "a fresh constitutional methodology,"[27] it did little more than summarize the twelve-year-old view that the Constitution includes no explicit right to an abortion and that therefore the Supreme Court was wrong to find one in its provisions.

On another level, it was a bold misrepresentation of the facts and law before the Supreme Court. "The courts of appeals betrayed unabashed hostility to state regulation of abortion and ill-disguised suspicion of state legislators' motives,"[28] the brief stated. But in the Pennsylvania case, it turned out, the Court of Appeals had struck down parts of only six of twenty sections in a twenty-four-page statute[29] which was described by State Representative Stephen Freind, its chief sponsor, as "the most comprehensive abortion control act in the United States, and the most publicized bill in Pennsylvania history."[30] Fried's brief did not say so, but most of the statute's provisions were left intact. They were as significant to the law as were the sections struck down. The lower court's ruling hardly amounted to "unabashed hostility."

As for the court's "ill-disguised suspicion," the history of the law indicated why the suspicion was justified. In 1981, the Pennsylvania legislature passed a bill designed to limit abortions that was based on a model statute written by an anti-abortion group in Chicago. Governor Dick Thornburgh vetoed the bill. In 1982, the legislature revised the bill to satisfy the governor, and passed it again. "Was my bill intended to discourage abortion?" Representative Freind asked rhetorically in an interview. "You use the word you want. It certainly counsels extreme caution to women and, by forcing them to understand what abortion is, tries to get them to think twice before going ahead with an abortion. I won't mince words: our goal is definitely to outlaw abortion."[31] Rather than supporting the view that Roe v. Wade and its progeny had been interpreted by state legislatures to require "free access to abortion," as the Acting SG's brief contended, legislatures like Pennsylvania's were testing to see how strongly their laws could discourage women from having abortions and still pass muster with the Supreme Court.

Instead of presenting a measured view about a vexing question of fact and law, Charles Fried had submitted a piece of advocacy that was marked by taunting phrases (like his comparison, already noted, of constitutional adjudication to a "picnic") and irrelevant asides (a comment on the meaning of the Establishment Clause, for example)[32] that made most sense as tips of the hat to the Attorney General and his ideological circle. In the estimate of many longtime observers of the SG's office, Fried's brief was more strident than any ever submitted by a Solicitor General.[33]

In a speech to federal judges in Little Rock, Arkansas, the month after the government entered the Pennsylvania and Illinois cases as a friend of the Court, Justice Blackmun called Fried's submission "a very amazing brief."[34] (Blackmun did not yet know that the SG assistant who had helped Fried write the brief was Albert Lauber, an ex-Blackmun clerk who kept his name off it so as not to offend the Justice.)[35] Blackmun also suggested that the Supreme Court was not likely to overturn Roe v. Wade. "There are always four votes" to hear an abortion case, he said, referring to the Court's rule to hear a case presented for review through a petition for certiorari if four Justices agree to.[36] "And the other five of us heave a deep sigh and wish we didn't have to go through this traumatic experience again."

Among the many amicus briefs filed on the other side from the government in the Thornburgh and Diamond cases, the best publicized was by Senator Bob Packwood, a Republican from Oregon; Congressman Don Edwards, a Democrat from California; and eighty other Republicans and Democrats from both Houses of Congress. It was written by four professors at Harvard Law School: Susan Estrich, Martha Minow, and Kathleen Sullivan, with Laurence Tribe as lead counsel.[37] Tribe is the author of a widely used treatise on constitutional law. Through the 1986 Term, he had argued fourteen cases before the Supreme Court—a notable accomplishment for anyone but a lawyer in the SG's office.[38]

At a press conference sponsored by Planned Parenthood in September of 1985, the day his brief was filed, Tribe described what Blackmun might have found amazing about the SG's submission. "The basic proposition" of the Tribe brief was "that the government's plea that the Supreme Court overturn Roe v. Wade is unprincipled, is divisive, and is dangerous." It was unprincipled "because it offers no coherent reason, at all, for the Supreme Court suddenly to repudiate this basic liberty." As the Tribe brief declared, "For the first time in the history of the Solicitor General's office, in a case in which the United States is not even a party, and a case in which the issue was not presented by the parties, the Department of Justice has urged the repudiation of a liberty long since declared fundamental by this Court." The SG's brief was divisive because it would "toss" the rights of women and of the unborn into "50 different political arenas, there to be resolved by a majority vote in 50 separate state legislatures." And it was dangerous because it threatened "every woman in this country with turning over her reproductive freedom to the powers that be in government," and because it advocated "radical surgery on our form of government and the body politic." The government had claimed that it wanted "to turn back the constitutional clock to 1973." It really called for turning back the clock "at least another half century," and repudiating "a long line of decisions about personal and family privacy which cannot be distinguished, in principle, from Roe v. Wade."[39]

A footnote in Tribe's brief emphasized the anomalous character of the role Fried had chosen to play:[40]

> In argument before this Court in Akron, the Solicitor General expressly refrained from asking the Court to overrule Roe v. Wade:
>
> Question: Mr. Solicitor General, are you asking us to overrule Roe v. Wade?
>
> Mr. Lee: I am not, Mr. Justice Blackmun.
>
> Question: Why not?
>
> Mr. Lee: That is not one of the issues presented in this case, and as amicus appearing before the Court, that would not be a proper function for us.

In an interview on National Public Radio in 1985, Lee was asked the same question. "When you come to cases like that," he said, "it's simply a question of 'Do you want to blow the bugle?' or 'Do you want to win the war?'"[41] In a draft of a speech he planned to give once he was out of office, written before his successor filed the government's abortion brief, Rex Lee made the point one more time, in the plainest possible language.[42] Bringing together in an organized way ideas he had expressed in various interviews, he wrote, "Let me give you the practical reasons why I don't think the Solicitor General can or should take it upon himself to tell the Supreme Court what he may very well believe are its errors of constitutional doctrine.

"The Solicitor General, unlike his critics, cannot afford to lose sight of the fact that he is a lawyer, an *advocate*, whose first duty is to see that his client, the federal government, prevails in the case at hand. There is, I admit, a place for announcement of pure principle, and from time to time that place is in a Supreme Court brief. But a Solicitor General is a *Solicitor* General, not a 'Pamphleteer General,' and his role is to persuade the Court by legal arguments to decide cases in the way that best serves his client, the people of the United States. His audience is not one hundred million people; his audience is nine people, or more specifically, nine Justices, all of them sophisticated, capable lawyers who are not about to be influenced by lectures or slogans. You just don't win cases that way.

"The law, especially constitutional law, is made incrementally, on a case-by-case basis. No lawyer worth his salt would think of going before the Supreme Court, or any appellate tribunal, and telling its members point blank that they were wrong on some case they decided just several years before, even if the lawyer strongly believes they were. That approach would simply not be in his client's best interest, and the reason is obvious: the Court as an institution would find it offensive. In a close case—as so many of the cases are in the Supreme Court—the lawyer's impertinence might well cost the client the one or two votes needed to win. It would therefore be both a tactical mistake and a professional violation of the lawyer's ethical duty to advance his client's cause. But more than that, it would deeply injure the Solicitor General's personal credibility with the Court, without which the government would cease to enjoy its remarkable success both in getting the Court to review its cases and in winning on the merits.

"And so my practical argument against those who would have the Solicitor General rail against the perceived excesses and errors of the Supreme Court is simply that it would be bad lawyering, period. And I think most lawyers, and certainly most seasoned litigators, would agree. In his speeches, in his writings, or, in later life, in the classroom (if that's where he ends up), the Solicitor General has the right of every citizen and the duty of every lawyer to speak his mind on the issues, and to say where he thinks the law is going and where it should be going. He has no business doing so as an advocate, however, and I challenge any scholars or researchers to find an example of a Solicitor General, beginning with

Benjamin Bristow in 1870, who has ever let politics or personal beliefs interfere with his advocacy in the Supreme Court." [43]

After Fried filed his brief, in July 1985, Lee toned down the text of the speech which he eventually delivered at Franklin and Marshall College. [44] While uncompromising about the Solicitor's need to preserve his "unique standing" with the Supreme Court, Lee went on, "This is not to say that it is never advisable for a Solicitor General to take a position that he knows the Court will reject. There could be long-range objectives to be served by such a filing. All I am saying is that there are large costs, and it is rarely advisable. In my four years I never did it," Lee said, "though I always held open the possibility that in a sufficiently compelling case I might." Lee restricted his disagreement with Fried to the area of tactics. At a conference about constitutional law in Washington, Lee said, "The one thing you learn as Solicitor General is how to count to five." [45] When he joined the Akron case as amicus, he believed that the Administration couldn't win five of the Court's nine votes to overturn Roe v. Wade, so he didn't asked the Court to consider it—even though he was highly critical of the ruling. The makeup of the bench hadn't changed since Fried took over as SG, so it made little sense to ask the Justices to abandon Roe. The plea detracted from the SG's credibility, because it gave the Justices the impression he was using the Supreme Court as a political forum; and it gave the Court the opportunity to reaffirm the holding in Roe v. Wade, yielding "one more recent precedent to fight." Lee said his remarks were not meant as a criticism of his successor. "These are difficult judgments to make," he said, "and they can only be made by the current Solicitor General."

In time, both Fried and the Attorney General addressed Lee's points, but they responded differently. Terry Eastland, Meese's spokesman at the Justice Department, acknowledged that a majority of Justices were not likely to take the government's line in the case. "But a brief can stimulate public discourse on an issue," he said when he was asked about the abortion case. "Notice the commentary . . . that's already out there now. It wouldn't be there except for our brief." [46] Eastland corroborated Lee's belief that some in the Reagan Administration wanted the SG to serve as a Pamphleteer General, using submissions in the Supreme Court to address the larger audience of voters beyond the capital.

Fried tried to keep discussion on a higher plane than that of a pamphlet. "Some legal conclusions are compelled by logic," he said, "and candor requires us to present them squarely to the Court. That's the duty of the government, don't you think?"[47] In the circle of lawyers who once served in the SG's office, Fried's line recalled a story about one of his predecessors, William Mitchell.[48] The SG was out for a stroll in Washington, and he met Justice Holmes on the street. "Mr. Solicitor General," the Justice said, "I admire your candor before our Court." As Mitchell drew himself up proudly, Holmes quickly added, "I have always thought that candor is the best form of deception."

As far as the SG's tradition was concerned, however, Fried insisted that his brief was business as usual: the commotion about it said more about his critics than about his views. At a speech to the Chamber of Commerce in Washington, Fried said, "I haven't discussed our brief in the abortion cases, and I'm not going to, but you might actually be interested to read it, and see whether it has any bearing on what I've said. The press, which does not like to read things, but prefers to call people up on the telephone and provoke them into indiscretions, called me a lot when the brief was filed, and they said, 'Well, what was the reason for you to take the position you did?' And that gave me the chance to say, 'You don't understand. A brief is not like a symphony. It's not like a directive. It's not even like a proclamation. A brief is nothing but reasons. And to ask "What are the reasons for your position?" is to ask "May I read it?" ' "[49]

During his remarks, Fried presented a sketch of the outlook informing his judgments as SG. He referred to Herbert Wechsler, his former professor at Columbia Law School, and a giant in the field of American constitutional law, who is noted especially for his theory of neutral principles related to the traditional idea of judicial restraint. In an essay published in 1959, Wechsler argued that unless courts could find reasons that were general and neutral enough to apply beyond the immediate case, they had no grounds for overturning the judgments of the other branches of government.[50] "I'm a reverent student of Herbert Wechsler," Fried volunteered, and he indicated that his abortion brief was an expression of his belief in neutral principles.

One of the scholars who read Fried's brief was Wechsler. "On balance," he said in February of 1986,[51] "my opinion is that the Solicitor General made a mistake in the abortion case. The recency of the reaffirmation of Roe v. Wade coupled with the fact that there had been no change in the membership of the Court suggested to me that the government was posturing rather than practicing good law when it asked for a complete re-examination of the issue. It's one of the oldest traditions of the Court, going way back to Chief Justice Taney, that the Court stands ready to reconsider its judgments if they are shown to be wrong. Over and over again, this has been done and the notion persists. But I can't really believe that Charlie Fried thought that this was an appropriate case for the Administration to ask the Court to restate the law. You've got to see the thing in long perspective. On the one hand, you've got the tradition that the Court is prepared to reexamine its decisions. And, on the other hand, that the Court considers that it speaks the last word in cases about interpreting the Constitution. Where to draw the line—between persistence and presumption—is more a matter of common sense than abstract thinking, and I think the Solicitor General was presumptuous in the abortion case."

Wechsler recalled, "I myself was in the SG's office during the late thirties and early forties, and I briefed and argued cases. I got the Court to overrule the Newberry case, in U.S. v. Classic.[52] That was a case which was crucial in doing away with lily-white primaries in Southern states. There had been ballot-stuffing in a Louisiana primary, and the Newberry case held that the election statute outlawing that kind of shenanigan didn't apply to primaries, but only to general elections. We got that overturned. Charles Evans Hughes was then Chief Justice, and he had been the winning counsel in Newberry. I had no reason to believe he would think differently as a judge, and I was happily surprised. We were engaged then in asking the Court to overturn a precedent, but how and when we did it marked the difference between persistence and presumption.

"Charlie Fried was a student of mine in the fifties, and a very brilliant fellow. I think his views as to what is right are close to Meese's. But I was surprised he took the job as Solicitor General, because he must have known he would confront the conflict between the office's and the Court's institutional values versus Administration policy. If Charlie Fried really believes that he has things to say about Roe v. Wade that have not been said, and that he has a fresh objection to the case that the Court might consider determinative, then he has a right to say it. But he's obviously a damn fool if he thinks he has anything to say that hasn't already been said."

The review of the government's brief that Fried favored was an article by the politically moderate Edwin Yoder that appeared in the Philadelphia *Inquirer.* [53] "Needless to say, it strikes me as an accurate and balanced discussion," the Solicitor General said about the piece. [54] Yoder is a syndicated columnist who has won a Pulitzer Prize for editorial writing, and he opened his assessment with a disclosure. "I can, for once, shed some first-hand light on a relationship that threatens to generate an obscuring excess of steam," he began. "Charles Fried, an old friend, has come to Washington from a distinguished teaching career to serve as U.S. Solicitor General—chief legal advocate—for the Reagan Administration. Fried is a kind, jolly, and brainy man. He is, however, addicted to dialectics as others are to bourbon or baseball. Those unaccustomed to his manner tend to find him contentious." Yoder's thesis, however, was that the "misimpressions" about the SG's brief had more to do with the abortion issue itself than with Fried's personality. "To argue that the Court should return the power to regulate abortion to the states, as Fried does, is not to argue for an outright ban on abortion," Yoder wrote. "In fact, the judicial debate is only secondarily about abortion."

From the vantage of the SG's office, and several lawyers whom Fried had inherited as members of the staff, the problem with Yoder's column was that it missed an essential fact. When the columnist hazarded that "the brief undoubtedly represents Fried's best thought on the law of abortion, not a pose forced on him by Attorney General Ed Meese" and that "[i]nsinuations to the contrary drastically underestimate Fried's commitment to principled debate and the Constitution," Yoder wrote with the confidence of an old friend and not, apparently, with the conviction held by many people in the SG's office: if Fried wanted to be named Solicitor General, and shed his conditional status as Acting SG, he had no choice about what position to take in the abortion case. [55]

In the speech that Edwin Meese gave to the American Bar Association where he discussed the government's submission in the abortion case, the Attorney General tied it to his primary initiative at the Justice Department.[56] A lawyer in the SG's office, who became one of Fried's main supporters after he was named Solicitor General, explained that Meese's expectations inside the Justice Department matched his public comments, and that Fried acted accordingly. "The Attorney General made it absolutely clear how far the government was going to go. Charles couldn't afford to give a hint of ambivalence about the position or he would have dropped out as a candidate for the post."[57]

Fried had a different view about his freedom as SG to write what he wanted. With longtime colleagues at Harvard Law School, he was cavalier. "I have no trouble saying what the Attorney General and his crew want me to, because I'm much more conservative than they are," he said.[58] When former Solicitor General Erwin Griswold, who had hired Fried for the Harvard faculty a quarter of a century before, expressed the view that the Acting SG's abortion brief so clearly flouted the deference of his office to the Court that it "apparently was filed pursuant to instructions," Fried called the Dean's comment "a shameful thing for him to say."[59] Another time, he said, "Anyone who says I was forced to write what I did in the abortion brief doesn't know what the hell he's talking about."[60] His vehemence was prompted by, among other things, a story in the *Wall Street Journal* ("Justice Department sources say Mr. Fried wasn't immediately nominated in June so department officials could test his willingness to advocate administration positions")[61] stating the view that was common in the SG's office and elsewhere at the Justice Department: to Meese and company, the abortion case was Fried's loyalty test.

ON THE MID-OCTOBER morning in 1985 when Charles Fried appeared before the Senate Judiciary Committee for his confirmation hearing, committee members came and went, and there were never more than a half-dozen present at any one time.[62] Of the committee's eighteen members, only ten took part in the proceedings. Fried said afterward, "The fix was in."[63]

Fried's testimony was careful and well prepared, and he controlled the give-and-take. "Mr. Chairman,"[64] he said, in answer to

a question from Strom Thurmond about his legal qualifications to be Solicitor General, "I think that of all the experience that I have had, that which qualifies me most, if I am qualified, is an experience I had twenty-five years ago, when it was my privilege to be law clerk to I think one of the finest Justices in the history of the Supreme Court, John Marshall Harlan, and I hope to carry his standards, and his values in my heart and mind, as I do this work." Like his invocation of Wechsler in speeches, Fried's reference to Harlan was shrewdly made, for Harlan was widely respected for his legal craftsmanship.

How did Fried plan to conduct himself if confirmed by the Senate?

"Nothing would be more important to me than to maintain that sense of confidence which I believe the Supreme Court has always had in the Office of the Solicitor General. That the Supreme Court can believe that the work that comes from the office represents the most objective, the most accurate, and the fairest presentation of the issues before it. To be sure, the Office of the Solicitor General is an advocate's office. Nevertheless, I think though we are the government's lawyer, we are also handmaidens to the Supreme Court, and the Supreme Court has always reposed a very special confidence in the quality of our work, in the accuracy of our work, and in the objectivity and restraint of our judgments, and I would hope very much to keep that up."[65]

What about the charges that "urging the abandonment of Roe versus Wade was an indication that the Office of the Solicitor General is being somewhat politicized?" Thurmond asked.

Fried answered, "Senator, I do not believe that our office has been politicized, and I would not wish to serve as Solicitor General in order to further a process of politicization. I suppose that the President has nominated me because he has some sense of what my philosophy is, and that philosophy enters my judgment of what the law is on a particular matter, and what arguments should be made. But certainly partisan political considerations have never entered into our judgments, never should enter into our judgments, and I would never allow them to enter into our judgments."

At one point, Joseph Biden, the senator from Delaware who was the committee's ranking Democrat, said, "I want to make sure you are rooted in Harlan and not in Meese. Do you understand my concern?"[66]

Fried replied deliberately, "I have been rooted in Harlan for a very long time."

A few days later, when told how comfortable he seemed answering questions from the committee, Fried scoffed, "These people don't have follow-up questions because they don't decide which questions to ask in the first place."[67] The quiet that greeted one of his remarks to the senators suggested the accuracy of his comment in this instance: either they knew little about the tradition of the Solicitor General, or were willing to accept Fried's recasting of it. "The office is, always has been, must remain independent," he said at the hearing. "I would like to explain what that means," Fried went on, "because the statutes and regulations which set up the Office of the Solicitor General plainly indicate that the Solicitor General is a subordinate official of the Attorney General. I think the original . . . 1870 statute speaks of the Solicitor General as a helper to the Attorney General, 'learned in the law.' Now, the way in which the Solicitor General serves the Attorney General, which he does, is by giving his own best independent judgment. That is how he renders that service. Now, the Attorney General does not have to accept that judgment, and he has got to make his own judgments, and that means that there will be occasions—there always have been and there will continue to be—in which the Attorney General, in rare cases, concludes that the judgment that his Solicitor General has given him is a judgment with which he does not concur, and in that event, he has the clear statutory authority to direct the Solicitor General to take a contrary position. There is no doubt about that."[68]

Until then, Fried's lesson had been unremarkable, a reading from a nuts-and-bolts chapter in a textbook. Then he turned the post of Solicitor General from a position of independence into the job of a good-natured mouthpiece.

When the Attorney General directs the Solicitor General to take a contrary position, Fried judged, "I think it would be *peevish* and *inappropriate* for the Solicitor General to be anything but *cheerful* in accepting that reversal."[69] His voice supplied the emphasis. He said that frequent reversals would give the SG "a right to wonder" whether the Attorney General had confidence in his judgment, and that the SG "should simply not" take a position "which he feels is influenced by improper factors, or, cannot conscientiously be urged to the Court," but the message he delivered most assertively was that he had already assumed a loyal position on the Reagan team.

Fried was also asked how the Justice Department determined its position in a case before the Supreme Court, and how he intended to resolve any differences of opinion within the Department. Again he gave a textbook answer. Some part of the government "will have won or lost a case in a court below, and will then request that our office take the matter to the Supreme Court." The request usually came on paper, and it was assigned to an assistant in the SG's office. "The assistants in the office are an extraordinary group of men and women," Fried said, "professional career lawyers of the highest degree of competence. That memorandum is then reviewed by one of the deputies who are even more remarkable than the assistants, and fewer in number, and that deputy and the assistants together make a recommendation to the Solicitor General, who then proceeds to make a final disposition whether the request of the agency or the department to bring a case to the Supreme Court will indeed go forward. If we determine it shall go forward, then we proceed to draft the papers, draft the brief, and argue the case." [70]

What Fried neglected to tell the committee—since he had never known the arrangement to be otherwise, he might not have thought there was any reason to mention it—was how differently from the textbook description the SG's office now worked. To anyone who knew about the change (none of the senators, apparently), Fried's answer sounded almost like part of a cover-up. He was frank about the deference he thought he owed the Attorney General (it would be "peevish" and "inappropriate" for the Solicitor to be anything but "cheerful" about taking orders from the AG), but he said nothing about how closely the Attorney General was keeping tabs on the SG's work. Nor did he refer to the agent selected for the task. The agent's name—William Bradford Reynolds—would have astounded at least the members of the Senate Judiciary Committee who had voted against his confirmation as Associate Attorney General four months before.

When Rex Lee was SG, Reynolds exercised influence far beyond his official status in deliberations about the government's position before the Supreme Court in civil rights cases, and many other cases where the President's agenda was at stake. Soon after Charles Fried replaced Lee, in June of 1985—and almost immediately after the Senate Judiciary Committee rejected Reynolds's promotion to Associate Attorney General—the civil-rights chief was rewarded for his past vigilance. The Attorney General announced he was giving Reynolds "important new duties" beyond his role as Assistant Attorney General and that he would be "part of our senior management team" with "a number of assignments."[71] Meese did not detail the new work, but he gave a large hint: Reynolds would operate on a par with the Deputy Attorney General and the Solicitor General, he said—above the rank of Assistant Attorney General and at the same level as Associate Attorney General. The arrangement had been set down in the memorandum describing what Reynolds's duties were supposed to be after he was confirmed as Associate AG. Reynolds could no longer use the Associate's post as a way station to becoming Solicitor General, as some of his allies in the Administration had planned he would and as many lawyers in the Justice Department and some senators on the Judiciary Committee expected him to do as well.[72] (Reynolds was asked, "Can you assure the Committee, that if you are appointed Solicitor General at a later date, you will come before the Committee for confirmation?")[73] But, instead of resigning, as some senators thought he should, Reynolds stayed on at the Justice Department. He was written up in a series of newspaper features in which the Attorney General praised Reynolds's "strength of character" and "tremendous statesmanship," and said how much he relied on his advice in a wide range of legal matters.[74] (In May 1987, Meese appointed Reynolds Counselor to the Attorney General, to supplement his title of Assistant Attorney General and finally make official the longtime close relationship between them.)

The week of the Fried hearing, and days before he was confirmed as SG, a lawyer in the SG's office reported matter-of-factly, "Reynolds now sits in on most meetings dealing with sensitive political cases."[75] One of Reynolds's assignments was to monitor Charles Fried's submissions as Solicitor General.

X

The Celestial
General

TO SOME CONNECTED with the SG's office, questions about their personal background seem beside the point. The details they like to talk about (where they went to law school, whom they clerked for, what cases they have argued before the Court) relate to the law. Louis Claiborne has a more spacious concept of autobiography. He has a handsome, weatherworn face, a dime-size scar on one cheek, and a charming, offhand manner, and he often wears casual clothes that give him the air of a man dressed for a summer evening on his porch. He is also a storyteller and his accent reveals his travels from New Orleans, where his family is from, to Europe, where he grew up, and from Washington, D.C., to London, between which he has shuttled half his life. In 1985, at fifty-eight, he was the oldest of five deputies. He had worked for six Solicitors and, within a tradition-minded institution, he was an institution himself.

"I theoretically come from Louisiana, but was in fact born in Europe and went to the University of Louvain, in Belgium—the Most Catholic University of Louvain—the head of which is usually called the Magnificent Rector, who is usually an Archbishop," Claiborne said in 1985.[1] "It was founded by Martin the Fifth, one of the Popes, or at least it was blessed by him, and mere attendance gives you something like a hundred days' indulgences in purgatory. As you can gather, I'm not a very good Catholic, but I was born Catholic and I went to the university not because it was Catholic but because it was meant to be the best university in Belgium. My father was an international banker representing a New York bank. He had been in Belgium before the war, which is why I was born there, in 1927, and he returned after the war, which is why I went to school there. I went there for a year, and did more social than academic things. Then went to the Science Politique in Paris, which was certainly more social than academic. That was three years. And then came back and went to Tulane Law School, which was the proper, traditional thing for me to do, being nominally from New Orleans, but not generally viewed anywhere outside Louisiana as a prime law school. I was blissfully unaware of that at the time.

"I practiced for a bit, and went into the local state district attorney's office, doing mostly appeals. Then there was a change in the local administration, and we in the reform group were removed for a more corrupt lot. I formed a little law firm and one of my cases took me to the Supreme Court of the United States in 1959, when I was thirty-one years old. It was called Louisiana Power & Light Company v. City of Thibodaux,[2] and it was an odd case. The city had expanded and annexed the territory next door. The city had a power authority of its own, but the new territory it was taking over was serviced by a private utility, the Louisiana Power & Light Company, and the city decided to appropriate the property of that company and integrate the system into its own. It invoked some relatively obscure Louisiana statute which seemed to cover the matter, but the Attorney General of Louisiana had ruled that it didn't. Anyway, it was not clear-cut what was the right answer. The case was removed to federal court, where J. Skelly Wright was then a district judge. He did what was unexpected from him of all people—he was not noted for his deference to state courts, because those were the days when Southern courts were pretty backward when it came to people's rights—and he abstained, and said this is a question of local law that ought to be settled by the Louisiana courts, and therefore required the parties to go to the Louisiana courts and find out what the answer was. Well, that stunned both sides, neither one of which had argued anything related. So the case went to the U.S. Court of Appeals for the Fifth Circuit, and that's the point at which I was brought into the case on behalf of the City of Thibodaux. I appeared before Judge Hutcheson, who was then a very senior judge in the Circuit, and he asked me how long I needed to argue the case. I said half an hour, or something like that, and he said, 'If I told you Wright was wrong, how long would you need?' I said, 'Five minutes,' argued, and he told me he'd heard enough. The judges decided promptly to reverse Wright, and said Wright must proceed to trial. Very nice for me.

"The Power & Light Company filed a petition with the Supreme Court, which decided to review the case. Once more the case fell to me, and I came to Washington and argued my first case, as a relatively new lawyer, before the Supreme Court. I prepared like mad and I argued the case, and on one side of the bench there was Felix Frankfurter, who thought I was twelve years old and treated me like a law student and had fun by doing a very academic exercise, and at the other end there was Hugo Black, who said 'I don't know about the points of my brother Frankfurter, but doesn't it make sense to let the state courts figure this out? The Attorney General of the state couldn't make head nor tail of it, and Judge Wright couldn't—isn't it common sense to leave it to the state courts?' So I had common sense and academia against me, and my chances were very poor. In the end, I did get three votes— from Brennan, Douglas, and Warren.

"The performance apparently amused Frankfurter, and the next time he saw Skelly Wright, he said, 'Who's this young lawyer from New Orleans?' To which Skelly Wright said, 'Never heard of him.' Frankfurter told him he ought to do better and know the people in his jurisdiction who were up and coming and all that, and why didn't he try to persuade me to come and clerk for him. Wright wasn't interested in hiring me, and I wasn't interested in clerking, but we agreed, for the sake of Frankfurter, to try it out for six months. It lasted two years. We got along fine. In the meantime, the desegregation crisis had arisen and I was helpful to him. Thanks to Wright's strong stand on desegregation—he was famous for his fight against the powers of Louisiana to get them to comply with Brown v. Board of Education—the move to get him the hell out of New Orleans, where he was stirring too much trouble, and promote him to the Fifth Circuit, where his influence would be diluted, or, even better, to the District of Columbia Circuit, where he'd be out of harm's way, became very popular. Bobby Kennedy, who was by then Attorney General, and Jack Kennedy acquiesced in this latter idea, which was a promotion for the judge and meant getting somebody more tractable in the district court in Louisiana. The judge wanted me to remain his clerk in Washington, but I thought the time had come to move on.

"Louis Oberdorfer, who is now a trial judge in Washington and was head of the Tax Division at the Justice Department and a great friend of Bobby Kennedy's, came down to New Orleans just about then, and Skelly Wright persuaded me to invite him to dinner, which I did. Over dinner, Oberdorfer suggested I join the Solicitor General's office. I'd never heard of the Solicitor General, and I wasn't particularly interested in a government job, and I wasn't interested in Washington, but Oberdorfer kept on about it and Skelly Wright said what a glorious opportunity this was, so finally I found out that somebody called Archibald Cox was the Solicitor General and I wrote myself a letter to Cox saying that Louie Oberdorfer had suggested I might be interested in a position under him. I got a very swift note back from Archie Cox telling me that Mr. Oberdorfer was head of the Tax Division, and if I wanted to work for the Justice Department, perhaps I should apply to the Tax Division, and that he was *the Solicitor General*, and he didn't need Oberdorfer as a scout making offers for his office.

"There were a few vacancies, because a longtime staffer named Oscar Davis had just gone on the Court of Claims, and another named John Davis—not *the* John Davis—had just become Clerk of the Supreme Court. By now, we're in early spring of 1962. I was rather annoyed at Cox's rebuff, having decided that I did want the job, so I was as stubborn as Cox. I got John Minor Wisdom, who became a great Fifth Circuit Judge, and Skelly Wright, and others to write on my behalf, but it produced very little—a halfway polite correspondence. Ultimately, I was invited to come up for an interview, but I didn't get much more out of Cox than a suggestion that I go into training for a year with the Tax Division. At which point, Skelly Wright alerted Frankfurter to this impasse, and apparently Frankfurter picked up the phone and told Cox that he had no choice but to hire me. Frankfurter, being Harvard Incarnate, overcame the prime objection, which was that I wasn't from Harvard, or even Columbia, which is where many of the lawyers in the SG's office had come from until then. There's an unproved belief among staff lawyers that I was the first non–Ivy Leaguer ever hired by an SG. What is more, most of the people Cox took had been Supreme Court clerks, as opposed to a clerk for a district judge, and they had been a year or two training at Covington & Burling, or some such fancy place, and had started it all on the *Law Review*. I didn't fit any of these. When Frankfurter told Cox 'Never mind all that,' Cox swallowed hard and reluctantly agreed that he would take the enormous risk. We in fact got along fine.

"When Cox left, in the summer of '65, there was a farewell party, at which three people said very different things, but all of them appropriate for Cox. One of them was Hugo Black, one was Bobby Kennedy, and one was a fellow named Ralph Spritzer, who had been Cox's first deputy, even though we didn't have titles like that in those days because there were only nine lawyers in the office, including the Solicitor General. What Hugo Black said about Cox was what Hugo Black thought about this office. A slightly exaggerated view, but still. He said Cox had distinguished himself in this office because he had not been 'the attorney for the parochial interests of the federal government but the lawyer of the people of the United States.' Bobby Kennedy told the story of his brother calling him up to ask for a legal opinion. 'I'll get right on it,' Bobby said. 'No, Bobby,' the President explained. 'You don't understand. I want a *legal* opinion. *Ask Archie.* He's the Solicitor General.' It was all said very nicely. Ralph Spritzer, in a more serious vein, said, 'There is only one word that describes Archie Cox. That is *rectitude.*' A very old-fashioned word, but it was true. Cox's own comment to me at this gathering was that he had thought when he was so brave as to take me on that I might end up as Cox's Folly, but that it had turned out all right. That was as generous as you could get from Archibald Cox, who was the best Solicitor General I ever worked for."

Another lawyer at the SG's office said about Claiborne, "He's of the Skelly Wright school: You do what you think is right." Though Wright was an activist liberal judge, who believed that the role of law is to serve human ends, he tried to place decisions he reached in the line of legal principles on which he drew. In legal terms, he tried to make sure that "the doctrine lined up."[3] Claiborne came early in a long string of gifted lawyers who worked for the judge as a law clerk (from 1975 through 1985, Wright was the only lower-court judge in the country who sent all his aides—

thirty of them—on to clerk at the Supreme Court),[4] and he was schooled by the judge in this practice.

Claiborne made his mark as a young assistant to the Solicitor General arguing cases dealing with problems of race. An early case of his was reported by Tom Kelly, a columnist for the Washington Daily News.[5] "Mr. Claiborne," Kelly wrote, "stood in his braided frock coat, slim as a sword cane, his manner as aristocratically militant as General Pierre Gustave Toutant Beauregard, and his voice as Southern as Terrebonne Parish." In Claiborne's native Louisiana, blacks could register to vote in the southern parishes "as easily as they sign up to cut cane." But in the northern parishes they had been "discouraged from voting so well that in West Feliciana [no black had been] on the rolls for ten years." Between 1956 and 1958, the registrars in the northern parishes and some white groups known as "citizens councils" had purged about thirty thousand blacks from the voting rolls. No whites had been removed. To get back on, blacks had to pass a test that whites were not required to take. Claiborne told the Court, "Any test is harder than no test." He also quoted the late Governor Earl Long speaking to the state legislature: "There ain't ten people looking at me, including myself, who, if attacked, could qualify to vote."

On the list of parishes before the Supreme Court was Claiborne Parish. Justice Arthur Goldberg asked the attorney about it. "I regret to say Claiborne Parish is one of the worst," the Daily News quoted Claiborne as saying. "It is named after my great-great grandfather who was the first Governor of Louisiana." The paper had skipped a generation. "An upwardly mobile pol," Claiborne called his great-great-great grandfather. The story was that Aaron Burr and Thomas Jefferson received the same number of electoral votes to be President in 1800. Those were the days the candidate with the most votes became President and the runner-up Vice-President. Jefferson and Burr agreed to run as a team, with Burr expecting to serve as Jefferson's second. When the vote came in tied, Burr reneged, and the election was thrown into the House of Representatives. On the thirty-sixth ballot, Jefferson was elected President and Burr Vice-President, and, not long after, Congress proposed the Twelfth Amendment to the Constitution, which provided for separate balloting for the two offices.

One of the deciding votes for Jefferson was cast by Claiborne's forebear, William Charles Cole Claiborne, who was then under twenty-five years old and therefore unconstitutionally representing Tennessee. His payoff was an appointment as Governor of Mississippi and, a few years later, when he was twenty-eight, he became the first non-French Governor of Louisiana.[6] Tom Kelly, who wrote the column about the parish voting case, kept up with Claiborne long after. "My wife is a sprig off the old aristocracy of New Orleans," Kelly said in 1985, "and she's always said that the Claibornes are the first family of Louisiana society."[7]

Claiborne's genealogy has exotic shoots as well as deep Louisiana roots. His brother Omer sells primitive art and antiques in Santa Fe.[8] His sister is Liz Claiborne, and in her world Louis is the one who needs an introduction. In 1976, Liz and her husband founded a women's clothing company named after her. On the strength of its elegant line, the company took less than a decade to climb into the Fortune 500 with over half-a-billion dollars of sales.[9]

In 1970, after eight years of arguing civil rights cases, Louis Claiborne left the SG's office for the first time. He said, "I left with a pull and a push."[10] The push was his sense after a year working for the Nixon Administration that his role in shaping arguments before the Supreme Court had been diminished. He was not the only valued lawyer to leave the SG's office during the Nixon years. The impression given by some senior Administration officials that they considered themselves above the law prompted rapid turnover in the SG's office. At one point, Erwin Griswold noticed that he was the only lawyer left who had graduated from Harvard Law School. At a dinner for his staff, the former Harvard dean went around the table introducing everyone by his credentials. When he came to Claiborne, he said, "And then there's Louie. Louie and I are the Alpha and Omega of the office. I won't say which is which."[11]

The pull was that Claiborne had an English wife who wanted to go home. The Ford Foundation had offered him a fellowship to write about the law, and he took it. "Three or four years later," Claiborne said, "I became a barrister and practiced for a few years with modest success."

In the mid-seventies, Claiborne began to come back to the SG's office during summers to make some extra money by filling in for lawyers on vacation. Once, he arrived before the close of Term and had the chance to argue a case in the Supreme Court. With a nudge from a colleague,[12] he proposed a departure from the SG's traditional garb. He had already set himself apart from other men in the office by buying his own formal outfit. (Most pass around five sets of hand-me-down gear, distinguished by size and wear and tear; they put on the one that fits best and, fastened in with safety pins, appear elegant only when they are viewed from a generous distance.)[13] With his own sense of folderol, Claiborne had another thought.

He explained: "I was a full-fledged barrister. The rules of the bar of England and Wales are that whenever you appear, whether in Great Britain or at a distant bar, you must always appear in the wig and gown. Using that as a pretext, I called Warren Burger's chambers at the Supreme Court and asked if I could have audience with him. His secretary was rather testy, so I told her it was to talk about a subject dear to the Chief Justice's heart: proper dress in the courtroom for lawyers. He called me back immediately, all ears. By way of asking him if I could appear in my wig and gown, I told him about the British rules. Then he said that he himself should be in a wig and gown, and had been cheated out of it by Thomas Jefferson. I didn't follow, so he told me about an exhibit in the Supreme Court lobby showing Chief Justice John Jay in a magnificent red robe, with a proper gentleman's wig. It followed that Burger should be so adorned, and would be, if Jefferson hadn't changed the rules. I wasn't sure whether he was being humorous or not, but I brought him back to my predicament, and asked him what I should do. He said he thought it was entirely appropriate for me to appear in my wig and gown, but warned that others might disagree. I went down to the Solicitor General's office—he was then Bob Bork—and told about this conversation. He said I had been a damn fool to ask permission, that I should have just done it. In any case, discretion got the better part of valor: I, not forbidden either by the Chief Justice or the Solicitor General, decided to go back to the standard getup of the SG, and so I did."[14]

In 1978, Claiborne returned full-time to the SG's office. He was put in charge of cases rising from the Environmental Protection Agency, the Department of the Interior, and the Lands Division at the Department of Justice, dealing with Indian affairs, environmental questions, and so on. "My cases dealt with the land and the water and the air," he said. The subject appealed to his sense of grandeur, and it fit his arch prose. "With this decision," he wrote about a case dealing with a lagoon near Venice, California, over which the state had exercised authority he thought it didn't have,[15] "the California Supreme Court appears enthusiastically to have embraced a new legal Renaissance, in which modern 'humanists' rediscover old texts and invoke the distant past to liberate the spirit from the confining 'shackles' of a more conventional era. But we are not witnessing Petrarch, mildly unorthodox in reviving Cicero, or Boccaccio retelling irreverent stories borrowed from Ovid. Here, the half-forgotten ancient models are the codes of the Emperor Justinian and Alfonso the Wise of Castile, the Magna Carta wrested from King John and the treatise of Henry de Bracton. We may question whether such a revolution, not in literature or philosophy, but in the law of property, even on the claim of returning to an earlier wisdom, is equally to be applauded."

Claiborne also took responsibility for an area known as original jurisdiction. It was a classic SG assignment: becoming expert in a hidden area of the law that can have deep importance to the parties before the Court. (According to the *Stanford Law Review*,[16] the Justices decided 123 cases under original jurisdiction between 1789 and 1957, for an average of between one and two a Term, but even the Supreme Court does not know how many OJ cases have now been before the Justices.)[17] Though Claiborne was linked to Judge Skelly Wright as a liberal activist, and was sometimes accused by colleagues of taking liberties with the law to see justice done, original jurisdiction showed him to be as meticulous a craftsman as anyone in the SG's office. "Louie's one of those gemstones with a number of facets not all of which you'd expect on the same rock," a former assistant to the SG said.[18]

"In all cases affecting Ambassadors, other public Ministers and Consuls, and those in which a State shall be a party," the Constitution reads, "the Supreme Court shall have original jurisdiction." The idea was that cases about the structure of the federal government or controversies between the United States and foreign countries should be resolved by a tribunal worthy of the parties before it. Because diplomats have immunity from most lawsuits, only three cases involving Ambassadors have arisen,[19] but OJ cases have raised serious questions about the relationship between the states and the federal government.

In recent years, the big OJ cases have involved disputes about America's offshore boundaries, because the limits on the territorial lines of the United States determine where states can allow drilling for oil and gas, and huge sums of money (three billion dollars in some cases) are at stake. By coincidence, given Claiborne's native state and his expertise, a good number of conflicts involved Louisiana and its craggy, inverted coast. For many years, the Solicitor General has delegated OJ cases to one lawyer. The part calls for thinking and writing about arcane notions that change little over long spans of time, and the Supreme Court almost always takes the lawyer's advice. Out of the limelight, Louis Claiborne became the world's leading expert on original jurisdiction.[20]

The Solicitor General who asked Claiborne to pick up the OJ brief was Wade McCree, in the Carter Administration. Claiborne admired his commitment to the SG's office. "He was very conscious of the independence of the office. He never hesitated to make the decision that might well stir questions. He took the position that, as SG, you didn't need to seek permission for a judgment, you just made it. Nobody would have dared ask him to fudge his views."[21]

When the Reagan Administration came in, and Rex Lee became SG, Claiborne wondered what his impact on the office would be. "Frankly, I was apprehensive, not because it was Rex Lee, but because it was a new Administration. But I was pleasantly surprised to find Lee extraordinarily likable and pretty clear about maintaining the independence of the office. He even took the advice of the civil servants, for which he was hounded. One assumes that some of the grumbling voiced in the legal press represented the views of the political leaders: that he was too timid about forcing the President's agenda in the Supreme Court, that he preferred to tap on the door instead of kicking it down. Unlike any other Administration, with the possible exception of the Kennedy Administration, this one has a clear idea where it wants to go and thinks it sees how to get there. The law is one of the obvious tools, and the Supreme Court is an obvious forum, and it's quite unacceptable for the Solicitor General or anyone else to filter the message."

Soon after Lee arrived, he arranged a breakfast so that Attorney General William French Smith could meet the Deputy SGs. He asked each one to say something about his background and responsibilities. "When my turn came," Claiborne said, "I told him I was a holdover from the Thomas Jefferson Administration. French Smith apparently lacked my sense of humor: he looked as if I had just uttered an obscenity. An aide leaned over and said, 'He means Kennedy,' not knowing about my comings and goings during most of the Nixon era as well, and that was worse."

In the fall of 1981, Claiborne caused Lee what the SG later called his "first major crisis." [22] "Here was a case that shows the unpredictable twists that there are more of in the Reagan Administration than in any other," [23] Claiborne recalled. In Nevada, a federal district judge had parceled out water rights to the Carson River. An irrigation project had diverted water from that and another river, "to increase irrigation for Sunday farmers who waste water at a scandalous rate," Claiborne said, and, because of the project, water had fallen in Pyramid Lake, "which is a great natural wonder." The drop had jeopardized the fishery of the Pyramid Lake Paiute Indian tribe.

In the Alpine case, as it was called, the government originally argued that the farmers were entitled to no more water for irrigation than certain long-term contracts provided. The trial judge ruled that the farmers could take as much water as they needed. "That was a preposterous notion that ought to have agitated the Department of the Interior," Claiborne recalled, "but it chose not to appeal the case." Senator Paul Laxalt, the Republican from Nevada, also urged the government not to appeal. Laxalt wrote a "Dear Bill" letter to William French Smith:

RE: ALPINE APPEAL

While it's fresh in my mind . . .

—This has immense political overtones out there. All those ranchers—who are our friends—feel they're finally going to get some relief from this Administration. To have to go through the legal expense and hassle of an appeal will be a real "downer" for them.

And:

—If Rex's shop thinks the Indians can intervene, let them. Even have Justice assist in fulfillment of whatever fiduciary responsibility exists, if any. Then at least the monkey won't be on our political backs.

—Lastly, this would be a badly needed signal—that in a proper case the Attorney General will overrule the careerists in Justice who have never been with us and will never be. [24]

Having the man known as President Reagan's best friend on Capitol Hill serve as a lobbyist for the farmers put extraordinary pressure on Lee. But the Solicitor General took the advice of Claiborne and another lawyer, and appealed. He lost.

In an internal memo recommending that the Solicitor General join the Indians in asking the Supreme Court to consider the case, Claiborne wrote, "It is, of course, arguable here—as in most cases—that 'enough is enough' and that we ought not to pursue a hopeless cause, however meritorious, to the bitter end when four judges below have rejected our arguments. But, needless to say, there can be no such inflexible rule." [25] Though the Department of the Interior had "never favored" the SG with "a complete report," there were "at least 350 *recent*" cases in which the trial judge's ruling in favor of the farmers would raise serious problems. If the judge's decision stood, the amount of water available for the Pyramid Lake fishery would be diminished. If the government pulled out of the case, the Indians would not be represented in the case, since the tribe had failed to gain permission to intervene. To Claiborne's mind, the U.S. government was "not as free as otherwise we might be to abandon ship, leaving the tribal interest to sink uncaptained." The memo was initialed in Claiborne's Declaration of Independence–worthy hand: a swooping "LC."

While Rex Lee believed that the Court of Appeals had been wrong to favor the farmers, he also thought that the holding had limited importance. He approved the request of the Indians to intervene as a formal party, but opposed their petition asking the Supreme Court to take the case. The Justices declined certiorari, and the case rested as the lower courts had decided. "In the Court of Appeals, Rex did the bold thing," Claiborne said, "and stayed with the case. But he learned the wrong lesson. Instead of realizing his independence, he figured he should be more politically sensitive. In those days, with James Watt running the Interior Department, they wanted to give away the store: to grant mineral leases that should not have been; to grant leases at lower royalties than was warranted; to let developers exploit land instead of preserving it in its natural state; to let oil companies drill on the outer continental shelf, on the theory that the United States should be independent of Arab oil. They wanted to favor the white farmer over Indian tribes regardless of legal rights. They cut corners in indefensible ways."[26]

Claiborne had never interpreted his responsibility as a lawyer in the SG's office to mean he should engage in no-holds-barred advocacy for either the Administration in power or the government. He sometimes gave what he called "my lecture on the self-destructive habits of the American legal establishment, both lawyers and 'jumped-up lawyers' sitting on the Bench, calculated to bring the law into disrepute by encouraging needless complexity, indulging in undue prolixity and tolerating endless procedural maneuvering," in the service of unjust results. He took the lecture to heart. A case about the decision to restart a nuclear power plant in Pennsylvania, after another one partially melted down in the 1979 accident known as Three Mile Island, particularly bothered him. Claiborne's judgment about the slowness of the nuclear regulatory process convinced him to support the government's position that the plant should go on line again. In an internal memo with his recommendation, he explained "that our system permits scandalously protracted and costly proceedings, even at the administrative level, and the consequence of acquiescing in the present decision would be to delay restart for much too long." But he also said, "Accordingly, I must agree that we should ask the Supreme Court to announce a rule that no non-lawyer will ever understand: that THE LAW does not care whether people living next door to a nuclear power plant, whose twin has recently gone bad, lose their peace of mind (or even their sanity), their family harmony, their community cohesion, or their property values. As it happens, the prospects of the High Court so ruling are very good.

And so," he concluded, "I cannot counsel against seizing the opportunity to win a predictable 'victory.' " The government won the Court's unanimous backing. [27]

As the Alpine case suggested, the problems created for the SG's office during the Reagan Administration were often of a different order. With William Bradford Reynolds setting the example, Claiborne's adversaries in the Environmental Protection Agency, the Lands Division of the Justice Department, and the Department of the Interior pressed the Solicitor General to approach the law as radically as they did. Claiborne said, "In the past, more often than not, when an assistant to the Solicitor General or a deputy disagreed with other parts of the government, he could persuade them to go along. He was that much better a lawyer, and they respected his judgment about the law. In the Reagan years, if there has been disagreement, the SG has been seen as a pushover. It's often been done nicely, but still, Lee didn't like to say no to the political appointees. Maybe he felt vulnerable because of all the carping from the New Right. He wanted to show himself as independent of the careerists. But everything became a controversy, and it made for a lot more work. The truth is that nine out of ten times this office got it right. That's our job. The telling point was the predictability with which the staff, when they wanted to hold the line, lost ground because of the Solicitor General. The old-time practice in the SG's office usually succeeded at keeping politics at bay. The Reagan style seemed to accent the politics, and sometimes made the law an afterthought. In the end, I think Lee was quite happy to call it a day and be free of the nagging from both sides. I doubt he had a single day of peace." [28]

In the fall of 1985, Claiborne announced he was retiring from the SG's office. The fun had gone out of the job for him, he said, and his wife was eager to move back to England. The last argument he made on behalf of the government came in December. The case was called U.S. v. Maine, No. 35, Original Jurisdiction, but Maine had long since dropped out of the case, so the cover of the SG's brief included a parenthesis identifying it as a Massachusetts boundary case. [29] The more accessible of the questions before the Court was whether, under a doctrine called "ancient title," the waters of Nantucket Sound qualified as "high seas" or as inland waters, as

Massachusetts insisted. The more remote of the questions dealt with the standard of evidence the Justices should impose.[30]

Before the argument, in his morning coat, a starched white shirt, and a striped silver tie, Claiborne admitted,[31] "It's of no practical importance, unless they find gold there, or buried treasure. The truth is that the case is still before the Court because of an ambiguity that arose through an accident of timing. When the last decision was shaped, one law clerk to the Court's special master wrote the first part but couldn't finish before his year ended. Another wrote the second, and therein lies the problem." The two clerks had adopted different theories of the case, according to Claiborne, and confused a special master appointed by the Justices to help resolve the case on a key point of law.

The government's brief was vintage Claiborne.[32] "In light of our acquiescence in the Special Master's recommendation that Vineyard Sound be declared part of the inland waters of Massachusetts, the only issue now before the Court is whether the waters of Nantucket Sound also qualify as inland (as the Commonwealth asserts), or, rather, constitute territorial sea and high seas (the Master's conclusion, which we support)." And: "That single question, alas, has spawned a dozen sub-issues and no lack of words, some apparently self-contradictory and many of them wide of the mark as it seems to us. Our endeavor will be to put the case back on track in as short a space as possible."

In his argument before the Justices, as well as his brief, Claiborne tried to do that and he eventually won the case.[33] His opposing counsel was Henry Herman, a lawyer for Massachusetts who also made a well-spoken presentation. After the argument, while Claiborne was catching his breath in the SG's office at the Supreme Court, Herman knocked on the door and asked Claiborne if he was free to meet later for a drink. They made a date, and the Massachusetts lawyer said, "The Great Claiborne. I've always wanted to argue a case against you, and now I have."[34]

Several weeks before, at the Officers' Club of Fort McNair in Washington, many current and former members of the SG's office had gathered for an event labeled "A Farewell Buffet upon his Departure to Reside in England," in Claiborne's honor.[35] A quartet of SGs (Erwin Griswold, Robert Bork, Rex Lee, and Charles

Fried) made generous remarks about Claiborne, and then Claiborne spoke. He offered a challenge for the future instead of nostalgia. He had written out his remarks in longhand on small sheets of buff-colored paper, in stanzas of blank verse, and, in bright yellow Magic Marker, had highlighted the words he wanted to stress.[36] "I fear that most of you are here under some *deception*," he began, "that I am about to *fade* into the wilds of Essex, never to be seen again on this side of the Atlantic. Which perhaps argues for a last look at this disappearing species, and certainly explains the extravagant remarks I have heard this evening: they were obviously spoken in the firm expectation that their truth would never be tested." He announced his intention to begin a transatlantic practice as a private counselor. ("Louis Fenner Claiborne, onetime public and private practitioner in Louisiana, sometime common lawyer at the bar of England and Wales, longtime Deputy Solicitor General of the United States, is now resuming the occasional private practice of law before the American appellate courts and international tribunals [standing, sitting or off-stage parts],"[37] read the formal announcement he soon mailed: it came with a Claiborne sonnet titled "Have Quill, Will Travel," which argued that it was not foolhardy to hire a lawyer based in England ["Why care about proximity today?/Concorde exists and so does Express Mail"] to argue in the United States Supreme Court, and ended: "If this be puffery, make the most of it./Or, better still, reward the joke of it.") Eventually, he shifted to a more serious tone.

"So far as my education in the law is concerned," he said, "I am proud to say that my principal post-graduate tutor was Judge Skelly Wright, who is here tonight." Judge Wright's health was poor, and though he had not yet notified the President, he had decided to take senior status as a judge. The Reagan Administration would be able to name a replacement who would give the President's appointees a conservative majority on the D.C. Circuit, which, two decades before, Wright had helped make the most liberal in the country. "For better or worse, he is responsible for my coming to the Solicitor General's office some twenty-three years ago," Claiborne continued. "With such a tutor, it follows that I was raised right, as they say in the South, and have, by and large, behaved accordingly. For me, it is too late in the day to cast off what we call the Old Humility in order to take up the New Arrogance that now prevails. And so I leave with no reluctance."

Claiborne asked a young member of the SG's staff to fetch a large, oddly shaped crate, made from cardboard boxes used by laundries to pack clean shirts, and went on, "So you will not forget me too quickly, I have something to leave behind, which I hope the new Solicitor General will put on display, perhaps in his office. The object inside the box is one of a very rare species called *Egretta Caelesis Generalis*. You will notice its pure white coat and its aloof stance. Originally, I painted him showing only his left profile, but, in deference to the times, I decorated the other side as well. He is therefore reversible, but he will not bend or stoop for anyone. I am encouraged to think that my creation bears a strong resemblance to the next Solicitor General. But, just in case, I leave him behind to watch over you all."

To understand Claiborne's gift, it was necessary to know a story from the SG's past. Robert Jackson was Solicitor General before becoming Attorney General and then a Justice on the Supreme Court. Justice Louis Brandeis thought that Jackson was so skilled an advocate he should be made SG for life.[38] During Jackson's tenure, a letter addressed simply to "The Celestial General, Washington, D.C.," found its way to him.[39] Until the Reagan Administration, the lofty title was an emblem of the Solicitor General among lawyers in the office.

Out of the box Charles Fried took a wooden cutout of an erect white egret, of the Celestial General species. The room filled with delighted clapping, and brows were raised in mild astonishment. Fried was momentarily speechless.

XI

Charles Fried

CHARLES FRIED'S DÉBUT as Solicitor General was a
celebration of the Reagan Right. It took place at the Hyatt Re-
gency Hotel at the foot of Capitol Hill one November night, and
it was convened not in honor of Fried but as an event called
"Saluting an American Hero: A Tribute to Wm. Bradford Reynolds."[1] The buffet for Louis Claiborne a few weeks before had
been a quiet affair dedicated to memories and tradition. The Reynolds salute was a campaign rally, a great time, an exercise in
forgetting. The pretext was the presentation to Reynolds of the
Winston Churchill Award, but the hum of voices, the glee and
rounds of applause, brought to mind a giddy political roast where
all the speakers had been guaranteed they could say whatever they
wanted about their absent nemeses with no ill consequences. The
tables were set with lilies, the head table was draped in red so it
would show up well on TV, and about six hundred people gathered in a large hall to let the world know, as the evening's host put
it, "When anyone attacks Brad Reynolds, they're attacking us."[2]

The host was Burton Yale Pines. He is chairman of the National Center for Public Policy Research, the group that sponsored
the dinner, and a vice-president of the Heritage Foundation, of
which the Center for Public Policy Research is a neutrally named
part, and he gave the welcome to the network of New Righters,
Religious Righters, Cultural Conservatives, Pro-Lifers, and others
who helped pay for the party: Joseph and Holly Coors, whose
family controls Coors beer; the Liberty Institute; World Youth
Crusade for Freedom; National Pro-Life PAC; National Right to
Life Committee; and other organizations whose names filled a

page in the evening's program.[3] In the audience, among others, were former civil rights lawyers who had become allies of Reynolds while working on cases with the Justice Department, and who paid fifty dollars each to show their admiration. Some realized they had crossed a line by attending the dinner. "Coming here was harder than it would have been to tell my mom I'd come out of the closet," one said, with an embarrassed laugh. "I'd just as soon people didn't know I was here."[4]

The master of ceremonies was Representative Henry Hyde, a Republican from Illinois, whose amiable liberal-bashing set the evening's tone. "One of the senators that gave Brad rather an unpleasant time over in the Upper Chamber, as we laughingly call it—I don't want you to think he was liberal, but I once asked him what he thought of the Indianapolis 500, and he said, 'They're not guilty!' "

Congressman Hyde initiated the list of Reynolds's virtues, and others took the next several hours to fill it out: courage; integrity; brilliance; idealism; patriotism; morality; incandescence; faithfulness to public service; commitment to important and traditional values; conservatism; warmth; genuineness; honesty; painstaking concern; humanitarianism; humor; and, the evening's theme, heroism.[5] Hyde also read a telegram from Ronald Reagan, who declared that "Brad has fought the good fight with energy, enthusiasm, and an unflinching commitment to the principle of equality under the law." His "dedication to justice, to professional excellence, and to civil rights for all Americans is a shining example for public servants." The President told everyone that "Nancy joins me in sending best wishes for a memorable event," and signed his greeting, "God bless you."

On the dais sat a rainbow coalition of Reagan conservatives: Roy Innis, black chairman of the Congress of Racial Equality; Madeleine Will, Assistant Secretary of Education in charge of services for the handicapped; Clarence Pendleton, chairman of the U.S. Civil Rights Commission; Senator Orrin Hatch; and Attorney General Edwin Meese. Pendleton was the most prominent black in the Reagan Administration, and he summarized the Reagan-Meese-Reynolds line on civil rights. He took as his text a passage from Rousseau.

"People once accustomed to masters are no longer in condition to do without them," he read. "If they try to shake off the yoke, they still move farther away from freedom, because they confuse it with an unbridled license and their revolutions nearly always deliver them into the hands of seducers who only make their chains heavier than before." The specific "yokes and chains" he had in mind were goals and timetables in affirmative action. He ended, "Brad, I'm proud to be your colleague and your friend, and together we will make this country a place where, as Langston Hughes once said in a poem, 'Freedom,' where 'Freedom is just the frosting on someone else's cake, till we learn how to bake.' Let's turn the ovens on, Brad!"

Hatch made the keynote speech. He asserted that the Senate Judiciary Committee owed Reynolds a deep apology. He made no mention of the reasons that had led a majority of the members, including two Republicans, to doubt Reynolds's truthfulness and commitment to the law. Hatch joked that the Democrats had voted against Reynolds to keep him on the civil-rights watch. He also suggested that they had "tarred and feathered" Reynolds. The Assistant Attorney General's was the "toughest" confirmation hearing Hatch had ever taken part in, and during it "Brad sat stoic as a bust at Mount Rushmore." Hatch stated that Reynolds had done "more than anyone to shape civil-rights policies in the United States since Abraham Lincoln."

When Reynolds spoke, he sounded shy and almost wary. The day before, the Washington *Post* had run a story under the banner "REYNOLDS SAYS HE'S BEEN TO THE MOUNTAINTOP," in which he advised that he was extending the tradition of Martin Luther King, Jr., and other civil-rights leaders of the nineteen-sixties. "I was pretty much in lockstep with that whole effort," he said.[6] At the tribute, Reynolds did not mention Dr. King. He called the event "a great affair," and identified himself as a "foot soldier" in Reagan's army. His "battle scars acquired in our struggle to preserve for all Americans those fundamental ideals that distinguish this country from all others" were "badges of honor." Reynolds also invoked Lincoln. "Let every man remember that to violate the law," he read without irony from the President's words, "is to trample on the blood of his father, and to tear the character of his own, and of his children's liberty."

As part of the program before Reynolds spoke, his onetime aide and Assistant Attorney General–designate, Charles Cooper, offered ornate reflections on "the contemporary state of the 'public man.' "[7] The quote was from a 1760 speech by James Otis denouncing the British. Reynolds was cast as an American revolutionary. "The only principles of public conduct that are worthy of a gentleman," Cooper pronounced with Otis's help, "are to sacrifice estate, ease, health, applause, and even life, to the sacred calls of his country." In Cooper's eyes, Reynolds had met this standard. He was "an honorable man who has had his integrity called into question." He was "a sensitive and friendly man who was cruelly defamed, excoriated, and ridiculed." Skipping to the words of Edmund Burke, Cooper said that the "slander" was all right: "obloquy is a necessary ingredient in the composition of all true glory"; "calumny and abuse are essential parts of triumph. . . . He may live long, he may do much more; but here is the summit: he never can exceed what he does this day." Cooper paused to let his words sink in, and, in a hushed voice, finished, "Brad, dear friend, here is the summit."

Charles Fried introduced Cooper. To most of the lawyers in the Solicitor General's office, few of whom were invited to the dinner or later heard about Fried's appearance, it would have been an enlightening performance. Among staffers in the SG's office, Cooper was known for his hot temper and his habit of fighting to the limit on every issue.[8] Like Reynolds, his friend and compatriot from the Bob Jones team, Cooper seemed to see every case involving a disagreement between the Civil Rights Division and the SG's office under Rex Lee as a test of will. Fried noted only that Cooper was "famous in Alabama as one of the most brilliant graduates" of the University of Alabama Law School, where he was editor-in-chief of the *Alabama Law Review*, and "famous at the Supreme Court as one of the most brilliant law clerks to Justice Rehnquist."

Before Fried praised Cooper, he made general remarks that drew applause. For an academic without much experience at political rallies, it was a good outing. To the assembly of Reynolds and Reagan supporters, Fried's talk confirmed what they had figured from his briefs: he was a team player.

"By 1980," Fried lectured, "this country was in danger of becoming a quota society. By 1980, we were in danger of a situation with jobs—private and public sector—educational opportunities, housing, judgeships—all the good things were being handed out, not on merit, but by a racial and ethnic and religious and gender spoils system. The American people elected Ronald Reagan to restore the idea of equality of opportunity and the great ideal of the unity of all mankind. Today that danger is further from us than it was in 1980. And if Ronald Reagan has been able to keep his promise, it is largely because of the work of Brad Reynolds. It has been a great honor to have Brad as a collaborator in the Department of Justice. It has been a great honor to agree and disagree with Brad, to learn from him, to persuade him, and be persuaded by him. It has principally and overwhelmingly been an honor to have Brad as a friend. It is that friendship, after all, that we are all here to acknowledge and celebrate. Let me say that in the last few months we have all learned that Reagan people make the very best friends."

CHARLES FRIED is a vivid, angular man who makes expansive gestures. His admirers call him passionate and charming. When he arrived as the political deputy in early 1985, lawyers who worked in the SG's office described Fried as "strange."[9] In November, not long after the start of his tenure as SG and the week following the Reynolds dinner, this writer had an experience with him that led me to think that, at least sometimes, he floated in his own world. When I came into the Solicitor General's suite one morning to keep an appointment,[10] Fried was sitting in a chair pulled up to the middle of an oblong conference table, looking through a large window to a spectacular vista down Constitution Avenue toward the east. In the foreground was the classical headquarters of the National Archives (with a Corinthian portico, a huge pediment framing statues of "Heritage" and "Guardianship," and the largest bronze doors in the world);[11] in the middle distance was the marble palace of the National Gallery of Art; and, a mile away, against a background of sky, the United States Capitol. The Supreme Court peeked over trees to the left of the Capitol dome.

Compared to every office at the Justice Department except the Attorney General's, the SG's is a dominion. Soon after former

Solicitor General William Mitchell became Attorney General, in 1929, he took charge of the design for the Justice Department building, which opened in 1935. Since the SG was then the second-ranking officer in the department, and served as Acting AG when the AG was out of town, Mitchell thought that the SG's suite should match the Attorney General's. Right up to the private elevator, it does.[12] The ceilings are twenty feet high, the decoration is aluminum Art Deco, and the space extends into a nook which holds a standard lawyer's desk, to a back room with a TV, and up a flight of stairs to a hideaway equipped with a sofa bed. The day of the visit, the space over the mantelpiece was bare. "John W. Davis used to be there," Fried explained with a smile, either amused by what he was about to say or anticipating future pleasure from a higher form of art. "Even though he was one of my predecessors and said to be a very good lawyer, and had hung there a very long time, I thought I could do better." Fried strode to his desk to get a copy of a letter he had written to the Chief Curator of the National Gallery of Art, in which he compared his office to Charlie Chaplin's quarters in *The Great Dictator*, and asked for a fine painting to hang over the fireplace.

We talked for a while in the office, and then Fried suggested we continue over lunch nearby. The restaurant at the National Gallery where we planned to eat was crowded when we got there, so we decided to try someplace else. But on the way, Fried said, "Have you got time? I want to show you a picture that captures the feeling of my view down Constitution Avenue." We entered the Gallery's old West Building, threaded through a series of galleries, and stopped in front of a painting by Nicolas Poussin, done in 1648.[13] "There!" Fried said. "That's my view."

Called "Holy Family on the Steps," it was a portrait of the Virgin Mary and Jesus Christ, and Joseph, Elizabeth, and her son John the Baptist. I had expected a literal depiction of the view from Fried's window, and was faced with a historical painting by the dominant French artist of the seventeenth century. It required a leap of imagination to see the painting in relation to the view from the SG's office.

While the ground for the figures of the Holy Family included a brilliant sky and the classical temple before which they were

pictured had a portico with Corinthian columns, the painting
focused on the boy Jesus accepting an apple from the young John
and other symbols of Christian tradition. It seemed to have far
more to do with religion and humanity than with architectural
vistas. As in his understanding of the law, Fried made a connection
that was grand and idiosyncratic, and spurned the obvious.

"Don't you see?" Fried asked. "The temple is in the place of
the National Archives, and there's the sky, just like mine." He
paused, and beamed at the painting. "I'm in your hands," he said.

AT THE GREAT HALL in the Folger Shakespeare Library, a
couple of blocks from the Supreme Court, one February evening
in 1986, Charles Fried gave an address called "Framers' Intent: A
Meditation on Sonnet 65 and the Constitution."[14] It was a cold,
blowy night, and the audience was small: regular library patrons,
graduate students, and a corps of Fried's friends, including writers
like Henry Brandon, formerly with the *Times* of London; William
Safire, of *The New York Times;* and columnist Edwin Yoder.

Fried describes himself as a polymath ("I've probably taught
more subjects and practiced less law than anyone who's been SG,"
he said),[15] and, like many academics, he had noted similarities
between debates about constitutional interpretation and debates
about literary theory. He wanted to share his thoughts about
them.[16] Fried asked, Does the meaning of a poem reside in the
author's intent, or of the Constitution in the Framers'? Or does it
spring from "the critical reader's free response to contemporary
conditions, whether it be in the Constitution or a poem?" He
began with the poem, Shakespeare's Sonnet 65:

Since brass, nor stone, nor earth, nor boundless sea,
But sad mortality o'ersways their power,
How with this rage shall beauty hold a plea,
Whose action is no stronger than a flower?
O, how shall summer's honey breath hold out
Against the wrackful siege of battering days,
When rocks impregnable are not so stout,
Nor gates of steel so strong, but time decays?

O fearful meditation! where, alack,
Shall Time's best jewel from Time's chest lie hid?
Or what strong hand can hold his swift foot back?
Or who his spoil of beauty can forbid?
    O, none, unless this miracle have might,
    That in black ink my love may still shine bright.

"Well," Fried said, "let's take a first and, I apologize, rather obvious cut at what the poem is about, and you will see in a moment why I burden you with these perhaps obvious observations." There was the contrast between the solid and the extremely transitory: brass, stones, rocks, and gates of steel versus beauty, the strength of a flower, honey breath, and love. As time was to brass and steel, so stone and steel were to beauty and love, which showed how transitory and weak the latter were. Fried said, "So what we have in the end is yet another poem about the potency of time, a poem about change and about decay. And, really, it's about the potency of time and its cunning, its kind of implacable potency, for if you try to hide from time, the way Jonah tried to hide from the Lord in the belly of the whale, you can't evade it. Time's chest is not a place for safekeeping, but an engulfing, kind of an active force, a voracious rage, which sucks up matter and puts it into nowhere."

The rage of impermanence seemed unstoppable, except by "black ink." A pot of ink dumped into the sea might disappear immediately, but that was Shakespeare's miracle. On paper, it could outwit time, and save what was flimsier than stones. "And for how long?" Fried queried. "Well, for about four hundred years." He observed offhandedly, "Now, this of course is the standard poet's theme. One might almost say that it is the perennial theme of poetry. The ravage of time, the impermanence of things, and the reason for that is worth pondering for a moment, because time is after all the greatest mystery of human experience, because it is the sense of time which animals do not have which allows us to plan, which allows us a sense of our own continuity, which gives us a sense of the future, and makes us human." Fried paused, and said, "Well, all of that is rather obvious, so let's change the subject."

Referring to Justice William Brennan in particular, whose work he presented in caricature, Fried went on, "There are those who say that to attempt to understand the words of the Constitution according to the intention of those who conceived it almost two hundred years ago is so obviously, so hopelessly unavailable, that the invocation of that is either foolish or a subterfuge, what has been called 'arrogance cloaked as humility.' The objection is that we cannot know the intention of those so distant from us in time's circumstance. I think the objection is not that it is inconvenient or even bad to ask about the original intention of the Framers, but that the 'wrackful siege of battering days' has made that very enterprise devoid of sense. Words simply cannot now mean what they did then, surrounded as they now are by new contexts. They may seem comprehensible and familiar, but a proper historical sense reveals that they are mere homonyms of their present counterparts. And so meaning too cannot hold out 'when rocks impregnable are not so stout, nor gates of steel so strong, but Time decays.' And that, of course, is a 'fearful meditation' indeed."

On the one hand, Fried conjectured, perhaps it was not so fearful after all. "Maybe in our impotence is potency, since freed of past meanings we are free, quite marvelously free, to make new ones, according to our present needs, visions, whims, what have you—so the idea that we cannot know the Framers' intent is perhaps a great liberation from the chains of the past." He asked, "Should we accept this line of argument? Is it true? Recall for a moment my exegesis of the obvious—the transparent meaning of Sonnet 65. Put aside for the moment the contents of that exegesis and recall just the act of it. You went along with it, or you didn't, and if you didn't, it was perhaps because you had a different, perhaps a better sense of what the poem meant. And in a way I tricked you, because in following along with me in my exegesis, whether you agreed with it or not, you agreed with my unstated, major premise—that the poem had meaning and that we could understand it, and that the intent to do so, rather than making up the meaning as we went along, was not arrogance cloaked as humility, but an ordinary act of human intelligence."

To Fried, the sonnet was not about the perennial theme of poetry at all, but about the nature of writing. "I think it's about words," he said. "The miracle that black ink can make the most fragile and evanescent of entities shine bright and that it can do so through time. But how do we know this? Why do we believe it? The poem is like one of those logician's tricks where the thing provides its own proof. The poem proves itself, for I contend that we all understand what the poem is claiming, and in understanding what the poem claims, we prove Shakespeare's contention that black ink can perform the miracle of causing meaning to shine bright across years. So it seems to me that the final meaning about the poem is about the power of poetry, and it proves its own thesis, just as the enterprise of discoursing about the Constitution and the possibility of understanding it, or not, proves that such discourse is possible. In addition, understanding the subject of the discourse, whether it's a poem or the Constitution, is also possible."

He went on, "Well, what about freedom?" As a straw man, Fried admitted, he had said that our inability to understand Shakespeare or the Constitution might be liberating. It might allow us to be creative and innovative. But, he continued, the ability to create something, like Shakespeare's poem, was an ability to stress thoughts and actions in words and transmit them over time. Fried declared, "It is the ability to transmit original intentions, if you like, Framer's intentions, across the void of time. Without that ability, we would be powerless to create and innovate."

Then Fried addressed the claim that "the Framers of the Constitution no more envisioned every application of their general terms than Shakespeare did the use I am making here of his sonnet. I think that's a dreadful red herring, which does indeed ignore the miracle of language and the miracle of general terms. For it's the very essence of language and the very essence of general terms to govern particular cases which were not envisaged by their authors. General terms are not mere compendia of the very specific instances which those who first employed them had in mind when they spoke them. If it were otherwise, we could never generate meanings." He continued, "What the miracle of language requires is that words, ideas, concepts reach new instances but that they do so definitely. Those who deny that language can reach new cases and those who claim that they can reach new cases but only indefinitely are really in the same camp. They are the enemies of meaning, and therefore the enemies of the very conditions of human creativity."

To Fried, a great deal was at stake here: "the integrity and meaning of human communication in general," and "the integrity of the tools of legal and political discourse." If he was correct about Shakespeare's meaning, then politics and law were not just a matter of power, but could be bound by words and reason as well. "And this is what law is," Fried stated. "It is a constraint, not of force but of reasons. The reasons that one man offers to another for his judgment and his action, the reasons that one age offers to another for its judgment and its action. So it means that the enterprise which the Framers embarked on in Philadelphia two hundred years ago was a possible enterprise, the establishment of a foundation of government, the structure for relations of power in a written Constitution—that is, in black ink." If we could understand Shakespeare's meaning in Sonnet 65, we could understand the Framers' meaning in the Constitution. "Not necessarily without difficulty," Fried admitted, "but that is not an objection in principal to making the effort. And the effort is what we owe to the texts of both."

Fried said, "The striking thing is that the courts are physically able, they can ignore the provisions of the Constitution, as can the President or a sheriff." The law was not a machine gun. It did not disable anyone from disagreeing. Whatever coercion the law exercised was guided by reason. "That's why the suggestion that we cannot understand the intentions of framers of laws, whether it's the Constitution or a law in its humbler manifestations, whether twenty years ago or two hundred years ago, is such a disturbing suggestion," Fried insisted. "It is that suggestion which I think Shakespeare refutes in Sonnet 65, and it is that miracle of meaning which we as free persons whose freedom is underwritten by the rule of law should celebrate."

Fried's lecture was intended as a contribution to the ongoing debate about the Jurisprudence of Original Intention between Attorney General Edwin Meese and Justice William Brennan, among others, and to throw in his lot with Meese. For many lawyers who heard about it in subsequent weeks, the most tactful

thing to say was that, whatever the current vogue among scholars for using the techniques of literary criticism to explain the law, Fried had skipped over the obvious point that the Constitution is not a sonnet and that the meaning of a law is different from that of a poem. Like the Attorney General, Fried had also declined to answer the hard question of how you interpret America's fundamental law when the text is ambiguous about its meaning. As David Lauter, then of the *National Law Journal,* put it, the Solicitor General had displayed a gift for phrases that rose like perfect bubbles, and then burst, leaving nothing behind to help solve the problem they were meant to address. [17]

But cast in terms of constitutional metaphor rather than text, and in metaphor generally (with the word "intention" redefined to mean not the "mere compendia of the very specific instances which those who first employed them had in mind when they spoke them"—that is, Meese's understanding of the Framers' intent—but as the Framers' general "concepts" that could grow to cover "new instances"), the lecture sounded surprisingly like an affirmation of Brennan. The answer Fried gave to a question from William Safire strengthened this view.

" 'O fearful meditation,' " Safire said. "In Shakespeare's time, the word 'fearful' meant 'filled with fear,' not 'striking fear,' so 'O fearful meditation' might mean 'O meditation that strikes us with fear,' though, in his time, it meant 'the thought is filled with fear.' Now, the question, recognizing the ambiguity, is what do you think we ought to do about it? Do you think we ought to find out what the context was in 1660 to determine what he meant by that? Or do you think we ought to have that creative tension between that meaning and the one of today?" Fried replied, "If you were to persuade me that in 1660 it meant 'filled with fear' instead of 'striking fear,' and, in fact plainly so, but it reverberates with other meaning for you, so much the better."

Earlier, Fried had declared, "I think the nature of the legal debate is this: Are we people of the law, people of the book, if you like, or people who are governed by judges? I think that is very much the issue. Maybe the text isn't the last word, but it certainly ought to be the first." Yet when a "judge"—in this case, a reader and columnist and man who writes best-selling books about the meanings of words—posed a choice between a meaning from the time Shakespeare used it in a text and one from today, Fried told him to choose the contemporary meaning, if it "reverberated" for him, and "so much the better."

It was a confusing answer. As with other examples from Fried's scholarly and government record, the specific advice was ambiguous, and seemed to contradict his general pronouncement on the law. If not, the point was lost in nuances that the Solicitor General did not clarify.

XII

Friends
of the Court

CHARLES FRIED summed up the events that shaped his
outlook as a lawyer in March of 1985, at a seminar titled "Crisis
in the Courts," sponsored by the Manhattan Institute for Policy
Research. "I think by now there is a large measure of agreement
that many significant, yet misguided, policy trends developed in
the law during the mid-1960s,"[1] he said, and "a growing institutional paralysis—a kind of celebration of self-hatred for national
values and institutions—was fed by the emergence of what many
have called the 'new class,' a class in which lawyers and judges
played a large role." Fried reduced his ideas to a caustic phrase.
"Looking back at that time," Fried said about the sixties and
seventies, "I think it is clear that judges were among those who
'did it to us.' "

Judges "did it to us" by creating too many new rights, and by
"departing from common sense and moving in the direction of
elaborate rule systems," through landmark decisions like Miranda.
They did it by saying a psychiatrist could be sued for not warning
a woman that one of his patients had threatened to kill her. (The
doctor went to the police instead.) They did it by declaring that
every product on the market carried an implied warranty that
could never be disclaimed, or, after a business ran into trouble, by
undoing good contracts made by executives in moments of bad
judgment, to protect them from their folly.[2]

To Fried, these examples of "judicial activism" represented "an
attitude." He told the Chamber of Commerce at a speech in 1985,
"It's an attitude which says that everybody is constrained by law
except the judges. The judges do justice. The rest of us are con-

strained by law. Now, I think that is the philosophy which is so dangerous to us, and which, in a sense, represents"—here Fried digressed to another example before making his point—"lawlessness." As Solicitor General, the "most important function" he could serve was to fight this "attitude" and help "maintain the rule of law." He came to Washington "to do something about this terrible drift."[3]

In some ways, Fried's critique went wider than the Attorney General's. Meese directed his attack at the Supreme Court, and faulted the Justices for interpreting the Constitution more broadly than the Framers intended. Fried contended that judges in state courts whose responsibility was to make law in areas like torts and contract were just as blameworthy. "If somebody is hurt, you find a way to put money in their pocket,"[4] he said. "That's the crudity of the logic." As SG, Fried could do little about the drift in judge-made, or common, law except through lecturing. The Constitution was a different matter, and he recognized the choice he faced.

"If you are to respect other institutions, be less activist, and adhere to precedent," he observed at the Manhattan Institute, "you're going to be stuck with many of the ill-conceived legal decisions which occurred between 1960 and 1980. If you're less activist, you're going to be less creative about interpreting some really silly statutes which were passed during this period, which could do with a dose of negative activism." To return the law to its proper role in society, he believed that lawyers with his beliefs had to urge federal courts to undo doctrine left over from ill-founded decisions by liberal judges during the past generation. Putting the idea in the negative, he said, "Judicial restraint may require judges to be faithful to a lot of things which, in the abstract, don't deserve fidelity."[5]

The Solicitor General with whom Fried often compared himself in the first year of his tenure was Archibald Cox. He knew how well-regarded Cox was as SG, and Fried thought it would be instructive to show how his approach to the job closely followed Cox's.[6]

Both had come from Harvard Law to serve as Solicitor General in Administrations with well-defined notions of what they hoped to accomplish in the Supreme Court, he pointed out, and, as Cox had done a generation before, Fried believed that the role of the SG was to enter into a Socratic dialogue with the Justices—what he called "a conversation with the Court." Both men cut stern, impressive figures when they argued cases before the Justices, and the lawyers who worked for each described their bosses as pompous but dedicated, and eager to take an active hand in shaping the briefs submitted by the government under their names. Instead of writing briefs in longhand on yellow pads, as Cox did, Fried composed on his computer, but he was equally engaged in the business of his office.[7]

In the field of constitutional law, Cox made a study of the Warren Court that raised questions related to Fried's complaints about that Court's decisions. In a series of lectures delivered not long after his term as SG, Cox said that Earl Warren's appointment as Chief Justice "marked the opening of a new period in our constitutional development. In the next 15 years the Supreme Court rewrote, with profound social consequences, major constitutional doctrines governing race relations, the administration of criminal justice, and the operation of the political process."[8] To Cox, the Court's choice was whether to play a role equal to Congress's and the President's in shaping the nation's destiny, or leave new departures in social policy to the political branches. In theory, Cox found the predicament insoluble. The "extraordinary character" of the issues presented to the Warren Court meant that the Justices could not "ignore the political aspects" of their decisions, yet the best result for the country, according to social consensus, was often inconsistent with what was required by current law. In practice, in times like the fifties and sixties when the Justices felt obliged to act because the other branches of government hadn't, the Supreme Court could best uphold its constitutional duty through far-reaching decisions—and by searching for principles that gave the decisions the force of law. "I cannot prove these points," Cox granted, "but they are the faith to which we lawyers are dedicated."[9]

According to Fried, the costs of the Warren Court era were evident in the social tatters left by the explosion of law since the nineteen-sixties. The rate of crime was up, the amount of litigation had multiplied, the costs of insurance for doctors had driven some of them out of practice because of the rise in malpractice suits.[10] Too much law had stripped the law of its power, and, in Cox's term, led people to withhold their "consent" from judicial opinions when consent was essential to the authority of courts in society. Writing in the late sixties about constitutional law, Cox had wondered if this might come about as a result of the Warren Court's activism. The majority had sometimes been "notably unsuccessful in rationalizing new departures" and, "when cynically minded," Cox confessed, "one wonders whether it has made much effort. Occasionally decisions seem to turn on intuitive judgments of right and wrong rather than the impartial application of principle."[11] Without the power of reason to command consent, the Justices' opinions undermined the rule of law. They robbed the Justices of authority to solve problems when the Court became the institution of last resort.[12]

For all their agreement, Cox and Fried acted differently as SGs. As a former law clerk to Judge Learned Hand and a onetime junior lawyer in the SG's office, Solicitor General Cox believed it was his duty to restrain the recommendations for activism that rose through the rest of the Justice Department, and to exercise similar restraint on the arguments it made to the Supreme Court.

At the Kennedy Justice Department, according to Victor Navasky, in *Kennedy Justice*, Cox was known as the Solicitor "who couldn't see beyond the law."[13] He regularly challenged proposals of Attorney General Robert Kennedy and his aides by insisting that the law constrained them from doing what they wanted. In a series of suits known as the sit-in cases, the question appeared to be whether the government should file an amicus brief to support civil-rights protesters who had staged sit-ins at lunch counters, stores, and other Southern establishments that refused to serve blacks. To Cox, the question was not so elementary. The Fourteenth Amendment guaranteed equal protection of the laws against state action, but what was that? Cox equated state action with official action—the deeds of police, the rules governing city parks, admissions policies to state universities. The NAACP Legal Defense and Educational Fund, Inc. and other liberal groups equated state action with "public" action and distinguished it from private action, so that even if a restaurant or a hotel was privately owned, its services and legal character were public. If the owner of a segregated restaurant called in the police to throw out blacks who had staged a sit-in, the combination of the public nature of the restaurant and the official help of the police in getting rid of the protesters amounted to state action. The Civil Rights Act of 1964 removed the issue from the Supreme Court to Congress, which resolved the question as the civil-rights groups wanted.

Burke Marshall, who is now a professor at Yale Law School, was the head of the Civil Rights Division during Cox's tenure. Though he disagreed with Cox about the sit-in cases, he respected the SG's concern about the law. "He was determined to understand and be persuaded that these pro-civil-rights positions were the right positions to take because they were constitutionally and legally sound," Marshall said. "His concern was 'Don't mislead the Court into doing something that might look right now, but wrong a hundred years from now.' "[14] Cox fretted that advocates who thought the new definition of state action would benefit blacks had paid no attention to its potential costs. He thought that blacks as well as whites might lose the safeguard of private law if doctrines like trespass were eclipsed by expanding the notion of state action.[15]

Cox rarely made an argument as SG until he was convinced it was the logical solution to a legal problem, and when he could not make up his mind, he refused to choose a position just to have one. In one government case, he presented both sides to the Supreme Court. This was an antitrust suit against the St. Regis Paper Company, in which the Federal Trade Commission had subpoenaed records including the firm's confidential responses to questions from the U.S. Census Bureau. The FTC and the Justice Department's Antitrust Division said the reports could be subpoenaed. The Census Bureau and the Bureau of the Budget said they couldn't, because they contained privileged information. As Navasky told it, Cox "chose to go before the U.S. Supreme Court, and as the nine robed men sat there slightly awe-struck he commenced to argue both sides of the case as fully and honestly and persuasively as he knew how." With some pique, Justice Frankfurter asked, "How do you expect us to decide this matter if you can't even get an agreement inside the Justice Department?" Cox replied, "Oh, Mr. Justice. If the dispute were only inside the Justice Department, I'm sure I could settle it." [16]

The major clash between a favored social policy of the Kennedy Justice Department and Cox's judgment about the constraints of the law came in a series of cases dealing with reapportionment of state legislatures. The first case was Baker v. Carr, [17] in which the plaintiffs claimed that they had been denied the equal protection of the laws guaranteed by the Fourteenth Amendment. In Tennessee, where the case arose, legislative districts were apportioned according to a 1901 state law. Though major changes in the pattern of the population had occurred since then, the legislature had failed on many occasions to redraw district lines. As a result, the votes in some parts of Tennessee, where districts were sparsely settled, counted much more than votes in others.

The issue for Cox was not whether the district lines in Tennessee were fairly drawn. He recognized that in Tennessee, and in many other states as well, the votes of many citizens had been seriously diluted with the passage of time. In Tennessee, the population had quadrupled. The number of voters in a district ranged from 2,340 to 42,298. [18] He also believed that the case involved "one of the most basic rights in any democracy, the right to fair representation in one's own government." [19]

The legal constraint for Cox was that the Supreme Court, less than two decades before, had called reapportionment "a political question" best left to the legislature. Even though Cox's predecessor, Lee Rankin, had decided that the government should enter the case as an amicus on behalf of the plaintiffs, Cox was not sure he should argue the case. After overcoming his misgivings, he did, and, according to Navasky, the government's amicus brief was "crucial in persuading at least two members of the U.S. Supreme Court—Justices Potter Stewart and Tom Clark. Without their vote the decision below would have been reaffirmed and there probably wouldn't have been any reapportionment cases." [20] The Supreme Court ruled that the plaintiffs were entitled to a decision in federal court.

Philip Heymann served as an assistant to the Solicitor under Cox. In 1985, he said, "Archie took the biggest cases, and he liked

to argue a lot. [Between 1942 and 1981, Cox argued eighty-seven times in the Supreme Court, sixty-seven as SG.][21] He was a very good advocate—exceptionally orderly, upright, clear. He was always a teacher. He would say, 'There are three issues here,' and what was happening was that, above all, he was imposing his structure on the question. He gave a very sharp sense of definition. The impression of the Justices was that he was telling the Supreme Court what the law was. He would tell the Court what was acceptable and persuasive, as a professor in the best sense. To some of them, it must have been very irritating, though Archie was very much in tune with the Warren Court. Baker v. Carr was one of his big cases. My impression in the courtroom was that a majority of the Court wanted to take jurisdiction in the case, but they were afraid of what they were getting into because of Frankfurter, who had objected to that position and who was a very powerful intellect. Archie unlocked the door for that majority, and Frankfurter ended up dissenting. Archie stood up and said, 'It is respectable and nothing terrible will happen if you take on reapportionment.' He wrestled with it—he spent a lot of time wrestling with questions because he sensed his influence on the Court. He wrestled with Baker v. Carr a long time, and it's one of those cases where the lawyer made all the difference."[22]

Cox's second struggle in the reapportionment cases was with the standard the Court should adopt as the measure of apportionment in a district. The question arose in Reynolds v. Sims,[23] which dealt with the constitutionality of the apportionment of legislatures in six states. Robert Kennedy and his aides believed that each person should have one vote, and that districts should have basically the same number of voters. According to Cox's estimate, that standard would lead to an extreme outcome, because the makeup of forty-six of the fifty state legislatures would be found unconstitutional,[24] requiring each of them immediately and at the same time to face the volatile task of reapportionment. The Solicitor General also thought the Attorney General's standard was simplistic. It would do nothing to avoid the problem of gerrymandering, because districts could be drawn so that they were equal in population but favored one party or the other. (In 1986, a generation later, the Supreme Court decided that federal courts could review gerry-

mandering by a state legislature.) [25] It ignored special circumstances presented by geography, because in some states mountains
divided areas that might be required to vote as a unified district if
the one person/one vote standard was adopted. The SG's hesita-
tions were supported by liberal and conservative scholars. [26] But
Bruce Terris, the assistant in the SG's office who was working
with Cox on the case, disagreed. "I think it is plain that it would
significantly benefit the country if our state legislatures were reap-
portioned on the basis of population," he wrote. "It would be a
tragedy if the great victory in Baker v. Carr were thrown away by
our persuading the Supreme Court to accept a weak substantive
standard." [27]

Terris anticipated by fourteen years what the Office of Legal
Counsel said the Solicitor General should do in a case like Reynolds v. Sims. (As noted earlier, in the 1977 document called "The
Role of the Solicitor General," the Office of Legal Counsel advised, "If the independent legal advice of the Solicitor General is
to be preserved, it should normally be the Solicitor General who
decides when to seek the advice of the Attorney General or the
President in a given case.") [28] In 1963, Terris wrote, "I recognize
that the choice between the various standards largely depends on
questions of policy. I have therefore gone on to suggest that the
population standard is, as a matter of policy, best for the country
because it is most consistent with contemporary concepts of democracy and with a strong federal system. However, despite my
views on the correct policy, I recognize that this vital issue is
largely outside my province. It seems to me to be a political decision properly made at the highest levels of government. Until that
decision is made, I do not believe that our legal position can be
formulated." [29]

Terris's memo was one of several documents sent to Cox to
persuade him to argue on behalf of the one person/one vote standard. Unwilling to order Cox to make an argument the SG did not
believe in, Robert Kennedy orchestrated a quiet campaign to
change the Solicitor's mind. Cox responded by drafting a memo
of his own, in which he argued that the one person/one vote
standard was sound social policy but questionable law. "In a state
constitutional convention my vote would go to apportion both

houses of a bicameral legislature in accordance with population," he wrote, "but I cannot agree that the Supreme Court should be advised to impose that rule upon all 50 states by judicial decree. In my opinion any such decree would be too revolutionary to be a proper exercise of the judicial function and too rigid to comport with the principle of federalism." In a meeting with the Attorney General and his advisers, Navasky reports, Cox lectured about his views until Kennedy interrupted, "Archie, isn't the real issue: 'Should some people's vote count more than other people's vote'?" [30]

That was as close as Cox and Kennedy ever came to a confrontation. The Attorney General never told Cox what to argue before the Court ("Archie, I know you can put this issue in a way that will convince the Supreme Court," he said), and when Cox faced the Justices, he stopped short of advocating one person/one vote. He said, ". . . my appraisal of sentiment within the legal profession—and probably outside—is that while the invalidation of the egregiously malapportioned legislatures would command a consensus of opinion, a 'one man, one vote' decision would precipitate a major constitutional crisis causing an enormous drop in public support for the Court." [31]

Cox says the meeting with Kennedy did not take place. "The one case that got sticky," he recalled in 1985, "and where my views of what good lawyering required and where the political views of others came into collision was here. I—I now think wrongly—I thought one really couldn't press a one person/one vote rule in a clear-cut form. I thought we couldn't ask the Court to require that legislatures draw district lines so that each person's vote counted the same. It wasn't that I didn't like the idea. I just doubted whether the Constitution required it. I had my heels dug in, and I wasn't going to budge. On the other hand, the President's aides were all gung ho that we push that standard. There was a meeting all set up in Bob Kennedy's office, and we were all going to thrash out the case. As I say, my heels were dug in. Well, that conference in Bob's office never happened. Burke Marshall and I happened to ride an elevator together one day. We were walking down the hall, and he said, 'We can't let this come to a head. You ought to recognize that Bob won't file a brief in the Supreme Court that you won't sign. You ought to recognize that he can't get into a position of filing a brief against the groups that have been pressing for one person/one vote.' I said, 'All right. I've got the germ of a solution, and I think I can work it out.' As I remember it, we filed a brief that didn't press that standard, but suggested a close alternative. Our brief provided the basis for much of the Court's decision, but the Justices took the final leap, which my intellect wouldn't allow me to. Poor prophet." [32]

Voting was a fundamental right, the Justices ruled, and any inequality of treatment for voters should be subjected to strict scrutiny. They ordered the states to establish districts with equal numbers of voters. Cox was not confident about the prospects for compliance with the Court's 1964 order, but far from causing a citizens' revolt, the Court initiated an orderly modernization of state government. Reapportionment in every state was virtually complete within two years. [33] Cox said, "I dug in my heels on one person/one vote, and I'm not especially proud of it. But my stubbornness was based on my sense of the law." [34]

A decade after the reapportionment cases, Cox's sense of the law was intensified by Watergate. He sees a close relationship between the secret of American constitutionalism and the resolution of that crisis. In a 1985 lecture, he asked, "Upon what does our constitutionalism ultimately rest? Why have the Constitution and the Supreme Court served so successfully for almost two centuries that the people, at least until now, have always rejected attacks upon the Court? The question confronted me with extraordinary personal intensity during the Watergate crisis." In the summer of 1973, the investigation he led as Watergate Special Prosecutor was stalled. Allegations that Richard Nixon and his White House aides had planned the Watergate break-in and then engaged in a conspiracy to obstruct justice through a cover-up hinged on the credibility of suspect witnesses like Nixon's onetime counsel John Dean. Then another aide disclosed that the President had installed a taping system in the Oval Office, which raised the possibility that hard evidence existed by which to judge the witnesses. When Cox subpoenaed the tapes, Nixon refused to cooperate, and continued to stonewall after federal trial Judge John Sirica and the U.S. Court of Appeals ordered him to turn them over. Cox said, "The habit of compliance—the notion that a powerful executive official has no choice but to comply with a judicial decree—is a fragile bond. Who could say in an age of Presidential aggrandizement that if one President succeeded in his defiance, others might not follow that example until ours was no longer a government of law?" [35]

On a Friday night, Nixon announced that he would not give up the tapes. He also ordered Cox "never again to resort to judicial process" to get White House evidence. Cox explained that he was obliged to pursue the inquiry as he had pledged he would to the Senate, and Nixon ordered Attorney General Elliot Richardson to fire Cox. After Richardson and William Ruckelshaus refused, on Saturday night, in Cox's words, the "third in command carried out the President's wish"—Solicitor General Robert Bork.

To Cox, what happened next is crucial: "Public support for the rule of law was then put to the test. A firestorm of public outrage overwhelmed the White House." By Tuesday, the President had promised to comply in all respects with the court order that he turn over the tapes. He did not in fact do so, but nine months later, when the Supreme Court itself ordered him to turn over the withheld tapes, he finally did. His resignation swiftly followed.

"The rule of law prevailed," Cox wrote, "because the people did rise up morally and politically. The response doubtless flowed from many sources; but I think there was present a deep and enduring realization, partly conscious and partly intuitive, that all our liberties depend upon compliance with law, because the principal bulwark of those liberties against executive or legislative oppression is respect for constitutionalism: the law and the courts." [36]

EVEN AS CHARLES FRIED compared himself with Cox, he sometimes tried to chip away at Cox's reputation for rectitude. "Why has Archie Cox been picked on by the right?" Fried asked. "He's been very partisan lately. At Common Cause"—for which Cox served as spokesman while criticizing Edwin Meese's fitness to be Attorney General—"he's Mr. Clean turned into a regular pol running a nickel-and-dime lobby." [37] Fried's apparent purpose was to show that Cox was no more a saint than Fried was a sinner: the similarities between their practices as SG outweighed any differences. The example Fried selected was their respective uses of amicus briefs in the Supreme Court. [38]

Part of the complaint that Fried had "politicized" the SG's office was the charge that he had submitted amicus briefs in agenda cases where the federal government's interest was "attenuated" rather than "direct." [39] Responding to this, Fried would ask, "What was the federal interest in the abortion case? Why, it was the same interest Archie Cox was required to articulate when he filed his brief in the reapportionment cases like Baker v. Carr and Reynolds v. Sims." [40] The answer was double-edged. It could mean that Cox had stated no federal interest in Baker v. Carr, so that Fried did not have to either, or, cutting the other way, that the interest Cox stated in Reynolds v. Sims was no less general than Fried had declared in some of his briefs. Fried's assertion raised a technical point. As a matter of Supreme Court procedure, Cox did not have to state a federal interest as part of a government brief. The rules under which Cox operated were issued in 1954. [41] When Cox was SG, from 1961 to 1965, no rule required him to state a federal interest, though he usually did. The Supreme Court rules were changed in 1970, and the new ones obliged Fried to declare the government's interest in every case.

Even when Fried discussed points less technical than the federal interest, he was concerned with a subject that draws the attention of only a small group of lawyers. But its significance has grown considerably in recent years. Since 1823, when the Justices let Henry Clay argue as an amicus, the Supreme Court has allowed lawyers to argue for clients as friends of the Court. The main requirement imposed on all friends of the Court (except the government) is that they present facts and law not well addressed by the parties. Amicus briefs answer a shortcoming of the adversary system: specific cases raise general questions that the parties do not always reckon with. [42]

During the presidency of Theodore Roosevelt, beginning in 1907, Attorney General Charles Bonaparte entered fifty-six cases before the Supreme Court in a little over two years, to press for an increase in the rights of blacks. [43] This was the first attempt by the government to spur social change as a friend of the Court. The Justices mentioned amicus briefs in the Court's rules of procedure for the first time in 1937, and by the forties, when cases arose dealing with desegregation, the Supreme Court began to ask the Solicitor General to give counsel through amicus briefs. [44]

Until the sixties, however, the subject of amicus filings was largely academic to the government. In 1956, for example, the government was an amicus in only two cases decided by the Justices. [45] From 1961 through 1966, the number of amicus filings by the government began to climb, and averaged seventeen a year. About one-fifth of the government's appearances in the Court during that period were as amicus curiae. The number in that era peaked in 1963, when the government filed twenty-eight amicus briefs, representing one-third of the cases in which it appeared before the Court in that Term.

In a speech before the Chicago Bar Association in 1962, when the subject of amicus briefs was as topical to lawyers as it became again during the Reagan Administration, Archibald Cox described the standards he followed as Solicitor General in deciding which cases to enter as a friend of the Court. [46] First, the question had to be important to constitutional law. Next, a large number of people should be affected. Then, the case had to have an impact on the government's "more direct interests"—this last standard being the hardest to define. (Though Cox did not cite them, Baker v. Carr and Reynolds v. Sims provided ready examples of cases meeting all three requirements. The government had a general interest in the suits because of the fundamental constitutional issues they raised, but that interest was also "direct" because the federal government would be directly affected by the outcome of the cases. What the Supreme Court decided about the apportionment of state legislatures would apply to Congress as well.) Finally, Cox asked, "Can we really help the Court?"

In 1985, Cox said about the government's use of amicus briefs during his tenure, "We had the feeling when we filed an amicus brief that we had an even stricter responsibility to the guardians of the law than we normally did. We couldn't just take a strong position on behalf of a state, for example. We had to be especially careful about what we said the law was or should be." Cox did not raise issues that were doomed to fail, because he thought it was the Solicitor General's duty not to waste the Court's time. He didn't raise issues not raised by the parties to the suit, or inject new issues not raised at trial. [47]

Though Cox felt constrained, the use of amicus briefs by private attorneys during his tenure was not constrained. In 1963, Samuel Krislov wrote in the *Yale Law Journal* that "the amicus is no longer a neutral amorphous embodiment of justice, but an active participant in the interest group struggle." [48] Between the late sixties and the early eighties, on average, amicus briefs were cited in almost one-fifth of the Supreme Court's opinions, and the average number of amicus briefs filed each Term was over sixty. [49] In that period, according to Karen O'Connor and Lee Epstein, who are professors of political science at Emory University, liberal groups like the American Civil Liberties Union and the NAACP Inc. Fund took part in over 40 percent of the Supreme Court's cases either as parties or as friends of the Court. Conservative groups played a role in almost 20 percent. In the dozen years from 1969 to 1981, while liberal participation stayed relatively steady, the percentage of appearances by conservative groups tripled. In civil-rights cases, defined to include abortion, affirmative action, and other topics on the Reagan agenda, conservatives played no role at the start of the period. They entered almost half by the end. Conservative groups became as accomplished in using amicus briefs to push their agenda as they had in mastering the use of political action committees, direct mail, and other new tools of politics. As O'Connor and Epstein put it, "Conservative as well as liberal groups now aspire to be 'private attorneys general.'" [50]

After the number of amicus filings by the government rose in the Cox era, it leveled off and did not jump to the next plateau until Robert Bork was Solicitor General. [51] The average number of cases in which there were amicus filings by the government between 1973 and 1977 rose to thirty-two, or 30 percent. The figures stayed about the same during the Carter Administration, and then they leaped again under Reagan, to an average of forty-three amicus filings, or 37 percent, through the 1984 Term. In short, between Cox's era and Bork's, amicus filings as a percentage of all of the government's briefs went from around 20 to 30 percent. Between

Cox's era and Rex Lee's, they doubled to almost 40 percent. And in the 1985 Term, the first full year Charles Fried was Solicitor General, the number of briefs climbed again to a rate of almost 50 percent of the government's filings in the Supreme Court for most of the Term, until the rate dropped off during the last few months to yield an annual figure of 41 percent. [52]

The increase in amicus filings in the seventies and eighties can be explained by several factors: the constitutionalization of the law; the growth in the number of federal statutes; and the tendency by government, private lawyers, and citizens alike to view the courts, and the Supreme Court in particular, as a proper forum for addressing social issues. But the Nixon, Ford, and Carter Administrations, in office when the number of filings began to increase, showed no special urgency about changing the law through amicus filings. [53] In many areas, lawyers in those Administrations believed the law was in equilibrium. Where the Solicitors General sought new doctrine, they were careful not to upset the general balance. The Reagan Administration, on the other hand, took a new tack, and used the amicus brief as a tool of change.

By Fried's time, according to a lawyer in the SG's office who was appointed by the Reagan Administration and who studied the filings of its predecessors, the type of amicus briefs filed by the Reagan team spelled a significant difference between how it viewed the office and how prior Administrations had. Fried defined the federal interest as broadly as possible—"threadbare," the lawyer called this definition—in order to enter any case where the Administration and the Solicitor General wanted to make a point. Instead of submitting briefs that were seen as attempts to help the Court, Fried filed position papers to put the Administration on record about questions of law it considered important for whatever reason. "I don't think you've been useful or not useful in terms of just wins or losses," he said. "It's a question of whether you've told the truth in a way that is persuasive and effective, and if in the end it's wrong, at least it's clearly wrong, not just a muddle." [54]

While the nature of practice before the Supreme Court had changed since Cox's day, the behavior of Reagan's second Solicitor General was not fully explained by this shift. Both Cox's staffers and Fried's agreed that the cardinal difference between the two Solicitors was that while both men declared beliefs in law as a constraint, Cox's record underscored that he felt bound by what the courts said was law, while Fried's showed that he did not. [55]

Cox often tells a story about his days as a law clerk to Learned Hand. "Sonny," Hand asked him, "to whom am I responsible? No one can fire me. No one can dock my pay. Even those nine bozos in Washington, who sometimes reverse me, can't make me decide as they want. Everyone should be responsible to someone. To whom am I responsible?" Then the judge pointed to the shelves of his law library. "To those books about us!" he answered. "That's to whom I'm responsible!" [56] Judges had a body of law to which they were accountable. They could change it, but they had to recognize their duty to the ideal of law or it would lose its force. [57] In the SG's post, Cox believed he stood halfway between the Supreme Court and the President, and he owed a duty to each. He kept the President and the Attorney General from ignoring what the Court said the law was, and from asking the Justices to reach judgments that, in his view, could harm the Court. He also argued the Kennedy Administration's position in terms he thought were consistent with the Court's reasoning about the law.

Philip Heymann can draw on as much experience as anyone in commenting about the difference between the Cox and Fried outlooks on the law. He has known both men well since the early sixties. It was Heymann who noted that, unlike Cox, Fried believes that "the law is not necessarily what the Supreme Court says it is," that "the law is something that any right-minded person can see." [58] As Fried put it, "Law is nothing but reasons." [59] The divergence between Cox's and Fried's views about the law and the Supreme Court led to a difference in their stewardships as Solicitors General that was summed up in their use of amicus briefs.

For Cox, representing the government required caution, patience, and steps of moderation. He tried to fulfill the SG's responsibility to the Supreme Court as well as the President, and by Republicans and Democrats, liberals and conservatives, he was hailed as a great SG. Serving an Administration that governed during the midst of a revolution in constitutional law, when he might have been expected to call for radical changes in the law,

Archibald Cox believed that, for the good of the Court and the SG's office, he should advocate restraint.[60]

Charles Fried, on the other hand, felt no such compunctions. "There are two reasons why you don't file an amicus brief in an important case," Fried said in 1986 when asked to explain the high number of filings he had made compared to his predecessors. "Either you are very deep and have too much to say to reduce it to a simple brief. Or you have nothing to say at all."[61] Except for his regular references to Archibald Cox, who said the "choice of words" in Fried's briefs ran ahead of "sober reasoning," was "too polemical" and "strident," and was "weakening the rule of law,"[62] Fried declined to comment on the appraisals of him made by some of his predecessors. He did not answer the charge of Erwin Griswold that the Reagan Administration "intervenes too often, a) for the good of the law, and b) for its own good." (Fried described a piece on NBC News that reported Griswold's view—"Three former U.S. Solicitors General accuse the Reagan Administration of turning that historic post into little more than a political mouthpiece for the President"—as "a hatchet job.")[63] He did not respond to the comment of President Carter's Solicitor, Wade McCree, that the SG's briefs appeared to be less "dispassionate" and "objective" than they had been "traditionally." Fried, however, contended that his briefs made arguments compelled by logic, and not by overt pressure from the Attorney General and his circle, or by the instinct to placate his masters,[64] as Louis Claiborne called it, that might overtake a Solicitor General trying to get along in an expressly ideological Administration.

"Take our brief in the Wygant case," Fried said about an amicus filing he made in Wygant v. Jackson.[65] "The reaction of some of our critics to that brief shows you how bad the polarization has become. Compared to the bland stuff that Archie Cox submitted, the Wygant brief was wonderfully well written. And that was my main problem. If that's the problem, I plead guilty." The Wygant case dealt with affirmative action. In 1972, the Board of Education and the teachers association in Jackson, Michigan, agreed on a plan: ". . . at no time will there be a greater percentage

of minority personnel laid off than the current percentage of minority personnel employed at the time of the layoff."[66] The goal
of the plan was to have at least the same percentage of minority
teachers on the staff of each Jackson school as there were minority
students throughout the Jackson public schools.

Though the SG's brief did not say so, until 1954 no black
teacher taught in the Jackson schools. By 1969, minority teachers
accounted for less than 4 percent of the school system's faculty,
and the Michigan Civil Rights Commission found that the school
board had discriminated in hiring. The board worked to improve
its record, and two years later the share of minority teachers had
doubled to almost 9 percent. But Jackson had to lay off some
teachers, and because the minority teachers were the most recently
hired, according to the superintendent of schools, the layoffs "literally wiped out all the gain."[67] In 1972, racial tension in the
Jackson schools tripped over into violence, and the school board
decided to integrate students and faculty. When teachers were
asked to consider abandoning the "last hired, first fired" layoff
scheme, all but a small fraction voted to retain it. The board and
the teachers' union negotiated, and they came up with the Jackson
plan.

In 1974, some white teachers in Jackson were laid off under the
agreement. They sued in federal court, and a judge ruled against
them. He found "a sound basis" to conclude that "minority under-
representation is substantial and chronic," that the "handicap of
past discrimination is impeding access of minorities," and that the
affirmative-action plan met standards laid down by the Supreme
Court. The U.S. Court of Appeals for the Sixth Circuit upheld the
trial court's ruling.

The core of the Solicitor General's argument asking the Supreme Court to overturn the lower courts was familiar. The white
teachers in the Wygant case had been laid off solely because of
their race, and because the school board had bound itself "to an
absolute layoff preference for 'employees who are Black, American, Indian, Oriental, or of Spanish descendancy.'" Neither the
school board, the lower courts, nor anyone else had found that
members of these groups had been victims of discrimination by the
school board, the city of Jackson, or the state of Michigan. "All

there is by way of justification for the racially based misfortune visited upon petitioners are references by the district court and the court of appeals to a history of 'societal discrimination' . . . 'under-representation' of minority teachers . . . and the need to supply 'role-models' for minority students." [68]

The conclusions of the SG's brief went as follows: "So casual a waving aside of the fundamental Fourteenth Amendment principle of equal treatment for all persons regardless of race and of our republic's basic moral vision of the unity of all mankind cannot be countenanced." [69] What Fried meant by the phrase "the unity of all mankind" was not explained. In any case, he went on, the courts below had "drawn a wholly unwarranted connection between the general history of racial discrimination in this country, and the statistical underrepresentation of minority group members in the teaching corps relative to the student body—without even the semblance of an attempt to relate that disparity to some pattern or practice of conduct by the school board." Then the courts used this "suppositious discrimination to justify a remedy which further undoes the connection between wrongdoer and victim," and let a person, "say of Asian descent whose ancestors suffered discrimination in the early history of California," gain an advantage over the white petitioners. "The third and final step in the shambling logic of this enterprise would justify the explicitly racially based layoff of petitioners on the ground that this is necessary to provide 'role-models' for minority group students. Stripped of its veneer of unsupported psychological and sociological conjecture, this justification can only mean one of two things. It may mean that black, Hispanic, or Asian students learn better if they are taught by black, Hispanic, or Asian teachers. Or it may mean that such students, conscious of the injustices done to the groups of which they are members, will draw encouragement and a practical moral lesson from seeing members of their own (or some other) minority group in positions of authority and respect."

To Fried's mind, the claim about role models missed the point that the "most powerful role models are those who have succeeded without a hint of favoritism." It also begged the question at issue in the case. "For one must assume that these students will be aware of the very system of racial preference which delivers role models in supposedly sufficient numbers. But what is the moral lesson that such a system teaches? Surely not that ours is a society in which each person can succeed as a result of his or her own work and talent. On the contrary, one may likelier suppose that such a system (its actual working laid bare) will teach a different and more sinister lesson: that one hundred and twenty years after the end of slavery government may still advance some and suppress others not as individuals but because of the color of their skin." [70]

Much of the SG's brief came off as a lesson about morals and role models rather than as a statement about law. But the brief reached a legal conclusion: "Equality before the law, so magnificent in principle, is often a difficult and uncomfortable concept in practice. There have always been and perhaps will always be voices seeking to carve out special exceptions to this principle based on history, prevailing social conditions, temporary need, or expediency. After the era of Reconstruction, such voices prevailed, and the true meaning of the Equal Protection Clause was long suppressed. In 1896, this Court approved the concept of 'separate but equal' facilities for blacks and whites and thus upheld the arrest of Homer A. Plessy for occupying a railroad coach reserved for whites. . . . In one of the most famous and prescient dissents in the history of this Court, the first Justice Harlan wrote . . . : 'Our Constitution is color-blind, and neither knows nor tolerates classes among citizens. In respect of civil rights, all citizens are equal before the law. The humblest is the peer of the most powerful. The law regards man as man, and takes no account of his surroundings or of his color when his civil rights as guaranteed by the supreme law of the land are involved.' This vision became the creed of the Civil Rights Movement, and eventually the nation." [71]

To brighten its argument, the SG's brief also included an attention-grabbing example: "Henry Aaron would not be regarded as the all-time home run king, and he would not be a model for youth, if the fences had been moved in whenever he came to the plate." [72] In a brief about the kind of affirmative action used by the school board in Jackson, Michigan, the example was wholly misleading. It implied that affirmative action in the case of a Henry Aaron would mean moving in the fences, as if minority teachers in the schools were permitted to impart less knowledge to their students than other teachers. For the analogy to work, however, it had to describe how a black athlete like Aaron might realistically benefit from affirmative action—how he might get a special chance to prove his talents as a ballplayer and earn a job as a major leaguer. A minority teacher hired through affirmative action in Jackson was expected to perform in the classroom at the same level as his colleagues. Similarly, once an athlete whose entrée to the majors had been helped by affirmative action stepped up to the plate, he would face the same pitcher and have to hit a home run over the same fence as anyone else.

At the Justice Department, the Wygant brief stirred a lot of talk. Some lawyers agreed with Fried's judgment that it was "wonderfully well written." Others did not. Lawrence Wallace commented on Fried's style, "His writing is of a more disputatious nature, written with an admixture of styles you might find in the *New Republic* or the *National Review.*"[73] And one senior lawyer in the department remarked, "It doesn't read like SG stuff. It reads like a combination of what you'd see in a neo-con editorial and a snarky Harvard book review."[74]

The strongest criticism of the Wygant brief faulted it on the grounds described by Charles Fried and Philip Heymann as the basis for the Solicitor General's legal arguments—that is, legal philosophy. In a 1964 lecture called "Civil Rights and the Limits of Law," Paul Freund addressed the question "Is not the Constitution color-blind? Can a preferential treatment of Negroes be squared with the requirement of equal protection of the laws? Is it not an unconstitutional discrimination in reverse?" Freund instructed, "The first thing to note about Justice Harlan's phrase is that it is not a constitutional text, it is a constitutional metaphor." No reference to the "color-blindness"of the law appears anywhere in the Constitution. The phrase had been taken by the Justice from a brief written by Albion Tourgée, a lawyer and novelist. (Tourgée's collaborator in the case, though not on the brief, was Samuel Phillips, an admired former SG whose thirteen-year tenure toward the end of the nineteenth century was almost twice as long as that of any other Solicitor either before or since.) Harlan's reading of the Constitution (for example, in a case where he judged that the right of an employer to hire and fire at will could not be tampered with by a statute protecting an employee's right to join a labor union) was not so pure that a lawyer should take the Justice's metaphorical teachings over the lessons of the text itself. As for the text, Freud said, "the most obvious fact" about the Fourteenth Amendment was that "it grew out of the Civil War in an effort to raise Negroes from the level of legal inferiority." In two cases, at least, there could be little doubt about the lawfulness of preferential treatment: where public facilities were unequal and de facto segregation shunted blacks to inferior ones; and where de facto segregation was "a product in part, a remnant, of the governmental discrimination in the past." Freund also said, " . . . if pushed to a drily logical extreme," the phrase "the Constitution is colorblind" can become "the reverse of liberal." He noted what Charles Fried did not: ". . . the moral, and it may be the legal, difference between a preference in favor of a minority and one against it." [75] The Supreme Court had acknowledged the distinction and, by authorizing affirmative action, turned it into law.

Laurence Tribe, the professor who filed a brief against Fried in the abortion case, who holds the only chair in constitutional law at Harvard Law School, and who is seen by some lawyers as the private lawyer's equivalent of an SG, was quoted by NBC News as saying, "The Solicitor General now is hardly a friend of the Court. He is a friend of the Administration and of Ed Meese." [76] When he was asked to comment about the Wygant brief, he said, "What's striking about the Wygant brief is not that it explores the underlying philosophies of equality that might give rise to either a condemnation or an acceptance of affirmative action on constitutional grounds. What's striking is its pamphlet-like quality: the offhand discussion of Hank Aaron as a role model, the cavalier assertion that life would have been different for Plessy if only he had lived in another state besides Louisiana, because he was just one-eighth black. Those are things I would have expected to find in a public speech by an Attorney General, or by a President, and not in a Solicitor General's brief. Not because it is wrong or unhelpful for a brief to have a colorful flourish here or there, but because, at least in my conception of a powerful brief, more work must be done to connect the flourishes to substantial and careful examination of law, and to the underlying philosophical issues in the case. What is striking in the Wygant brief is that those observations float free of any anchor in the law itself. There is a casual examination of three or four arguments made by various people chosen almost at random who are in favor of affirmative action, and then a rather sweeping non sequitur defending the principle that the Constitution should be color-blind."[77]

Tribe also commented, "It seems to me that the problem isn't that the SG's briefs are philosophical, it's that their rhetoric is not carefully connected with a legal theory that is made coherent and brought to bear on cases themselves. In Wygant, for example, the fact which is clear from the record that prior to 1954 there were no minority teachers at all in Jackson is surely not irrelevant. The case is about whether an agreement entered into by the local government which is designed to assure a more integrated society is lawful. And yet from the SG's brief you wouldn't even know that that was an aspect of the case. The use of a case pending in the Supreme Court as an occasion for a grand pronouncement about a subject in ways not connected to the case, or to the history of legal development on the matter, unbolstered by a careful, comprehensive, and rounded statement of the relevant philosophy is less than one is entitled to expect from the Solicitor General's office operating at its best."

When the Supreme Court decided the Wygant case, in the spring of 1986, the Justices handed down the kind of mix of opinions that normally appeals to the Court-watchers in the SG's office. There were five opinions, and none was joined by more than three Justices. A majority of five struck down the Jackson scheme, on the ground that the school district had never proved how its affirmative-action plan was justified by discrimination against minority teachers in the schools. Writing a separate opinion to explain her part in the Court's majority, Justice Sandra Day O'Connor was clear about the evidence that would have accomplished that end. For her, proof that the share of minorities in the Jackson work force was much greater than the percentage of those hired as teachers could have settled the case of "deliberate discrimination."[78] Three Justices who formed the core of the majority were represented by Justice Lewis Powell, and he addressed another defect of the Jackson plan. While hiring goals diffused the burden of affirmative action throughout society, he said, making a large concession to those who favor affirmative action, goals in layoffs requiring whites to give up their jobs to blacks imposed "the entire burden of achieving racial equality on particular individuals, often resulting in serious disruption of their lives." Powell wrote, "That burden is too intrusive." In sum, the Jackson scheme was not "sufficiently narrowly tailored."[79]

The Court's opinions otherwise amounted to a rejection of the Reagan Administration's views about affirmative action. Attorney General Meese had boiled the Administration's position down to one line: "The idea that you can use discrimination in the form of racially preferential quotas, goals and set-asides to remedy the lingering social effects of past discrimination" was "nothing short of a legal, moral and constitutional tragedy."[80] Even the Powell opinion in the Wygant case refuted him. "In order to remedy the effects of prior discrimination," the Justice wrote, "it may be necessary to take race into account. As part of this nation's dedication to eradicating racial discrimination, innocent persons may be called upon to bear some of the burden of the remedy."[81] For the first time, eight of the Court's nine Justices (only Justice White signed no opinion commenting on the subject) appeared to endorse the voluntary use of hiring goals by government employers, like public schools, to correct their past discrimination against minorities.

Justice O'Connor explained, "[T]he Court has forged a degree of unanimity: it is agreed that a plan need not be limited to the remedying of specific instances of identified discrimination for it to be deemed sufficiently 'narrowly tailored,' or 'substantially related,' to the correction of prior discrimination by the state."[82] Though the Court's holding was no ringing endorsement of affirmative action, and it favored the side supported by the SG's brief, the O'Connor opinion explained why the case was a defeat for the Administration. The Solicitor General had taken a position that none of the Justices endorsed.

To Charles Fried, the style and substance of the Wygant brief was a fair sample of the amicus briefs that he filed in the 1985 Term.[83] He told the *Congressional Quarterly*, "There are cases where what is at stake is not some particular government program but an important and pervasive view of the law or the Constitution." While Fried suggested that his goal was to win cases instead of grandstanding ("The really important part of the story," he said, before the Court gave him his report card in the Wygant case, "is whether we got it right"), Steven Puro, a political scientist who studies amicus briefs, said it was notable that people often read about the substance of the government's filings in the newspapers, as if they were speeches or position papers, before the briefs ever made it to the Supreme Court. [84]

Burt Neuborne, a professor at the New York University School of Law who was then legal director for the American Civil Liberties Union, offered another judgment. He said that Fried had "demoted the Solicitor General's office to our level, the level of an ideological interest group, a salesman for a partisan line just like the ACLU is." [85]

XIII

The SG's Lawyers

LAWYERS IN THE SG's office describe themselves as nerds, wonks, and idiot savants,[1] who wear dull gray suits and thick-soled wing-tips, and sometimes relieve the intensity of analyzing cases with a quick game of darts.[2] They have an aversion to simplicity, one said, but in 1985 and 1986 some were anxious about what the SG's office was becoming and they spoke about it plainly.

In discussing their reasons for finding the traditions of the office to be under assault, the assistants meant to be careful. They balanced the list of wrongs against the office with an acknowledgment that the laws and cases in dispute could usually be interpreted in several ways. But they seemed to be a wounded, bewildered lot. They were contemptuous of what they considered crude legal notions emanating from the AG's office and often supported by Charles Fried as SG, yet fully aware that Meese and Fried had the power and they did not. These were smart, highly trained, articulate people who had a passion for the law. Though some expected to go into private practice or to teach, many hoped to spend their careers right where they were. They took the challenge to the way of doing things in the SG's office as an affront to a great institution and, because of the SG's role, an attack on the integrity of the law.

Edwin Kneedler, then a six-year veteran, explained the value that the SG's office had long attached to process.[3] He sketched how the SG's office traditionally worked and added a new dimension to the standard description. Ordinarily, an agency like the Department of Health and Human Services would recommend to a division of the Justice Department, say the Civil Division, that the government appeal a case. The Civil Division would then make its recommendation to the SG about what should be done. The case would be assigned to an assistant to the SG, like Kneedler, who would write a memo assessing the pros and cons of the recommendation. Making a proposal of his own, he sent the memo to a deputy, who added his thoughts in a brief note that was sometimes handwritten on a modest slip of yellow paper. The memo and note went to the SG, who made a decision. If there was any disagreement about what to do, lawyers from the agency and division involved might be invited to a meeting with the assistant to the SG, the deputy, and, perhaps, the Solicitor General, to resolve the case. In rare instances, the Attorney General was asked to help decide.

These steps represented a form of due process. The assistant to the SG would seek out the views of officials from all parts of the government with a stake in the case, to make sure his recommendation was informed by their experience. He had the freedom to write his own thoughts, but he was forced to put down on paper his assessment of the position the government should seek, making it clearer and easier to grasp than it would have been if he had made only an oral report, and harder to ignore if it ran counter to a claim with support elsewhere in the bureaucracy. The deputy was forced to articulate his ideas on paper, as well, if they clashed with the assistant's. Each point of view had a chance to be aired, and when there was a reckoning, it was with ideas rather than some form of posturing. The Solicitor General could rely on both the balanced approach of his aides and the clarity of the record as a foundation for his judgment. Being independent, as the Solicitor General usually prided himself in being, did not require riding roughshod over the rest of the government. The SG's office sat at the top of a very large pyramid—with lawyers in the ninety-four U.S. Attorneys' offices at the base, the Justice Department's trial divisions in the middle, and its appellate sections just below the apex—and a skillful SG used the government to help make a reasoned decision about the law.

"If you think about it," Kneedler reflected, "there are few occasions when one branch of government speaks directly to the other: the State of the Union address; proposals for new laws; vetoes of legislation. There is a great deal of diplomacy about them. Our filings in the Supreme Court are on this short list, and our faith in the separation of powers requires us to be respectful as well. For justice to be done, it must be seen to be done, too, and that's what this process is about."

Harriet Shapiro also talked about what had been. Her commitment to the SG's office was as serious as Kneedler's. Shapiro was editor in chief of the *Columbia Law Review* in 1955, when less than 10 percent of Columbia's law-school classes were women, and in 1972 she became the first woman hired as a regular attorney by the SG's office. (The highest number who have served at one time is four, and by 1986 there had been nine in all.) On her own hiring, she explained, "The young Turks in the office persuaded the SG it was time to hire a woman. They said he had never hired a woman before because nobody qualified had ever applied." [4]

The aspects of the SG's work that animated Shapiro, like Kneedler, dealt largely with the lawyer's craft. "In some sense," she said, "authorizing appeals in the lower federal courts may be the most important thing we do. Once a case gets to the Supreme Court, we have an information-gathering function, because the government as a whole is a repository of specialized information about all kinds of law: the Social Security Act, the Freedom of Information Act, and so on. One role we play is to translate this information for the Supreme Court, to tell the Justices about the impact of a possible decision on the workings of the government. On the other hand, the Justices sure as heck can read cases. They've got a terrific staff of law clerks who can help them with the reading, and in many cases they can get along without us. But when we're deciding about an appeal in the lower courts, we've got to decide whether the government should swallow a defeat or, if not, why we should take a crack at a case in an appeal. We serve a kind of judicial function, and it's ours alone."

In Shapiro's view, the SG's office served as a well-placed information booth, advising judges about the law (in the Courts of Appeals and the Supreme Court), answering questions from law reviews about legal developments worth noting, fielding questions from major newspapers about how to improve their coverage of Supreme Court cases. [5] What set it apart was its judicial function, and its attention to process. "The office makes decisions on paper," she said, "because it couldn't function otherwise. It's important to have a written record, because the government tries to take consistent positions—or, if it takes an inconsistent one, to know why." And: "Anyone who wants to talk to the SG's office about a case he has a part in, especially from the government, is welcome. The door is always open." Like many assistants, Shapiro took pride in her ultimate accountability for the office's work. "After a brief comes back from the printer in final form," Shapiro said, "it comes back to the assistant who worked on it. He's responsible for final checking—of proofreading, substantive stuff, everything. When he's done, he marks it 'O.K. for Filing,' and initials it. For me, that's a very special moment in the process. I look at the paper and say, 'This is the best I can do.' I believe in the process. When I put my initials on some paper, that's my stamp of approval."

David Strauss spoke shortly before he left the SG's office in 1985 to teach at the University of Chicago Law School. "I wanted to say what the office meant to me,"[6] he said soon after a farewell lunch in his honor. "It's been a huge experience working for the Solicitor General. More important than law school at Harvard, working on the *Harvard Law Review,* or clerking for Judge Irving Goldberg on the Fifth Circuit, whom I greatly admire. I believe, when I look back on my career, this will have been the formative experience. So there was something I wanted to say: the office believes in the sovereignty of reason. It's very much the ethos, and Ken Geller and Andy Frey, who are deputies, represent it best, since almost 70 percent of the work goes through them. In the SG's office, what you know is that you don't say anything or write it on paper unless you can defend it. If you do, and you can't, you'll be attacked and torn to shreds. But if you can defend it, you say it and, more importantly, you write it, so it's down in black-and-white. No one can misrepresent or mess with it. And even if your colleagues aren't predisposed to agree with you, even if they disagree with your larger judgments about policy, if you're right on the law and you convince them, they'll listen and back you."

Kenneth Geller came to the SG's office in 1975, after serving as a member of the Watergate Special Prosecutor's force.[7] By 1985, he was in charge of civil cases, and he was known at the Justice Department for his intense dedication.

"Reviewing cases from the Civil Division," one assistant said, "is very hard. It deals with a lot of really boring, technical things that are difficult to grasp, and Geller had a remarkable ability to see ill-founded notions the division wanted to push that no one else caught. A case came up from the Second Circuit on the question whether a resident alien"—someone without American citizenship living in this country—"could get Social Security benefits. A district court said yes. The Second Circuit said yes. To anybody but the political folks at the Civil Division, the answer seemed to be yes. The division wanted to appeal, and Geller wanted to avoid a big fight. No one else could figure out how to avoid it. So he asked about the alien, and what was likely if the Supreme Court ruled the way the division wanted. The alien turned out to be seventy-two years old and very sick, and she had been in the United States for twelve years. She qualified for benefits on a number of grounds, and it wasn't likely she would be deported, even if Geller took the division's side and won the case. So what was the point of the suit? If she wouldn't be deported, it was a lousy suit to push. It was such a simple point, yet nobody had thought of it."[8]

In his dealings with the Civil Division, Geller was often acerbic. "As usual," he sometimes began notes about the division's papers to the SG, "the Civil Division has missed the point."[9] Lawyers who received this sort of note hoped that they were not supposed to take it personally. Ridicule and sarcasm sharpened Geller's principal tool—reason—and if work from these lawyers gave him grounds to exercise it, they were willing to be corrected. One government lawyer, whom Geller described as "dumber than a stone" after they met about a case, called Geller the rudest person she had ever talked to. She said he was arrogant, and told him so, and he was not surprised. But generally his professional reputation (monklike devotion to the law, firm commitment to the government's interests, competence to match) was excellent. Some of his colleagues held him to be the best lawyer they had ever worked with.

Geller created a series of notebooks that played a characteristic part in the due process of the SG's office.[10] In a special binder he kept statistics about his caseload, the names of pending cases, and the outcomes in cases already resolved. Then came pages from a

loose-leaf publication called *U.S. Law Week,* showing a table of Supreme Court opinions from 1978 to the present, so Geller could quickly locate a citation in the Supreme Court's *United States Reports* for each, and memos written at his request by assistants to the SG about various topics of legal analysis that were frequently of use.

The heart of the book was a collection of aphorisms. They were quotations taken from Supreme Court opinions and copied by Geller into his book during the course of the previous few years. "These are the sorts of things you could never find by standard legal research," Geller said. "Opinions aren't indexed by aphorism," he pointed out, but he wanted to have them at hand. His entries included one in particular that appealed to him: " 'Unless we wish anarchy to prevail within the federal judicial system, a precedent of this Court must be followed by the lower federal courts no matter how misguided the judges of those courts may think it to be.' Hutto v. Davis." It summarized a traditional view now under attack by Edwin Meese and his supporters.

Geller also recorded in his book statistics that were available nowhere else in the government. Among other things, they revealed that for the judicial year beginning on June 30, 1984, and ending June 28, 1985, of 2,089 appeals handled by the Office of the Solicitor General, Geller had been in charge of 782, or 117 more than any other deputy in the office.[11] He had overseen about 37 percent of the office's work, and with Andrew Frey 69 percent. Of 110 briefs on the merits filed by the government in the Supreme Court, he handled 27, or almost a quarter of the government's primary statements about the law.

On file carts parked by the side of his desk, Geller kept rows of black binders storing all the memos he had reviewed as Deputy Solicitor, and all the memos dealing with civil matters going back more than a decade. Though they lacked the force of law, because they were internal documents used only to decide what position to take in a federal court, the papers made up a bank on which Geller and other lawyers in the SG's office could draw to ensure that the government took consistent positions before the courts (or, if not, could say why it had departed from previous submissions). The binders were part of the record of the SG's due process. They were a piece of the SG's memory, to which Geller served as the index, and they helped the office play its role in the law.

Andrew Frey was the office den leader: almost every day around twelve-thirty, he would knock on doors along the SG's corridor, and in an announcer's voice—"Lunch!"—round up a half-dozen lawyers for a session about the law over sandwiches in the Justice Department cafeteria. He was in charge of criminal appeals, and in that area was known as a persistent, sometimes obstinate, conservative. When Wade McCree became SG, he was told by people in the Carter Administration to "watch out for Andy Frey," McCree said, "because he just wasn't a liberal." (Frey became a favorite of McCree's.) Frey's job was to argue for rules that "promote efficient law enforcement," Frey said. "Everybody agrees that these aren't the only goals of the law, but I generally tried to move the law in the direction of helping the police do their job and prosecutors get accurate verdicts." [12]

Like Edwin Meese, Frey was preoccupied by problems caused by the Miranda decision. In an article for the *University of Pittsburgh Law Review* in 1978, he contended that, instead of trying to identify and punish those who commit crimes, the "first principle" of the law about confessions had become "solicitude for the interests of the arrested suspect." In the best of circumstances, confessions were difficult to obtain, Frey judged, and the "central inquiry" for lawyers should be how to balance the interest of police in obtaining "honest" confessions against the interest of a suspect in not being coerced to confess. Unlike the Attorney General, Frey acknowledged that the concerns prompting Miranda were "real and valid." But he also advised that the law should be changed to take a more "realistic view of society's needs"—that is, the needs of the police as opposed to suspects. The police should not be restricted to taking "statements only from those suspects who are unequivocally willing to give them." [13] Frey used SG briefs to guide the Court toward this view of Miranda, and if the Justices had not intended to strike the balance that Frey counseled when they handed down the landmark, as some legal scholars believe, [14] they did in cases he argued a decade later. By 1985, with a traditional, evolutionary approach, Frey had already helped accomplish without fanfare what the Attorney General contended was still left to do.

The most compact example of Frey's ability to persuade the Justices to take a position on the side of the government and against criminal defendants came in the area of double jeopardy. The principle of double jeopardy is reputedly the oldest of the procedural guarantees included in the Bill of Rights ("The laws forbid the same man to be tried twice on the same issue," Demosthenes wrote in the fourth century B.C.), [15] but, as a field of constitutional law, it was only sketchily developed before Frey joined the SG's office. Until then, most American lawyers with reason to think about the subject assumed that the Double Jeopardy Clause of the Fifth Amendment ("nor shall any person be subject for the same offense to be twice put in jeopardy of life or limb") meant that a criminal defendant had almost complete protection from further proceedings after any ruling in his favor by a federal court.

Frey's concern about double jeopardy was spurred by events that prompted the Supreme Court to re-evaluate this area of law as well. In 1969, the Court ruled that the clause applied to the states, where the vast majority of crimes are prosecuted. [16] In 1971, an omnibus crime law sponsored by the Nixon Administration included a provision explicitly allowing the federal government to challenge rulings by judges that raised questions about double jeopardy. [17]

The Double Jeopardy Clause protects a defendant against a second prosecution for the same offense after he has been acquitted; against a retrial for the same offense after he has been convicted and the conviction has been overturned; and against more than one punishment for the same offense. But the meaning of terms like "acquittal" and "conviction" is not always simple, and the Supreme Court has struggled to define them in this context. [18] Frey persuaded the Justices to read the clause as he did in most cases and limit the reach of this safeguard. His theme was that unless there was the threat of an entirely different trial, there was no second jeopardy, because the Double Jeopardy Clause does not bar the continuation of proceedings that could be carried on without making a defendant go through a new trial. Balancing the defendant's interest in receiving a final judgment and the state's interest in effective law enforcement, the Court accepted Frey's proposal that the latter be given more weight.

According to Peter Westen, a professor at the University of Michigan Law School and an expert on double jeopardy,[19] "The truth about Frey's work is that it was just highly intelligent advocacy. It didn't raise any red flags, because his were the same arguments that someone could make who was not pro-government, so few scholars in the law, let alone anyone else, picked up on it. He just tested old myths about doctrine, and came up with ideas based on good legal reasoning. It was a careful, methodical, incremental process."

To Westen's mind, the process that Frey used at the SG's office to craft his arguments was reflected in the Supreme Court's development of the law. Retired Supreme Court Justice Potter Stewart concurred with this judgment. "While a seat on the Supreme Court may be the best job in American law,"[20] Stewart said, "the Solicitor General's office provides the best lawyers' jobs. It's a small office, and it's independent. The Solicitor General has his own staff, and they argue fully half the cases before the Court. They participate in the development of the law. Andy Frey is a good example how they do it."

In March of 1986, it had been nine months since Charles Fried took over as Acting Solicitor General and five since he was confirmed as SG. In that period, over one-quarter of the lawyers in the office had left and been replaced. On a Wednesday during the first week of March, Andrew Frey, Kenneth Geller, and an experienced assistant named Kathryn Oberly, three of the most respected lawyers in the office, announced to Fried that they, too, had decided to leave. A lawyer in the office recounted,[21] "At three-thirty the next afternoon, a couple of secretaries wandered down the hall and told us we were wanted in Mr. Frey and Mr. Geller's offices immediately. People knew something was afoot. There was an inkling. But we weren't sure what. We all crammed into the suite where Andy and Ken worked next door to each other in adjoining offices, and Charles said there were some announcements. Andy started, and told us that he and Ken and Kay were going to be leaving to join Mayer, Brown & Platt"—the Washington, D.C., branch of that Chicago law firm. It also employs former Acting Solicitor General Robert Stern and former Deputy SG Stephen Shapiro, who are two of the three co-authors of Stern, Gressman, and Shapiro on *Supreme Court Practice;* former (political) Deputy SG Paul Bator, who now teaches at the University of Chicago Law School and who is of counsel to the firm; and former assistant to the SG Mark Levy.

"Andy said it was a bittersweet moment for all of them, because the SG's office meant a lot to them. But the law firm had offered a wonderful opportunity. Then Charles piped up, and that's when the offensiveness began. He said, 'We're sorry to see Andy and the others go, but I have some really good news.' Then he told us about their replacements. He went on for a long time, and finally Larry Wallace, who hadn't planned to speak, felt compelled to deliver a kind of apology for Charles. There was a lot to apologize for. The combination of Charles's remarks and his press release about the new appointments, which didn't mention Andy or Ken or Kay, made it seem as though he had asked them to leave. Neither he nor anyone else said the unspoken, but it was definitely there. Of course, that was the farthest thing from the truth and it was a terrible thing for him to do. It was as if somebody had given a eulogy and he had said, 'The deaths of this trio are too bad, but life goes on and besides there are three less mouths to feed. And let me tell you about my three *new* friends.' He must know that it's bad for the office to lose three first-rate, experienced professionals in one blow, but he had no idea of the depth of feeling that people have about all this. It is going to mean the end of an era, and I blame Charles."

The press release the lawyer had in mind was dated Thursday, March 6, 1986. It began, "Solicitor General Charles Fried today announced the appointment of three new deputy solicitors general—a United States attorney from California, the former chief appellate lawyer for the Justice Department's Criminal Division, and a partner in a prestigious Washington law firm. All three have clerked for justices of the United States Supreme Court." [22] On the face of it, the release justified Fried's enthusiasm about the new appointments. The three lawyers were very well qualified and showed every promise of meeting the standards set by the deputies they were going to replace. But, according to an official of long tenure in the Justice Department, [23] the release departed from Justice Department tradition by failing to mention the three lawyers leaving the SG's office to join Mayer, Brown & Platt. It was also misleading. The release suggested that the new deputies were each directly replacing the three who were departing. In the case of William Bryson, a Special Counsel to the Organized Crime and Racketeering Section of the Criminal Division, and a onetime assistant to the SG, who was taking the place of Andrew Frey as deputy in charge of criminal matters, it was true. In the others it was not. Donald Ayer, the U.S. Attorney in Sacramento for the Eastern District of California, was filling the job of political deputy held by Carolyn Kuhl. Louis Cohen, a partner in the law firm of Wilmer, Cutler & Pickering, and, like Fried, a former law clerk to Justice Harlan, was assuming the post vacated by Louis Claiborne five months before. Oberly and Geller were not being "replaced."

A few days later, *The New York Times* ran a small article about the new appointments. [24] It mentioned the outgoing trio, but it reversed the order of the departures and arrivals, and implied that the former lawyers had been dismissed. ("Two top deputies in the Solicitor General's Office have said that they are leaving for a private law firm after the Solicitor General, Charles Fried, announced their replacements," it began.) A lawyer outside the Justice Department who deals regularly with the SG's office commented about this gloss on the departures of Frey and Geller, "It really irritates me that a lot of lawyers are asking whether they were forced to leave, or whether they resigned. They were the top lawyers in the government, and people should know they weren't fired." [25]

From Fried's vantage point, Geller and Frey had brought the problem on themselves. While the SG had known for months that Oberly and Geller were thinking of leaving (Geller was a candidate for a judgeship that he was not offered), Fried said that neither they nor Frey had given him adequate notice. (When the lawyers told Fried they were leaving, they said they would stay as long as he wanted.) Fried also said that Frey's decision was a complete surprise. [26]

To others, Frey had seemed the most likely to leave. In 1984, he had been nominated for a judgeship on the local, as opposed to the federal, Court of Appeals in Washington. According to an official familiar with the District bench, as a former editor of the *Columbia Law Review* who had won Columbia's award for its outstanding graduate and then risen to become Deputy Solicitor General, Frey had the "best legal credentials" of anyone ever nominated to that court. [27] But after the Washington *Post* reported that Frey was a member of the National Abortion Rights Action League, the National Coalition to Ban Handguns, Planned Parenthood, and the Legal Aid Society of D.C., conservatives opposed him and the Reagan Administration asked the Senate Governmental Affairs Committee to cancel the hearing it had scheduled to confirm Frey. [28]

He had done more than any advocate since the mid-seventies to persuade the Supreme Court to take conservative positions in criminal law, [29] and his views about criminal law were relevant to his possible duties as a judge: half the docket in the D.C. court is made up of criminal cases while less than one-sixth of the cases deal with criminal law in the average federal appeals court. [30] Frey's thoughts on social issues like abortion and birth control were close to irrelevant, because few of the cases before the local court were likely to involve them. But the nomination lapsed at the end of the Congressional session in 1984, and after President Reagan was reelected, he chose not to follow the local bar's recommendation and name Frey again for the judgeship. The experience embittered Frey (about the press, about the New Right senators who attacked him, about the members of the Reagan Administration who sympathized with them and made his life difficult at the SG's office). Almost everyone who worked with him in the SG's office expected he would eventually leave.

The *American Bar Association Journal* wrote up the departures under the banner "SOLICITOR GENERAL: HAS OFFICE BEEN POLITICIZED?" [31] The piece was neither trenchant nor harsh, but after it was published, the SG followed his habit of correcting the reporters of pieces he did not like ("You hit all the sour notes," he complained to the reporter from a newspaper about a story on the departures) and wrote the *ABA Journal* to protest the opinion of its feature. A lawyer from Alaska, who had once worked with

Kathryn Oberly on a Supreme Court brief, also read the account of the departures, and wrote her a letter.[32] He had just finished reading the *ABA Journal,* he began, "and by luck opened to page 20 and saw your picture at the bottom of the page so I read the article. The article disturbed me greatly—I would hate to see the 'most prestigious little law firm' in the United States lose that great institutional credibility it has both with the court and with members of the practicing bar. So much for the myth that conservatives protect our institutions, values, and traditions!"

With the departures of Claiborne, Frey, and Geller, the SG's office had lost three of its four nonpolitical deputies in five months. They had a combined total of over forty years of experience as government lawyers, and in the history of the SG's office there had never been a wave of departures like the one under Fried.[33] Oberly had four years of experience in the SG's office, and she had thought about making a career in the government.[34] After she and her colleagues left, three-fourths of the lawyers in the office had been there less than two years.[35] Counting all the lawyers who had left on Fried's watch, the rate of turnover in the office was 50 percent in his first year, or double the normal rate.[36]

Lawyers in the SG's office recognized that Frey, Geller, and Oberly had each left for different reasons, but they also believed that the trio had been increasingly disturbed by Charles Fried's advocacy and had finally lost patience with him. No matter how lawyers who were left behind rationalized the departures ("Andy is a splendidly capable lawyer, but he's a very hard grader," said one, "and the only SG he's ever worked for who measured up to his standard was Bob Bork"), the lawyers took them as a judgment on Fried that spoke for itself.[37]

During the week after the changing of the guard, lawyers in the SG's office said: "Charles is hiring very good people, but there's a sort of affirmative-action program for right-wingers. He gives them a big preference. He's on a hot seat. He wants to maintain professional standards and not everything he does is indefensible or plainly wrong, but something always grates." "Geller didn't know the difference between himself and the United States. He was about as loyal and dogged a civil servant as you can find in the government. His slot won't be easy to fill. It can't be done by a mere mortal. You've got to have real penetration and quickness to do the job. I'd heard he was looking, but this is a sure sign that he was disgusted." "The people and the traditions in the SG's office can be dispensed with. There's nothing that makes it so special that can't be changed overnight." [38]

Not long afterward, the pitch of emotion fell and leveled off. Many of the SG's assistants were exhausted from months of pressure generated by work and worry, and some wondered if they should remain to uphold traditions that newcomers might not know about, or if they should take a hint from Fried's decision to hire all but one of his deputies from outside the staff. ("Why am I here at 2 a.m. if I'm not appreciated?" one assistant asked.) Others were struck by a newfound grace in Fried. On the last day that Frey, Geller, and Oberly spent in the SG's office, the Solicitor held a small ceremony to honor them and told his full staff that the trio was irreplaceable. "It was something that needed to be said," an assistant commented. To fill the assistant's slot for a tax specialist that recently belonged to Albert Lauber, Fried chose a career lawyer from his permanent staff. (Lauber had planned to return to private practice, but he decided to stay when the SG asked him to replace Geller as a deputy.) The SG used the hire to soothe the feelings of the civil servants who worked for him. Fried also let the new tax lawyer know he was not the first who had been offered the job, and turned a bright note flat. [39]

IN AN ARTICLE ABOUT the SG's office, Robert Stern once wrote, "The Office, experience proves, molds the Solicitor General, who usually comes from an entirely different background from that of his staff, but almost invariably prides himself on conforming to the standards of the Office. The consequence is that the Office operates pretty much the same way no matter who is Solicitor General." [40] Through the end of the Carter Administration, longtime lawyers in the office later said, Stern was essentially correct. The SG's office held the image of a talented, hard-working, compulsive band who put great store in legal reasoning and who were accustomed to almost total deference from the rest of the government. In reality, the assistants and deputies knew, they got their way more often in dry technical cases about tax law than they did in front-page tests of the Constitution, and they thought this was appropriate. Some admitted they were occasionally less punctilious than tradition suggested, and counseled the government to override the interests of other litigants in court. They could also be high-handed about basic details. If they did not like the draft of a brief written by a lawyer elsewhere in the Justice Department, they often discarded it and wrote one they liked instead. But the lawyers admitted their lapses because they were confident about the general value of their prudent ways. [41]

Under Rex Lee, Bradford Reynolds's frequent clashes with lawyers in the SG's office led to his "running to the AG" on an almost regular basis, and the SG's office became the subject of increasingly common front-office arbitrations. When Charles Fried became SG, Reynolds didn't have to go to the AG, because Edwin Meese had designated him the SG's overseer. "It used to be that the SG's slip"—the piece of paper on which the Solicitor General announces his judgment in a case—"represented the last word," an assistant said. In Lee's time, if Reynolds disagreed with the SG, it was grounds for a new debate. By Fried's day, lawyers in the SG's office expected that in almost any controversial case the SG would have made the SG's slip an afterthought: by the time a case reached him for decision during his first year as SG, according to some of his assistants, Fried had figured out what was expected of him in the front office by speaking with his "kitchen cabinet." This was composed of lawyers from the Bob Jones team—Reynolds; Carolyn Kuhl, whom Fried promoted from Deputy Assistant Attorney General for the Civil Division to take his place as political deputy; and Charles Cooper, who was promoted from his post as Reynolds's deputy to be Assistant Attorney General for Legal Counsel. (Fried saw the same facts differently. He often turned to Reynolds for advice because he respected the lawyer's judgment, he said—Reynolds was one of the few top officials as old and experienced as Fried at the Justice Department. The others were talented lawyers whose ideas he valued.) [42]

Lawyers in the SG's office especially resented what one called the "shadow process"—Fried's freewheeling method of taking part in the office's development of positions. It came about slowly. Soon after Fried arrived as political deputy, he asked an assistant to rewrite a memo because he did not like its tone. ("There is a standard set of tropes to characterize the arguments of an adversary which I don't like," he said later. "I can't stand 'multiply flawed.' I can't stand any suggestion that an argument is made in bad faith. In my book, that charge is inadmissible.") The assistant reminded him of the office tradition that every lawyer was responsible for his own arguments, and said that if Fried didn't like what he'd read, he was welcome to set his own thoughts on paper and append them to the memo bound for the SG, according to the practice of the office. Fried asked the lawyer once again, emphasizing it was the tone and not the outcome of the argument that he disagreed with. What happened next suggested otherwise. After the lawyer submitted a milder statement of the case, Fried made it appear toothless by flatly disagreeing with it on substance. [43]

Once Fried was confirmed as SG, the shadow process was stepped up. In some cases, according to lawyers in the SG's office, he picked up the phone and called the general counsel of the agency with a grievance in a sensitive case, so they could work out a deal. The lawyers in the agency, the division with responsibility for the case at the Justice Department and especially at the SG's office, who had laid the groundwork for the judgment of the Solicitor General, were left in the dark about the arrangement he had made. In the agenda cases, lawyers in the SG's office were certain, the problem of ad hoc negotiation was worse. Fried held secret meetings with his kitchen cabinet and others to set a position for the government, or excluded lawyers in the SG's office from meetings that were not secret. He did not consult assistants who had written the basic memos for cases, and used their papers to legitimize the agreements he struck on his own. He also undermined the status of his assistants with the rest of the Justice Department. Where they had been accustomed to dealing as equals with older and more senior officials (an admiral would come in from the Coast Guard to ask a young assistant to forward his service's appeal in a case about the placement of a navigation buoy; [44] an Assistant Attorney General would realize he had to persuade an assistant about the merits of his case if he wanted the Solicitor General to rule his way), [45] the assistants became prey to phone calls from the Attorney General's special assistants, fresh off clerkships, who took their cues from other front-office lawyers checking up on the Solicitor General. [46]

"Part of our being upset over this is the arrogance of the people in the SG's office," one lawyer admitted. "We think we're good lawyers. But there's also a value to putting arguments on paper, so everyone knows what the choices are and other lawyers are forced to deal with the merits or get the chance to offer a counter-view. We're also the only lawyers in the government who take a relatively neutral view. The agencies have axes to grind, because their programs are at stake in litigation. This Administration's senior executives are so political their legal views are colored as well. That leaves the SG's office, and one of the things that people in the office like least is that Fried gets advice from the agency involved, the responsible part of the Justice Department, his kitchen cabinet, and us, as if they were all on the same footing. He treats us like any other part of the government. That is what people in the office find most difficult to take." [47]

Through most of 1985, some assistants and deputies to the SG did not want to believe that the office was changing. They re-criminated about the pressures that drove Rex Lee out of office but insisted that the SG's office would regain its form if only the Administration would appoint someone, like Charles Fried, whose legal credentials assured that his mandate was to serve the law and not politics. [48] Then they detailed the pressures on Fried to submit briefs that carried the Administration's message beyond the Su-preme Court to American voters, and said Fried would declare his independence once he was elevated from Acting Solicitor General to SG. After Fried was sworn in, they contended that the agenda briefs he filed were distinguished from the great majority of gov-ernment papers, and that the Supreme Court would separate the former from the latter as long as the SG's filings on traditional subjects met the government's longtime standards. When the com-pass of the Administration's agenda expanded so it appeared to include almost any topic that caught the attention a member of the Reagan team, the lawyers in the SG's office came up with new reasons why what many other observers of the office thought was happening there was not as bad as it looked. The lawyers in the SG's office believed so strongly in the tradition of the place that they were sure Fried would come around. "Optimism springs eternal," explained one assistant to the SG after he was reminded about this series of rationalizations. [49]

Despite Fried's obvious intellectual quickness and his eagerness to engage in the work of the office, he did not make this brand of loyalty easy for his staff. In February of 1986, the Justice Department advertised the opening for an assistant to the Solicitor to handle tax cases. [50] The notice carried six requirements for candidates who wanted to fill the job. The next week, the government sent out an amended notice, which the Solicitor General had written. Fried had added a seventh requirement ("On occasion will be expected to work on special assignments of particular difficulty or delicacy outside the field of tax") that announced to lawyers they should be ready to work without qualms on agenda cases. Assistants still retained their optimism. They often spoke in melodramatic terms ("Not long ago, I thought Charles was going to succeed in destroying the traditions of the office") tempered with hope ("but I think things have finally turned the corner"). A Supreme Court law clerk harshly criticized Fried one day in an interview. "I resent the fact that there is any suggestion that Fried is an honorable man," he said. "He is an opportunistic, scheming, manipulative, mean-spirited man, and he's led a great institution into disgrace." One of the lawyers in the SG's office was asked how he thought Fried could continue to serve the government's interests if anyone with even modest influence in the law held such a black view. "Things are turning around," the lawyer said. [51]

Lawyers in the office volunteered a range of explanations for Fried's behavior: When he became Acting SG, in June of 1985, he still knew relatively little about how the government worked or about litigation; the first case he had ever argued was in the Supreme Court the winter before, as Rex Lee's deputy; he didn't know enough to see the fault in the political arguments pushed on him. [52] Or: He wanted to win the favor of the Meese team so they would appoint him SG, and "he went to absurd lengths to accommodate them." Or: Once he became SG, he meant no harm to the SG's office, but he was insensitive and didn't realize that the manner he used to ingratiate himself with members of the Bob Jones team "insulted lawyers who weren't targets of his charm." He also, at least at work, seemed unconcerned and neglectful of social skills or small courtesies—hello's, goodbye's, please's, thank-you's. He was an impetuous, enthusiastic official who had never managed an office before, and he appeared to overlook the value of basic plea-santries.[53] Or: He had little appreciation for good lawyering and cared less about a tight analysis than a bold, memorable declara-tion.[54] "He's very smart, he's very conceptual, he likes to put things in a general framework, which is always a help," Paul Bator said about his friend; "he's stronger on the conceptual side than on the detail side."[55]

On the other hand, Lyle Denniston, a legal correspondent for the Baltimore *Sun,* and now the dean of Supreme Court reporters, described Fried as an upbeat, naïve, refreshing intellectual, who believed deeply in the principles he espoused and was oblivious to pressure from political officials who wanted him to push ideas he had already come to on his own.[56]

The most sympathetic appraisal of Fried from career lawyers in the SG's office, which was shared by some who followed it from outside the government, was an explanation about circumstances: in the Meese Justice Department, Fried had little room to maneu-ver between the Attorney General's inner circle and the tradition-alists in the SG's office—social revolutionaries with no regard for the law, on the one hand, and intransigent holdovers, on the other, as they saw each other. It was a clash of forces, and Fried was caught in the middle. He was the right man at the right time, in this appraisal, because his cleverness, good nature, and intelligence equipped him as well as anyone to satisfy both sides. ("You don't survive by appearing disloyal to the Meese team," observed a lawyer in the SG's office who was in Fried's corner. "You've just got to fool them.") Fried might join a group within the Attorney General's inner circle known as the Committee on Religious Lib-erty for regular meetings to discuss how to promote their extreme version of that concept before the Supreme Court. But he also recog-nized, on advice from his deputies, the value of hiring lawyers who met the standards of the SG's office. Aligning Fried with Meese missed the complexity of his role, his appreciation for the tradition of the SG's office, and the moderation of his lawyering, even though the Attorney General went beyond valuing the Solicitor General's "intellectual breadth" and considered Fried a reliable member of his inner circle.[57] While Fried always insisted that he was frank when he spoke about his judgments as SG, one of his allies advised that the SG's need to satisfy Meese often prevented Fried from saying what he truly believed about his advocacy for the Administration.[58]

One of Fried's critics was asked to comment on the theory of his supporters. The lawyer said, "Charles sees himself as a consensus-builder. He thinks he hammers out deals that make everyone happy. The problem is they leave no one happy." The defiant edge of this remark seemed to bear out Fried's explanation for the bad feeling expressed about him at the SG's office: it was grousing from a bunch of prima donnas who were angry they had lost their sway. Fried said that making the SG's office more accountable to a democratically elected President was bound to cause resentment. Several former aides to the Solicitor, including one who shared and one who criticized Fried's ideas, supported this view. One former deputy, who is now a federal judge, said that the Solicitor General was inevitably engaged in judgments about policy; the surprise about the office was that it did not get more guidance from the White House. Surely Charles Fried was correct, though deputies like Andrew Frey and Kenneth Geller disagreed, that the job of the Solicitor General was not to extend the power of the government virtually every time it went to court. That was not the meaning of "doing justice." It was to represent the policies of the current government as well as he could, and still perform his other duties as SG.[59]

To some observers of the office, the deputies and assistants were finally getting their comeuppance. They invariably judged someone by how smart he was (when lawyers in the office heard a comment they considered worthy, they said, "That's a thought,"[60] as if awarding a star), and sometimes forgot that the clever answer was not always the right one. The real tradition of the office was a clubby sense of self-importance—what one ex-assistant called "a collective smugness."[61] Some of the SG's aides from Columbia, Harvard, and other élite law schools looked down their noses at political officials like Bradford Reynolds, Charles Cooper, and Carolyn Kuhl, as if where the three studied law (Vanderbilt, Alabama, and Duke) were enough to explain why they failed to defer to the wisdom of the office's career lawyers. ("They don't know any better because they didn't go to the right schools," one of the SG's lawyers explained seriously.) A bunch of well-credentialed white men (no matter how calmly the women in the office took their poor representation among the regular attorneys, it was conspicuous—and, since 1870, the office had employed only five blacks, including two SGs) had used a vague tradition as a cover for insisting on arguing whatever made sense to them in the law. "Their sort of know-it-all stuff is O.K. for a law clerk who is drunk from his first proximity to power," one legal reporter said about the SG's lawyers, "but at some point you've just got to grow up."[62]

However compelling some of the criticism about the career lawyers in the SG's office, Fried consistently brought the focus back to himself. "I'm feeling very upbeat about the office,"[63] he said one day in April of 1986. "The Term is coming to a wonderful end." Not long after, he talked about the changes he had weathered. He said, "When Andy and Ken and Kay walked in and said they were leaving, my heart fell into my shoes. I thought, This is a potential disaster. The buzzing about the office would have just what it wanted: a sign of vulnerability. I was very upset, and I was hurt because they'd given me no warning. If the word got out, the vultures, very much in the press—they like to see an event, a trend that corresponds to a cartoon-like quality—if the word got out, the event would prove itself. Those were five of the worst days of my life, but today I think we are in very good shape. After the assistants got over the shock, they were entirely with me." Confident that the office was finally under his control, he downplayed continuing rumblings as the harmless mutterings of a temperamental staff. Repeating a phrase some assistants used to describe their efforts to persuade Fried not to send one of his flightier notions to the Court,[64] the SG gamely made fun of himself. "Of course I appreciate it when the assistants 'scrape me off the ceiling,' " he said, as if it were the job of the young lawyers, a few years out of law school, to protect the Solicitor from his foibles, and not the other way around.

He went on, "I have a sense that when this Justice Department got started five years ago, the SG's office pictured itself as a bulwark against the barbarians. An embattled station. That seems to me just an untenable way to talk about your work. It's poisonous. If that's the way you feel, you shouldn't have the job. When I took it, I thought I should develop collegial relations with the rest of the department. I thought the rest of the people in it were serious and impressive, and I was sympathetic to their agenda. They got into government for the same reason I did. I don't push the views I do because I'm their Solicitor General, but they probably picked me to be SG because I have these views. I also thought there was a difference between saying that the SG's office contained the vestal virgins of the law, and that it could maintain its own special standards while representing the President's interests. Don't you think we've done that?"

The image Fried wanted to convey was of a Solicitor General who served both the Reagan Administration and the tradition of the SG's office. He blamed the lawyers in the office for the problems they had encountered in dealing with political officials at the Justice Department before he took over. An observer of Fried at the office was asked why he thought the SG did this. He explained that Fried said things like this for public consumption, to keep Attorney General Meese and the "idiots" around him happy, but that he actually relied increasingly on the lawyers in the office, especially the ones he had chosen.[65] "To get along in this Justice Department," the lawyer recounted, "you've got to be a hypocrite. You try to keep Meese and everybody happy, you try to operate by the traditions of this office, and you sometimes say things to grease the wheels that you'd rather not have to. Charles understands this."

Fried did not acknowledge that he faced anything like the dilemma described by his observer in the office. The observer was asked whether, in private, the Solicitor General ever spoke about either the unusual circumstances under which he served, or the different faces he presented to the front office at the Justice Department and to the office he led, in order to survive and carry on as SG. "I've never heard him mention a word about this," the lawyer replied. "You just have to intuit it from his behavior." The lawyer was told that Fried had defended the Attorney General and the

Meese team as energetically as he had criticized the SG's office under Rex Lee. The lawyer did not say anything for a moment and then answered, "Sometimes Charles goes beyond the call of duty." [66]

Fried emphasized the warmth and collegiality in the SG's office, as if the days of the Vestal Virgins v. the Barbarians ended when the disgruntled former deputies left, and a new era of harmony began. He made a point of going through the roster of lawyers in the office, and saying how well he got along with each one. Some of the lawyers he mentioned had different views.

"He's a bizarre fellow," one said. "To a lot of the assistants, Fried's actually gotten to the point where he can do no right. They are still upset over Geller and Frey leaving, and they blame Fried for that. They remain loyal to a couple of lawyers who were extremely able deputies. Fried is not seen as an ally of theirs. Even when he does something right—the new deputies he brought in are fine—he gets no credit. The case for him is that he has tried to maintain the quality of the office, but when there are get-togethers among lawyers who used to be in the office and lawyers who still are, you can see a closeness between Rex Lee and the staff that you don't see between them and Fried. You feel that you work for him, not with him. He has private meetings about cases. The collegiality Fried talks about is between him and the rest of the political appointees, not between him and the office. In the Department of Justice, there is a group that is in—in every section of the department—and there is everyone else, and Fried concentrates on the people who count. Most of them are not in the SG's office." [67]

"It's definitely the end of an era," another lawyer said, "in the sense that the SG no longer has the final say on what the law is. At least through the late sixties there were few challenges to the SG's authority, and there was little pressure on assistants and the deputies to change their minds about a legal problem. As recently as the tenure of Wade McCree, during the Carter Administration, you felt you could say what the law was, and be protected by the Attorney General. That was still true of Rex. You got the feeling that even if Lee felt pressure to take a different position, once he acted, one way or the other, the chance of reversal wasn't high. These days, it's pretty clear that Fried doesn't have free rein. Now there's a constant need to find a middle ground and accommodate the political folks. The SG is not making decisions that are the best for the government to take, in the best of all possible worlds. Sometimes the accommodations work fine. You also hear there are secret meetings that people in the office don't get invited to on political cases. From the Administration's point of view, that makes sense, because they came in with a prejudice against career people and thought the SG's office was trying to subvert the President's program. But it's still a big change.

"As for a sense of cohesiveness and spirit, it's hard to have that when only four of the seventeen assistants have been here for more than two years. It's hard to imbue the new people with the traditions of the place, even if they like tradition. Charles has come to appreciate the value of the organization more than he did when he came in as a loner, and he puts stock in collegiality. I don't see him as a captain on a bridge far removed from the deck. But he sees a different way of doing things. Even if the office isn't going down the tubes, the underlying question is: What is the role of the office? What is his job? How much independence should the SG have? Under Fried, you get the sense that he has less to say about how these questions are answered than do people outside the office. Even if he's not told what to do, there's a way of exerting pressure. An Assistant AG comes to see him over and over, and after a while Fried must get the idea he'd better do what the guy wants, or else. He has less authority to turn people down than the SG did in the past. If you're not willing to go along, you're obstructing the President's program. And Fried doesn't have trouble going along. He's not constrained by the government as a client, by precedent, or by standard legal reasoning. He takes a longer view, of who might be on the Court and what the law might become. If you're on the receiving end, that is, if you're up at the Court, it must be hard to distinguish between the abortion-type briefs and traditional ones. They get lumped together. That's the cost to the office, the cost of not having credibility."[68]

"It's difficult to draw any firm conclusions," said a third lawyer, "but my assessment isn't so rosy. In the first place, there is a low level of experience in the office. People just don't have the knowledge to draw on about how the government works, which makes it more difficult to resist badgering since they also don't know about what it means for the SG to be independent. In the second place, regardless of what Fried says about his support from the Attorney General and his independence, and I can't think of a recent case where he was overruled, there's a reason why we no longer have disagreements with the rest of the department as we did under Lee. Fried is completely in tune with Meese and company, who have a radical vision of the law. He has a very good sense of how far to go in pushing their agenda, so this office has become a tool of the Administration rather than the legal conscience of the government. In the third place, Fried loves talking about being in a dialogue with the Court. The idea of engaging in a dialogue with a judge is a peculiar view of the lawyer's role, but Fried doesn't take a traditional lawyer's view. He sees himself as being as much an originator of law as the Justices, and says he refuses to pander to the Court by telling them what they want to hear. But traditional lawyers don't see interpreting precedent that way. They see it as respecting the law." [69]

XIV

October Term, 1985

FROM THE DAY that Charles Fried filed the government's brief in the abortion case during the summer of 1985, the most often asked question about the SG's office was how the Solicitor General's aggressive advocacy would affect the office's standing with the Court. Whether the SG is seen as serving only the interests of the President who appointed him, as maintaining loyalty to both the Executive Branch and the Judiciary, or as serving all three branches of government through his duty to the law, the Solicitor General's credibility with the Justices is indispensable to him: he can be effective only as long as the Justices have confidence in his competence, integrity, and legal judgments.

Not long after the start of the 1985 Term, Charles Fried made a short argument before the Justices that some people at the Court cited as a good point of departure for a discussion about the SG's standing.[1]

One of the main tools of a courtroom advocate is his voice, and to observers at the Supreme Court, Fried's is his most distinctive physical feature. Fried speaks in the accent that some American Anglophiles pick up when they go to England for graduate school. Though he is married to an Englishwoman, it has been almost five decades since he lived briefly in England as a baby and refugee from Czechoslovakia en route to the United States, and almost three decades since he studied at Oxford. He grew up in Manhattan. Fried's accent strikes some as an affectation and it is singled out, even by people who like him, as a peculiar mannerism. When Fried-watchers at the Supreme Court recounted his performance in this case, they often imitated his voice.[2]

The case was Bender v. Williamsport, and it dealt with the right of a group of high-school students to meet during a free period at school and pray in a private club called Petros.[3] Bender drew attention because it was part of a series of divisive religion cases that had topped the Court's docket the previous Term. Attorney General Edwin Meese had discussed them at length in his speeches on constitutional law at the end of that Term, and his interest had influenced the government's position in Bender. When Fried took the podium to speak for five minutes as a friend of the Court, Justice Stevens immediately began to quiz him about problems of jurisdiction—the question of the Supreme Court's authority to consider the case. Fried's first answer was confusing. "I am not sure of what your answer is," the Justice told the SG. Fried tried again, and when Stevens began to correct him, Fried cut him off. "On the jurisdictional point," he said, "we do discuss that on page five of our brief. It is fairly intricate." The SG lingered on the last word, and then began his argument about accommodation of religion. Stevens heard him out, but at the end of Fried's speech he came back to the point that bothered him.

Stevens could not understand whether the case presented a true legal controversy for the Court to resolve. It was not clear to the Justice that John C. Youngman, Jr., who had pursued the appeal as a member of the school board and as a parent of a student, had shown how he or his son was harmed by the prayer meetings. To use Fried's word, the question was intricate, and it seemed that Fried was nervous or that he was not confident he knew the answer or that, from the vantage point of an amicus concerned with a lofty issue of constitutional law, he thought the Justice's preoccupation with this technicality was trivial—that the answer must exist somewhere in the case file.

"But at the time the appeal was taken," Stevens asked, "what was the controversy? Who was fighting with whom? Was there any allegation that any non-Petros child was offended by these meetings?" Fried replied, "Mr. Youngman, I believe, at that time was claiming on his behalf as a parent." Stevens persisted, "Where in the record do you find that?" Fried paused, and said, "I cannot point you to the section of the record."

During this second exchange, Stevens took off his glasses,

leaned over the bench to glower at Fried, and spoke in an increasingly agitated voice. Stevens does not have a naturally imposing presence, and he often seems grateful that lawyers before the Court are willing to help him and the other Justices solve the hard legal problems they consider. He normally addresses counsel in a respectful, easygoing manner. Now, however, he showed signs of anger at the SG's unsupported assertion and his attempts to dodge the question.

During the summer before the case was argued, Stevens had joined three of his colleagues in an extraordinary dissent from the Court's decision to let the SG argue in the Bender case as a friend of the Court. The senior deputy in the Court Clerk's office couldn't remember a similar dissent from any previous Term. [4] Stevens eventually wrote the Court's opinion dismissing the case, on the same procedural grounds that Fried had been unprepared or unwilling to discuss in response to the Justice's questions. [5] "A lot of people up here thought Fried's performance in the Bender case was shocking," said one law clerk. "He came in with a little speech about freedom of religion, and wouldn't answer Stevens's questions. He gave the impression that either he was a windbag or he was not telling the truth." [6]

Fried's performance in Bender was selected by career lawyers in the SG's office from the Supreme Court arguments, odd events, and amicus briefs submitted by the office in October of 1985 as what they called the "Embarrassment of the Month." [7] It was the first of a string of incidents that earned this sobriquet during the 1985 Term. The details of these encounters seemed to indicate that even if the career lawyers were not blameless in their disagreements with Fried and his allies, they understood better than anyone the long-term costs to the SG's office of his and the Administration's tenure. Under Fried, according to some of his aides, the SG's advocacy for the Administration often seemed to vanquish craftsmanship in the law.

Part of the new SG's problem was the insensitivity that he projected to the Court. During November, Fried argued for the government in a case called Davidson v. Cannon. [8] He later won it, and was proud of the victory. But at the oral argument, the SG began with what he judged a worthy piece of legal history, and what Justices and law clerks at the Court heard as tasteless commentary. [9]

The case concerned whether the negligence of a prison warden should make the government liable to a suit by an inmate. A prisoner had helped break up a fight between two other inmates, and one of them threatened to retaliate. The prisoner sent a note to the warden telling him about this threat; the warden read it, and passed it to one of his sergeants. The sergeant heard that the note was on its way and what it was about, but he did not bother to read it. Over the weekend, he forgot about it. Two days later, the inmate who had threatened the prisoner attacked him and beat him up badly, and the prisoner sued for damages. The Court eventually ruled that the warden's lack of care did not approach "the sort of abusive government conduct" that the Fourteenth Amendment's Due Process Clause was designed to prevent. [10]

Rather than going directly to the question of the government's liability, Fried opened his remarks with a comment about the prisoner who had been beaten up. "If I may," he began, "before I enter the details of what we consider to be the defects in petitioner's claim, may I suggest a more distant perspective on this case? A hundred years ago, Oliver Wendell Holmes began *The Common Law* by insisting on a distinction which he said was so basic that it is part even of our animal nature, the distinction, in his words, 'between being stumbled over and being kicked.' In this case, respondent"—that is, the warden—"can at most be said to have stumbled. If anyone kicked petitioner, it was his fellow prisoner, McMillan, against whom, of course, Davidson retains a cause of action." [11]

Fried saw his paraphrase of Holmes as a tribute to the scholarly tradition of the SG's office, but, as the opening comment on a case about the beating of a prisoner, the reference was jarring and crude. A number of Supreme Court law clerks mentioned it as an example of a Fried "snapper"—one of the showy fillips of language or law that he regularly employed. The Solicitor had the taste to sanitize Holmes's remark, by referring to "our animal nature" instead of quoting the Justice directly and saying it was "a dog" who knew the difference between "being stumbled over and being kicked." But, if not as a dog, was the Court supposed to think of the prisoner as another kind of animal? Did being a prisoner mean a man had to suffer incompetence from a warden, as an animal had to accept being stumbled over in the outside world? Although the SG's brief on the case was cited by some longtime lawyers in the SG's office as sound, Fried's oral argument in the case joined his performance in the Petros case as evidence of an odd insensitivity to his impact on the Court.[12]

In December, Fried's performance in two cases vied for honors as "Embarrassment of the Month," according to staffers in the SG's office.[13] The more poignant was called Batson v. Kentucky,[14] and it was argued by Lawrence Wallace. When Wallace became a target for the anger of Reagan conservatives after the Bob Jones debacle, they tried to link the source of his obstinacy to his political views, overlooking his loyalty to the SG's office. Wallace's sense of commitment was matched by his eagerness to get on with his work, and after an early period of uneasiness with Fried, he and the Solicitor formed a mutual-admiration society. Their legal experiences (Columbia Law School; Supreme Court clerkships; years as professors) were sufficiently alike to explain the alliance. Fried's quest for support among career lawyers in the SG's office also helped create this bond with Wallace, and each man praised the abilities of the other.

In the Batson case, the Supreme Court was being asked to revise a precedent set in the mid-sixties. During the heyday of the civil-rights movement, the Warren Court had held that prosecutors who systematically excluded blacks from juries solely because of their race, and "for reasons wholly unrelated to the outcome of the particular case on trial,"[15] violated the Constitution. But the Justices also held that it was lawful for prosecutors to strike blacks from juries by using peremptory challenges (a set number of challenges to potential jurors that prosecutors can exercise without any explanation) even if they excluded from the final panel all the blacks in a pool of potential jurors.

At Fried's request, Wallace argued in Batson. He had made his reputation as a civil-rights lawyer for the government, and, according to lawyers in the SG's office,[16] Fried believed that the Justices would think Batson was not an agenda case if Wallace represented the government. Wallace dutifully squared off against the

NAACP Legal Defense and Educational Fund, the American Civil Liberties Union, the Lawyers' Committee for Civil Rights Under Law, and other groups, and made the prosecutors' case— that peremptory challenges should be available even to exclude from a jury every black in the jury pool for no reason other than race. The Justices rejected his arguments.[17] In a seven-to-two ruling, the Court overturned a twenty-one-year-old decision and made it easier for black criminal defendants to keep prosecutors from excluding blacks from juries. Justice Lewis Powell wrote the Court's majority opinion, which united Justices from across the Court's spectrum. Although Wallace was embarrassed as the government's spokesman, the blame lay at Fried's door. He eventually accepted it. "I think the Supreme Court, on reflection, was right," he said. "I think they taught us something about adhering to our own principles more rigorously than we had thought to do."[18]

In another December case, Thornburg v. Gingles, Fried argued for the government.[19] In 1982, Congress amended the Voting Rights Act of 1965, which had let voters sue state governments for unfair districting, unfair registration, and other discriminatory election practices. With the help of the 1965 law, the percentage of blacks registered to vote in the South had almost doubled (from 29 to 57 percent between 1965 and 1980), and the number of blacks holding office increased from fewer than three hundred to over twenty-four hundred.[20] The Supreme Court had held that in order to win suits under the original law, voters had to prove that legislators who set district lines intended to discriminate against them when they diluted the voting power of minorities. The voters could not rely simply on a showing that the effect of the change was to dilute minority votes. In the wake of this ruling, Congress decided to amend the law. The Reagan Administration fought to have it retain the "intent" standard, on grounds that any form of an effects test would require "proportional representation" and lead to "a quota system for electoral politics." In 1982, both the House and the Senate rejected the President's view and voted overwhelmingly (389–24 in the House, and 85–8 in the Senate) to amend the law so that it allowed voters to use an effects test when seeking fairer elections. Under the 1982 amendment, voters had to prove that the "results" of redistricting denied them an equal opportunity to take part in elections and to choose the representatives they wanted.

The Gingles case arose in North Carolina, where several blacks challenged the state's redistricting plan for the North Carolina General Assembly, and a federal trial court found that the plan violated the new standard. The case was the first to test the 1982 amendment before the Justices, and it raised elementary legal questions. How should the Court interpret the new standard? What kind of evidence should it tell lower courts to rely on in making the judgment?[21] The state of North Carolina argued that the "results" that a voter had to show to get relief were the outcomes of elections in suspect districts. On that theory, if any blacks had been elected, the black voters could not have been victims of discrimination. The NAACP Legal Defense and Educational Fund, Inc., on the other hand, attempted to give substance to the new law's "totality of the circumstances"[22] test: even if some blacks had been elected, the lawyers contended, there were other factors to consider in assessing the "results" of an election.[23] In North Carolina, black districts had been submerged in white districts where voters elected several representatives, and blacks were only occasionally elected. The share of white voters who chose blacks on their ballots was extremely low. Even when whites voted for blacks, they ranked the blacks last or next to last. Blacks who won the highest number of votes from blacks regularly carried the smallest number from whites. After a century of official hostility to their voting in North Carolina, blacks still registered to vote less often than whites, and according to the Inc. Fund, black candidates sometimes lacked the money and know-how to compete against whites. As the lower court acknowledged, blacks occasionally won in the elections under scrutiny only because they picked up votes from whites who hoped to prove to the Court that the new districts treated blacks fairly. The Inc. Fund pointed out that North Carolina had long had the smallest percentage of blacks in its state legislature of any state with a sizable black population (blacks made up 22.4 percent of the state's residents, but had never been more than 4 percent of either house of the state legislature), and the first black had not been elected to the state House of Representatives until 1968.

In the Supreme Court, Fried articulated views primarily associated with Edwin Meese and Bradford Reynolds, and argued that North Carolina blacks should get elected "the old-fashioned way—through politics." [24] He agreed with the state of North Carolina that "results" meant "election outcomes." [25] Since blacks had been elected to office, he said, the new districting scheme could not have impeded the rights of blacks to play a role in politics. Fried's was a skillful presentation, and on the surface it was difficult to fault. But to lawyers interested in the case—and to civil-rights attorneys, because it dealt with the right to vote, Gingles was as important as any case on the Court's docket—the SG gave no help on the central question. As longtime lawyers in the Civil Rights Division at the Justice Department put it, it was impossible to tell from the SG's brief or from his argument how he thought the Supreme Court should interpret the amendment's new standard, except to rule that the districts in North Carolina were legal. [26] On the lawyer's issue, which a Solicitor General could be expected to see as the most significant in the case and the one on which the Justices might most value his counsel, Fried was silent.

The SG saved his voice for chiding the Republican Party of North Carolina; the then Senate Majority Leader, Robert Dole, Republican from Kansas; Senator Charles Grassley, Republican from Iowa; and eight other co-sponsors of the 1982 amendment, who together had filed an amicus brief siding with the NAACP Inc. Fund against the government. In their brief, the co-sponsors stated that the lower court had interpreted the new law as Congress intended.

On the steps of the Supreme Court after the argument, Julius LeVonne Chambers, the director-counsel of the NAACP Legal Defense and Educational Fund, Inc., who argued against the Solicitor General, observed that Gingles was the first case in his long career as a civil-rights lawyer in which he had faced the Solicitor General as "the enemy." [27]

The morning the Justices announced their decision in the voting-rights case, at the end of the 1985 Term, Charles Fried happened to be at the Court sponsoring a group of lawyers for membership in the Supreme Court bar. When he heard the Chief

Justice say that Justice William Brennan would announce the holding in the voting-rights case, Fried's back stiffened and involuntarily, it seemed, he sucked in his breath.[28] Brennan was a liberal and, if one of the Court's two liberals had written the majority opinion, Fried knew that it was not likely to favor the Administration's views. Brennan's first sentence confirmed this fear. Brennan handed down the Court's opinion on behalf of all his colleagues (though some filed separate opinions concurring or dissenting about peripheral questions), essentially rejecting the SG's interpretation of the law.[29] At forty-seven pages, the opinion was long. At least half of it was devoted to rebutting the Solicitor General's arguments, point by point.

The Court's opinion took care to identify and criticize the SG's departures from standard methods of legal reasoning. When the voting-rights case was briefed for the Supreme Court, the NAACP Inc. Fund complained that the Solicitor had offered "an account of legislative history" that was "substantially inaccurate." According to the Inc. Fund, in 1982 the entire Senate Judiciary Committee had favored amending the Voting Rights Act as it was ultimately amended, and two-thirds of the full Senate stood ready to support the bill in case any of the remaining senators should consider holding the bill in committee until it was changed to suit them. But the SG's brief focused on the views of a few senators who were overwhelmingly outvoted; it called the result of their stubborn bit of maneuvering a "deadlock"[30] instead of acknowledging the general harmony of the decision. After the amendment was passed, the Senate followed its usual procedure and wrote up the history of the new voting-rights legislation in an official Senate Committee Report. In his brief, the SG urged the Supreme Court to pay slight attention to this official Senate Report.

For the full Court, the Brennan opinion indicated that the disagreement about whose version of legislative history was accurate touched a deeper issue of law. "The Solicitor General urges this Court to give little weight to the Senate Report," the Justice wrote, "arguing that it represents a compromise among conflicting 'factions,' and thus is somehow less authoritative than most Committee Reports." The Court expressly rejected the SG's contention. "We have repeatedly recognized that the authoritative source for legislative intent lies in the committee reports on the bill." Later in the opinion, the Court again repudiated an argument presented by the SG, not because of any larger disagreement about philosophy but because of its faulty legal reasoning. "The United States," Justice Brennan complained about the SG's stated interpretation of the district court's original opinion in the case, "isolates a single line in the court's opinion and identifies it as the court's complete test."[31]

In January, February, and March 1986, the roster of agenda cases on the Supreme Court's docket expanded from school prayer, abortion, affirmative action, and other familiar topics, to include medical treatment of handicapped infants, land-use regulation, the conflict between federal labor law and local regulation, school discipline, and the legality of an established doctrine called associational standing, which makes it possible for an organization like the United Auto Workers or the Chamber of Commerce to sue on behalf of its members.[32] The agenda now seemed to include almost anything of interest to a member of the Reagan (and, really, the Meese) team. Though the cases raised eyebrows for different reasons, they were all notorious among regular observers of the Supreme Court. They continued to strengthen the concern that serious harm was being done to the SG's office.

In March, the talk was about the SG's brief in the case brought by the United Auto Workers against the Secretary of Labor. The government's filing prompted a united response by the improbable coalition of the Chamber of Commerce, the AFL-CIO, the American Medical Association, the NAACP, the Alliance for Justice, the Chemical Manufacturers Association, and the Sierra Club. At issue was a federal supplement to state unemployment insurance for auto workers who had lost their jobs because of foreign competition. In a highly unorthodox move, the SG's office waited until presenting its brief in the Supreme Court to raise the question of whether the United Auto Workers had standing to sue on behalf of its members. (According to the key precedent, an association like a union could sue on behalf of its members if members would have had standing to sue on their own, the suit brought by the association was related to the group's overall purpose, and the nature of the suit did not make it necessary for individual members to take part.)[33] The SG's approach was particularly odd, because when the government had earlier opposed the union's petition for certiorari, the SG had acknowledged that the Court of Appeals correctly applied the law of associational standing when it let the UAW represent its members and supporters in court, and appeared to endorse this doctrine, which it called "well-settled."[34]

Some of the associations that responded to the SG's brief had not planned to. They saw no reason to burden the Supreme Court "with a brief arguing that the Court should adhere to 'well-settled' principles that neither party had questioned in the Court of Appeals or at the certiorari stage."[35] Because of the surprise about-face by the SG, the associations suddenly saw a need to participate. Written by a trio of attorneys in the law firm of Sidley & Austin, which Rex Lee joined after he left the government, the amici's brief criticized the SG's office in unusually blunt terms for a paper filed at the Supreme Court. One of the brief's authors was the former assistant to the Solicitor, Carter Phillips ("that quota lover!"), who had tangled with Bradford Reynolds.

"Without any previous hint of doubt about the petitioner union's basic right as an association to have standing to represent its members' interests," the brief observed, "the federal government has asked this Court to hold as a matter of 'policy' that the petitioner union should be denied standing to assert the rights of its members in federal court. It is particularly inappropriate for the federal government to raise an issue as fundamental and important as the validity of associational standing without submitting the issue to the adversarial process at any time prior to the Court's grant of certiorari. Because the government's litigating tactics on an issue of such national importance are not proper, the Court should simply refuse to entertain the Solicitor General's suggestion, in this case."[36] (The Court did.)

In April, the case on the docket that captured the most attention at the SG's office was called City of Los Angeles v. Preferred Communications.[37] It was about the L.A. decision not to let that company provide cable TV service to city homes. The company's challenge to the city's judgment was based on the belief that Los Angeles had abridged the First Amendment's guarantee of free speech by insisting that the city had the authority to award a cable franchise to one company only, which was not Preferred. Bradford Reynolds and the circle of young lawyers around the Attorney General became interested in the case and, operating outside the sphere of civil rights once more, Reynolds urged Charles Fried to take a vigorous line in favor of competition and against regulation of the company's access to the city's cables.[38] He argued that the city's telephone poles, on which the winning cable company had hung its lines, had room for another set of cables as well, and that deregulation of cable and competition between companies would improve the choice of fare for viewers.

To lawyers involved with the case, the Reynolds argument had a number of problems. To begin with, it appeared to run counter to the Supreme Court's reading of the Constitution.[39] It also prevented the Solicitor General from defending a 1984 statute called the Cable Communications Policy Act. As a report by the Congress about the law announced, the act "expressly affirmed the authority of local governments to issue franchises for cable television service" and it reinforced their power "to determine the number of cable operators."[40] Reynolds wanted the SG to ask the Supreme Court to overturn the Court of Appeals' opinion upholding the city's cable regulations, and to overlook the new federal law about cable TV.

Charles Fried thought he should not push the Justices that far. He filed a brief advising the Supreme Court to do what it eventually did: to send the case back to the trial court to gather more facts as a basis for judgment about the First Amendment issue at the heart of the case. In contrast to the wave of cases in which he had appeared to capitulate to pressure within the Administration to promote the President's social agenda, Fried's decision in Preferred was hailed by lawyers in the SG's office as a sign of backbone.[41]

Nonetheless, the substance of Fried's brief had all but contradicted its conclusion. "What respondent seeks to do is to communicate messages—some of its own choosing, some of its own devising—on a wide variety of topics and in a wide variety of formats," the brief stated. "Surely this enterprise is every bit as much the enterprise of speech, of the communication of ideas, as are the traditional enterprises of newspaper and book publishers,

of public speakers, and of pamphleteers." The brief extolled the virtues of competition in the marketplace of ideas, and left to a footnote any discussion of the statute regulating cable TV that was central to the case. If not a pamphlet, the Solicitor's brief lacked the qualities of a traditional brief. The assistant to the SG assigned to the brief was unhappy enough about its contents to ask that his name be removed when it was filed with the Supreme Court. [42]

By late April, however, the Solicitor General was pleased with his performance on the job. His new team was in place and he was happily immersed in the details of the case that commanded attention outside the Justice Department. It dealt with the constitutionality of the Balanced Budget and Emergency Deficit Control Act of 1985, widely known as the Gramm-Rudman Act. [43] A panel of lower-court judges, in an opinion written by Antonin Scalia, had ruled that the feature of the act calling for automatic budget cuts made the act unconstitutional. [44] The judges found that the provision violated the Constitution's requirement for separation of powers between the branches of government by giving authority of the Executive Branch to the Comptroller General, who works for Congress.

The Comptroller General's task under the Gramm-Rudman law was to tell the Executive Branch how much it had to cut the federal budget to stay on schedule for eliminating the government's deficit. As head of the General Accounting Office, which is a nonpartisan agency of Congress founded in 1921 to monitor the Executive Branch's enforcement of the laws, the Comptroller General is appointed by the President for a fixed term of fifteen years. To assure his independence, the law setting up the agency says he can only be removed from office by impeachment or by a joint resolution of Congress. [45] Through the tenures of six Comptrollers, none had come close to being removed.

This fact made the appeals court's ruling appear speculative and largely abstract, and the lower-court judges knew it. "It may seem odd," Scalia commented, "that this current curtailment of such an important and hard-fought legislative program should hinge upon the relative technicality" of who had the power to remove the Comptroller General. "But the balance of separated powers established by the Constitution consists precisely of a series of technical provisions that are more important to liberty than superficially appears, and whose observance cannot be approved or rejected by the courts as the times seem to require." In their opinion, it was illegal for the Executive Branch to delegate power to the Comptroller General, because, no matter how farfetched it sounded, he could be fired only by the Legislature and thus was not an Executive official.

In Fried's argument in the Gramm-Rudman case, which was his last of the Term, he showed polish and admirable control. He supported the lower court's reasoning that the Act was unconstitutional, which eventually prevailed. [46] But he still drew the Justices into unusual exchanges. Early in his presentation, the SG tried to divorce himself from the contention he appeared to make in his brief that all independent agencies (not just the provision affecting the Comptroller General in the case) might be unconstitutional. The Attorney General had pursued the subject in speeches, and it was widely understood to be an agenda item. Fried began: "I would like to say at the outset that this second argument does not in our view in any way cast any doubt on the validity of agencies such as the Federal Reserve Board, the Federal Trade Commission, or any such agencies, and that the notion that the second argument in some sense endangers those agencies or would embark this Court on some constitutional adventure is simply a scare which we don't intend to throw into the Court and I don't think need be thrown there." To Justice O'Connor, the idea expressed in the SG's brief was "a novel doctrine" without precedent "in any of this Court's previous decisions." Drawing a nervous murmur from the courtroom gallery, she observed, "Well, Mr. Fried, I'll confess you scared me with it." (When the Court decided the case, it did not endorse the doctrine suggested by the brief.) [47]

Fried's "novel" approach came up again when the Supreme Court ruled on the Pennsylvania abortion case. By five to four, the Justices upheld the right to abortion. The Court's majority opinion was written by Harry Blackmun. He recalled that three years before, in the Akron case, the Justices had reviewed state and local laws regulating abortion. "In Akron, the Court specifically reaffirmed Roe v. Wade," Blackmun emphasized. "Again today, we reaffirm the general principles laid down in Roe and in

Akron." The Justice attempted to clarify why a majority of the Court thought that the Constitution protects the right to abortion. "Our cases long have recognized that the Constitution embodies a promise that a certain private sphere of individual liberty will be kept largely beyond the reach of government," Blackmun stated. "That promise extends to women as well as to men. Few decisions are more personal and intimate, more properly private, or more basic to individual dignity and autonomy, than a woman's decision—with the guidance of her physician and within the limits specified in Roe—whether to end her pregnancy. A woman's right to make that choice freely is fundamental. Any other result, in our view, would protect inadequately a central part of the sphere of liberty that our law guarantees equally to all." [48]

When the abortion case came down, Fried held the first major press conference ever given by a Solicitor General. He admitted that the case "was a defeat in the sense that the position we urged was not adopted by a majority of the Court." Now that the Court had spoken, Fried said, he wouldn't make a "pest" of himself by looking for another case that would allow him to press a similar claim. But he also hazarded that the government had done "a useful thing and a responsible thing in provoking a very restrained and a very probing constitutional inquiry which I believe is far from over." [49]

The inquiry he had in mind was a dissent by Justice Byron White—"one of the most remarkable and profound statements of constitutional principle which I have read for a long time," [50] Fried called it. Joined by William Rehnquist, White contended that decisions reading values and principles into the Constitution that are not explicitly stated usurp the power of the people, "for such decisions represent choices that the people have never made and that they cannot disavow through corrective legislation." The majority's was a "warped point of view," White concluded. "In my view, the time has come to recognize that Roe v. Wade," like other previously overturned Court decisions, " 'departs from a proper understanding' of the Constitution and to overrule it." [51]

The Solicitor General did not answer questions about the substance of another opinion criticizing White's. Justice John Paul Stevens dissected what he considered errors in White's logic. As

Stevens indicated, in 1965 Justice White had written for the Court when it struck down a statute outlawing birth control. In White's words, the law then in question deprived people of liberty without due process because of its "telling effect on the freedom of married persons." In the latest abortion case, White recognized that a woman's ability to decide whether to have an abortion was a "liberty" protected by the Constitution, but he announced that it was less fundamental than the rights associated with marriage. Stevens failed "to see how a decision on child-bearing becomes *less* important the day after conception than the day before. Indeed, if one decision is more 'fundamental' to the individual's freedom than the other, surely it is the post-conception decision that is the more serious." Stevens concluded, "In the final analysis, the holding in Roe v. Wade presumes that it is far better to permit some individuals to make incorrect decisions than to deny all individuals the right to make decisions that have a profound effect upon their destiny."[52]

The exchange between Blackmun, White, and Stevens about how the Court should interpret the Constitution carried wide significance, and it distracted attention from the Court's more focused response to the Solicitor General. Fried had asserted that the lower courts showed "unabashed hostility" to attempts by states to regulate abortion. For a majority of the Court, Blackmun found that the hostility came from the states. "In the years since this Court's decision in Roe," the Justice observed, "States and municipalities have adopted a number of measures seemingly designed to prevent a woman, with the advice of her physician, from exercising her freedom of choice." He added, "The States are not free, under the guise of protecting maternal health or potential life, to intimidate women into continuing pregnancies."

Like the Court's comments in the voting-rights case, Blackmun's statement transcended the question before the Court. A majority of the Justices seemed sufficiently concerned about the way the Solicitor General had argued for the Administration that they went out of their way to correct his presentation.

The Court's comments about the SG's arguments were prickly and virtually unprecedented, and they were restricted neither to cases the SG lost nor to agenda cases.[53] In a case where the Justices ruled in favor of the government, they corrected the SG on a technical doctrine known as equitable estoppel.[54] Explaining his understanding of a legal point endorsed by the Court, Justice Stevens instructed: "The [SG] has argued . . . that the remedy ordered by the District Court was improper because it rested on an equitable estoppel theory. The Court today correctly—and unanimously—rejects this argument, thus answering the central question of law that prompted it to grant certiorari in a way that completely repudiates the submission of the Solicitor General."[55]

To some lawyers in the SG's office, the opinions indicated that it was time for a statement of contrition from Fried and other senior Administration officials. The Solicitor General did not make one. When he commented on his record after the 1985 Term closed, he noted that he had won "a respectable 71 percent" and predicted that "the clarity of our arguments" would help shape the law in the future even though the arguments had not won the Court's "triumphant embrace."[56] Though the government's winning percentage had declined (in the 1984 Term, the government had won 77 percent of its cases, which was the average winning percentage during Rex Lee's four years as Solicitor General),[57] favorable holdings in uncontroversial cases about the details of government assured Fried a large enough share of victories that he seemed to feel comfortable reading the Court's high-profile opinions to find what he wanted.

After the voting-rights opinion was handed down, Fried declared that he was "very pleased" the Court had not endorsed the principle of "proportionate representation"[58]—which was never at issue in the case because, as briefs for all parties and the Court's opinion itself made clear, it was specifically excluded by Congress from the statute in question. In the wake of the affirmative-action cases, the Solicitor General explained the Court's holdings like this: "I think what they said is that while we feel using discrimination to get rid of discrimination is something you must never do, they said, 'No, not never, but hardly ever.' "[59] The Court had said nothing like Fried's interpretation. "To summarize our holding today," Justice Brennan wrote in Local 28 of the Sheet Metal Workers' International Association v. the Equal Employment Opportunity Commission, "six Members of the Court agree that a district court may, in appropriate circumstances, order preferential relief benefiting individuals who are not the actual victims of discrimination as a remedy for violations of Title VII" of the 1964 Civil Rights Act. [60] The Justice offered explicit directions on how to read the holding so no government official would do what Bradford Reynolds had done two years before, when he took a narrow decision and read it broadly as the basis for an attack by the Administration on affirmative action, [61] but Fried did not heed the Justice. The complexity of the Court's opinions about affirmative action gave Fried ample grounds for asserting that the Justices had been cautious in their judgments, but, instead, he pulled from the decision a strict limitation that simply was not there. [62]

It was not as far as Fried went to put his advocacy in the best light. He regularly emphasized that in Bowers v. Hardwick, [63] upholding a Georgia law that made oral and anal sex between consenting adults a criminal offense, the Supreme Court had used the same reasoning offered by the SG in the Term's major abortion case. Fried said the argument the Justices had adopted was that the Court should not "invent rights," and called this "the most dramatic example" of his salutary influence on the Court. [64] This claim astonished former and current lawyers in the SG's office. In the first place, Bowers was a case in which the government had not participated. (To former colleagues at Harvard Law School, Fried confided that the Attorney General and his aides didn't dare suggest that the SG file an amicus brief in the case, because they knew his reservations about the state law.) [65] In the second place, a reading of the opinions gave no reason to believe that any of the Justices, whether in the majority or in dissent, had actually relied on the Solicitor General's abortion-brief reasoning that rights should not be "invented."

Finally, to the extent that the SG's argument in the abortion case had any similarity to the holding of the majority in the sodomy case, it was like an argument that several Justices on the Court had been making for many years, and certainly did not reflect any novel contribution by the SG. [66] In fact, as one of Fried's deputies reminded him, the Justices in the majority in the sodomy case had done precisely what the SG had advised against in other cases when they read into the state law a distinction between homosexu-

als and heterosexuals that the law itself did not make, to uphold
the law's application to homosexuals. The SG had no basis for
taking credit for the Court's reasoning either way, and even one
of his unshakable defenders in the SG's office admitted that Fried
had engaged in "puffery" by doing so. (Another lawyer in the
office explained, "We got a run of bad decisions, so that was a
pretty bleak period for us. Charles meant to cheer the place up.") [67]
Attorney General Meese embellished the Solicitor General's line
and called the Court's decision to uphold the anti-sodomy law the
Administration's biggest victory of the Term. Meese and Fried
used identical language to present the Administration's public
position. They said, "We don't have to be in a case to get our view
across." [68]

Fried's habit of representing Court opinions to be as he wanted
them understood, and not as they were written, was related to the
theme of the Court's sharp criticism of him as Solicitor General—
serious concern about his repeated departures from settled practices of legal reasoning, in order to press for results favored by the
Administration. The pretense that the law is a system of scientifi-
cally applied rules was abandoned in the nineteen-thirties, [69] but
lawyers still agree on certain principles for reading cases and statutes. One of the most basic, as Fried regularly stated, was to begin
with the text of a decision or a law itself to understand its meaning.
Fried seemed not to do this when it did not suit his purpose. Not
long after decisions were issued in two cases on the Reagan agenda
(not because they were obviously part of the President's social
program, but because someone in the Justice Department had
added them to the list), Fried was asked what he thought of
the rulings. In each instance, a Justice representing the Court's
right or left flank had rejected a theory supported by the Solicitor
General.

"I'm gratified that Justice Rehnquist recognized the middle
ground we carved out," Fried said about the first case, which
concerned sexual harassment. [70] The main question before the
Court had been: When should a company be liable to one of its
employees for harassment by another employee? The Solicitor
General argued that unless someone let the employer know about
an incident of sexual harassment (for example, by filing official

charges), the company could protect itself from liability simply by declaring its opposition to harassment and setting up a grievance procedure. [71] Rehnquist had declined to rule on the question of liability. (The factual record in the case wasn't clear enough.) But, in his opinion for the Court, the Justice "reject[ed] petitioner's view"—and the SG's—"that the mere existence of a grievance procedure and a policy against discrimination, coupled with respondent's failure to invoke that procedure, must insulate petitioner from liability." [72] When Fried was asked about this apparent rejection, he replied, "Isn't it nice we can go to the written record, and let the words decide for us?" [73] While the Court may have "recognized the middle ground," its rejection of that position was as plain as words could make it.

Fried's second mischaracterization dealt with the Court's dismissal of the Solicitor General's request that the Justices overrule the precedent giving groups like the United Auto Workers the authority to represent their members in court under the doctrine of associational standing. "Well," Fried said, "I couldn't have been happier with the treatment the Court gave us. Read the Marshall opinion. He said, 'We are not prepared to dismiss the government's argument out of hand.' That was a very respectful thing to say.' " [74]

While some, with Fried, may have found respect in that single phrase of Marshall's, which Fried paraphrased, no one could find that quality in Marshall's complete statement. It closed, "[t]he Secretary" (by proxy, the Solicitor General) "has given us absolutely no reason to doubt the ability of the UAW to proceed here on behalf of its aggrieved members, and his presentation has fallen far short of meeting the heavy burden of persuading us to abandon settled principles of associational standing." [75]

By the end of the Term, the record showed that the Solicitor General's victories were less grand than he claimed, that his losses were more emphatic and severe, and that, in general, the Court had rejected the arguments of the Solicitor General more often than ever before in history. Coming from a moderately conservative Court, these judgments were all the more indelible.

XV

The View from
the Court

TOWARD THE END of the 1985 Term, a young lawyer who
had recently clerked for a Justice remarked that the question about
Charles Fried was not whether his advocacy had diminished the
standing of the SG's office before the Court, but how much he had
aggravated a problem that had started before his arrival. "Every
year,"[1] the former clerk said, "the law clerks from each chamber
have lunch with each of the Justices. Invariably, during the past
few years, the subject of the SG's office has come up. The impression the clerks get is that the Justices feel they can no longer trust
the SG's office as they once did. While the briefs dealing with the
merits of cases on the Reagan agenda are one thing, the skepticism
has spilled over to other sorts of filings. In some cases, clerks found
that the SG's statements carried the stamp of a sharp-edged advocate more than a dispassionate scholar. There were definitely papers that were less honest about the facts and case citations than
they should have been. In order to dissuade the Court from taking
a case, for example, a petition opposing certiorari would downplay
conflicts in the Circuit Courts and claim support for its argument
which existed only weakly in the cases the SG's office cited. On
the whole, the office continued to file good briefs and to make
more polished and confident arguments than other lawyers. But
from the Court's point of view the politicization of the SG's office
marked an important change. In the past, the Justices had counted
on the SG as a kind of partner, an officer of the Court whose
inclusion in the list of officials at the front of every volume of the
United States Reports symbolized his special duty and loyalty. By
filing amicus briefs in cases where the federal interest was attenu-

ated and asking the Court to overturn recently reaffirmed precedent, or by attacking landmark holdings, the SG turned himself into a partisan before the Court and a kind of adversary of the Court itself. This was a major topic of conversation at the Court. It was significant because it determined how the clerks and the Justices first looked at material from the SG's office, and it was clear that the Court didn't trust the SG's office the way it used to."

It would not have been surprising if observers' opinions about Fried conformed to their views about the desirability of the results he sought: liberal law clerks would be his biggest critics, conservative clerks his boosters, and moderates somewhere in between. Since liberal Justices do not necessarily hire liberal clerks, or conservative Justices conservative clerks, there was no foolproof way to test this theory. But when, at the end of the 1985 Term, law clerks from each of the nine chambers agreed to be interviewed, as long as they were not identified by name, the results *were* surprising.

Except for one clerk, known by others for his devotion to the Federalist Society (a meeting ground for rising and established Reagan conservatives),[2] who chose not to speak, with the comment that "most of the clerks up here are very liberal and aren't likely to give the Solicitor General a fair shake,"[3] every clerk interviewed said that Charles Fried had pushed the Administration's political agenda more aggressively than any SG they had heard of from the Justices and prior law clerks. Two clerks praised the SG's office and said that, for all Fried's excesses ("He is definitely a maniac," said one, with obvious overstatement. "Even staunch Republicans tell lawyers thinking about government service not to go near the Justice Department or the SG's office, because they are now bastions of extremism"), the Court paid little attention to the Administration's rhetoric and found little reason to fault the craftsmanship of most of the SG's work. Discounting the notion of a special role for the Solicitor, as if anyone familiar with the law realized that the days of dispassionate advocacy were long past, one clerk said that the SG's work met the highest standard for lawyers urging a hard line on the Justices.[4]

But the majority of the clerks, who described themselves variously as moderate conservatives, moderates, or liberals, gave

many reasons to conclude that the reputation of the Solicitor
General at the Court had slipped dramatically during the 1985
Term. From all nine chambers, and very different political visions, they accused him, or the office under his command, of bad
lawyering, intemperance, deceit, arrogance, extreme partisan-
ship, and disgracing a long, great tradition. The language they
used often seemed exaggerated, but a clerk who described himself as a moderate conservative commented, "A guy gets up there
and he flaps his arms like a duck and he quacks like a duck, what
do you think of his work? He claims, 'This contravenes all notions of legal history,' or says, 'This contradicts known principles of law.' The Justices aren't idiots, and neither are the clerks.
They know what he claims is often hyperbole. It just rolls off his
tongue, and sounds like a lot of rot. He's the one who uses
strong language without cause." One of his fellow clerks said
more succinctly about Fried's advocacy, "My government lies to
me. My government *lies* to me!"[5]

The clerks also offered wide agreement about a concrete measure of the erosion in the SG's influence at the Court. A principal
chore of the Solicitor's office is to help the Supreme Court set its
docket by screening petitions for writs of certiorari. In the 1985
Term, parties from around the country filed 3,876 cert. petitions;
the Court granted only 146 of them.[6] As in previous Terms, the
task of winnowing out about 96 percent of the petitions was
tedious but important. No party came close to matching the Solicitor General's record of success with cert. petitions. The government derailed some cases on their way to the Court by opposing
petitions from other parties; it boosted the chances of other petitions by joining at the request of the parties submitting them; and,
where only a tiny fraction of petitions from any other party succeeded, the SG's office persuaded the Court to take an extraordinary share—83 percent—of its own petitions.

The rate of success in the 1985 Term was slightly higher than
during Rex Lee's last Term as Solicitor, when the Court granted
80 percent of the government's petitions. But while the government filed about the same number of amicus briefs to support
petitions from other parties, the Court granted only 57 percent of
these petitions, as opposed to the 80 percent it had accepted on

average during the previous four Terms.[7] This fact suggested that while the SG continued to affect the Supreme Court docket through its cert. petitions, Charles Fried had pressed the Administration's agenda at the cert. stage more aggressively than Rex Lee, and certainly more than previous SGs, who rarely entered cases at the cert. stage as an amicus.

Fried appeared to pay a price for it. In most chambers, reading and thinking about cert. petitions is a job that the Justices share with their clerks. The chambers of Justices Brennan, Marshall, and Stevens handle petitions independently,[8] but during the 1985 Term and before, the other six Justices decided which petitions to grant by forming a pool of all their law clerks, assigning one clerk to write a "pool memo" about each position, and basing their individual votes largely on information provided by the pool memo. The clerks had legitimate firsthand views about the petitions, since they had a significant hand in helping the Justices rule on them.

A law clerk: "The SG's cert. petitions cause law clerks a lot of consternation. When the Court sees 'The United States' at the top of a petition, it tends to be especially interested. The Court respects the government. When you're up here, you assume that the United States knows when not to bring a case to the Court. That's one of the main purposes of the SG's office, to determine which cases to bring to the Court's attention. The problem is that a lot of the petitions the Court now gets from the SG aren't what the Justices expect. As a law clerk, you go over them with a fine-tooth comb, because the petitions don't cite cases and they make huge assertions that don't always stand up. A whole lot of cert. memos begin with phrases like 'It's puzzling why the SG is bringing this petition.' You see that language quite often. The Supreme Court grants cert. if four Justices vote in favor of hearing a case, and on the 1985 Court there were three Justices—Burger, Rehnquist, and White—who used to give the SG the benefit of the doubt and were usually inclined to vote for his petitions. But now clerks often suggest: 'We know you want to hear cases the government says to, but not this one.' When the year started out, sometimes there wasn't a fourth vote. Now, though there are no official statistics kept about this, sometimes the SG gets none at all."[9]

Another clerk: "The clerks resent Fried, in part, because he makes our job harder. We don't trust the SG's submissions the way previous law clerks told us they did. That's no big deal, really. We're supposed to be here to do legal research. But the people who do the work for the highest Court in the Judicial Branch of government can use the SG's help. Nine Justices, thirty-three law clerks, sixteen secretaries, the people in the Clerk's office, the messengers, the library staff—it's not very many. It matters that the SG is less trustworthy, because the Court tends to get a less balanced picture of the law and the facts than it expects. The SG used to play a valuable role of processing information about the impact on the law of a possible holding, but that's been changed. Now he omits key cases, which, in the law, is a form of dishonesty, or he sneaks around precedents. This is not just a bureaucratic squabble. It's a break with a long tradition." [10]

A third clerk: "As a little kid, I actually wanted to be a lawyer. The first time I saw a picture of the Solicitor General on the steps of the Supreme Court, I thought, That's great, I aspire to that kind of integrity. When I got a little older, I read about the office and it measured up. I wanted to go there. Now it's over. This isn't something I want to be part of. It's tainted. The office doesn't seem to be a place where integrity reigns. It might change, but not for a long while." [11]

When Fried was asked about the government's cert. submissions during his tenure, he said, "You make an assertion in a cert. petition, and not an argument, so you want to be especially sure you're confident about what you say in them. I will never stretch a point about a conflict between the circuits. I will never say something is important to the government if it's not. I don't think our record this year is any different from in the past. On the whole, I think we do a fine job. On that, I would be very distressed if I learned otherwise, because with cert. petitions I am trying to be the faithful servant of the Court." [12]

During the Term, the Justices made a number of other minor decisions that signaled a decline in the SG's status before the Court. In two major cases—the Wygant affirmative-action case and the Akron abortion case—the Justices denied the Solicitor General's request for time to present an oral argument as a friend of the Court. According to Richard Revesz, an assistant professor at New York University School of Law, the denials fit a larger pattern. From the 1953 Term through the 1985 Term, he discovered, the Supreme Court refused to let the Solicitor General argue as an amicus curiae only eighteen times. The Justices turned down the SGs' requests on twelve occasions in the first five Terms of the Reagan era, when the Reagan SGs had asked the Justices for permission to argue as a friend of the Court as many times as their predecessors had in the previous twenty-seven Terms. In a third major case during the 1985 Term—about a school's authority, consistent with the First Amendment, to punish a student for making lewd remarks in assembly—the Justices denied Fried argument time even after the school had agreed to his request for ten minutes to present his views in favor of civility in schools. According to the Clerk's office, it was the only time in the history of the Supreme Court that this had happened. [13]

The denials were the only public sign that a majority of the Court sometimes disagreed with Charles Fried's insistence that he had the prerogative of stating the government's position as a friend of the Court in cases where there was no federal interest. But inside the Court the topic was a regular source of tension among the Justices. One Justice explained, "In those instances where the SG had requested time to argue and had shown that one of the parties was willing to give him ten minutes, the Chief Justice invariably approved. When another amicus asked for the same thing, on the same grounds, he invariably said no. That created some flak among the Justices. It was an irritant. All the rest of us didn't always agree with the Chief, and there was at least one case where we decided the government should not be given time to argue, because there was no federal interest." In the cases where no party had given the SG time to argue, even the Chief sometimes agreed with his colleagues. When the SG asked for time in the abortion case, Warren Burger issued an unusual internal memo in which he said the government should not be allowed to argue before the Court because there was clearly no federal interest in the case. [14]

Behind the scenes, there were other events, too, that reflected on the SG's increasingly shaky standing with the Justices. The Solicitor General asked the Clerk of the Court for a second extension of time to file a brief in a minor case called DiNapoli v. Northeast Regional Parole Commission.[15] The Criminal Division of the Justice Department had handed in its draft brief to the SG's office behind schedule, so the SG thought he needed more time.[16] To Charles Haydon, the lawyer from New York City opposing the government on behalf of DiNapoli, the second request for an extension of the deadline appeared to have serious consequences. His client was in jail. If DiNapoli was to win his appeal, every day of delay before a decision meant more unwarranted time behind bars. Haydon wrote a letter of protest to the Clerk's office. "I strongly object to a further extension and request that the Court act on the petition for the reason that it is inconceivable that three months are required for the response," the lawyer declared.[17] "If Petitioner's position is correct, he is being held illegally while the government takes its time in reviewing a response."

The letter went to Thurgood Marshall, the Justice who oversees the business of the U.S. Court of Appeals for the Second Circuit. Marshall dismissed the lawyer's protest,[18] but the incident reminded the Justice how unhappy he was about the state of affairs at the SG's office. As a former SG himself ("It's the best job I've ever had," he once said, "bar none!"),[19] Marshall has unusually high expectations of the office. During the 1985 Term, he complained to other Justices that the office had grown noticeably sloppy under Fried, and had taken advantage of its special relation to the Court. Some Justices also knew that Marshall believed in playing by the rules. ("I never got any special favors when I was representing the NAACP," he would say.) He raised the DiNapoli question at the private weekly conference of the Justices, and then asked a deputy clerk to come see him about their decision. The clerk let the SG know that the Justices would no longer tolerate repeated requests by him for extra time to file.[20]

As the Term drew to a close, the opinions of the Court rejecting the government's positions in agenda cases provided detailed evidence about the SG's loss of standing with the Justices. But the SG's defeats in the agenda cases were accompanied by a series of rejections in other matters as well. It was one thing for the Solicitor General to be chastised by William Brennan in cases where the sides could be easily identified as liberal and conservative. Charles

Fried suggested as much when he dismissed as "nonsense" charges that his advocacy had hurt the standing of his office with the Court. That sort of talk came from people who were so opposed to the Administration's views that they could not "bear" to have them stated, he said. (Fried also attributed the talk to vindictive lawyers who had left the SG's office and were out to settle a score;[21] to "smart-aleck insiders" who showed "disrespect for the Court" by suggesting that the SG's tactics as an advocate had backfired, irritating some of the Justices enough to cost the Administration victories it might have had if the SG had softened his approach in the agenda cases;[22] and to a flock of unnamed critics—"You know, there is a certain desire on some people's part to get the SG," he said on TV at the end of the 1985 Term.)[23]

But other rejections occurred in cases not obviously on the President's social agenda. The opinions were written by Justices ranging from liberals (like Brennan and Marshall), to centrists (Blackmun and Stevens), moderate conservatives (Powell and O'Connor), and even the Court's strongest conservative (Rehnquist). "The worst possible result of the aggressive Reagan policy would be for the Justices to take out their frustrations with the Administration's filings in agenda cases on regular government cases,"[24] concluded one assistant to the SG. This is just what appeared to have happened by the close of the 1985 Term.

In an opinion about the government's "secretive" policy to deny mentally disabled people Social Security benefits, Justice Powell wrote for a unanimous Court. Although the government argued that it had properly handled the appeals at issue, Powell sternly disagreed. He insisted that the people were entitled by law to a "fair and neutral"[25] procedure, and that the government had not given it to them. "While 'hard' cases may arise," Powell concluded in his opinion, "this is not one of them." Clerks and Justices at the Supreme Court spoke about the Social Security case as if it were another one of Fried's forays on behalf of the Administration's agenda. In a sense, this proved how thoroughly the SG's credibility had eroded. For his part, Fried wrote off the case. "That was a standard government case," he said. "We got a client, the client's got a problem, and you do the best you can for your client. That struck me as a down-the-line case. I didn't even handle it. I let the career lawyers worry about the case." [26] Fried might not have worried about it, but the Justices held him responsible for the government's position.

In a criminal case, the Court criticized the Solicitor General for making an argument the Justices had "expressly rejected" [27] when the government had first tried it a few years back. In a case dealing with attorneys' fees—an area of law where the Supreme Court had recently adopted the government's position in almost every instance—four Justices ridiculed the SG. They noted that the formula he had recommended for awarding fees in a civil-rights case would have inevitably, and unacceptably, yielded a paltry amount to lawyers who had worked for years to vindicate the rights of the Chicano plaintiffs. The Justices declared, "We reject the Solicitor General's suggestion that the prospect of working nearly 2,000 hours at a rate of $5.65 an hour, to be paid more than ten years after the work began, is 'likely to attract a substantial number of attorneys.' " [28]

Fried stated publicly that his advocacy had not damaged the reputation of the SG's office at the Court, but behind the scenes at the SG's office, lawyers said, Fried was profoundly disturbed by the Supreme Court's criticism of his advocacy. Inside the Justice Department, the SG spoke as if he believed he had been sold a bill of goods by Reynolds and other political officials who, on behalf of Attorney General Meese, convinced him to make the arguments he did in some controversial cases. [29] He declared his intention of finding a middle path between what he called "being obdurate and being abject before the Court." [30]

Fried was encouraged to seek this prudent course by Donald Ayer, the new political deputy who arrived with a sterling reputation from his post as U.S. Attorney in the Eastern District of California. Despite Ayer's partisan charter and his description of himself as a Reagan Republican, when he came to the Justice Department, in the spring of 1986, he was unprepared for the intensity of interest from political appointees outside the SG's office who expected to play a large role in shaping the SG's briefs. Lawyers in the SG's office said that Ayer was "shocked" by the pressure from Reynolds. After Ayer got caught in a shouting match with Reynolds about the government's briefs in a trio of agenda cases, the usually reserved Deputy SG described Reynolds to some of his colleagues as "a jerk," "a horse's ass," and worse, and said that if Reynolds had been calling the shots throughout the Reagan years, he finally understood why the President had such a dismal reputation on civil rights. Ayer was loyal to the Solicitor General, and the contribution of the new conservative political deputy, ironically, was to remind Fried of his legal responsibilities, and to press him to give up pamphleteering. "I'm especially concerned with the integrity of papers the government files saying what the law is," Ayer said. "I think a lot of attention has to be paid to conservative standards in the legal sense." [31]

ALTHOUGH MANY LAWYERS deduced a tie between the changes in the SG's office and the Court's apparently negative response, few could show a direct link. Members of the Court themselves offered the evidence.

By the end of the 1985 Term, the Justices had each observed an average of five SGs, and had more experience together as a panel than any set of Justices in history, so they could provide well-informed views. Although one Justice decided the topic was "a sensitive one, too sensitive" [32] for him to discuss, and one did not break his policy of not granting interviews to talk about Court business, a majority of the Justices were willing to address the subject of the SG. One Justice observed that the SG's standing as an advocate was still relatively high, especially among members of the Court's right flank. ("His writing always has influence," the Justice said. "Chief Justice Burger, Justice O'Connor, Justice Rehnquist—they've always been interested in what the present SG says, and gain support from his briefs for positions they want to espouse.") Another Justice treated the changes in the SG's office as a faint bureaucratic rumbling in the Justice Department, barely audible on Capitol Hill where the Supreme Court sits. Focusing on the institution instead of the man, the Justice said that the Court's high respect for the SG continued as usual. [33]

But others acknowledged a decline in the standing of the Solicitor General, and spoke in detail about their own views and those of their colleagues on the topic. According to these Justices, the expressions of concern and disapproval in the Court's opinions were only a hint of the sadness and distress felt by at least a majority of the Justices (Brennan, Marshall, Blackmun, Powell, and Stevens, four of whom were appointed by Republicans) about the changes in the role of the Solicitor General. Interviews with Justices, law clerks, and other close observers of the Court also indicated that each of the four other Justices was sometimes put off by the SG's advocacy, because he had been too aggressive (O'Connor), too supercilious (White), or too willing to be spokesman for the "reactionary" Reagan Administration (Burger). [34]

While William Rehnquist was the only Justice who suggested that he was skeptical of the notion of the SG's dual responsibility, to the Executive Branch and to the Court [35] (to him, the SG is above all an advocate for the Executive rather than the Tenth Justice), apparently he, too, was somewhat critical of the role Fried was playing. When the Justice was asked whether he agreed with Rex Lee's statement that the SG should not be a Pamphleteer General, Rehnquist replied, "That's exactly right." [36]

"Charles Fried is a different type of Solicitor General," said one Justice. "I'm a little biased, I suppose. I think that Archibald Cox and Erwin Griswold got it right. They thought they had a basic responsibility to the Court as well as to the Administration, and they were not the political voice of the Executive Branch. They thought they had to say 'No' on occasion, and the Court was confident in them. Generally, until recent years, I've always welcomed any filing by the Solicitor General. Now the clerks tell me consistently that you can't trust the SG about the facts or the law the way you'd like, and I rely on their judgment. So we pause a bit longer in granting cert. just because the government says to, and we may grant a few less. I had always tended to apply the word 'integrity' to the SG's office. There was always an honest presentation made. When they took a position, even in the big policy cases, they were always straight on the law. I sense that there's less of that now. I've felt that I've had to watch for political overtones as I didn't from Wade McCree or other recent SGs. Of course, the current SG has taken a beating for it, more than in any Term I can remember. We're saying to him: 'Don't do this. You're going too far.' But if a couple of us old goats fall over, we'll be replaced—and who knows what will happen." [37]

Another Justice had been willing to speak the year before as well, and the turn in his opinions was conspicuous. At the close of the 1984 Term, he offered what he felt was a realistic view. "I don't criticize the SG for changing his views about policy matters from Administration to Administration," he had declared. "The Solicitor General is the government's attorney. I regret the shift that the SG's office was forced to make in the Bob Jones case, but it was not out of the question. There have to be some responsibilities on political grounds. Either the SG represents the Administration, or he quits."[38]

A year later, the Justice's tone had changed markedly. He was angry. He said, "I'm quite surprised that Charles Fried has departed so far from the standard that Rex Lee strived for, which is the standard that has governed the SGs since I've been here. While they were all very loyal to the Administration, they drew some lines. No one has ever gone as far as Fried.

"I get the impression that on abortion, affirmative action, and a whole range of other subjects, he's gone way out of his way to support the point of view of the Administration. On a lot of them, he has to know he faces an uphill climb to persuade us that the Administration is right. In a number of cases, we've already said rather definitely how we feel about them. In abortion, Justice Powell said what the Court thinks only a few years ago in the Akron case. But Fried came at us with the recommendation that we reverse ourselves as if it were old hat to do that. And in affirmative action he's persisted in reading into the Court's opinions ideas that our writings won't bear. It's hardly the mark of a reasoned approach to the law. It's ideology, pure and simple. It's an assault on settled practices. That's the thing that has distressed me most about it.

"I look at things from the SG's office a lot more closely than I felt I had to in the days of anyone else. I scrutinize the cert. petitions more so than I used to. Not that I don't think the government makes a case that we should grant its cert. petitions more often than we do for any other petitioner, but I don't give them the same benefit of the doubt I used to and I have to spend more time combing through their work. Now I don't have the feeling that every case is presented squarely. I'm not even sure that the facts are accurate, in some cases. In the past, I didn't have that uneasy feeling about the SG, but today I do.

"There's no question we've taken this SG to task in our opinions more than any of his recent predecessors. What we're saying to him and the other people in the Justice Department is simple: 'Listen, you guys, you're just dead wrong. This is an abdication of your responsibility.' The notion that the SG has no obligation to help the Court is an outrage. You might as well let the rest of the government argue its own cases. What good is the SG?

"The thing of it is, Fried hasn't learned a thing. He's really been boasting that he has an obligation to press on the Court the Administration's view. In the context of the traditional role of the SG's office, this is revolutionary. And he has persistently misstated what the Court has held in various opinions this Term. His suggestion that we had accepted the basic premise of the Administration except for a couple of wrinkles in the affirmative-action cases is irresponsible."

The Justice concluded: "Fried clerked for Justice Harlan, you know. Harlan had enormous respect for the SG's office, and if he were alive to see this, he'd be just as disappointed as some of the rest of us." [39]

XVI

The Rule of Law

NOT LONG BEFORE the close of the 1985 Term, Warren Burger unexpectedly announced his resignation as Chief Justice of the United States and Ronald Reagan selected William Rehnquist to succeed him. The President chose Antonin Scalia to take Rehnquist's place as Associate Justice. Though the appointments did not change the number of Justices who were likely to support the Administration's arguments before the Court (as does seem likely to happen with the replacement of Lewis Powell in 1987), they supplied an exclamation point to the Term. The end of the Burger Court prompted its students to compile some fascinating statistics about the era.

From 1801 to 1900, the average number of Supreme Court cases decided by a bare majority each Term was one.[1] During Warren Burger's tenure as Chief Justice, from the 1969 Term through the 1985 Term, the Court decided more cases by a plurality (a group whose opinion presents the Court's decision without commanding a majority of five) than ever before in its history, and in the 1985 Term one-quarter of the Court's cases were decided by a bare majority of five to four.[2] In the history of the Court, it had overruled its own precedents 184 times. Since 1950, it had overturned precedents 98 times, or more than half of the total. The Warren Court is generally thought of as reaching a high-water mark for judicial activism, but, according to the Library of Congress, the Burger Court overturned precedents more often (50 to 46), struck down more acts of Congress (31 to 21), overturned more state laws (288 to 150), and otherwise appeared to exercise its power to review the actions of government more actively than had the Warren

Court and, therefore, than any Court ever. Since the Burger Court decided about 15 percent more cases than the Warren Court, the absolute figures are less conclusive than they appear, but they are still significant as signs of evolution. [3]

As the Supreme Court's work shifted from resolving common-law questions of torts, property, and contracts (in the nineteenth century), to interpreting statutes and ruling on the meaning of the Constitution (during the twentieth), these numbers suggest that the Justices became increasingly divided about the substance of the law. During the past generation, when the number of cases dealing with important social policies like school desegregation and affirmative action rose considerably, the Court gradually exchanged a bold liberal outlook for a cautious, conservative one, and as the quest for neutral principles by which to decide these disputes foundered, the Justices settled for what Vincent Blasi, a professor at Columbia Law School, called "a rootless activism." [4] In cases about abortion, school prayer, and the rights of criminal suspects—principal items on the Reagan social agenda—Court decisions seen from afar as broad legal pronouncements appeared from close up to reveal an intense struggle among the nine Justices to agree on doctrine that expressed the most subjective human judgments.

The instability resulting from this struggle was underscored in 1986 by the Court's ruling in Bowers v. Hardwick, upholding the Georgia law that made a crime of oral and anal sex between consenting adults. [5] Justice Blackmun argued in dissent that the Constitution's concept of liberty includes a right of privacy requiring protection of intimacy among homosexuals as well as heterosexuals, and that the law should be struck down. For a five-to-four majority, Justice White dismissed that view ("We do not agree," he declared), and described one of the claims for the protection of privacy made by counsel as, "at best, facetious." [6] Soon afterward, Justice Lewis Powell confirmed a report by the Washington *Post* [7] that he had planned to vote with Blackmun, but because he thought the case wasn't the best on which to base a judgment about such a deep question of constitutional law, he had switched sides to join White. [8] As a result of this shift, instead of extending to homosexuals the full protection of the Constitution, the Court appeared to assent to an effort to push them to the margins of society. "This was the most exhausting Term of any since I've been on the Court,"[9] Blackmun said at the end of his sixteenth Term on the Supreme Court, and he attributed the exhaustion to bickering and arm-twisting about cases like this.

The Court's rightward drift occurred in a period of bitter and widespread political controversy about the law in general. While most of the disagreement focused on the federal courts, Americans expressed their conflicts about social issues by making the elections for judgeships in the forty states that held them increasingly contested affairs.[10] Rose Bird, Chief Justice of the California Supreme Court, was re-elected with only 52 percent of the votes in 1978, and in 1986 was removed by a two-to-one margin through the vigorous efforts of conservative critics and others. While her unqualified opposition to the death penalty marked her as a liberal, she said, "It doesn't make any difference if the court is liberal, conservative or somewhere in between. What [voters] want is somebody who will do exactly what they want on particular issues, so that when they push a button, you salivate on signal."[11] A majority of the American people appeared to want the same, according to a 1986 NBC News poll. A representative sample decided that the Chief Justice of the United States should be elected, too,[12] and overlooked the value of having the nation's highest judge be above politics.

There are many reasons for these developments, but one of the most dominant in the Reagan years has been the encouragement by the President himself of a partisan and divisive view of the law. His regular commentary about abortion provides a good example. When members of the right-to-life movement send roses to members of Congress and of the Supreme Court each year to protest the Roe v. Wade decision on its anniversary, and then gather on the Ellipse behind the White House for a rally, the President offers words of solidarity. When members of the movement gathered for the funeral of sixteen thousand aborted fetuses one year, he sent his condolences. Reagan's comment about abortion was "I don't feel that I'm trying to do something that is taking a privilege away from womanhood, because I don't think that womanhood should be considering murder a privilege." Through the eighties, as the number of bombings at abortion clinics rose, he did little to discourage such tactics, and continued to pledge his support to the pro-life and anti-abortion movement.[13]

In 1986, a pro-life clergyman publicly urged a prayer for the death of Justice William Brennan as part of the answer to the country's abortion problem. He reasoned that Brennan's passing would allow the President to appoint a pro-life Justice, and shift the balance of the Court to achieve a majority ruling against the right to abortion.[14] Brennan became a renewed focus of pro-life criticism after Edwin Meese singled him out (though it was Justice Blackmun who wrote the majority opinion in Roe v. Wade). It was hard not to see a chain linking the President's encouragement of the movement, Meese's criticism of Brennan as the symbol of the kind of judicial activism that led to that landmark decision, and the "prayer" of the clergyman.

The President's confusion of the law with his own moral and social agenda was often repeated by the Justice Department under Meese. Again and again, in situations where the Administration's desired social policy required it to make a choice between conflicting values, whether the subject was pornography, AIDS, the rights of criminal suspects or some other item on the President's expanding agenda, the Reagan Administration chose not to follow established legal practices while presenting its position. It read cases, construed statutes, and represented both trial records and legislative history in radically unorthodox ways, and the Solicitor General sometimes did so for the President.

Was it inevitable that the Solicitor General would become a partisan advocate for the administration in power if the law is increasingly seen as no more than an instrument of politics and so much of the Supreme court's docket now deals with the legal aspects of social policy? Shouldn't an Administration's election to office entitle it to have arguments carried directly to the Court, without being filtered by an obscure office of civil servants, in these circumstances? How can the SG expect to fulfill a dual responsibility to the Court and the Executive Branch when neither can claim to apply neutral legal principles?

One of the hallmarks of legal scholarship in the Reagan era, as well as in the judicial and political arenas, is political polarization.[15] It has become difficult for a young law professor to avoid choosing between one of the movements in the law that correspond to the political far left or right. Even by choosing to do old-fashioned doctrinal analysis, by scrutinizing cases for new and insightful principles that transcend politics, a gifted legal scholar risks being considered trivial or anachronistic. In 1986, an able lawyer in the SG's office was interviewed at first-rank law schools for a teaching job that almost certainly would have been his a decade ago, when the skills of analyzing and writing about legal doctrine that he cultivated in the government would have been highly valued. He was turned down by all the schools, in part, they indicated, because he did not bring to teaching the special insights that came from looking at the law from the vantage point of a movement. [16]

As a balance to the right's Law and Economics, a school favored by the Reagan Administration, a movement called Critical Legal Studies sprang up on the left. A basic premise of CLS, as it is known, is that the law is ultimately defined less by abstract principles than by the political and moral views of the judges and lawyers who apply them, and that in the endless process of interpretation that it requires, the law becomes a forum for resolving larger social conflicts rooted in passion, reason, and, most of all, power. [17] Since the volumes of legal cases and statutes are full of contradictory doctrine, CLS holds, it is possible to make a respectable legal argument leading to any desired result.

Ironically, the aggressive advocacy of Charles Fried during the 1985 Term seemed to prove the wisdom of CLS scholars: choosing to question, rather than to reason from, the premises of earlier Supreme Court rulings, the more controversial briefs that he endorsed as Solicitor General appeared nonetheless to make presentable legal arguments. By this theory, the filings of the SG's office should have provoked no more distress than much current American legal scholarship—Fried had merely aggravated the problem by attracting attention.

But the judgments of the Justices about Fried's advocacy during the 1985 Term suggested other conclusions. For half a century, American lawyers have lived with the tension between the need, on the one hand, for legal ideals that command respect because judges make them appear to come from some higher authority and the knowledge, on the other, that the law is the imperfect creation of imperfect human beings.[18] They have recognized that the law is an art, not a science. Though there may be few "right" legal answers dictated by formula, legal reasoning can be done well or badly. When done well and honestly, it has a greater chance of illuminating either the purpose of the statute under scrutiny or the principle at the heart of the most relevant precedents in case law. In turn, it can fulfill its role of helping give order to society by contributing stability, predictability, and determinability to the law. If there were no overarching "neutral principles" guiding lawyers who worked on the most controversial problems before the courts in the mid-eighties, there were standard practices of legal reasoning that assured the law some integrity and helped define it as law.

The Justices of the Supreme Court indicated repeatedly in opinions at the end of the 1985 Term that the Solicitor General's office had failed to honor these practices as faithfully as they expected it to. The law was unsettled in some cases where the quality of the SG's advocacy fell down, and this was why the Justices seemed especially upset: the process by which the law is shaped is particularly important when the outcome of a case may be subject to controversy. Members of the Court knew little about the changes within the office that led to the decline in its work, but the Justices willing to speak about the topic did not think this deterioration had been inevitable. Unlike Archibald Cox, who, they concurred, demonstrated high legal scruples as Solicitor General during a similarly divisive period a generation ago, President Reagan's second SG bent reason and spurned restraint in order to try for results. By misusing accepted principles of legal reasoning in major cases, he made the government's rationales suspect in run-of-the-mill matters, and he threatened the law's stability when the legal system was unusually vulnerable. Instead of envisioning the law as a means for building consensus, as Cox did, Charles Fried advanced the President's positions without regard to the divisions they deepened in American society.[19]

The 1985 Term would have been an extraordinary one for the Supreme Court even if the Reagan Administration had not tried to press its agenda so aggressively, because the Justices resolved an unusually high number of cases presenting distinct choices about major issues in the law. The 1986 Term promised to be quieter and, at its opening, Charles Fried made a comment about the results of his advocacy before the Court during the previous Term: "We spoke last year," he told the Washington *Post*, [20] "they answered, we heard, and we go from there," which was as close as he'd come to conceding in public any errors of judgment as Solicitor General.

Out of optimism or an accurate sense of change, lawyers in the SG's office who spoke about Charles Fried's approach to cases for the new Term—before he had filed enough briefs for anyone outside the government to judge how they compared to submissions of the previous one—picked up on this comment. The lawyers were struck by the SG's new resolve to use his talents in the tradition he had previously compromised, and, adopting the coloration of his surroundings, to give up his ornate, frenetic style in favor of the less flashy manner of a reliable government lawyer. He had picked first-rank deputies who reinforced each other's devotion to craftsmanship, the lawyers said, and though he still overruled the deputies in favor of advice from Bradford Reynolds and representatives of Attorney General Meese, and had to be canny about warding off incursions from political appointees when he did not agree with them ("One whiff of treason, and they boot you out," a lawyer in the office said), Fried usually heeded the advice of his new deputies. He was committed to guarding the SG's office as well as he could, they said. [21]

Fried's eventual record in a number of the 1986 Term's major cases about affirmative action and other agenda items, in which the Justices again seemed to go out of their way to correct the government's reasoning while firmly ruling against it, suggested that the change noted in the SG by his staff had to do with tone more than substance—with his apparent attitude toward the Court rather than with what he actually argued, since he rejected the logic of its opinions and the importance of those statements as guiding judgments about American law. [22] His testimony before Congress in March 1987 that public criticisms of his approach as Solicitor were merely "subjective judgments" and that, during the previous eighteen months, he hoped that "the style and the content of the advocacy, the quality of advocacy, the thoroughness of the argumentation" by the SG's office under his leadership was "as good as it has ever been," [23] raised questions as to how deeply his attitude had changed.

Still, for whatever it was worth, the change in tone, at least, was clear. At the end of the 1985 Term, according to the Philadelphia *Inquirer,* Fried had criticized one decision of the Justices by saying, "Who knows what these clowns mean?" [24] The words conveyed the disdain for the Court with which the SG was then increasingly associated. A year later, toward the close of the 1986 Term, the Attorney General's spokesman, Terry Eastland, commented that "a new appointment or two" to the Supreme Court would be the best way to reverse the Court's outlook on affirmative action. Fried called the remark "deeply troubling," and, drawing attention on the front page of *The New York Times,* the SG stated: "The way I should do my job is by crafting conscientious, scrupulous arguments in the light of the law. Personally, I wish every one of the Justices well." The Fried-Eastland exchange was only one of a series of minor incidents in which the Solicitor General and his right-wing allies within or outside the Justice Department not only acknowledged but magnified and seemed to relish a new distance between them. "I'm a very different man today than I was a year ago," Fried said after the Term ended. [25]

Lawyers in the SG's office also recognized a more general truth: the advocacy of Charles Fried, perhaps more than that of any other Solicitor General, could fairly be judged only by considering the Administration he served. Although he maintained that he had no grounds for complaint, the legal views pressed by Edwin Meese and the practices of Meese and Reynolds—which flabbergasted longtime observers of the Justice Department and exhausted the supply of synonyms for extremism in the law—severely limited Fried's independence.

Several weeks before the start of the 1986 Term, Reynolds gave a speech at the University of Missouri purporting to offer a serious comment about principles to apply in interpreting the Constitution. [26] Instead, Reynolds's remarks amounted to an attempt to blame one Justice for the discord between the Administration and the Supreme Court. In what a press spokesman at the Justice

Department later called the strongest personal attack on a member of the Court by any top member of the Administration, and what lawyers in the department described as the venting of an obsession, Reynolds denounced Justice Brennan for not reading the Constitution as Meese, Reynolds, and others thought it should be read. He declared Brennan's "radical egalitarianism" to be "perhaps the major threat to individual liberty" in the United States today.

The speech promoted the Attorney General's Jurisprudence of Original Intention more forcefully than Meese himself had done since its initial presentation, when critics on both left and right had given the theory low marks. After peppering his text with quotations from Brennan's major speech on the Constitution, Reynolds then accused the Justice of regarding the document as "a 'dead letter,' " placing quotation marks around this phrase so as to convey the false impression that it too was quoted from Brennan. In actuality, the Justice had argued the direct opposite.[27] Reynolds's speech was a reminder that the most powerful officials in the Reagan Justice Department sometimes skirted a practice without which the rule of law collapses—telling the truth.

A question about Meese, Reynolds, and their allies during the Reagan Administration that has often cropped up is this: Why did they do it? What moved them to defy the constraints of mainstream legal thinking, and sometimes the law itself, in their pursuit of the Reagan agenda? Neither the Attorney General nor his right-hand man would answer the question, in part because they did not grant its premise. They spoke about their reign in government as if they were meeting the highest standards of public service.[28] Because they were close allies of a President who was extraordinarily popular for almost six years and, perhaps, because many people who vilified them paradoxically wrote the pair off as unworthy of serious consideration, both men remained strong and untouchable long after the record warranted a harsher judgment.

In this period of free-for-all in the law, when a vocal group of scholars and advocates on the left joined Meese and Reynolds on the right in believing that, without cost, they could make almost any legal claim with a straight face, it was no wonder that the Solicitor General appeared to believe that, on behalf of the Administration, he could, too.

However much changes in the legal culture explain the transformation of the SG's office during the Reagan years, the story carries a lesson of its own. To understand how the Reagan Administration views the law, it is only necessary to know what it did to the office of the Solicitor General. If there is a thing called law, with a reassuring sense of continuity despite its contradictions, a measure of stability that contributes to social order, and an integrity provided by, among other things, the careful practice of legal reasoning, then one of the great misdeeds of the Reagan Administration was to diminish the institution that, to lawyers at the highest reaches of the profession, once stood for the nation's commitment to the rule of law.

A Note on Sources

Like many significant documents in American law, whether opinions of the Supreme Court or statutes passed by Congress, the briefs and other writings that express the legal views of Solicitors General were available to me, as they are to the public, at the Supreme Court and the Department of Justice libraries. These and other relevant books and papers are available at libraries around the country, and for this book I also used materials at the library of American University's Washington College of Law, the Boston Athenaeum, the Columbia University Oral History Project, the Georgetown University Library, the Harvard Law School Library, the Library of Congress, and the Montgomery County Public Libraries in Maryland. I used papers in the collections at the National Archives and the National Gallery of Art as well. I also relied on reports in newspapers, magazines, academic journals, and law reviews (in particular, on stories by David Lauter in the *National Law Journal*; Linda Greenhouse, Robert Pear, Philip Shenon, and Stuart Taylor, Jr. in *The New York Times*; Fred Barbash, Al Kamen, Howard Kurtz, and Loretta Tofani in the Washington *Post*; and James Stewart and Stephen Wermiel in the *Wall Street Journal*), and on radio and television reports (especially by Carl Stern for NBC News and Nina Totenberg for National Public Radio). Some papers on which I relied are not generally available to the public, and I'm grateful to the people who trusted me with these confidential documents.

Despite the value of this written record, much of the history of the Solicitor General's office has not been pieced together until now. To gather stories about past Solicitors and others who served in the office, during most of 1985, 1986, and part of 1987, I spoke with every living SG (nine in all), from Walter Cummings, appointed in the Truman Administration, to Rex Lee and Charles Fried, of the Reagan Administration; with Paul Freund, who ran the SG's office when he served there in the forties, and Robert Stern, who took charge during the early fifties; with scores of other lawyers who once worked in the office or do now; and with many other people who had facts and opinions about the Solicitor General to share. When I began this project, I expected to tell the unhurried and virtually unknown history of a tiny, great institution in the Justice Department. Not long after I started my reporting, it became clear that events at the SG's office were transforming the institution. The story took on an intense quality, and I began to concentrate as well on learning about the nature and significance of the changes.

Many in the SG's office or with special knowledge about it felt comfortable talking about general office lore, but believed they put themselves at risk by speaking with me about current events. In some cases, they cited their duty to honor the confidentiality of dealings between an attorney and his client (in this case, the government); sometimes they said they didn't want to be quoted criticizing lawyers they might deal with again in the future; sometimes they treated the questions I raised as if answering them required a breach of national security—which it never did, since none of the issues that interested me involved national security in the sense in which the phrase is ordinarily used.

In brief, some of the many people I spoke with did so on the record about subjects that they considered uncontroversial, but otherwise insisted on terms that would allow them to tell their stories without incurring the distrust of their colleagues or jeopardizing at least their ability to perform their jobs, if not the jobs themselves, through unwanted publicity. These are terms to which reporters regularly agree in Washington in order to get closer to the truth than official, on-the-record statements allow. They would talk about certain topics only if I promised not to name them as the source of their remarks.

In the past, some of the SG's former and current lawyers explained, they had cooperated with reporters for *The New York*

Times, the Washington *Post,* and other major news organizations to make sure the press accurately represented the meaning of Supreme Court opinions in cases in which the government had taken part. They thought that stories would be improved if the reporters knew how legal positions had developed inside the government. The lawyers protected themselves by providing this information on background only (i.e., not for direct attribution). A larger percentage of the lawyers in the SG's office told me that before they agreed to speak with me, they had never talked about their work with a reporter. They said that they had agreed to talk with me for one of two main reasons: they cared enough about the SG's office and how it was being changed to want to share their views about current events (even though some believed they would be fired if political officials in the Reagan Administration knew they had helped me piece together the story of the transformation); or they believed the story was more complicated than it seemed as it was passed along the grapevine of lawyers, judges, and journalists who follow the SG's office and the Supreme Court, and they wanted to counter the misimpressions they assumed I was gathering from other people.

Every reporter I know prefers to identify sources for readers so the readers can judge for themselves the sources' motives, biases, and reliability. Some reporters won't report the facts attested to by a source unless he is willing to be identified. In this case, I believe readers are better served by my reliance on some unnamed sources than they would have been had I ignored this material. I think the sense of the Solicitor General's office they gain is closer to the truth than it would otherwise be.

In every instance (and I asked permission to do this), I have tried to indicate a source's position, to let readers better judge the credibility of his observation ("a lawyer in the SG's office said"; "a Supreme Court law clerk commented"; "a Justice observed"). Although this may in given instances invite speculation about a source's identity, it seems a reasonable way of balancing the two concerns of protecting privacy and properly informing the reader.

Because this book focuses on the SG's office, I talked regularly with lawyers in that office during my reporting. In the heart of it, I spoke at length with more than half the current office staff and dozens of other lawyers who had served there and still kept up with the office. I tried to speak with at least three lawyers whenever my reporting centered on a controversial subject, to ensure that I heard several points of view. The lawyers from the SG's office identified in the notes are only some of those with whom I spoke during my reporting. I did not necessarily discuss other subjects with a lawyer who agreed to be quoted only about a certain topic.

Since this book was first published, three men who sat on the Court during the period the book covers have commented on my reporting about their views on the role of the Solicitor General. Because their statements drew attention from the press, I believe I should also comment.

Referring to my assertion that he was "sometimes put off" by Solicitor General Charles Fried's advocacy, because he had been "too willing to be spokesman for the 'reactionary' Reagan Administration" (page 265), former Chief Justice Warren Burger took exception to my use of the word "reactionary" in quotation marks. In a press release after excerpts of this book appeared in *The New Yorker*, and later in a letter to Fried, he said I "falsely attributed" to him "one statement never made."

My source in this instance was someone who had worked closely with Burger when he was Chief Justice, who had proved reliable on other matters I was able to verify, and who told me he had heard Burger say what I reported. While Burger held Fried accountable as the principal advocate for the Reagan Administration, he apparently used the word "reactionary" in particular to describe the views of Attorney General Edwin Meese and Assistant Attorney General William Bradford Reynolds. As this book details, evidence of Burger's disapproval of some of the SG's advocacy accumulated over time, and I stand by my reporting.

Former Justice Lewis Powell also disavowed views that I report, in a letter to Solicitor General Fried. Responding to excerpts published in *The New Yorker*, he stated in part: "I do not know Caplan, and he did not interview me. Nevertheless, my name was included in one article as a Justice critical of you. Of course, I have not agreed with all of your arguments, but I have not criticized you as Solicitor General."

On July 2, 1986, in answer to an inquiry from me dated May 12, the Justice wrote me a letter about his views on the Solicitor General's role, on the condition that I not quote from the letter without obtaining his permission. Soon after, I called him and we spoke by telephone. During the conversation, he clarified several key points in the letter and gave me permission to use with attribution his phrase describing the Solicitor's "dual responsibility" to the Executive Branch and the Supreme Court, and to cite his letter to me as the source of this phrase, as I do in notes to this book.

It may be fair in some usages of the word to say that Justice Powell didn't "know" me, as he wrote, and it is correct that I didn't interview him in chambers as I did some of his former colleagues, but I think it is plain that the exchange of correspondence and the conversation by phone I had with Justice Powell constituted substantive communication between us, and are facts at odds with the impression created by the Justice's letter to Fried. I believe it is also important to distinguish between Justice Powell's disavowal of any personal criticism about Charles Fried as Solicitor General (which I do not claim) and what I report as part of a summary of a number of Justices' views: "[T]he expressions of concern and disapproval in the Court's opinions gave only a hint of the sadness and distress that at least a majority of the Justices (Brennan, Marshall, Blackmun, Powell, and Stevens, four of whom were appointed by Republicans) felt about the changes in the role of the Solicitor General" (pages 264 and 265). I continue to believe this characterization is accurate as it applies to Justice Powell's views at the end of the 1985 Term, based on his explanation to me of the SG's "dual responsibility," his published opinions, and the observations of clerks and other Justices about Justice Powell, which I report in this book.

Justice Thurgood Marshall disavowed saying he felt "sadness and distress" about the change in the role of the Solicitor General during the Reagan Administration. "I never said any such thing about the Solicitor General," he told the *Legal Times,* in response to a reporter's inquiry. "I don't make statements about people. If I were to say anything about the SG, I would say it only in the

Court's Conference Room, and I don't even recall saying anything to any Justice about him."

Justice Marshall took exception to something I don't report: the sentence in my book that he disavowed is about his views on the institution rather than an individual, and it doesn't quote him; it reports, in my words, what I believe to be true based on a variety of sources—including a telephone interview I had with Justice Marshall.

On September 20, 1985, in response to a letter from me, the Justice phoned me. We spoke about many topics related to the SG's office. Among them were briefs recently filed by the Solicitor General, including the much-publicized 1985 Term abortion brief; decisions about the Court not to let the SG argue before the Court as an amicus curiae in cases where the Court would almost certainly have granted the government's request to do so in the past; and practices of the SG's office under Justice Marshall, such as the office's policy of letting the Court know about what he considered improprieties in wiretap cases, which symbolized to him the role he considered proper for an SG, as opposed to what he viewed as the approach of the Reagan SGs.

The descriptions the Justice gave of matters that disturbed him and the conclusions he stated about them support the characterization that he was saddened and distressed (and, even, angered) by the change in the SG's role under President Reagan, as does evidence from other sources presented in the book. In an interview with syndicated columnist Carl Rowan that was broadcast by WUSA-TV in Washington, D.C., on December 13, 1987, Justice Marshall also expressed this view. Referring to government briefs submitted by the Solicitor General, he said, "I think there are certain movements that the Department of Justice is making which could be interpreted as trying to undermine the Supreme Court itself, which is of course impossible. They can't separate the political from the legal. They write political speeches and put the word 'brief' on them." He said, "The Solicitor General is the government's spokesman in this Court. He speaks for the government. It's always been true until the past decade or so. Now it seems as though he speaks only for the President, and not for the rest of the government."

It is understandable that the views of Justices that I report in this book drew attention out of proportion to their limited place in the narrative when they were first published. However much the Justices have lifted the veil of secrecy at the Court in recent years, in television, radio, and print interviews, as well as in speeches and writing, they usually offer general, diplomatic pronouncements rather than direct answers to the questions they are addressing, as some did with me. But the strong, considered views I report only confirmed what I and other Supreme Court observers had learned from numerous publicly available Court opinions.

Much of this book's material is from the written public record, including Court opinions, books, current and historical government documents, and law review, academic, and news articles that are identified in the notes to the text. There are 923 notes. Thirteen percent, or 119, are based on confidential interviews, with other observers of the SG's office as well as with Justices.

I am grateful to the hundreds of people who told me about the history and lore of the Solicitor General's office, and what they thought happened there during the Reagan years.

Notes

The notes in this book conform to the following rules of citation: Brown v. Board of Education, 347 *U.S.* 483, 484 (1954), means that the Supreme Court decided the case in 1954, that the opinions begin at page 483 of volume 347 of the *United States Reports*, and that the passage quoted or mentioned begins at page 484. I occasionally cite old cases by the name of the official reporter of the case, which was the custom at the Supreme Court until 1875. Marbury v. Madison, 1 *Cranch* (5 *U.S.*) 137 (1803) means that the case was reported in the first volume compiled by William Cranch and the fifth volume of the *United States Reports*. The other reporters whose volumes I cite are Henry Wheaton and Benjamin Howard. Because there is a delay between the Supreme Court's decisions about cases and the publication of opinions in the official reports, I sometimes refer to one of two other publications of Supreme Court cases. 104 *S. Ct.* 2520 (1984) means that the case is reported at page 2520 in volume 104 of the *Supreme Court Reporter*, a service of West Publishing Company that includes a quickly available softcover edition. 54 *U.S. Law Week* 4095 means that the case is reported at page 4095 in volume 54 of *U.S. Law Week*, a loose-leaf publication of the Bureau of National Affairs. I also refer to some cases only by name and case number, without citing the volumes in which they are reproduced, because when I collected these cases, the sole version available was that printed by the Supreme Court. Finally, I sometimes refer to other volumes reporting lower-court opinions: *F. Supp.* refers to the *Federal Supplement* and *F. 2d* to the second edition of *Federal Reports*. Since 1932, district-court decisions have been reported in *F. Supp.*, and appeals-court decisions in *F. 2d*.

Books are cited by author, title, publisher, year of publication, number of pages, and pages of reference. Articles in law reviews and other journals are cited by author, title, volume, and name of the review, page, and date. In most instances, articles in newspapers are cited by paper, page, and date.

Some notes are labeled "Confidential interview." (These are marked "CI" after the first, or "CIs" for more than one.) I explain my reliance on these interviews in A Note on Sources, on page 280.

CHAPTER I

THE TENTH JUSTICE

1. In this note, "Government Litigation in the Supreme Court: The Roles of the Solicitor General," 78 *Yale Law Journal* 1442, 1442 (1969) means that the unsigned article appeared in 1969, in volume 78 of the *Yale Law Journal,* at page 1442, and the quotation appears on page 1442. Footnote 1 of the article quotes the original Act of Congress, passed June 22, 1870.

2. Interview with the late Justice Potter Stewart on June 5, 1985; confidential personal interviews with four Justices in 1985 and 1986; confidential phone interviews with two other Justices in 1985 and 1986; and a letter from Justice Lewis Powell to the author, July 2, 1986, quoted with his permission. After this book was first issued, the *Loyola Law Review* responded by publishing a symposium of articles from different points of view about the role of the Solicitor General, 21 *Loyola Law Review* 1047 (1988). Some of the articles attempt to define from a normative point of view the SG's responsibilities, and treat in detail the subject of the opening paragraph of this book.

3. Letter from Justice Powell to the author, July 2, 1986.

4. Interviews with Paul Freund on April 12, 1985, and October 10, 1985; Erwin Griswold on April 5, 1985; and other long-time students of the Supreme Court and the SG's office, and with lawyers currently employed in the SG's office. In 1984, an opinion by Judge Patrick Higginbotham referred to "the historically unique and functionally important relationship between the office of Solicitor General and the Supreme Court." (Cotner v. U.S. Parole Commission, No. 83–1757.)

5. Statistics from October Term, 1983, available in the Docket Management Section of the SG's office and in "Annual Report of the Attorney General of the United States" for 1984 (U.S. Government Printing Office). "October Term, 1983" refers to the Supreme Court Term beginning then and continuing until the summer of 1984: each year the Court's Term is identified by when it opens—now the first Monday in October—and the calendar year. Cases argued after the turn of the year thus belong to the Term begun the previous October, and so a February 1984 case was heard in October Term, 1983.

6. In 1955, the Justice Department began using its current system for keeping Supreme Court statistics, and it applied the method retroactively to October Term, 1943. In the forty years prior to the 1983 Term, the Solicitor General won an average of 69 percent of the cases that he argued or presented on the merits to the Court. "Annual Report of the Attorney General of the United States," 1955 through 1984.

7. Homer Cummings and Carl McFarland, *Federal Justice: Chapters in the History of Justice and the Federal Executive* (Macmillan, 1937, 576 pp.); and Thomas Thacher, "Genesis and Present Duties of Office of Solicitor General," 17 *American Bar Association Journal* 519 (1931); Charles Fahy, "The Office

of the Solicitor General," 28 *American Bar Association Journal* 20 (1942); Simon Soboleff, "Attorney for the Government: The Work of the Solicitor General's Office," 41 *American Bar Association Journal* 229 (1955); Erwin Griswold, "The Office of the Solicitor General—Representing the Interests of the United States before the Supreme Court," 34 *Missouri Law Review* 528 (1969).

8. Op. cit., "Roles of the Solicitor General," *Yale Law Journal* 1442.

9. Cong. Globe, 41st Congress, 2nd Session, 3035, by Representative Jenckes, cited in Griswold, 34 *Missouri Law Review* 527, 530 (1969).

10. Benjamin Helm Bristow, *Dictionary of American Biography* (Scribner, 20 v. 1928–1936), Vol. III, 55–56.

11. Mark Sheehan, Assistant Director of the Office of Public Affairs at the Justice Department, letter to the author, March 6, 1986.

12. Interviews with Rex Lee on June 11, 1985, and Virginia Bolling, of the Docket Management Section of the SG's office, on August 11, 1986.

13. Op. cit., Soboleff, "Attorney for the Government," 230.

14. U.S. v. Mendoza, 104 *S. Ct.* 568, 573 (1984).

15. Interviews with Louis Claiborne on June 12, 1985; Andrew Frey on June 29, 1985; Kenneth Geller on June 20, 1985; and Lawrence Wallace on May 24, 1985.

16. Erwin Griswold, "Constitutional Cases in the Supreme Court," 24 *Oklahoma Law Review* 353, 354 (1971).

17. Op. cit., Stewart interview.

18. Op. cit., Soboleff, 232.

19. According to Virginia Bolling, of the SG's office, during the 1984 and 1985 Terms the SG was invited to enter as a friend of the Court in thirty-seven and thirty-one cases, respectively.

20. This is a phrase used by Justices in personal interviews during 1985 and 1986, and by law clerks at the Court who repeated the words of the Justices.

21. Interviews with Kenneth Geller, op. cit.; Edwin Kneedler on November 25, 1985; Joshua Schwartz on March 20, 1985; David Strauss on July 30, 1985; and Harriet Shapiro on December 3, 1985.

CHAPTER II
LORE

1. Interviews with Archibald Cox on April 11, 1985; John Davis (a onetime lawyer in the SG's office who became Clerk of the Supreme Court—no relation to Solicitor General John W. Davis) on June 9, 1985; Oscar Davis on June 21, 1985; Philip Elman on October 19, 1986; Daniel Friedman on June 22, 1985; Paul Freund, op. cit.; Warner Gardner on May 22, 1986; Erwin Griswold, op. cit.; Ralph Spritzer on February 26, 1986; Robert Stern on May 20, 1986; and Charles Wyzanski on April 12, 1985, among others.

2. William H. Harbaugh, *Lawyer's Lawyer: The Life of John W. Davis* (Oxford University Press, 1973, 648 pp.), 92.

3. Ibid., 92, 107.

4. Interviews with John Davis, op. cit.; Oscar Davis, op. cit.; and Paul Freund, op. cit.

5. Archibald Cox, "The Government in the Supreme Court," 44 *Chicago Bar Record* 221, 225 (1963).

6. Interview with Robert Bork on May 22, 1985.

7. DeMarco v. U.S., 415 *U.S.* 449, 451 (1974).

8. Op. cit., Cox, 225.

9. Young v. U.S., 315 *U.S.* 257, 258 (1942).

10. The facts about the Peters case, unless otherwise noted, are from the "Memorandum for the Attorney General from the Solicitor General Re: Peters v. Hobby," January 14, 1955.

11. Joseph Rauh, "Nonconfrontation in Security Cases: The Greene Decision," 45 *Virginia Law Review* 1175, 1178 (1959).

12. Confidential interview (hereafter CI).

13. Op. cit., "Memorandum for the Attorney General," 1.

14. Ibid., 13, 22.

15. CI.

16. Interviews with John Davis, op. cit.; and Oscar Davis, op. cit.

17. In the *Dictionary of American Biography,* op. cit., Vol. II, 508, the Bowers entry states, "It is well known that only his death prevented his nomination by President Taft to the Supreme Court of the United States." According to Charles Wyzanski, op. cit., another former SG, William Mitchell, might also have gone to the Supreme Court, but he turned down Herbert Hoover's offer of a seat because he believed Benjamin Cardozo should be appointed instead, as he was.

18. Including Sobeloff, the number of SGs who either left the bench to take the job or who later became judges is at least thirteen, or over one-third of the total of thirty-eight. (The SG's office has no records about past Solicitors and the *Dictionary of American Biography* does not have entries for every SG.) Of those who have served since 1930, the fraction is over half—ten of eighteen. In 1986, there were ten federal judges on active duty who once worked as lawyers in the SG's office.

19. CI.

20. Op. cit., interview with Paul Freund.

21. Op. cit., interview with Charles Wyzanski.

22. CI.

23. Interviews with Paul Freund, op. cit.; Erwin Griswold, op. cit.; and Charles Wyzanski, op. cit.

24. Frankfurter memo, March 15, 1933, Harvard Law School Library Manuscript Collection.

25. Leonard Baker, *Brandeis and Frankfurter: A Dual Biography* (Harper & Row, 1984, 567 pp.), 282.

26. CI.

27. Op. cit., Leonard Baker, 283.

28. CI.

29. According to Paul Freund, op. cit., the Democratic Party in Rhode Island, which McGrath had represented in the Senate, was badly divided. The Democrats' plan was for McGrath to gain some prestige in the Justice Department and return home to unify the party.

30. Francis Lorson, Chief Deputy Clerk of the Supreme Court, arranged access to Court files. The Court's records are not complete (the Court notes the titles of cases that lawyers have argued on their certificates of membership, but the Court only began using these certificates in 1925 and the records concerning lawyers who argued at the Court before then are spotty) and the current notation system is not foolproof (the Clerk's office follows no uniform system for crediting lawyers with arguments and sometimes fails to note that an advocate has made an argument), but, according to Court records, this is McGrath's score.

31. Richard Rovere, *The American Establishment and Other Reports, Opinions, and Speculations* (Harcourt, Brace, & World, 1962, 308 pp.), 85.

32. Interview with Walter Cummings on October 22, 1986.

33. Interviews with John Davis, op. cit.; Oscar Davis, op. cit.; and Robert Stern, op. cit.

34. Francis Biddle, *In Brief Authority* (Doubleday, 1962, 494 pp.) 98.

35. Interview with Sandy Nelson, of the Court Clerk's office, on January 27, 1987.

36. Interviews with Daniel Friedman, op. cit.; Paul Freund, op. cit.; Warner Gardner, op. cit.; and Charles Wyzanski, op. cit.

37. Op. cit., interview with Paul Freund.

38. Paul Freund, "Felix Frankfurter: Reminiscences and Reflections," Harvard Law School, 5, 6 (1982).

39. Robert Jackson, *The Struggle for Judicial Supremacy: A Study of a Crisis in American Power Politics* (Knopf, 1941, 361 pp.), xix.

40. Edward J. Bander, *Justice Holmes Ex Cathedra* (Michie Co., 1966, 381 pp.), No. 425, 207. Also, op. cit., interview with Paul Freund.

41. Thomas Reed Powell, "Constitutional Metaphors," *New Republic*, 314 (February 11, 1985).

42. Robert Stern, Eugene Gressman, and Stephen M. Shapiro, *Supreme Court Practice* (Bureau of National Affairs, 1986, 1,030 pp.), vii.

43. Op. cit., interview with Robert Stern.

44. Op. cit., interview with David Strauss.

45. Interview with Mark Sheehan, Office of Public Affairs, Justice Department, on October 22, 1986.

46. Op. cit., Biddle, 97.

47. Peter Irons, *Justice at War: The Story of the Japanese American Internment Cases* (Oxford University Press, 1983, 407 pp.), 278–310.

48. CIs with Justices, and interviews with Robert Bork, op. cit.; Archibald Cox, op. cit.; Paul Freund, op. cit.; Erwin Griswold, op. cit.; Rex Lee, op. cit.; Alan Morrison on March 20, 1986; Burt Neuborne on June 24, 1986; Laurence Tribe on November 15, 1985; and other lawyers.

CHAPTER III
THE SG AND THE SUPREME COURT

1. According to Erwin Griswold, op. cit., this occurred when he first joined the office in 1929. Paul Freund, op. cit., said that when he joined the office in the thirties, the practice continued and lawyers there talked about it as if it had happened before. The practice ended after Griswold's tenure as SG. "No one told me about it," said his successor, Robert Bork, op. cit.

2. Op. cit., interview with Paul Freund.

3. CI.

4. Op. cit., interview with Andrew Frey.

5. Interviews with Daniel Friedman, op. cit.; and Philip Elman, op. cit., the Frankfurter clerk and longtime assistant to the SG.

6. Op. cit., interview with Lawrence Wallace.

7. "Memorandum to the Solicitor General: Thoughts on Advocacy," May 14, 1980. Interviews with Andrew Frey, op. cit.; Kenneth Geller, op. cit.; and Harriet Shapiro, op. cit.

8. This occurred in the fall of 1986, for example, when the late Justice Potter Stewart was honored.

9. Interviews with Kenneth Geller, op. cit.; and Lawrence Wallace, op. cit.

10. Interviews on May 15, 1986, with Francis Lorson and the staff of the Supreme Court Clerk's office who handle membership in the Court bar.

11. Robert Jackson, "The Law Catches Up with the Times," broadcast on NBC Radio on November 21, 1938, on the National Radio Forum, sponsored by the Washington *Star*.

12. Op. cit., Stern, Gressman, and Shapiro, [*Supreme Court Practice*,] 898, Rule 36.4.

13. Op. cit., interview with Francis Lorson.

14. William H. Allen and Alex Kozinski, "Rules of the Supreme Court of the United States," 94 *Harvard Law Review* 312, 316 (1980). Also, op. cit., Stern, Gressman, and Shapiro, [*Supreme Court Practice*,] 895, Rule 33.2b.

15. Op. cit., interview with Francis Lorson.

16. Interviews with Francis Lorson, op. cit.; and Lawrence Wallace, op. cit.

17. Op. cit., interview with Francis Lorson.

18. Interview with Carter Phillips on June 19, 1985.

19. Op. cit., interview with Kenneth Geller.

20. Interviews with Robert Bork, op. cit.; Raymond Randolph on June 27, 1985; and Stuart Smith on September 17, 1986. Gregg v. Georgia, 428 *U.S.* 153 (1976).

21. Op. cit., interview with Raymond Randolph.

22. Charles Goetz, *Law and Economics: Cases and Materials* (West Publishing Co., 1984, 544 pp.), 491, 492.

23. Interview with David Kendall on July 1, 1985.

24. White had relied on the SG's office to report in his opinion for the Court that converting codeine into morphine is routine and "produces an

extremely noxious and penetrating odor which would make concealment of such conversion operations virtually impossible." Turner v. U.S., 396 *U.S.* 489, 497 (1970).

25. The SG had stated that it was "advised that the reductions involved did not exceed $6 per month for a four-member household if the household remained eligible for benefits," Stevens observed. "It does not indicate where in the record this information is located; nor does it indicate the source of the 'advice.' " Atkins v. Parker, 105 *S. Ct.* 2520, 2524, note 8 (1985).

26. CI.

27. Philip Elman, Columbia University's Oral History Project, December 3, 1983, used with permission of Elman and Columbia University. Also, "The Solicitor General's Office, Justice Frankfurter, and Civil Rights Litigation, 1946–1960: An Oral History," 100 *Harvard Law Review* 817 (1987).

28. Plessy v. Ferguson, 163 *U.S.* 537 (1896).

29. Bernard Schwartz, *Super Chief: Earl Warren and His Supreme Court* (New York University Press, 1983, 853 pp.), 1–3.

30. Richard Kluger, *Simple Justice: The History of Brown v. Board of Education and Black America's Struggle for Equality* (Knopf, 1976, 823 pp.), 672.

31. Ibid. Also, op. cit., interview with John Davis.

32. *The New York Times*, A-30, March 24, 1987. See also Randall Kennedy, "A Reply to Philip Elman," 100 *Harvard Law Review* (1987): "Offered as a behind-the-scenes report on his activities as an attorney in the Solicitor General's Office, Elman's memoir is instead a classic example of the treachery of nostalgia. In the end, its combination of factual errors and poor judgment makes it unreliable legal history and bad reminiscence."

33. Roe v. Wade, 410 *U.S.* 113 (1973).

34. Brown v. Board of Education, 347 *U.S.* 483 (1954).

35. Philip Elman quoted the Eisenhower addendum in his oral history, Wade McCree supplied a copy of the draft on which Eisenhower had hand-written his comments, and the Justice Department library confirmed that the copy from McCree matched the official copy on file there. The Eisenhower comments edited by Elman match the final printed version of the government brief on file at the Justice Department as well.

CHAPTER IV
"INDEPENDENCE"

1. Interviews with Archibald Cox, op. cit.; Thurgood Marshall on September 20, 1985; Erwin Griswold, op. cit.; Robert Bork, op. cit.; Wade McCree on July 11, 1985; Rex Lee, op. cit.; and Charles Fried on November 11, 1985, and June 28, 1986.

2. Op. cit., interview with Archibald Cox. Also, see proclamation of the American Bar Association to Erwin Griswold when the group awarded him its gold medal in 1978.

3. CI.

4. Interviews with Louis Claiborne, op. cit.; and Nathan Lewin on March 15, 1985. Also, Richard Harris, *Justice: The Crisis of Law, Order, and Freedom in America* (E. P. Dutton, 1970, 268 pp.), 193, 194.

5. Interviews with Louis Claiborne, op. cit.; and Lawrence Wallace, op. cit.; and CIs.

6. CIs.

7. Op. cit., interview with Erwin Griswold.

8. Sanford Ungar, *The Papers and the Papers: An Account of the Legal and Political Battle over the Pentagon Papers* (E. P. Dutton, 1972, 319 pp.), 224.

9. *The New York Times*, B-16, December 11, 1986.

10. New York Times Co. v. U.S., 403 *U.S.* 713 (1971).

11. Op. cit., interview with Erwin Griswold; and National Public Radio report by Nina Totenberg on June 8, 1975. Gutknecht v. U.S., 396 *U.S.* 295 (1970); and U.S. v. U.S. District Court, 407 *U.S.* 297 (1972).

12. "Statement of Information," Hearings about Watergate before the House Judiciary Committee, Book II, H 521–39, May–June 1974.

13. Op. cit., "Statement of Information," Book II, 1–9, memorandum by Erwin Griswold dated February 26, 1971.

14. Op. cit., "Statement of Information," Book II, 312 et seq., transcript of April 19, 1971, meeting in Oval Office of Richard Nixon, John Ehrlichman, and George Shultz.

15. Jack Anderson, Washington *Post*, D-15, March 3, 1972. "I'm so sorry that we got that call from the White House," an ITT lobbyist named Dita Beard wrote to her boss. "I thought you and I agreed very thoroughly that under no circumstances would anyone in this office discuss with anyone our participation in the Convention." She continued: "I was afraid the discussion about the three hundred/four hundred thousand committment [sic] would come up soon"; and "Certainly the President has told [Attorney General John] Mitchell to see that things are worked out fairly." She closed with a request that was ignored: "Please destroy this, huh?" Op. cit., "Statement of Information," Book II, 447, Beard memorandum, June 25, 1971.

16. Op. cit. "Statement of Information," Book II, 853, Richard Kleindienst statement. Also, op. cit., interview with Erwin Griswold.

17. Op. cit., interview with Erwin Griswold.

18. Op. cit., "Statement of Information," Book II, 853, Richard Kleindienst statement.

19. Op. cit., interview with Erwin Griswold.

20. Op. cit., interview with Robert Bork. He summed up these ideas in "Neutral Principles and Some First Amendment Problems," 47 *Indiana Law Review* 1 (1971).

21. Op. cit., interview with Robert Bork. At Yale, Taft and Bork were Chancellor Kent Professors of Law.

22. Symposium, "The Fire of Truth," 26 *Journal of Law and Economics* 163 (1983). Also, interviews with Guido Calabresi, Henry Manne, Richard Posner, and George Priest in February, March, and April 1984. Also, see Lincoln

Caplan, "Is the Supreme Court Ready for This Kind of Free-Market Justice?," Washington *Post*, D-1, September 30, 1984.

23. Op. cit., "The Fire of Truth," *Journal of Law and Economics* 183.

24. Robert Bork, *The Antitrust Paradox: A Policy at War with Itself* (Basic Books, 1978, 462 pp.).

25. Gerald Gunther, *Constitutional Law: Cases and Materials* (Foundation Press, 1975, 1,653 pp.), 731.

26. Op. cit., interview with Robert Bork.

27. Confirmation of Federal Judges, Hearings before the Senate Judiciary Committee, Senate document J-97-52, 8, 9 (1982).

28. J. Anthony Lukas, *Nightmare: The Underside of the Nixon Years* (Viking Press, 1976, 626 pp.), 439, and generally, 437–46. Also, Richard Ben-Veniste and George Frampton, Jr., *Stonewall: The Real Story of the Watergate Prosecution* (Simon & Schuster, 1977, 410 pp.), 123–57, 150, 156. Op. cit., interview with Robert Bork, Washington *Post*, A-8, July 27, 1987.

29. Interviews with Robert Bork, op. cit.; Raymond Randolph, op. cit.; and Stuart Smith, op. cit. Also, op. cit., Gregg v. Georgia.

30. CI.

31. Op. cit, Bork hearing, 11 et seq.

32. Interviews with Robert Bork, op. cit.; Daniel Friedman, op. cit.; and Lawrence Wallace, op. cit.

33. Interviews with Robert Bork, op. cit.; Andrew Frey, op. cit.; Raymond Randolph, op. cit.; and Lawrence Wallace, op. cit.

34. Op. cit., interviews with Stuart Smith and Robert Bork.

35. Interviews with Robert Bork, op. cit.; Daniel Friedman, op. cit.; and Lawrence Wallace, op. cit. Also, see "The President, the Attorney General, and the Department of Justice," the report on a conference at the University of Virginia, January 4–5, 1980. On page 86, Edward Levi said that President Ford was involved in the busing decision and that the Department of Justice made its own decision because "the president wanted it that way."

36. Morgan v. Kerrigan, 509 *F 2d.* 580 (1st Cir. 1974), cert. denied, 421 *U.S.* 963 (1975).

37. Op. cit., interview with Robert Bork.

38. Op. cit., Bork; NPR report by Nina Totenberg.

39. Regents of the University of California v. Bakke, 438 *U.S.* 265 (1978).

40. Interviews with Paul Bator on April 11, 1985; Bruce Fein on April 17, 1986; Charles Fried, on November 11, 1985; and William Bradford Reynolds on January 9, 1986. Also, see Stuart Eizenstat, "White House and Justice Department After Watergate," 68 *American Bar Association Journal* 175, 176 (1982).

41. Timothy O'Neill, *Bakke and the Politics of Equality: Friends and Foes in the Classroom of Litigation* (Wesleyan University Press, 1985, 325 pp.), 22.

42. Ibid., 42, 45.

43. Justice Department Memorandum from Drew Days to file, February 28, 1977.

44. Frank Easterbrook, Memorandum to the Solicitor General, June 9, 1977.

45. Ibid., 29, 36.

46. Interviews with Wade McCree, op. cit.; and Drew Days on July 1, 1985.

47. Press conference No. 12 of President Jimmy Carter, July 28, 1977.

48. Interviews with Drew Days, op. cit.; Stuart Eizenstat on July 3, 1985; Ben Heineman on July 24, 1985; Wade McCree, op. cit.; Lawrence Wallace, op. cit.; and others.

49. Interviews with Drew Days, op. cit.; Brian Landsberg on June 12, 1986; and others at the Civil Rights Division.

50. Joseph A. Califano, Jr., *Governing America: An Insider's Report from the White House and the Cabinet* (Simon and Schuster, 1981, 474 pp.), 237.

51. Ibid.

52. Griffin B. Bell, with Ronald J. Ostrow, *Taking Care of the Law* (William Morrow & Co., 1982, 254 pp.), 29.

53. Interviews with Drew Days, op. cit.; Frank Easterbrook on June 21, 1986; and Lawrence Wallace, op. cit. Also, see Easterbrook memorandum.

54. Stuart Eizenstat and Robert Lipshutz, "Memorandum for the President," September 6, 1977.

55. *The New York Times*, A-1, September 12, 1977.

56. Op. cit., Califano, 241.

57. Eizenstat notes of the meeting. He let the author copy his notes at his law office in Washington, D.C., and gave permission to quote from them.

58. Op. cit., Califano, 241; interview with Stuart Eizenstat; and Eizenstat notes.

59. Op. cit., Califano, 241.

60. Op. cit., Bell, 28–32. Also, interview with Terrence Adamson on July 10, 1985.

61. Letter from Chief Justice William Rehnquist to the author, October 2, 1986, used with permission of the Chief Justice.

62. Op. cit., Bell, 31.

63. TVA v. Hill, 437 *U.S.* 153 (1978).

64. Op. cit., interview with Wade McCree.

65. Ibid.

66. Op. cit., interviews with Terrence Adamson and Wade McCree.

67. Brief for the United States as amicus curiae, Regents of the University of California v. Bakke, No. 76-811, October Term, 1977.

68. Op. cit., O'Neill, 57.

69. Op. cit., Califano, p. 243.

70. "Memorandum for the Attorney General Re: The Role of the Solicitor General," September 29, 1977. Published as "77-56 Memorandum Opinion for the Attorney General: Role of the Solicitor General," in "Opinions of the Office of Legal Counsel," Vol. 1, 228 (1977).

71. Interviews with Miles Foy on July 23, 1985; Larry Hammond on June 28, 1985; and John Harmon on July 23, 1985.

72. Op. cit., Office of Legal Counsel, memorandum. The quotations cited in the rest of this chapter are on pages 1–11 of the memorandum.

73. Letter from Erwin Griswold to Attorney General Griffin Bell, May 13, 1977, used with permission of Erwin Griswold.

CHAPTER V
THE BOB JONES CASE

1. Brief for the United States, Goldsboro Christian Schools, Inc. v. U.S. and Bob Jones University v. U.S., No. 81-1 and 81-3, October Term, 1981, 1.

2. Interviews with Rex Lee. op. cit.; and Lawrence Wallace. op. cit.

3. Interviews with Andrew Frey, op. cit.; Kenneth Geller, op. cit.; Albert Lauber on July 30, 1985 and February 20, 1986; and Lawrence Wallace, op. cit.

4. Interviews with Francis Lorson, op. cit.; Supreme Court reporters; and Lawrence Wallace, op. cit.; and author's observations.

5. Interviews with Francis Lorson, op. cit.; and Lawrence Wallace, op. cit.

6. Louis Claiborne had about fifty in 1981, and was second to Wallace. As of 1987, Wallace had 97. Griswold used the figure of 127 cases, because he counted as two different cases some that were consolidated and argued at the same time. Other records, including the Supreme Court's, said 117. Also, op. cit., William H. Harbaugh, *Lawyer's Lawyer*, 531.

7. Kennedy School of Government, Harvard University, Center for Press, Politics, and Public Policy, "Ronald Reagan and Tax Exemptions for Racist Schools," 14 (1984).

8. Joint appendix in Bob Jones University (Nos. 81-3), A2–A3, A40–A41.

9. Washington *Post*, D-2, March 30, 1986.

10. Harvard Law School, Program on the Legal Profession, "Segregated Schools: Government Lawyers and Politics," 4 (1983).

11. Op. cit., Bob Jones joint appendix, 84.

12. Bob Jones University v. U.S., 468 *F. Supp.* 890, 894 (1978).

13. Op. cit., Kennedy School study, 25, quoting transcript of January 30, 1980, speech at Bob Jones University.

14. Op. cit., Kennedy School study, 14.

15. Op. cit., Harvard Law School study, 4.

16. CIs.

17. Op. cit., Kennedy School study, 9.

18. Ibid., 17.

19. CIs.

20. Bob Jones University v. U.S., 461 *U.S.* 574, 595 (1983).

21. Op. cit., Harvard Law School study, 8; quoting letter from Trent Lott to Rex Lee, October 30, 1981.

22. Op. cit., Harvard Law School study, 41.

23. Ibid., 10, 11.

24. Ibid., 23, 12.

25. CIs.

26. Op. cit., Harvard Law School study, 18, 54.

27. CIs. Also, see op. cit., Harvard Law School study, 26.

28. Op. cit., Bob Jones University v. U.S., 595. Also, Coit v. Green, 404 U.S. 997 (1971).

29. Hearings on the nomination of William Bradford Reynolds to be Associate Attorney General, Senate Judiciary Committee, No. J-99-29, 32, June 4, 5, and 18, 1985.

30. Interviews with Bruce Fein, op. cit.; and William Bradford Reynolds, op. cit. Also, see op. cit., Harvard Law School and Kennedy School studies.

31. CIs with Justices.

32. Op. cit., Kennedy School study, 49, 50.

33. Op. cit., Kennedy School study, 67.

34. Ronnie Dugger, *On Reagan: The Man and His Presidency* (McGraw-Hill, 1983, 616 pp.), 214.

35. Op. cit., Harvard Law School study, 48.

36. Op. cit., Dugger, 213–14.

37. Op. cit., Kennedy School study, 76.

38. Ibid., 107.

39. St. Louis *Post-Dispatch*, 1A, January 12, 1982.

40. CI.

41. Op. cit., interview with Lawrence Wallace.

42. Letter from Marvin Frankel to Lawrence Wallace, February 5, 1982, used with permission of Frankel and Wallace.

43. Op. cit., Bob Jones University v. U.S., 595, 598.

44. Op. cit., Kennedy School study, 111, 113.

45. Ibid., 115.

46. Interviews with Albert Lauber, op. cit.; and Lawrence Wallace, op. cit.

47. Interview with Brian Landsberg, op. cit. Also, see his remarks at Civil Rights Division farewell reception in his honor, June 20, 1986.

48. CIs.

49. *Wall Street Journal*, 16, September 6, 1984, quoting James McClellan.

50. Interviews with Paul Bator, op. cit.; Bruce Fein, op. cit.; Bradford Reynolds, op. cit.; and others.

51. CI.

52. CI.

53. Interviews with Paul Bator, op. cit.; Bruce Fein, op. cit.; William Bradford Reynolds, op. cit.; and others.

54. Op. cit., interview with Paul Bator. Also, see résumé of Paul Bator, March 1985.

55. Remarks by Paul Bator at the swearing-in of Kenneth Starr as a judge of the U.S. Court of Appeals for the D.C. Circuit, 2, 3–5.

56. Op. cit., interview with Paul Bator.

57. Interviews with Paul Bator, op. cit.; Charles Fried, op. cit.; and William Bradford Reynolds, op. cit.

58. Interview on January 27, 1987, with Jewel Lafontant.

59. Interviews with Andrew Frey, op. cit.; Kenneth Geller, op. cit.; and Lawrence Wallace, op. cit.

60. Op. cit., interview with Paul Bator.

CHAPTER VI
JUDICIAL RESTRAINT

1. Op. cit., interview with Robert Bork.

2. Interviews with Archibald Cox, op. cit.; Paul Freund, op. cit.; and others.

3. Council on the Role of Courts, *The Role of Courts in American Society* (1984).

4. Ibid., 1, 3.

5. Ibid., 4, 101.

6. Ibid., 6, 118–20.

7. See Joel Klein, "The Lawyers' Plot," *New Republic* 29 (February 4, 1985).

8. Remarks of the Attorney General before the Federal Legal Council, Reston, Virginia, October 29, 1981, 1.

9. Ibid., 14, 15, 17–18.

10. Ibid., 12.

11. Hearings on Justice Department confirmations, hearing on the nomination of Rex Lee to be Solicitor General, Senate Judiciary Committee, No. J-97-7-Part 2, June 19, 24, and July 17, 1981, 2.

12. Rex Lee, *A Lawyer Looks at the Equal Rights Amendment* (Brigham Young University Press, 1980, 141 pp.) and *A Lawyer Looks at the Constitution* (Brigham Young University Press, 1981, 229 pp.).

13. CIs.

14. Op. cit., Rex Lee, *A Lawyer Looks at the Constitution*, 9.

15. Op. cit., Lee hearings, 43.

16. Ibid., 45, 47.

17. CI.

18. Op. cit., interview with Rex Lee.

19. Op. cit., "Annual Report of the Attorney General," 1955 through 1985. The average percentage from the 1943 through 1983 Terms was 69. Except for the 1983 Term, the winning percentage was over 79 only twice: in the 1953 Term the percentage was 81; and in the 1981 Term the percentage was 82. Also, op. cit., interview with Virginia Bolling. She reports that some former lawyers in the SG's office claim the office did as well in the early years of this century.

20. Gerald F. Uelmen, "The Influence of the Solicitor General Upon Supreme Court Disposition of Federal Circuit Court Decisions: A Closer

Look at the Ninth Circuit Record," 69 *Judicature* 361 (No. 6, April–May 1986).

21. CIs.

22. "Judging the Judges," 1 *Benchmark* 1 (Nos. 4 and 5, July–October 1984).

23. Washington *Post*, A-2, March 8, 1982.

24. Los Angeles *Times*, A-1, July 25, 1983.

25. Ibid.

26. Learned Hand, *The Bill of Rights* (Harvard University Press, 1958, 82 pp.), 15, 29.

27. Hamilton wrote that limitations on the federal government contained in the Constitution "can be preserved in practice no other way than through the medium of courts of justice, whose duty it must be to declare all acts contrary to the manifest tenor of the constitution void." Charles A. Beard, ed., *The Enduring Federalist* (Frederick Ungar, 1959, 396 pp.), 333. Also, Marbury v. Madison, 1 *Cranch* (5 *U.S.*) 137, 177 (1803).

28. Charles Black and Eugene Rostow at the Yale Law School were key articulators of this view in the nineteen-fifties and -sixties.

29. Robert Jackson, *The Supreme Court in the American System of Government* (Harvard University Press, 1955, 92 pp.), 53.

30. Alexander Bickel, *The Least Dangerous Branch: The Supreme Court at the Bar of Politics* (Bobbs-Merrill, 1962, 303 pp.), 19.

31. James Bradley Thayer, "The Origin and Scope of the American Doctrine of Constitutional Law, 7 *Harvard Law Review* 129 (1893).

32. Reynolds v. Sims, 377 *U.S.* 533, 589 (1964).

33. Op. cit., Hand, 73.

34. Baker v. Carr, 369 *U.S.* 186, 270 (1962).

35. Op. cit., Bickel.

36. William Leuchtenburg, "Franklin D. Roosevelt's Supreme Court 'Packing Plan,' " in *Essays on the New Deal*, compiled by Harold M. Hollingsworth (University of Texas Press, 1969, 115 pp.), 76.

37. Interviews with Daniel Friedman, op. cit.; and Erwin Griswold, op. cit.

38. Op. cit., Leuchtenburg, 80.

39. Op. cit., Leuchtenburg, 75: "The question was debated at town meetings in New England, at crossroads country stores in North Carolina, at a large rally at the Tulsa court house, by the Chatterbox Club of Rochester, New York, the Thursday Study Club of La Crosse, Wisconsin, the Veteran Fire Fighters' Association of New Orleans, and the Baptist Young People's Union of Lime Rock, Rhode Island."

40. Richard B. Morris, *Encyclopedia of American History* (Harper & Row, 1970, 850 pp.), 356.

41. Interviews with Norman Dorsen on June 10, 1986; and Albert Sacks on June 9, 1986.

42. Karl Llewellyn, *The Common Law Tradition: Deciding Appeals* (Little, Brown, 1960, 565 pp.), 4.

43. Interview with Rex Lee, op. cit.; and CIs.

44. Speech by Rex Lee at Franklin and Marshall College, October 24, 1985, 23.

45. Op. cit., Los Angeles *Times.*

46. "Crisis in the Courts," *Manhattan Report,* 1985, p. 6.

47. Richard Posner, *The Federal Courts: Crisis and Reform* (Harvard University Press, 1985, 365 pp.), 210.

48. Résumé of Richard Posner, January 30, 1984.

49. Op. cit., Caplan, "Free-Market Justice."

50. George L. Priest, "The Rise of Law and Economics," a paper for a Conference on the Place of Economics in Legal Education, October 28–30, 1982, 49.

51. Richard Posner and Elisabeth Landes, "The Economics of the Baby Shortage," 7 *Journal of Legal Studies* 323 (1978).

52. Op. cit., interview with Richard Posner.

53. Los Angeles *Times* interview, released by the White House press office on June 23, 1986.

54. Knights of Columbus speech, August 5, 1986, released by White House press office.

55. Bruce Fein, "Why Ed Meese Is Right About the Supreme Court," Los Angeles *Herald-Examiner,* F-1, November 17, 1985.

56. Op. cit., *Benchmark,* 1. Also, see Bruce Fein, "Selecting a Supreme Court Justice Devoted to Judicial Restraint," 1 *Benchmark* 1 (No. 6, November–December 1984).

57. Op. cit., Los Angeles *Times.*

58. CI.

59. Op. cit., *Wall Street Journal,* 16, September 6, 1984.

60. Thomas Ferguson and Joel Rogers, "The Myth of America's Turn to the Right," *Atlantic Monthly,* 45–46 (May 1986).

CHAPTER VII

THE SHADOW SOLICITOR

1. Hearings on nomination of William Bradford Reynolds to be Associate Attorney General, Senate Judiciary Committee, No. J–99–29, 3, June 4, 5, and 18, 1985.

2. Op. cit., interview with William Bradford Reynolds.

3. CIs. Also, see *Legal Times,* 1, August 18, 1986, on Griffin Bell's testimony during the Rehnquist Chief Justiceship hearings.

4. Op. cit., interview with William Bradford Reynolds. Also, see op. cit., Reynolds hearings, 3.

5. Op. cit., interview with William Bradford Reynolds.

6. Interview with John Wilson, Office of Public Affairs, Justice Department, on January 9, 1986.

7. CIs.

8. Washington v. Seattle School District No. 1, 458 *U.S.* 457 (1982).

9. Interview with Gordon Foster on May 12, 1986. Also, see Fact Sheet About Busing, School of Education and Allied Professions, University of Miami, and "Covering School Desegregation," Educational Equity Project, Vanderbilt University.

10. Charlotte *Observer*, 1A, October 9, 1984.

11. "President's Busing Remarks Anger Schools Superintendent," Charlotte *Observer*, 1A, October 9, 1984.

12. "You Were Wrong, Mr. President," Charlotte *Observer*, 10A, October 9, 1984.

13. Carl Stern, "Nofziger memo," NBC News, October 16, 1981.

14. CI.

15. Robert J. D'Agostino, memorandum to William Bradford Reynolds about U.S. v. Yonkers, July 21, 1981.

16. Petition to William French Smith and William Bradford Reynolds about D'Agostino's July 21 memo.

17. CIs. Also, see letter from William Bradford Reynolds to the Civil Rights Division staff on September 17, 1981, using the same term.

18. CIs.

19. CIs.

20. Op. cit., Bakke, 407.

21. Glenn Loury, "The Color Line Today," *Public Interest*, Summer, 1985.

22. "The State of Black America 1986," National Urban League, i.

23. In 1986, Justice Thurgood Marshall took the occasion of a speech to the judges of the U.S. Court of Appeals for the Second Circuit, where he once sat, to explain why affirmative action was a required step toward the ultimate goal of a color-blind society. "We still have a very long way to go" before the United States finally closes the gap between whites and blacks that was brought about by slavery, he observed, and the "vestiges of racial bias in America are so pernicious and so difficult to remove that we must take advantage of all the remedial measures at our disposal." Remarks by Justice Thurgood Marshall, September 4, 1986, 3.

24. Op. cit., Interview with William Bradford Reynolds. Also, see remarks of William Bradford Reynolds before the Seventh Annual Convention, National Association of Police Organizations, August 1, 1985; before the Wilmington Rotary Club, October 31, 1985; and before the University of Chicago's Chapter of the Federalist Society, January 10, 1986.

25. Op. cit., interview with William Bradford Reynolds. Also, see file of news clips about Reynolds at the Leadership Conference for Civil Rights.

26. Interviews with Paul Bator, op. cit.; and William Bradford Reynolds, op. cit.

27. CIs.

28. Boston Firefighters Union, Local 712 v. Boston Chapter, NAACP et al., 461 *U.S.* 477 (1983).

29. Op. cit., interview with Carter Phillips.

30. CI.

31. CI.

32. Interviews with Rex Lee, op. cit.; and William Bradford Reynolds, op. cit.; and CIs.

33. CIs.

34. Op. cit., 461 *U.S.* 477 (1983).

35. "Assault on Affirmative Action," a production of WGBH broadcast in June 1986 by WETA in Washington, D.C.

36. Firefighters Local Union No. 1784 v. Stotts, 104 *S. Ct.* 2576 (1984).

37. Op. cit., WGBH.

38. CI.

39. Op. cit., Stotts.

40. CIs.

41. Op. cit., interview with William Bradford Reynolds.

42. 103 *S. Ct.* 3221 (1983).

43. CIs.

44. CIs.

45. CI.

46. Vasquez v. Hillery, 54 *U.S. Law Week* 4068 (decided January 14, 1986).

47. CIs.

48. Joshua Schwartz, Memorandum to the Solicitor General About Vasquez v. Hillery, No. 84–836, April 26, 1985.

49. Author's observation at oral argument on October 15, 1985.

50. Hillery v. Pulley, 563 *F. Supp.* 1228, 1234 (1983).

51. Op. cit., Vasquez v. Hillery, 4070, note 3.

52. Walter Barnett, Cover Memorandum About Vasquez v. Hillery to Charles Cooper, March 28, 1985, 1.

53. CIs.

54. William Bradford Reynolds, Memorandum for the Solicitor General Re: Vasquez v. Hillery, April 11, 1985, 2. All quotations in this paragraph are from this page.

55. CI.

56. Op. cit., Schwartz, 8, 9.

57. Strauder v. West Virginia, 100 *U.S.* 303, 308 (1880).

58. Rex Lee, Memorandum to the Attorney General, May 7, 1985.

59. Op. cit., Vasquez v. Hillery, 4070, 4072.

60. Op. cit., *Wall Street Journal*, 1, September 6, 1984.

61. Lynch v. Donnelly, 104 *S. Ct.* 1355 (1984).

62. Interviews with Paul Bator, op. cit.; Rex Lee, op. cit.; and Michael McConnell on May 28, 1985.

63. Lemon v. Kurtzman, 403 *U.S.* 602 (1971).

64. 525 *F. Supp.* 1150 (D.R.I. 1981) and 691 *F. 2d* 1029 (1st Cir. 1982).

65. Brief for the United States as amicus curiae supporting reversal, Lynch v. Donnelly, No. 82-1256, October Term, 1982, 23–24, 24–25, 1.

66. Norman Dorsen and Charles Sims, "The Nativity Scene Case: An Error of Judgment," *University of Illinois Law Review,* No. 4, 837 (1985).

67. CIs.

68. William Lee Miller of the University of Virginia argues that the religion clauses reflect a commitment to a liberty encompassing much more than religion. The religion clauses were intended to help guarantee the freedom of thought that is the foundation of free government. William Lee Miller, *The First Liberty: Religion and the American Republic* (Knopf, 1986, 373 pp.)

69. Op. cit., *Benchmark.*

70. Daniel Popeo, a contributing editor to *Benchmark* and a founder of the Washington Legal Foundation, one of the New Right centers that began during the Reagan years, said, "The Justice Department calls me up to go on the MacNeil/Lehrer Show, and I go." Interview with Daniel Popeo on November 14, 1985.

71. *Washington Post,* A-6, August 9, 1985.

72. Editor's brief, "A Lawyer Looks at Rex Lee," 1 *Benchmark* (No. 2, March–April 1984), 1 et seq.

73. Ibid., 5.

74. Ibid.

75. Jaffree v. Board of School Commissioners of Mobile County, 554 *F. Supp.* 1104, 1113, note 5 (1983). Also, interview with Forrest McDonald on March 17, 1987.

76. Op. cit., Lee, *A Lawyer Looks at the Constitution,* 31.

77. Op. cit., Editor's brief, 1–2.

78. Op. cit., interview with Paul Bator.

79. Interviews with Paul Bator, op. cit.; and Rex Lee, op. cit.

80. Op. cit., *Wall Street Journal,* 16.

81. William Bradford Reynolds, Memorandum to Rex Lee about Jaffree v. Wallace, June 29, 1983.

82. William Bradford Reynolds, Memorandum to Rex Lee about Jaffree v. Wallace, October 3, 1983.

83. Op. cit., *Wall Street Journal,* 16.

84. Op. cit., interview with Paul Bator.

85. Wallace v. Jaffree, No. 83-812, decided June 4, 1985; 4, note 22, 14.

86. Ibid., 10.

87. Ibid., O'Connor opinion, 11.

88. Op. cit., Editor's brief, 5.

89. Ibid., 16, 12, 15.

90. Op. cit., "Annual Report of the Attorney General" for 1938: "It is evident, therefore, that on the basis of reversals the percentage of success obtained by the Government at the last Term was better than at any time" since 1927. "It far exceeds that secured by its opponents as well as that obtaining in all cases, Government and non-Government. . . . Taking all cases decided on the merits at the last term in which the Government was a party, . . . the Government won, in actual numbers 91 cases and lost 23, a

percentage of 80," 37. In October Term, 1938, the government won 64 percent; in October Term, 1939, 84 percent. Robert Jackson's overall record as SG was 76 percent.

91. Eugene Gerhart, *America's Advocate: Robert Jackson* (Bobbs-Merrill, 1958, 545 pp.), 145.

92. Op. cit., Editor's brief, 2; 4–5, 14.

93. Ibid.

94. Richard G. Wilkins, "Another Lawyer Looks at Rex E. Lee: A Reply to James McClellan," 15.

95. Op. cit., Editor's brief [McClellan], 3.

96. "No Friend of the Court," *The New York Times*, A-22, August 4, 1982.

97. Brief Amicus Curiae of Senator Bob Packwood (R-Ore.), Representative Don Edwards (D-Calif.), and Certain Other Members of the Congress of the United States in Support of Appellees, Thornburgh v. American College of Obstetricians and Gynecologists, No. 84-495, October Term, 1985, 8.

98. Op. cit., Los Angeles *Times*, July 25, 1983.

99. City of Akron v. Akron Center for Reproductive Health, 103 *S. Ct.* 2481 (1983).

100. Op. cit., interview with Rex Lee.

101. Ibid.

102. Op. cit., Reynolds hearings.

103. Statement submitted, with testimony of Thomas D. Barr, by Lawyers' Committee for Civil Rights Under Law, June 4, 1985.

104. Interview with Thomas Barr on November 14, 1985.

105. Op. cit., Lawyers' Committee, 3–4.

106. Ibid., 6.

107. Ibid., 4.

108. CIs.

109. Op. cit., Reynolds hearings, 17.

110. Op. cit., Lawyers' Committee, 30.

111. Op. cit., Reynolds hearings, 887.

112. Ibid., 888, 889.

113. Ibid., 996.

114. Ibid., 997.

115. On page 208 of the hearing transcript, a Mathias sentence begins, "Now, they may be happy with the result, but the result really was the opposite of the way you started, and that is my concern." In the printed hearing record at page 997, the sentence reads, "Now, they may be happy with the result, but my concern is that the result really was what you originally wanted." The printed version is a misleading correction of the sentence the author heard Mathias speak, which the transcript records. It should read, "the result was *not* what you originally wanted."

116. News release from Dennis DeConcini, June 19, 1985.

117. Staff office, Senate Judiciary Committee.

118. Op. cit., interview with Rex Lee. Also, Rex Lee interview with Nina Totenberg on National Public Radio, May 28, 1985.

119. Op. cit., Office of Legal Counsel memorandum.

120. CIs.

121. A second good example is the Lands Division, but the Antitrust, Civil, and Criminal Divisions also did the same.

122. Op. cit., interview with Rex Lee.

123. Rex Lee, Memorandum to William Bradford Reynolds About *Irving Independent School District v. Tatro*, No. 83-558, February 3, 1984, 1.

124. "Inside: The Justice Department," Washington *Post*, A-23, May 3, 1985.

125. In the federal-court year that ended June 28, 1985, only six of the 110 briefs on the merits filed by the SG's office concerned civil rights. The low number was misleading as an index of Reynolds's dealings with the SG.

CHAPTER VIII
MEESE'S LAW

1. Hearings on Confirmation of Edwin Meese III to be Attorney General, Senate Judiciary Committee, No. J-99-1, January 29, 30, and 31, 1985, 723–725.

2. Ibid., 713. Also, *The New York Times*, A-1, July 23, 1985, quoting William Clark, who was National Security Adviser and then Secretary of the Interior in the Reagan Administration, and an old friend of the President. He observed about Caspar Weinberger and Meese that neither expressed purely personal views: "The thing to emphasize is that Cap and Ed Meese, for the past 18 years, have been the great articulators of the Reagan view of life, whether it be national security or domestic issues. They mirror the President on all the key issues. No one else can even come close."

3. Ibid., 713–763.

4. CIs.

5. Report of Independent Counsel Concerning Edwin Meese III, submitted to the U.S. Court of Appeals for the District of Columbia, Division for the Purpose of Appointing Independent Counsels, Ethics in Government Act of 1978, No. 84-1, September Term, 1984.

6. Common Cause, "The Case Against Edwin Meese for Attorney General," December 1984, 2.

7. Op. cit., Independent Counsel report, 8–12. Also CIs.

8. Ibid., 339–351.

9. Ibid., 151–225.

10. Op. cit., Common Cause, 4–5.

11. See Lincoln Caplan, "The Meese Affairs," Baltimore *Sun*, January 29 and 30, 1985.

12. CIs.

13. Op. cit., Meese hearings, 713–763.

14. "Theorists on Right Find Fertile Ground," Washington *Post*, A-1, August 9, 1985.

15. Address of Edwin Meese before the American Bar Association, July 9, 1985, 14–15.

16. Ibid., 15, 17, 12, 10.

17. H. Jefferson Powell, "How Does the Constitution Structure Government?: The Founders' Views," *A Workable Constitution* (forthcoming), 7.

18. McCulloch v. Maryland, 4 *Wheat.* (17 *U.S.*) 316, 407 (1819), 415.

19. Op. cit., Meese address, July 9, 18.

20. Address of Edwin Meese to the American Enterprise Institute, September 6, 1985, 1.

21. Address of Edwin Meese to Dickinson College, September 17, 1985, 10.

22. *U.S. News & World Report*, 67, October 14, 1985.

23. Office of Public Affairs, Justice Department.

24. Sidney Zion, "A Decade of Constitutional Revision," *The New York Times Magazine*, November 11, 1979, 27–28.

25. Interview with Yale Kamisar, professor of criminal law, Michigan Law School, on January 23, 1987.

26. "Interrogations in New Haven: The Impact of Miranda," 76 *Yale Law Journal* 1519, 1613 (1967). Also, op. cit., Zion, 28.

27. A few months before Meese's attack on Miranda, Justice William Brennan dissented from a decision in which the Supreme Court ruled that in some cases the police could ask questions first and later warn the accused of his rights. This limitation on Miranda prompted Brennan to write that the Supreme Court was "increasingly irrelevant in the protection of individual rights." Washington *Post*, A-17, April 4, 1985.

28. Op. cit., "Impact of Miranda," 1613.

29. Op. cit., interview with Yale Kamisar.

30. William J. Brennan, Jr., "The Constitution of the United States: Contemporary Ratification," October 12, 1985, 1.

31. Ibid., 4.

32. Ibid., 7.

33. Address of John Paul Stevens to the Federal Bar Association, October 23, 1985, 9.

34. NBC News, October 25, 1985.

35. Thornburgh v. American College of Obstetricians and Gynecologists, No. 84-495, decided June 11, 1986, White opinion, 4. Also, interviews with Terry Eastland on November 13, 1985; and Bruce Fein, op. cit.

36. Edwin Meese, *Policy Review*, 34, Winter, 1986.

37. Ibid.

38. Op. cit., Meese, *Policy Review*, 34.

39. Op. cit., Bickel, *Least Dangerous Branch*.

40. Op. cit., Meese, *Policy Review*, 34.

41. Brief for the United States as Amicus Curiae in Support of Appellants, Thornburgh v. American College of Obstetricians and Gynecologists, Dia-

mond v. Charles, Nos. 84–495 and 84–1379, October Term, 1985, filed July 15, 1985.

42. Address of Edwin Meese to the American Bar Association, July 17, 1985, 11.

43. Op. cit., Roe v. Wade, 410 *U.S.* 113 (1973).

44. John Hart Ely, *Democracy and Distrust: A Theory of Judicial Review* (Harvard University Press, 1980, 268 pp.), 1–2.

45. John Hart Ely, "The Wages of Crying Wolf," 82 *Yale Law Journal* 920, 949 (1973).

46. Akron v. Akron Center for Reproductive Health, Inc., 462 *U.S.* 416 (1983).

47. Interview with John Hart Ely on April 24, 1986.

48. Op. cit., Packwood-Edwards abortion brief, 3.

49. Address of Edwin Meese to the Federal Bar Association, September 13, 1985, 4.

50. Cooper v. Aaron, 358 *U.S.* 1, 18 (1958).

51. Lecture by Edwin Meese on "The Law of the Constitution," Tulane University, October 21, 1986, 12.

52. Op. cit., McCulloch v. Maryland, 401.

53. Saul Sigelschiffer, *The American Conscience: The Drama of the Lincoln-Douglas Debates* (Horizon Press, 1973, 488 pp.), 226, 133, 188.

54. Op. cit., Meese lecture, 9.

55. Op. cit., Cooper v. Aaron, 18.

56. Washington *Post*, A-3, February 16, 1987.

57. Op. cit., Meese lecture, 6–7, 11.

58. Op. cit., Gerald Gunther, *Constitutional Law,* 32.

59. Op. cit., Meese address, July 9, 14.

60. Roger Clegg, Memorandum to Charles Fried About U.S. v. District of Columbia, September 26, 1985.

61. CIs.

62. Op. cit., Cox, *Chicago Bar Record,* 229.

63. *The New York Times,* A-13. December 9, 1986.

64. See reports in the Washington *Post* about lax enforcement of environmental, occupational health and safety, civil rights, antitrust, and other laws, from 1981 through 1987.

65. Washington *Post*, D-2, December 7, 1986.

66. Letter from Edwin Meese to Dwight D. Opperman, December 13, 1985, supplied by the Office of Public Affairs, Justice Department.

67. Ibid., 2.

68. Letter from Dwight Opperman to Edwin Meese, December 26, 1985, supplied by the Office of Public Affairs, Justice Department.

69. Letters from Benjamin Civiletti to Walter Mondale on January 13, 1981, and from William French Smith to George Bush on November 21, 1984, supplied as public documents by Michael Davidson, Counsel in Office of Senate Legal Counsel, March 27, 1986.

70. Op. cit., Civiletti letter.

71. Op. cit., Smith letter.

72. CIs.

73. Letter from Edwin Meese to Thomas P. O'Neill, Jr., May 1, 1985.

74. Sheldon Goldman, "Reagan's Second Term Judicial Appointments: The Battle at Midway." 70 *Judicature*, April–May 1987.

75. Speech by Paul Simon, "Judging Judges: The Senate's Role in Judicial Appointments," National Press Club, March 10, 1986, 2.

76. Op. cit., Office of Legal Counsel memorandum, 11.

CHAPTER IX

THE ABORTION BRIEF

1. Interview with Charles Fried on January 22, 1987.

2. *Harvard Law School Bulletin*, 12, Winter, 1986.

3. Interviews with Paul Bator, op. cit.; and Charles Fried, op. cit., on November 11, 1985.

4. Charles Fried, curriculum vitae, 2; and op. cit., *Bulletin*.

5. Op. cit., vitae, 5–7.

6. Charles Fried, "Curbing the Judiciary," *The New York Times*, A-23, November 10, 1981.

7. Charles Fried, "The Trouble with Lawyers," *The New York Times Magazine*, D-56, February 12, 1984.

8. UPI, May 26, 1985.

9. David Lauter, "A Champion of the Reagan Agenda," *National Law Journal*, 1, 30, January 27, 1986. Also, CIs with Harvard Law School students and professors.

10. Charles Fried, "The Lawyer as Friend: The Moral Foundation of the Lawyer-Client Relation," 85 *Yale Law Journal* 1060 (July 1976).

11. CIs; op. cit., Lauter, 31.

12. Alasdair MacIntyre, review of *Right and Wrong*, *New Republic*, 29, May 6, 1978.

13. Charles Fried, "Privacy," 77 *Yale Law Journal* 475 (1968).

14. Charles Fried, *Right and Wrong* (Harvard University Press, 1978, 226 pp.), 1.

15. 88 *Yale Law Journal* 647 (1979).

16. Interviews with Charles Fried, op. cit., on November 11, 1985, and Philip Heymann on April 12, 1985. Also, Poe v. Ullman, 367 *U.S.* 497, 539, 542 (1961).

17. CI.

18. Washington *Post*, A-8, January 7, 1986.

19. Op. cit., interview with Charles Fried.

20. Interview with Philip Heymann on February 14, 1986.

21. Op. cit., interview with Charles Fried; and news accounts.

22. The Supreme Court dismissed Diamond v. Charles on jurisdictional grounds, and decided only Thornburgh v. American College of Obstetricians and Gynecologists.

23. Op. cit., SG's Thornburgh brief, 2.

24. Ibid., 3.

25. Ibid., 20, 21, 23.

26. Ibid., 24, 29.

27. Op. cit., interview with Charles Fried; and news accounts.

28. Op. cit., SG's Thornburgh brief, 3.

29. No. 1982–138, Chapter 32, Abortion, to amend Title 18, act of November 25, 1970 (Pennsylvania Law 707, No. 230).

30. Interview with Stephen Freind on June 12, 1986.

31. Ibid.

32. Op. cit., SG's Thornburgh brief, 26.

33. Interviews with Archibald Cox, op. cit.; John Davis, op. cit.; Erwin Griswold, op. cit.; Wade McCree, op. cit.; and others.

34. Washington *Post*, A-25, September 20, 1985.

35. CIs.

36. John Paul Stevens, "Deciding What to Decide: The Docket and the Rule of Four," *Views from the Bench: The Judiciary and Constitutional Politics*, edited by Mark W. Cannon and David M. O'Brien (Chatham House, 1985, 330 pp.), 81.

37. Op. cit., Packwood-Edwards abortion brief.

38. Interview with Laurence Tribe, op. cit., and summary of briefs and arguments from Tribe.

39. Planned Parenthood conference, September 3, 1985, 3, 17.

40. Ibid., 8.

41. Op. cit., Lee NPR interview with Nina Totenberg, May 28, 1985.

42. Rex Lee, draft of "History of the Office of the Solicitor General," 32.

43. Ibid., 32–34.

44. Op. cit., speech by Rex Lee at Franklin and Marshall College.

45. Notes of author from Bureau of National Affairs conference September 13 and 14, 1985.

46. *New Republic*, 11, October 7, 1985.

47. Op. cit., interview with Charles Fried; and CIs.

48. A letter from Paul Freund to the author, May 8, 1985, tells this story. Also, op. cit., Bander, *Justice Holmes Ex Cathedra*, No. 402, 195. After Fried's submission in the abortion case, and his comments about it, other lawyers who once served in the SG's office and who knew the Mitchell story told it in this context.

49. Audiotape of remarks by Charles Fried to the Chamber of Commerce on November 19, 1985, provided by Winston Leavell, Manager, News Department, Public Liaison, Chamber of Commerce, and transcribed by the author.

50. Herbert Wechsler, "Toward Neutral Principles of Constitutional Law," 73 *Harvard Law Review* 1, 19 (1959).

51. Interview with Herbert Wechsler on February 26, 1986.

52. 313 *U.S.* 299 (1941).

53. Philadelphia *Inquirer,* 15-A, January 17, 1986.

54. Letter from Charles Fried to author, January 21, 1986.

55. CIs.

56. Op. cit., Meese address, July 17, 17.

57. CI.

58. CIs with several of Fried's former colleagues at Harvard Law School.

59. Stuart Taylor, Jr., *The New York Times,* A-8, July 18, 1986.

60. Op. cit., interview with Charles Fried.

61. *Wall Street Journal,* 1, September 26, 1985.

62. Author's observation.

63. Comment by Charles Fried to author at party for Louis Claiborne on October 21, 1985.

64. Transcript of hearing on the confirmation of Charles Fried to be Solicitor General, Senate Judiciary Committee, October 17, 1985, 71.

65. Ibid., 72.

66. Ibid., 76, 88.

67. Comment of Charles Fried to author at party for Louis Claiborne on October 21, 1985.

68. Op. cit., Fried hearing, 94.

69. Ibid., 95.

70. Ibid., 73, 74.

71. Washington *Post,* A-7, August 9, 1985; A-1, August 25, 1985.

72. Op. cit., *Wall Street Journal,* September 6, 1984.

73. Op. cit., Reynolds hearings, 135.

74. Washington *Post,* A-7, August 9, 1985. Also, *The New York Times,* B-3, October 3, 1985.

75. CI.

CHAPTER X

THE CELESTIAL GENERAL

1. Op. cit., interview with Louis Claiborne on June 12, 1985.

2. Louisiana Power & Light Co. v. City of Thibodaux 359 *U.S.* 25 (1960).

3. CI.

4. Information supplied by Judge Wright's chambers.

5. Tom Kelly, Washington *Daily News,* April, 1965.

6. Joseph T. Hatfield, *William Claiborne: Jeffersonian Centurion in the American Southwest* (University of Southwestern Louisiana Press, 1976, 393 pp.).

7. Interview with Tom Kelly on December 12, 1985.

8. Claiborne Gallery, Santa Fe, New Mexico.

9. *The New York Times,* Business Section, 1, May 4, 1986.

10. Interview with Louis Claiborne on June 18, 1985.

11. CI.

12. Interviews with Louis Claiborne, op. cit.; and Raymond Randolph, op. cit.

13. Interviews with Edwin Kneedler, op. cit.; Joshua Schwartz, op. cit., and Lawrence Wallace, op. cit.

14. Op. cit., interview with Louis Claiborne.

15. Brief for the United States as amicus curiae urging reversal, Summa Corporation v. State of California, No. 82-708, October Term, 1982, 4.

16. "The Original Jurisdiction of the United States Supreme Court," 11 *Stanford Law Review* 665 (1959).

17. Interviews with Francis Lorson, op. cit.; and with Clare Bailey on February 18, 1986.

18. Interviews with Charles Fried, op. cit.; Edwin Kneedler, op. cit.; Rex Lee, op. cit.; and Joshua Schwartz, op. cit.; also, CIs.

19. Op. cit., "Original Jurisdiction," 665, 667, note 24.

20. Interviews with Louis Claiborne, op. cit.; and Michael Reed on June 5, 1986; and CIs with Supreme Court Justices.

21. Op. cit., interview with Louis Claiborne.

22. Rex Lee remarks at party for Louis Claiborne on October 21, 1985, and interview with Rex Lee on October 23, 1985.

23. Op. cit., interview with Louis Claiborne.

24. Letter from Paul Laxalt to William French Smith, October 7, 1981, reproduced in the appendix to the reply brief of the Pyramid Lake Paiute Tribe of Indians, in Pyramid Lake Paiute Tribe of Indians v. Truckee-Carson Irrigation District, No. 82-1723, October Term, 1983.

25. Louis Claiborne, Memorandum to the Solicitor General about U.S. v. Alpine Land & Reservoir Co., April 14, 1983.

26. Op. cit., interview with Louis Claiborne.

27. Louis Claiborne, Memorandum for the Solicitor General Re: Pane v. NRC, August 16, 1982, about that case, which was eventually decided by the Supreme Court and reported at 460 *U.S.* 766 (1983).

28. Op. cit., interview with Louis Claiborne.

29. Reply brief for the United States, U.S. v. Maine, No. 35, Original, October Term, 1985.

30. As the Washington *Post* summed up in the box labeled "Supreme Court Calendar," which it runs on days that arguments are scheduled, "No. 35 Original. U.S. v. Maine. Boundary dispute. Must state establish claim to coastline jurisdiction by 'clear beyond doubt' evidence?"

31. Comment by Louis Claiborne to author before oral argument on December 12, 1985.

32. Op. cit., reply brief, 1.

33. U.S. v. Maine, 54 *U.S. Law Week*, 4173, decided February 25, 1986.

34. Author's observation.

35. October 21, 1985.

36. From handwritten remarks of Louis Claiborne, which he gave to the author.

37. From announcement that Louis Claiborne mailed to associates and friends, and to the author.

38. Op. cit., interview with Paul Freund, a onetime Brandeis law clerk. Also, op. cit., Eugene Gerhart, *America's Advocate: Robert Jackson*, 199.

39. Op. cit., Gerhart, 143.

CHAPTER XI
CHARLES FRIED

1. November 6, 1985, sponsored by the National Center for Public Policy Research.

2. Videotape of the dinner provided by Amy Moritz, Executive Director of the National Center for Public Policy Research. All quotations from speakers at the dinner are taken from the videotape. Comments to the author are from the author's notes.

3. Program, Reynolds dinner, 3.

4. Comment to the author.

5. These are taken from the author's notes, and checked against the videotape.

6. Washington *Post*, A-3, November 5, 1985.

7. Remarks of Charles Cooper at Tribute to William Bradford Reynolds, November 6, 1985.

8. CIs.

9. CIs.

10. November 11, 1985.

11. Public Information Office of the National Archives.

12. Op. cit., Griswold letter to Griffin Bell.

13. Background on the history and contents of the painting provided by the National Gallery of Art. Also, see Colin Eisler, *Paintings from the Samuel H. Kress Collection: European Schools Excluding Italian* (Phaidon Press for the Samuel H. Kress Foundation, 1977, 639 pp.), 274–280.

14. February 10, 1986.

15. Op. cit., interview with Charles Fried on November 11, 1985.

16. The author taped and transcribed Fried's lecture; all quotations in this section are taken from the tape and transcription, and checked against notes provided to the author by Charles Fried.

17. Comment by David Lauter to the author on January 22, 1986, used with Lauter's permission.

CHAPTER XII
FRIENDS OF THE COURT

1. Op. cit., "Crisis in the Courts," *Manhattan Report.*

2. Fried Chamber of Commerce speech, op. cit.; and interview with Charles Fried, op. cit., on November 11, 1985.

3. Op. cit., Fried Chamber of Commerce speech. Also, Fried speech to the Academy of State and Local Government, February 13, 1986, reported by staff members and others who attended.

4. Op. cit., Fried Chamber speech.

5. Op. cit., *Manhattan Report.*

6. Interviews with Philip Heymann, op. cit.; Abram Chayes on October 9, 1985; and other members of the Harvard Law School faculty. Also, interviews with Charles Fried, op. cit., on November 11, 1985; and CIs.

7. Interview with Charles Fried, op. cit.; interview with Potter Stewart, op. cit.; author's observation of Fried and comments of Potter Stewart and other Justices about Cox; interviews with Philip Heymann, op. cit.; Nathan Lewin, op. cit.; Carolyn Kuhl, op. cit.; and Albert Lauber, op. cit.

8. Archibald Cox, *The Warren Court: Constitutional Decision as an Instrument of Reform* (Harvard University Press, 1968, 144 pp.), 1.

9. Ibid., 22.

10. Op. cit., interview with Charles Fried on November 11, 1985.

11. Op. cit., Cox, *The Warren Court,* 22–23.

12. To some scholars, Cox's criticism of the Warren Court played into the hands of its detractors by oversimplifying the role of the Supreme Court in American democracy. "Contemporary constitutional debate is dominated by a false dichotomy," John Hart Ely argued in the preface to *Democracy and Distrust:* "Either, it runs, we must stick close to the thoughts of those who wrote our Constitution's critical phrases and outlaw only those practices they thought they were outlawing, or there is simply no way for courts to review legislation other than by second-guessing the legislature's value choices." To Ely's mind, it missed the point to write off the cardinal decisions of the Warren Court as exercises in social policy. The accomplishment of the Supreme Court between 1954 and 1969 (the dedication of Ely's book to Earl Warren—"You don't need many heroes if you choose carefully"—emphasized that he considered it an accomplishment) was to fill in gaps left by other branches of the federal government and by state governments. The Court returned fairness to the political process, guaranteed that blacks and other minorities could vote, and otherwise safeguarded the workings of democracy.

13. Victor S. Navasky, *Kennedy Justice* (Atheneum, 1977, 482 pp.), 280.

14. Ibid., 291; and interview with Burke Marshall on May 20, 1985.

15. Op. cit., interview with Archibald Cox.

16. Op. cit., Navasky, 286, 296.

17. Op. cit., Baker v. Carr.

18. Op. cit., Navasky, 301.

19. The SG's brief, Reynolds v. Sims brief, 17.

20. Op. cit., Navasky, 299.

21. Supreme Court records.

22. Op. cit., interview with Philip Heymann.

23. Op. cit., Reynolds v. Sims, 533.

24. Op. cit., Navasky, 298.

25. Davis v. Bandemer, No. 84–1244, decided June 30, 1986.

26. Alexander Bickel, Paul Freund, Philip Kurland, and others.

27. Op. cit., Navasky, 308.

28. Op. cit., Office of Legal Counsel memorandum, 11.

29. Op. cit., Navasky, 309.

30. Ibid., 311, 314.

31. Ibid., 315, 313.

32. Op. cit., interview with Archibald Cox.

33. Herbert Wechsler, "Report of the Advisory Commission on Intergovernmental Relations," January 1967, footnote 25.

34. Op. cit., interview with Archibald Cox.

35. Archibald Cox lecture at Hunter College, "Storm over the Supreme Court," 1985, 18, 19.

36. Ibid., 20.

37. Op. cit., interview with Charles Fried on June 28, 1986.

38. Op. cit., interviews with Charles Fried. Also, according to lawyers in the SG's office and several of Fried's former Harvard Law School colleagues, he made the same point to them.

39. These are standard lawyer's terms, used by people in the SG's office and outside.

40. Op. cit., Fried speech to the Academy of State and Local Government, as reported by members of the Academy staff and by others at the event. Also, op. cit., interview with Charles Fried on November 11, 1985.

41. Interview with Steven Shapiro on March 27, 1986. According to Rule 42 of the 1954 Supreme Court rules contained in *Supreme Court Practice,* 2nd Edition, 1954, anyone who wanted to file an amicus brief in a case before the Court either had to obtain consent of the parties to the case, or to file a motion for permission to file a brief, which had to include a statement of interest. As one of the SG's prerogatives, on the other hand, the SG did not have to obtain permission to file an amicus brief, so he was never obliged to state a federal interest in a case. The rules changed in 1970. The Justices moved the location of the statement of interest. Instead of requiring that it be included in the motion for permission to file a brief, they directed that the statement of interest be included in the brief itself. The SG was still free to enter any case he chose without permission of the parties—he is one of the few advocates who enjoy that privilege—but he had to declare the government's interest just like any other advocate. The upshot was that when Cox was SG, no rule

required him to state a federal interest. By Fried's time, the rules had changed, and they obliged the SG to declare the government's interest.

42. Samuel Krislov, "The Role of the Attorney General as Amicus Curiae," in Luther A. Huston, ed., *Roles of the Attorney General of the United States* (American Enterprise Institute, 1968, 153 pp.), 89.

43. Ibid., 80.

44. Ibid., 85.

45. "Annual Reports of the Attorney General," 1920 through 1985.

46. Op. cit., Cox, *Chicago Bar Record*, 226.

47. Interview with Archibald Cox on August 5, 1985.

48. Samuel Krislov, "The Amicus Brief: From Friendship to Advocacy," 72 *Yale Law Journal* 694, 703 (1963).

49. Karen O'Connor and Lee Epstein, "Court Rules and Workload: A Case Study of Rules Governing Amicus Curiae Participation," 8 *Justice System Journal* No. 1 (1983), Table 2.

50. Karen O'Connor and Lee Epstein, "The Rise of Conservative Interest Group Litigation," 45 *Journal of Politics* 479, 481 (1983). The facts cited in the rest of this paragraph are on pages 482–487.

51. Op. cit., "Annual Reports of the Attorney General."

52. Clerk's office of the Supreme Court and Docket Management Section of the SG's office.

53. Interviews with Paul Bator, op. cit.; Andrew Frey, op. cit.; Charles Fried, op. cit.; Stephen Shapiro, op. cit.; and others.

54. CI; op. cit., interviews with Charles Fried; op. cit., David Lauter, *National Law Journal*, 24.

55. Interviews with Philip Heymann, op. cit.; and Nathan Lewin, op. cit.; and CIs.

56. Op. cit., Cox lecture, "Storm over the Supreme Court," 17; and interview with Archibald Cox, op. cit.

57. Op. cit., interview with Archibald Cox.

58. Interview with Philip Heymann on February 14, 1986.

59. In his Chamber of Commerce speech, Fried said, "A brief is nothing but reasons," and in an interview with the author, Fried said, "The law is nothing but reasons."

60. Op. cit., interview with Potter Stewart; and CIs with other Justices. Also, CIs with former lawyers in the SG's office. Op. cit., interview with Archibald Cox.

61. Op. cit., interview with Charles Fried on June 28, 1986.

62. Carl Stern, NBC News, October 21, 1985, transcript, 4.

63. Op. cit., interview with Charles Fried on November 11, 1985.

64. Comment of Louis Claiborne at the party in his honor on October 21, 1985.

65. Op. cit., interview with Charles Fried on November 11, 1985; brief for the United States as Amicus Curiae Supporting Petitioners, Wygant v. Jackson, No. 84–1340, October Term, 1985, and slip opinion, Wygant v. Jackson, decided May 19, 1986.

66. Op. cit., Wygant brief, 2.

67. Op. cit., Wygant decision, Marshall opinion, 4.

68. Op. cit., Wygant brief, 4.

69. Ibid., 5.

70. Ibid., 5, 6.

71. Ibid., 7, 8.

72. Ibid., 23.

73. Op. cit., interview with Lawrence Wallace.

74. CI.

75. Paul Freund, *On Law and Justice* (Harvard University Press, 1968, 251 pp.), 33, 44, 45, 46, 47. Also, Robert D. Miller, "Samuel Field Phillips: The Odyssey of a Southern Dissenter," vol. LVIII, No. 3, *North Carolina Historical Review*, 263, 273–79 (July 1981).

76. Op. cit., Carl Stern, NBC News, 2.

77. Interview with Laurence Tribe on November 18, 1985.

78. Op. cit., Wygant decision, O'Connor opinion, 3.

79. *The New York Times*, A–21, May 20, 1985.

80. Op. cit., Meese address to Dickinson College, 10.

81. *The New York Times*, A–28, May 21, 1986.

82. Op. cit., Wygant decision, O'Connor opinion, 3.

83. Op. cit., interviews with Charles Fried.

84. Elder Witt, "Reagan Crusade Before Court Unprecedented in Intensity," *Congressional Quarterly*, March 15, 1986, 616, 617.

85. Washington *Post*, A–7, July 7, 1986.

CHAPTER XIII
THE SG'S LAWYERS

1. Interviews with Kenneth Geller, op. cit.; Edwin Kneedler, op. cit.; Albert Lauber, op. cit.; Andrew Pincus on May 25, 1986; Joshua Schwartz, op. cit.; and David Strauss, op. cit.

2. During the seventies, for several years, five lawyers in the SG's office (Frank Easterbrook, Andrew Frey, Kenneth Geller, John Rupp, and Stephen Urbancyzk) held a regular dart game at 5:30 p.m.

3. Op. cit., interview with Edwin Kneedler.

4. Op. cit., interview with Harriet Shapiro.

5. According to Boisfeuillet Jones, general counsel of the Washington *Post*, he and Al Kamen, who covers the Supreme Court for the paper, had lunch with Kenneth Geller and Andrew Frey to discuss how the paper could improve its coverage of the Court.

6. Op. cit., interview with David Strauss.

7. Op. cit., interview with Kenneth Geller.

8. CI.

9. The facts in this paragraph are from CIs.

10. Op. cit., interview with Kenneth Geller and author's observation.

11. Deputy in charge
    of review:

	Bator	Claiborne	Frey	Fried	Geller	Wallace
Number of appeals (Total: 2089)	38	142	665	49	782	413
Number of briefs on the merits (Total: 110)	8	23	23	7	27	22

12. Op. cit., interviews with Carter Phillips, Wade McCree, and Andrew Frey.

13. Andrew Frey, "Modern Police Interrogation Law: The Wrong Road Taken," 42 *University of Pittsburgh Law Review* 731, 732, 733 (1978), 736.

14. Op. cit., interview with Yale Kamisar.

15. Peter Westen and Richard Drubel, "Toward a General Theory of Double Jeopardy," *Supreme Court Review* 81 (1978), 81.

16. Peter Westen, "The Three Faces of Double Jeopardy: Reflections on Government Appeals of Criminal Sentences," 78 *Michigan Law Review* 1001, 1005, and 1006 at note 18, for description of Benton v. Maryland, 395 *U.S.* 784 (1969).

17. In 1971, Congress passed 18 U.S.C. 3731, Title III of the Omnibus Crime Control Act of 1970, explained at page S—146 of the Library of Congress "Constitution of the United States, 1978 Supplement," edited by Johnny Killian.

18. During a double-jeopardy argument, the then Associate Justice William Rehnquist asked, "Mr. Frey, you are not suggesting that all of the authoritative answers, as you refer to them, that have been given by this Court to these questions are consistent with one another, are you?" Transcript of U.S. v. Scott, No. 76–1382, October Term, 1977, 5, 6.

19. Interview with Peter Westen on July 11, 1985.

20. Op. cit., interview with Potter Stewart.

21. CI.

22. Press release, March 6, 1986, Department of Justice.

23. In a confidential interview, the official said the release "cavalierly disposed of" the three longtime SG lawyers.

24. "U.S. Solicitor General Announces Top Aides," *The New York Times*, March 7, 1986.

25. CI.

26. The facts in this paragraph are from an interview with Charles Fried on June 28, 1986, and from CIs.

27. CI.

28. Op. cit., interview with Andrew Frey; Ed Bruske, Washington *Post*, A-15, July 26, 1984; letters to Senate Majority Leader Howard Baker from Senators Jeremiah Denton, John East, Charles Grassley, and Orrin Hatch on August 9, 1984; to Andrew Frey from Senator Jeremiah Denton on September 7, 1984; and, eventually, to President Ronald Reagan from Senators Steve

Symms and Jeremiah Denton on March 6, 1985; CIs and Memorandum to the Full Committee Staff from John Duncan, the staff director of the Senate Governmental Affairs Committee, announcing the committee's plan to consider the Frey nomination, September 6, 1984, until the White House asked the committee to cancel the hearing.

29. Op. cit., interview with Potter Stewart.

30. Statistics in letter to the author from Alan Herman, Clerk of the Court, D.C. Court of Appeals, and from the Statistics Office of the Administrative Office of the U.S. Courts.

31. Nancy Blodgett, "Solicitor General," 72 *American Bar Association Journal* 20 (May, 1986).

32. CI; Charles Fried, Letter, 72 *American Bar Association Journal* 12 (July, 1986); letter from LeRoy E. DeVeaux to Kathryn Oberly, May 7, 1986, used with permission of DeVeaux and Oberly.

33. Interviews with John Davis, op. cit.; Oscar Davis, op. cit.; Philip Elman, op. cit.; Daniel Friedman, op. cit.; Paul Freund, op. cit.; and Erwin Griswold, op. cit.

34. Interview with Kathryn Oberly on March 13, 1986.

35. CI.

36. Until this change, most Deputy Solicitors General had served for many years. The SG's office generally hired three new assistants a year. From June 1, 1985, through April 1, 1986, excluding Solicitor General Rex Lee, eleven out of twenty-two lawyers left the office, for a 50 percent turnover. Though normal turnover before this wave was more like 15 percent a year—that is, three of twenty-three—the author assumed that an office of seventeen assistants who have an average tenure of three years, and whose arrivals and departures are spread evenly over the years, may have to replace four members in some years, which is 23 percent. Taking the figure of 50 percent and the figure of 23 percent as a basis for comparison, the author concluded that the rate of turnover jumped from about a quarter to half.

37. The facts in this paragraph are from CIs.

38. CIs.

39. The quotations and facts in this paragraph are from an interview with Charles Fried and CIs.

40. Robert Stern, "The Solicitor General's Office and Administrative Agency Litigation," 46 *American Bar Association Journal* 154 (1960).

41. The facts in this paragraph are from CIs.

42. The quotations and facts in this paragraph are from an interview with Charles Fried and from CIs.

43. The quotations and facts in this paragraph are from an interview with Charles Fried and CIs.

44. Interview with Bruce Kuhlik on November 1, 1985.

45. Op. cit., interview with Philip Heymann.

46. Unless otherwise indicated, the quotations and facts in this paragraph are from an interview with Charles Fried and from CIs.

47. CI.

48. Interviews with Andrew Frey, op. cit.; Kenneth Geller, op. cit.; and Lawrence Wallace, op. cit.

49. Unless otherwise indicated, the quotations and facts in this paragraph are from CIs.

50. Announcement of Career Opportunities, Justice Department, February 21, 1986.

51. Unless otherwise indicated, the quotations and facts in this paragraph are from CIs.

52. Author's observation and CIs.

53. Unless otherwise indicated, the quotations and facts in this paragraph are from CIs.

54. A lawyer, who claimed to be Fried's ally and whom the SG said he relied on, observed, "Charles has no patience for the intricacies of legal argument."

55. Interview by David Lauter with Paul Bator, used with permission of David Lauter.

56. Interview with Lyle Denniston on April 14, 1986.

57. Interview with Terry Eastland on June 26, 1986.

58. Unless otherwise indicated, the quotations and facts in this paragraph are from CIs.

59. Unless otherwise indicated, the quotations and facts in this paragraph are from CIs.

60. Interviews with Andrew Frey, op. cit.; and Kenneth Geller, op. cit.

61. Interview with Harlan Dalton on June 27, 1985.

62. Unless otherwise indicated, the quotations and facts in this paragraph are from CIs.

63. Interview with Charles Fried on April 28, 1986.

64. CIs.

65. CI.

66. CI.

67. CI.

68. CI.

69. CI.

CHAPTER XIV
OCTOBER TERM, 1985

1. CIs.

2. The facts in this paragraph are from interviews with Charles Fried and from CIs.

3. Bender v. Williamsport, No. 84-773, decided March 25, 1986.

4. Op. cit., interview with Francis Lorson.

5. Washington *Post*, A–8, March 26, 1986.

6. CI.

7. CI.

8. Davidson v. Cannon, 54 *U.S. Law Week* 4095, decided January 21, 1986.

9. Op. cit., interview with Charles Fried on June 28, 1986; CIs.

10. Op. cit., Davidson v. Cannon.

11. Op. cit., Davidson, transcript, 26.

12. Op. cit., interview with Charles Fried on June 28, 1986; CIs; interviews with Andrew Frey, op. cit.; Kenneth Geller, op. cit.; and Edwin Kneedler, op. cit.

13. CIs.

14. Batson v. Kentucky, 54 *U.S. Law Week* 4425, decided April 30, 1986.

15. Swain v. Alabama, 380 *U.S.* 202, 209–222 (1965).

16. CIs.

17. *The New York Times*, A–1, May 1, 1986.

18. Transcript of MacNeil/Lehrer News Hour, 6, July 2, 1986, provided by WETA.

19. Slip opinion, Thornburg v. Gingles, No. 83–1968, decided June 30, 1986.

20. Op. cit., Ronnie Dugger, *On Reagan*, 212.

21. CI.

22. Section 2(b), as amended, provides that Section 2(a) of the Voting Rights Act of 1965 is violated where the "totality of the circumstances" reveals that "the political processes leading to nomination or election . . . are not equally open to participation by members of a [protected class] . . . in that its members have less opportunity than other members of the electorate to participate in the political process and to elect representatives of their choice." Op. cit., slip opinion summary.

23. Brief for Appellees, Thornburg v. Gingles. Also, see press packet from the NAACP Inc. Fund.

24. Author's observation and transcript of argument.

25. Washington *Post*, A–4, December 5, 1985.

26. CIs.

27. Author's observation.

28. Ibid.

29. Op. cit., interview with Charles Fried on June 28, 1986; op. cit., Thornburg decision.

30. Op. cit., NAACP Inc. Fund brief, 32, referring to SG's brief, 8, note 12.

31. Op. cit., Thornburg decision, Brennan opinion, 10, 22.

32. Heckler v. American Hospital Association, No. 84-1529, October Term, 1985; MacDonald v. Yolo, No. 84-2015, October Term, 1985; Golden State Transit v. Los Angeles, No. 84-1644, October Term, 1985; Bethel v. Fraser, No. 84-1667, October Term, 1985; United Auto Workers v. Brock, No. 84-1777, October Term, 1985.

33. Hunt v. Washington, 432 *U.S.* 333 (1977).

34. Motion for leave to file on behalf of the Chamber of Commerce et al., UAW v. Brock, by Sidley & Austin, 3.

35. Ibid., 2.

36. Ibid., 5.

37. City of Los Angeles v. Preferred Communications, No. 85–390, decided June 2, 1986.

38. CI.

39. In the Red Lion case, 395 *U.S.* 367 (1969), the Justices ruled that the government could regulate media like radio and TV where there was a scarcity of broadcast frequencies. Instead of undermining the First Amendment, they judged, the government's commitment to assigning frequencies could enhance the freedoms of speech and press by assuring access for individuals and groups who might otherwise not get on the air. The Red Lion decision also approved government regulation of the content of broadcasts, which was a more difficult question for the Justices than the matter of awarding licenses.

The lower-court opinion in the Preferred case found an analogy between Los Angeles's rules for awarding its cable franchise and the federal government's policy about granting radio and TV licenses. The Supreme Court's prior judgment that the government could limit the number of licenses to avoid a cacophony of voices seemed to settle the case. If the government could control radio and TV licenses, a city could regulate cable. Experts also said that regulation of cable improved the content of programs. If the rules enforced by Los Angeles were upheld, they said, the city's cable company would have to maintain time for community programs. If the bid for competition prevailed, the need to win customers with commercial fare might squeeze public-service programs off the air.

40. Brief for United States and the FCC as Amicus Curiae Supporting Affirmance, No. 85–390, 12. One of the reasons for the federal law was to help companies like Preferred. Before the law was passed, cities had extracted from companies bidding for cable franchises pledges to build production studios, to train citizens how to produce cable programs, and to provide other benefits, as part of deals awarding the franchises. It was a form of "holdup," according to a lawyer in the SG's office familiar with the practice. The federal law was designed to settle the process for awarding cable franchises across the country.

41. CIs.

42. Op. cit., SG's Preferred brief, 9, 11; CI.

43. Interview with Laura Kopelman, of the General Accounting Office, on June 19, 1986.

44. Synar v. U.S., 626 *F. Supp.* 1374 (D.C. 1986).

45. Impeachment requires a majority vote in the House of Representatives and a two-thirds vote in the Senate. A joint resolution requires a majority vote of both houses, unless the President vetoes it, in which case Congress can override the President by a two-thirds vote.

46. Washington *Post*, A–1, February 8, 1986.

47. Bowsher v. Synar, No. 85–1377, transcript, 51, decided July 7, 1986.

48. Op. cit., Thornburgh v. American College of Obstetricians and Gynecologists, No. 84–495, decided June 11, 1986, 10, 23.

49. Transcript provided by Justice Department, 8, 9, 11.

50. Ibid., 5.

51. Op. cit., Thornburgh decision, White opinion, 2, 3, 29.

52. Op. cit., Thornburgh decision, Stevens opinion, 2, 5, 10.

53. Stuart Taylor, Jr., "Tasting the Salty Air of Politics and Criticism," *The New York Times*, A–8, July 18, 1986. Also, Al Kamen, "A Series of High Court Rebuffs for Reagan," Washington *Post*, A–7, July 7, 1986. Also, CIs with Justices.

54. Lyng v. Payne, No. 84–1948, decided June 17, 1986.

55. Ibid., Stevens dissent, 3. The case dealt with a claim by some Florida farmers that the government had failed to tell them about a program of emergency loans for disaster relief that could have helped the farmers recover from torrential rains that caused major losses of crops and property. By an eight-to-one margin, the Justices held that the Secretary of Agriculture had given the farmers sufficient notice about the program. But the Justices took the SG to task for misusing the doctrine of equitable estoppel. The classic example of the doctrine occurs when a government official conceals an important fact from a potential recipient of federal aid and, relying on the official's word, the applicant fails to qualify for help. Since the government misled the citizen, a court will hold that the government is "equitably estopped" from arguing that the citizen should have known better. Courts now frown on the doctrine and allow individuals to use it only when a misrepresentation is grave. In any event, in the Florida case equitable estoppel was not obviously relevant. The Secretary of Agriculture had not advertised the government's relief program, but in no instance had a farmer been misled. The heart of the farmers' case, which was the basis for the ruling in their favor in the lower courts, was that the government had failed to follow basic rules of administrative law and give the farmers proper notice about the existence of the relief program. Nonetheless, on appeal to the Supreme Court, the SG's office framed the farmers' case as one that rested on the outmoded doctrine of equitable estoppel, and argued that the farmers should lose. The Court unanimously criticized the SG for this mischaracterization. Writing for the majority, Justice O'Connor rejected the idea that any claim that was like an equitable estoppel could be thrown out as the SG had advised. If the Justices accepted that notion, she said, they would take from the courts a power that Congress had specifically given in order to let judges correct obvious government wrongs. In case the Solicitor General missed the reprimand, Justice Stevens made the comment quoted in the text above.

56. Op. cit., Stuart Taylor, Jr., "Tasting the Salty Air of Politics."

57. Docket Management Section, SG's office.

58. CIs. Also op. cit., interview with Charles Fried on July 1, 1986; and news accounts.

59. Op. cit., transcript of MacNeil/Lehrer News Hour, 3, July 2, 1986.

60. Local 28 v. EEOC, No. 84–1656, decided July 2, 1986, Brennan opinion, 57.

61. When Justice Brennan handed down his opinion for the Court in Local 28 of the Sheet Metal Workers' International Association v. Equal Employment Opportunity Council, he took pains to explain why a majority agreed, even though he wrote only for a plurality.

62. " 'Hardly ever?' " asked a onetime chairman of the U.S. Equal Employment Opportunity Commission, Eleanor Holmes Norton, at a symposium in Manhattan to celebrate the centennial of the Statue of Liberty, not long after the New York affirmative-action case came down. "Hardly ever," the SG repeated, according to the Philadelphia *Inquirer*, though he observed that while the Justices were "paid to make things a little clearer," they hadn't in the New York case. He said, "Who knows what these clowns mean?" Carlin Romano, Philadelphia *Inquirer*, July 7, 1986.

63. Bowers v. Hardwick, No. 85–140, decided June 30, 1986.

64. Op. cit., Stuart Taylor, Jr.

65. CIs.

66. Justice White's dissent in Roe v. Wade often comes to mind when scholars discuss this.

67. CIs.

68. John Jenkins, "Mr. Power: Attorney General Edwin Meese," *The New York Times Magazine*, 18, 92 (October, 12, 1986).

69. Edward H. Levi, *An Introduction to Legal Reasoning* (University of Chicago Press, 1949, 104 pp.).

70. Op. cit., interview with Charles Fried on June 28, 1986; Meritor Savings v. Vinson, No. 84–1979, October Term, 1985, decided June 19, 1986.

71. Ibid., Rehnquist opinion, 14.

72. Op. cit., Rehnquist opinion, 14.

73. SG's Meritor brief, 26: "If the employer has an expressed policy against sexual harassment and has implemented a procedure specifically designed to resolve sexual harassment claims, and if the victim does not take advantage of that procedure, the employer should be shielded from liability absent actual knowledge of the sexually hostile environment (obtained, e.g., by the filing of a charge with the EEOC"—that is, the government's Equal Employment Opportunity Commission—"or a comparable state agency)."

74. Interview with Charles Fried on June 28, 1986.

75. Op. cit., UAW v. Brock, Marshall opinion, 15.

CHAPTER XV

THE VIEW FROM THE COURT

1. CI.

2. The Federalist Society for Law and Public Policy was founded in 1982 by law students, law professors, and judges to challenge "the orthodox liberal ideology which advocates a centralized and uniform society." According to

the society's brochure, "In working to achieve these goals the Society has created a conservative intellectual network that extends to all levels of the legal community."

3. Interview with Paul Cassell, a law clerk to Chief Justice Warren Burger, on June 23, 1986.

4. Unless otherwise indicated, the quotations and facts in this paragraph are from CIs.

5. The quotations in this paragraph are from CIs.

6. Docket Management Section of the SG's office.

7. Figures provided by Virginia Bolling, in the Docket Management Section of the SG's office.

8. CIs.

9. CI.

10. CI.

11. CI.

12. Op. cit., interview with Charles Fried on June 28, 1986.

13. Op. cit., interview with Francis Lorson; *Legal Times*, 3, August 18, 1986; op. cit., Bethel v. Fraser.

14. CIs.

15. Letter from Charles Fried to Joseph F. Spaniol, Jr., about DiNapoli v. Northeast Regional Parole Commission, No. 85–335, October 29, 1985.

16. CI.

17. Letter from Charles Haydon to Joseph F. Spaniol, Jr., October 31, 1985, used with permission of Haydon and the Supreme Court.

18. Letter from Joseph F. Spaniol, Jr., to Charles Haydon, November 12, 1985.

19. Op. cit., interview with Justice Thurgood Marshall.

20. Unless otherwise indicated, the quotations and facts in this paragraph come from CIs.

21. Op. cit., Stuart Taylor, Jr.

22. *The New York Times*, A–1, July 11, 1986.

23. CBS TV, "Nightwatch," July 15, 1986.

24. CI.

25. Bowen v. City of New York, No. 84–1923, decided June 2, 1986, 9, 19.

26. Op. cit., interview with Charles Fried on June 28, 1986.

27. Maine v. Moulton, No. 84–786, decided December 10, 1985, 15.

28. Riverside v. Rivera, No. 85–224, decided June 27, 1986, 16, note 10.

29. CIs.

30. Op. cit., interview with Charles Fried on June 28, 1986.

31. Interview with Donald Ayer on September 10, 1986; CIs.

32. Confidential letter to the author.

33. Unless otherwise indicated, the quotations and facts in this paragraph are from CIs.

34. CIs.

35. U.S. v. Mendoza, op. cit., 573, and DeMarco v. U.S., op. cit. Also, CIs.

36. CIs.

37. CI.
38. CI.
39. CI.

CHAPTER XVI
THE RULE OF LAW

1. Interview with Johnny Killian, of the Congressional Research Service, Library of Congress, on September 10, 1986.

2. In 37 of 151 cases.

3. Op. cit., interview with Johnny Killian.

4. Vincent Blasi, *The Burger Court: The Counter-Revolution That Wasn't* (Yale University Press, 1983, 326 pp.), 6.

5. Op. cit., Bowers v. Hardwick.

6. Ibid., White opinion, 8, 9.

7. Al Kamen, Washington *Post*, A–1, July 13, 1986.

8. "The respondent had not been tried or convicted, and we had no occasion to consider possible defenses, such as one based on the Eighth Amendment, to an actual prosecution," the Justice explained at an American Bar Association conference. Address to the ABA Litigation Section, August 12, 1986.

9. Remarks of Justice Harry Blackmun to the Eighth Circuit.

10. Roy A. Schotland, "Elective Judges' Campaign Financing: Are State Judges' Robes the Emperor's Clothes of America Democracy?," 2 *Journal of Law and Politics* 57 (1985).

11. *The New York Times*, E–2, December 22, 1985.

12. NBC Nightly News, August 10, 1986.

13. Annual reports in the Washington *Post* on January 23, the day after the anniversary, from 1982 through 1987; Los Angeles *Times*, 1–3, October 7, 1985; Los Angeles *Times* interview on June 23, 1986; addresses on the State of the Union in 1985 and 1986.

14. Los Angeles *Times*, 1–17, June 2, 1986.

15. Op. cit., Richard Posner, *The Federal Courts*, 218, 219, and note on 219, where he reports that Georgetown University Law Center professor Mark Tushnet claims that judges should rule on the basis of whether a result will advance the cause of socialism, and that University of Texas law professor Lino Graglia claims that constitutional review should be abolished, taking away a principal function of federal courts.

16. CIs.

17. See Roberto Mangabeira Unger, *The Critical Legal Studies Movement* (Harvard University Press, 1986, 128 pp.). Also, *The New York Times Book Review*, 1, February 16, 1986.

18. Daniel Boorstin, "The Perils of Indwelling Law," in Robert Paul Wolff, ed., *The Rule of Law* (Simon & Schuster, 1971, 254 pp.), 75.

19. CIs.

20. Washington *Post*, A–1, October 7, 1986.

21. CIs.

22. U.S. v. Paradise, No. 85–999, decided February 25, 1987; Johnson v. Transportation Agency, Santa Clara, California, No. 85–1129, decided March 25, 1987; School Board of Nassau County, Florida v. Arline, No. 85–1277, decided March 3, 1987; Immigration & Naturalization Service v. Cardoza-Fonseca, No. 85–782, decided March 9, 1987.

23. Oversight Hearing on the Solicitor General's Office, U.S. House of Representatives, Committee on the Judiciary, Subcommittee on Monopolies and Commercial Law, March 19, 1987.

24. Op. cit., Carlin Romano, Philadelphia *Inquirer*, July 7, 1986.

25. *The New York Times*, A–1, March 28, 1987. Also, interview with Charles Fried, July 6, 1987.

26. Lecture by William Bradford Reynolds, "Securing Liberty in an Egalitarian Age," September 12, 1986.

27. Op. cit., Brennan Georgetown symposium speech.

28. Remarks by Edwin Meese and by William Bradford Reynolds at the Reynolds dinner on November 6, 1985. Also, op. cit., interviews with William Bradford Reynolds and Terry Eastland. Also, op. cit., Jenkins profile of Meese in *The New York Times Magazine*.

Acknowledgments

Many people helped me during the two and a half years I researched and wrote this book, and I want to thank them.

Nathan Lewin, a Washington lawyer and a onetime assistant to the Solicitor General, suggested that I write about the SG's office and got me started on my reporting.

At the SG's office, Virginia Bolling, Elizabeth Werling, and others in the Docket Management Section were regularly helpful in answering my requests for legal papers filed by the SG's staff. In the Public Information office of the Justice Department, Mark Sheehan, who was responsible for answering questions about the SG's office while I did my reporting, was similarly cooperative. Frank Lindh, who worked as a researcher at the SG's office, gathered speeches by past SGs, bar-journal articles about the office, and other relevant materials as part of his own work, and made copies for me. Quinlan J. Shea, Jr., who runs the Library at the Justice Department, shared with me his knowledge of the Library's resources and helped me learn how to use them.

At the Supreme Court, Toni House and her staff at the Public Information office, including Kathleen Arberg, Susan Coss, and Sheryl Farmer, were also regular sources of assistance. Elsewhere at the Court, Clare Bailey on the Technical Services staff, Francis Lorson in the Clerk's office, Linda McElroy in the Curator's office, and Sara Sonet on the Library staff, among others who answered my questions, gave especially useful help. Secretaries to a number of Justices were patient in helping me arrange or request interviews.

Many other people also eased my research or provided me with material, and I would like to thank several in particular: Nancy Broff, at the Judicial Selection Project; Erika Chadbourn, when she was Curator of Manuscripts at the Harvard Law School Library; Florence Coman, of the National Gallery of Art; Eddie Correia, Mark Gitenstein, Chip Reid, Phil Shipman, and Laurie Westley, on the staff of the Senate Judiciary Committee; Olive James, Abram Boni, and other staff members in the Loan Division of the Library of Congress; Johnny Killian, at the Congressional Research Service of the Library of Congress; Jeanne Smith at the Public Information office of the Library of Congress; Susan Liss, of People for the American Way; Benna Solomon, at the Academy for State and Local Government; and Joanne Zich, a librarian at American University's Washington College of Law. Staff members of the American Enterprise Institute, the Bureau of National Affairs, the *Congressional Quarterly*, the Heritage Foundation, the Los Angeles *Times*, *The New York Times*, and the Washington *Post* also responded quickly and courteously to my requests for information.

Others helped to improve my work by responding to my questions, suggesting material for reading, or otherwise acting as counselors. Some of these people are my friends, and others spoke with me because of their interest in the SG's office. They don't necessarily share my views about the SG's office or other topics in the law, but all made contributions for which I'm grateful: Stephens Broening, Paul Freund, Daniel Friedman, William Goodman, Jamie Gorelick, Philip Heymann, David Ignatius, Vicki Jackson, Bill McKibben, Daniel Meltzer, Ellen Semonoff, Robert Shapiro, William Shawn, and the late Charles Wyzanski. Raphael Sagalyn served as a first-rate agent for this project, and his assistants, Deborah Billig and Ann Sleeper, proved to be mine as well. At Knopf, Ashbel Green edited my manuscript and, with tact and intelligence, guided me to tell as well as I could the story I found in my reporting. Mildred Maynard and Melvin Rosenthal copy-edited the manuscript, and they skillfully improved the substance and presentation of this book. At *The New Yorker*, with verve and clarity, Robert Gottlieb helped me streamline the book into a two-part series of articles; Patrick Crow gave me excellent and welcome editorial counsel; and Richard Sacks carefully checked my assertions of fact and, very much a colleague, did much to ensure the book's accuracy. Peter Dimock of Vintage Books suggested I write the new foreword to this edition, gave fine advice about its shape and content, and was otherwise helpful in shepherding this book into print.

There are several more people whom I'd like to include on this list, and to thank publicly for their help. But because of the nature of their current or past jobs, we've agreed that I should not mention them by name. I owe deep thanks to two in particular. They are both fine and insightful teachers, assiduously balanced in their judgments, and they exemplify in their work the commitment to the law represented by the SG's office at its best.

Finally, I want to thank my family. My parents, Lewis and Jane Caplan, encouraged me to make my way as a writer and to find the confidence to try a project as challenging as this. My sisters Joanna and Margi gave me strong and constant support. My brother-in-law Bob Blaemire guided my reading about some key questions of politics and law. My nephew Nicky was a wonderful companion on afternoons when the rest of the world seemed hard at work and I needed a break from mine. My cousin Dorothy Leavitt carefully read an earlier version of this book, and gave me valuable suggestions on how to improve it.

Most of all, my wife, Susan, to whom this book is dedicated, gave me help as a keen and patient editor, and spurred me on with faith and love.

L.C.

Index

ABOUT THE AUTHOR

Lincoln Caplan's first book was *The Insanity Defense and the Trial of John W. Hinckley, Jr.* As published in *The New Yorker*, it won in 1985 the American Bar Association's Silver Gavel Award, presented annually to works that make "an outstanding contribution to public understanding" of American law. Mr. Caplan was born in New Haven, Connecticut, in 1950, was graduated from Harvard College and Harvard Law School, and is a former White House Fellow. He is a staff writer for *The New Yorker* and has written for the Baltimore *Sun*, the Los Angeles *Times*, *The New York Times*, and the Washington *Post*, among other publications. He lives with his wife and daughter in Washington, D.C.